❦ The Holocaust and Historical Methodology ❧

MAKING SENSE OF HISTORY
Studies in Historical Cultures
General Editor: Stefan Berger
Founding Editor: Jörn Rüsen

Bridging the gap between historical theory and the study of historical memory, this series crosses the boundaries between both academic disciplines and cultural, social, political and historical contexts. In an age of rapid globalization, which tends to manifest itself on an economic and political level, locating the cultural practices involved in generating its underlying historical sense is an increasingly urgent task.

Volume 1
Western Historical Thinking: An Intercultural Debate
Edited by Jörn Rüsen

Volume 2
Identities: Time, Difference, and Boundaries
Edited by Heidrun Friese

Volume 3
Narration, Identity, and Historical Consciousness
Edited by Jürgen Straub

Volume 4
Thinking Utopia: Steps into Other Worlds
Edited by Jörn Rüsen, Michael Fehr, and Thomas W. Rieger

Volume 5
History: Narration, Interpretation, Orientation
Jörn Rüsen

Volume 6
The Dynamics of German Industry: Germany's Path toward the New Economy and the American Challenge
Werner Abelshauser

Volume 7
Meaning and Representation in History
Edited by Jörn Rüsen

Volume 8
Remapping Knowledge: Intercultural Studies for a Global Age
Mihai I. Spariosu

Volume 9
Cultures of Technology and the Quest for Innovation
Edited by Helga Nowotny

Volume 10
Time and History: The Variety of Cultures
Edited by Jörn Rüsen

Volume 11
Narrating the Nation: Representations in History, Media and the Arts
Edited by Stefan Berger, Linas Eriksonas and Andrew Mycock

Volume 12
Historical Memory in Africa: Dealing with the Past, Reaching for the Future in an Intercultural Context
Edited by Mamadou Diawara, Bernard Lategan, and Jörn Rüsen

Volume 13
New Dangerous Liaisons: Discourses on Europe and Love in the Twentieth Century
Edited by Luisa Passerini, Liliana Ellena, and Alexander C.T. Geppert

Volume 14
Dark Traces of the Past: Psychoanalysis and Historical Thinking
Edited by Jürgen Straub and Jörn Rüsen

Volume 15
A Lover's Quarrel with the Past: Romance, Representation, Reading
Ranjan Ghosh

Volume 16
The Holocaust and Historical Methodology
Edited by Dan Stone

Volume 17
What Is History For? Johann Gustav Droysen and the Functions of Historiography
Arthur Alfaix Assis

Volume 18
Vanished History: The Holocaust in Czech and Slovak Historical Culture
Tomas Sniegon

Volume 19
Jewish Histories of the Holocaust: New Transnational Approaches
Edited by Norman J.W. Goda

The Holocaust and Historical Methodology

Edited by
Dan Stone

berghahn
NEW YORK · OXFORD
www.berghahnbooks.com

First published in 2012 by
Berghahn Books
www.berghahnbooks.com

© 2012, 2015 Dan Stone
First paperback edition published in 2015.

All rights reserved. Except for the quotation of short passages for the purposes of criticism and review, no part of this book may be reproduced in any form or by any means, electronic or mechanical, including photocopying, recording, or any information storage and retrieval system now known or to be invented, without written permission of the publisher.

Library of Congress Cataloguing-in-Publication Data

The Holocaust and historical methodology / edited by Dan Stone.
　　p. cm. — (Making sense of history ; v. 16)
ISBN 978-0-85745-492-8 (hardback : alk. paper) — ISBN 978-1-78238-678-0 (paperback : alk. paper) — ISBN 978-0-85745-493-5 (ebook)
　　1. Holocaust, Jewish (1939–1945)—Historiography. I. Stone, Dan, 1971–
D804.348.H646 2012
940.53'18072—dc23

2011052128

British Library Cataloguing in Publication Data

A catalogue record for this book is available from the British Library.

Printed on acid-free paper.

ISBN: 978-0-85745-492-8 hardback
ISBN: 978-1-78238-678-0 paperback
ISBN: 978-0-85745-493-5 ebook

Contents

Preface to the Series   vii
    Jörn Rüsen

Introduction: The Holocaust and Historical Methodology   1
    Dan Stone

Part I: Memory and Culture in the Third Reich

Chapter 1. A World Without Jews: Interpreting the Holocaust   23
    Alon Confino

Chapter 2. Holocaust Historiography and Cultural History   44
    Dan Stone

Chapter 3. The Invisible Crime: Nazi Politics of Memory and Postwar Representation of the Holocaust   61
    Dirk Rupnow

Chapter 4. The History of the Jews in the Ghettos: A Cultural Perspective   79
    Amos Goldberg

Chapter 5. National Socialism, Holocaust, and Ecology   101
    Boaz Neumann

Part II: Testimony and Commemoration

Chapter 6. Bearing Witness: Theological Roots of a New Secular Morality   127
    Samuel Moyn

Chapter 7. Transcending History? Methodological Problems
in Holocaust Testimony   143
    Zoë Waxman

Chapter 8. Studying the Holocaust: Is History Commemoration?   158
    Doris L. Bergen

Part III: Another Look at a Classic of Holocaust Historiography

Chapter 9. An Integrated History of the Holocaust: Some
Methodological Challenges   181
    Saul Friedländer

Chapter 10. Truth and Circumstance: What (If Anything) Can Be
Properly Said about the Holocaust?   190
    Hayden White

Chapter 11. Modernist Holocaust Historiography: A Dialogue
between Saul Friedländer and Hayden White   203
    Wulf Kansteiner

Part IV: The Holocaust in the World

Chapter 12. The Holocaust and European History   233
    Donald Bloxham

Chapter 13. Fascism and the Holocaust   255
    Federico Finchelstein

Chapter 14. The Holocaust and World History: Raphael Lemkin
and Comparative Methodology   272
    A. Dirk Moses

Select Bibliography   290

Contributors   310

Index   313

Preface to the Series

JÖRN RÜSEN

At the turn of the twenty-first century the term "history" brings extremely ambivalent associations to mind. On the one hand, the last decade has witnessed numerous declarations of the end of history. Whether in reference to the fundamental changes in the global political situation around 1989/90, or to so-called postmodernism, or to the challenge to Western dominance by decolonization and multiculturalism, "history" as we know it has been declared to be dead, outdated, overcome, or even a myth at its end. On the other hand, there has been a global wave of intellectual explorations into fields that are "historical" by their nature: the building of personal and collective identity through "memory"; the cultural, social, and political use and function of "narrating the past": and the psychological structures of remembering, repressing, and recalling. Even the subjects that seemed to call for an "end of history" (globalization, postmodernism, multiculturalism) quickly turned out to be intrinsically "historical" phenomena. Moreover, "history" and "historical memory" have entered the sphere of popular culture, from history channels to Hollywood movies, becoming an ever more important factor in public debates and political negotiations (the discussions about the aftermath of the wars in the former Yugoslavia, European unification, or the various heritages of totalitarian systems, to name but a few). In other words, after "history" was declared to be, like god before it, dead, "historical matters" have come back with a vengeance.

This paradox calls for a new orientation or at least a new theoretical expression. Indeed, it calls for a new theory of history; and such a theory should serve neither as a subdiscipline reserved for historians nor as a systematic collection of definitions, "laws," and rules claiming universal validity. What is needed is an interdisciplinary and intercultural field of study. Hayden White's deconstruction of the narrative strategies of the nineteenth-century historicist paradigm somehow came to be regarded by many as historical theory's famous last words, as if the critique of the discipline's claim to rationality could put an end to the rational self-reflection of that discipline—as if this critique were not a rational self-reflection in itself.

In the late 1980s the "critical study of historical memory" began to be substituted for historical theory. Overlooked in this trade-off is the fact that any exploration into the ways that historical memory in different cultural contexts not only crosses over into the field of critical studies, but also contains the keystones for a more general theory of history. Analysis of even a simple instance of historical memory cannot avoid questions pertaining to the theory and philosophy of history. And vice versa: the most abstract thoughts of philosophers of history have an intrinsic counterpart in the most secular functions of memory (for example, when parents narrate past experiences to their children, or when an African community remembers its own colonial subordination and eventual liberation from it). As long as we fail to acknowledge the fundamental connection between the most sophisticated historical theory and the process of historical memory most deeply imbedded in the culture and the everyday life of people, we remain caught in an ideology of linear progress which regards cultural forms of memory simply as some intriguing objects of study instead of recognizing them as examples of "how to make sense of history."

The series "Making Sense of History" aims at bridging this gap between historical theory and the study of historical memory. It is not exclusively related to historical studies; contributors, from virtually all fields of cultural and social studies, explore a wide range of phenomena that can be labeled "making historical sense" (*Historische Sinnbildung*). As such, the series crosses the boundaries between academic disciplines as well as those between cultural, social, political, and historical contexts. Instead of reducing historical memory to just another form of the socio/cultural "construction of reality," its contributions deal with concrete phenomena of historical memory: it seeks to interpret them as case studies in the emerging empirical and theoretical field of "making historical sense." Along the same line, rather theoretical essays are also included with the aim of not only establishing new methods and theories for historical research but also to provide perspectives for a comparative, interdisciplinary, and intercultural understanding of what could be called the "global work of historical memory" or the "cultural strategy to orient human life in the course of time."

This does not imply the exclusion of critical evaluations of the ideological functions of historical memory; however, it is not the primary objective of this series to find an ideal, politically correct, ideology-free mode or method of how to make sense of history. The goal is rather to explore the cultural practices involved in generating historical sense as an extremely important realm of human thought and action, the study of which may contribute to new forms of mutual understanding. In an age of rapid globalization that manifests itself primarily on an economic and political—and, much less so, on a cultural level—finding such forms is becoming an urgent task.

It is for this reason that the series begins with a volume documenting an ongoing intercultural debate. It is the aim of the first volume to question whether or not the academic discipline of "history"—as developed at Western universities over the course of the last two hundred years—represents a specific mode or type of historical thinking that can be differentiated from other forms and practices of historical consciousness. Subsequent volumes present history as a genuinely interdisciplinary field of research. Historians, anthropologists, philosophers, sociologists, psychologists, and literary theorists, as well as specialists in fields such as media and cultural studies, explore such questions as: What constitutes a specifically historical "sense" and meaning? How do different cultures throughout various historical periods conceptualize time? Which specific forms of "perception" inform these conceptualizations, and which general problems are connected with them? What are the dominant strategies used to represent historical meaning? What function does the generating of historical sense fulfill in practical life?

Ranging from general overviews and theoretical reflections to case studies, the essays cover a wide range of contexts related to the question of "historical sense," among them topics such as collective identity, the psychology and psychoanalysis of historical memory, and the intercultural dimension of historical thinking. Additionally, the books of this series address the place of history in the humanitites, and the humanities in general as an essential place for sense generation in modern societies. Even modes of sense generation that are not specifically historical can be dealt with, as long as they share with history the concern for coming to terms with time as it pertains to human life. For the most part, historical memory is not an arbitrary function of the cultural practices used by human beings to orient themselves in the world in which they are born, but covers, rather, those domains of human life that seek to orient existence temporally. These domains demand mental procedures for connecting past, present, and future that became generalized and institutionalized in the West as that specific field of culture we call "history." The areas of human thought, action, and suffering that call for a specifically "historical thinking" include (1) the construction and perpetuation of collective identity, (2) the reconstruction of patterns of orientation after catastrophes and events of massive destruction, (3) the challenge of given patterns of orientation presented by and through the confrontation with radical otherness, and (4) the general experience of change and contingency.

In accordance with the collective aim of the series "Making Sense of History" to outline a new field of interdisciplinary research (rather than to offer a single theory), the volumes in the series are not designed to establish a new historiographical approach; rather, they seek to contribute to an interdisciplinary study of historical cultures and related subjects. One focus, for instance, is on the notion of collective identity. General theoretical aspects and problems in this field are considered, most importantly the interrelationships among identity, otherness, and representation. But case studies of the construction of gender identities (especially those of women), of ethnic identities, and of different forms and politics of national identity are also included. The essays on this subject point out that any concept of identity as being disconnected from historical change not only leads to theoretical problems, but also covers over the fact that most modern forms of collective identity take into account the possibility of their own historical transformation. Thus the essays in this series that are concerned with identity suggest that identity ought to be regarded not as a function of difference, but as a concrete cultural and ongoing *practice* of difference. They show that the production of "sense" is an epistemological starting point, as well as a theoretical and empirical research-field in and of itself.

Another volume focuses on the psychological construction of time and history, analyzing the interrelation between memory, morality, and authenticity in different forms of historical or biographical narration. The findings of empirical psychological studies (on the development of temporal and historical consciousness in children, or on the psychological mechanisms of reconstructing past experiences) are discussed in the light of attempts to outline a psychological concept of historical consciousness around the notions of "narration" and the "narrative structure of historical time."

This first volume of the series is dedicated to psychoanalytical approaches to the study of historical memory. It reconsiders older debates on the relation between psychoanalysis and history and introduces more recent research projects. Instead of simply pointing out some psychoanalytical insights that can be adopted and applied in certain areas of historical studies, this volume aims at combining psychoanalytical and historical perspectives, thus exploring the history of psychoanalysis itself, as well as the "unconscious" dimensions underlying and informing academic and nonacademic forms of historical memory. Moreover, it puts special emphasis on transgenerational forms of remembrance, on the notion of trauma as a key concept in this field, and on case studies that may indicate directions for further research.

Cultural differences in historical thinking that arise from different concepts of temporality are the subject of another volume. With a view to encouraging comparative research, this volume offers general essays and case studies written with the intention of providing comparative interpretations of concrete material, as well as possible paradigmatic research-questions for further comparisons. In the light of the recent resurgence of ethnocentric world-views, this volume focuses on the question of how cultural and social studies should react to this challenge. It aims at counteracting ethnocentrism by bridging the current gap between a rapid globalization manifesting itself in ever increasing political/economic interdependencies of states and continents, and the corresponding lack of mutual understanding in the realm of culture. The essays illustrate the necessity of intercultural communication pertaining to the various historical cultures and their shared semblances as well as the differences between them. Such communication seems not only a possible, but indeed a necessary presupposition of any attempt to negotiate cultural differences on a political level, whether between states or within the increasingly multicultural societies in which we live.

The special emphasis the series fixes on the problem of cultural differences and intercultural communication reveals the editors' desire to aim beyond the realm of merely academic concern. Building intercultural communication represents a formidable challenge, as well as a great hope, to a project committed to general theoretical reflection on the universal phenomenon of "remembering the past." Despite the fact that "cultural difference" has become something of a buzz phrase since the 1990s, the topic itself is characterized by a paradox quite similar to that underlying the current fate of the notion of history.

The past fifteen years have witnessed escalating interference by the industrialized states in the political and economic affairs of the rest of the world, as well as an increased (if sometimes eccentric) appropriation of modern economic and political structures by developing countries, including the former or still officially "communist" states. But this process of mutual rapprochement on the political and economic fronts is characterized by a remarkable lack of knowledge of, or even interest in, the cultural and historical backgrounds of the respective nations. Thus, the existing official forms of "intercultural" communication lack an adequate cultural dimension, leaving the themes and problems analyzed in this series of volumes (identity, memory, cultural practices, history, religion, philosophy, literature) outside of what is explicitly communicated; as if such matters would not have powerful affects on political as well as economic agendas.

On the other hand, the currently dominant approaches found among the cultural theorists and critical thinkers of the West either claim that an intercultural *rapport* concerning the common grounds of cultural identities is impossible—based on the assumption that they have nothing in common (the hypostatization of difference)—or they politicize cultural differences in such a way that they are relegated to mere *stuff*, out of which may be constructed various cultural subject-positions. Despite their self-understanding as "critique," these approaches amount to the exclusion of culture on the level of national politics and economic exchange alike. Thus, cultural theory seems to react to the marginalization of culture by way of its own self-marginalization.

The series "Making Sense of History" intends to challenge this marginalization by introducing a form of cultural studies that takes the term *culture* seriously again, without dissolving it into identity politics or into a hypostatized concept of unbridgeable difference. At the same time the goal is to reintroduce a notion of "historical theory" that no longer disconnects itself from historical memory and remembrance as concrete cultural practices, but seeks instead to explore those practices, interpreting them as different articulations of the universal (if heterogeneous) effort to make sense of history. Thus, the series relies on the idea that an academic contribution to the problem of intercultural communication should assume the form of an academic discourse newly awake to its own historicity and cultural background, as well as a fresh acknowledgement that other cultural, but nonacademic, practices of "sense-formation" are equally important forms of human orientation and self-understanding (in their general function, in fact, not much different from the efforts of academic thought itself).

Such a reinscription of the universal claims of modern academic discourses into a variety of cultural contexts, the objective of which is the providing of new starting points for intercultural communication, is an enterprise that cannot be accomplished or even outlined in a series of a few books. Consequently, "Making Sense of History" should be regarded as something like a first attempt to map out one possible field of research—the field of "historical cultures"—that might help us to achieve this aim.

The idea of the book series was born in the wake of the successful completion of a research project on "Making Sense of History: Interdisciplinary Studies in the Structure, Logic and Function of Historical Consciousness—an Intercultural Comparison." This project took place at the Center for Interdisciplinary Studies (ZiF) of the University of Bielefeld, Germany, in 1994/95. It was partly supported by the Kulturwissenschaftliches Institut (KWI) Essen (Institute for Advanced Study in the Humanities at Essen). The project's conferences and workshops generated many of the chapters included in the books in this series. The arranging, revising, and editing of the different texts occupied the next several years, with the first volume coming out in 2002. In the meantime the series has enlarged its perspectives by bringing in other projects of the Kulturwissenschaftliches Institut and of its partners all over the world.

I would like to express my gratitude to the staff of the Center for Interdisciplinary Study at the University of Bielefeld and of the Institute for Advanced Study in the Humanities at Essen. I also want to thank the editors and co-editors of each of the volumes in this series and, of course, all the contributors for the effort and patience they expended to make these books possible. Finally, my thanks go to Angelika Wulff for her engaged management of this series and to my wife Inge for her intensive support in editing my texts.

Introduction
The Holocaust and Historical Methodology[1]

Dan Stone

> *Dictatorships, wars, and cruelty drive whole countries to madness. My theory is that the human species was crazy from the very first and that civilization and culture are only enhancing man's insanity. Well, but you want the facts.*
> —Isaac Bashevis Singer, "A Tale of Two Sisters"

Twenty years ago, Saul Friedländer published his edited volume, *Probing the Limits of Representation: Nazism and the "Final Solution."* The book has become justly famous not as the first but as the most stimulating collection of essays on the problem of how to represent an event which seems to outstrip the ability of language or art to do so. As Hannah Arendt wrote of the Holocaust, "For those engaged in the quest for meaning and understanding, what is frightening is not that it is something new, but that it has brought to light the ruin of our categories of thought and standards of judgment."[2] This was a problem that exercised many scholars at a time (the late 1980s and early 1990s) when debates over postmodernism and its impact on the humanities were at their height. Friedländer's book basically turned on Hayden White's claims, in his well-known works *Metahistory* (1973), *Tropics of Discourse* (1978), and *The Content of the Form* (1987), that there were no grounds to be found in the historical record itself for construing the meaning of the past one way or another. In the charged atmosphere of the time, this claim was widely misunderstood to mean that White—who also advocated a rediscovery of the sublime in history, despite its association with Fascism—was an extreme relativist who had no defense against Holocaust denial. If one narrative of the past was as good as any other, then one might as well say that truth is no more than the force of prevalent opinion.[3] In the face of the inevitable attack on this position (which reason-

---

Notes for this section begin on page 15.

able person would not attack it?), many were satisfied when White appeared to back down somewhat and to suggest in his chapter in *Probing the Limits of Representation* that an appeal to the facts themselves would, in the case of the Holocaust, prevent a narrative of the events being written in, say, the comic or pastoral mode.[4]

White, however, did not think that, in Martin Jay's words, he "undercuts what is most powerful in his celebrated critique of naïve historical realism."[5] In other words, he still held to his view that one cannot look to the historical record in order to reveal the meaning of the past.[6] Meanings are given through aesthetic and moral choices by historians in the present. With reference to such major events as revolutions and wars, Jay argued that there is "virtually no historical content that is linguistically unmediated and utterly bereft of meaning, waiting around for the later historian to emplot it in arbitrary ways."[7] That is quite so, but White does not think that the narrative emplotments constructed by historians are arbitrary. He also admits that the narratives historians tell about the past can be altered by the evidence; for all that, there are more meanings available to historians in the present than there are constraints placed upon potential narratives by the linguistic content and mediation of events. The range of possible narratives—of "true stories" to use Paul Veyne's famous term[8]—is exceptionally wide, if not unlimited, so that the historian's narrative freedom is not confined by some dictate in the sources. In any case, with respect to the Holocaust, the range of possible narratives far exceeds those that have been produced, for, as I will discuss below, Holocaust historiography, for all its size and sophistication, remains dominated by a more or less positivist—that is to say, untheorized empiricist—historical method.[9]

Although few historians have engaged directly with White on the level of theory or philosophy of history,[10] his claims have come to inform accepted historical practice. Holocaust historiography is something of an exception, as we will see, even though (or precisely because) it is in the field of Holocaust history (or more precisely, with respect to the phenomenon of Holocaust denial) that his ideas have been most hotly debated. This book investigates the many ways that the historical record can be engaged with, not just to show that there are many ways to do history, but to demonstrate that the meanings we give to the past are not provided for us, ready-made, by the past itself, but are forged through the creative act of writing history. But, as a volume in the theory of history, this emphasis on the "creative" or "poetic" does not contradict a rigorous reliance on the evidence. White himself never suggested, contrary to some of his bowdlerizers, that one is justified in inventing the past if that is what people want to hear. "Events happen," wrote White, but "facts are constituted by linguistic description."[11] But events and facts, even as White defines them, are not unrelated! As Allan Megill explicates: if the historical text is itself "a 'fictive' creation," that does not mean that "'there is no *there* there'; it is an assertion that the historian makes (but not out of nothing) the particular historical objects presented in her work."¹² *The Holocaust and Historical Methodology* thus confirms White's basic standpoint, not through philosophical analysis but through reflections on historical method and discussions of the varied methodologies that can be employed to write about the Holocaust. The different chapters show, by virtue of their wide range and different approaches, that many different meanings emerge out of the historical record, without having to worry that anyone doubts that "the event" occurred in the first place. As Robert Berkhofer, talking of history in general, noted, "historians must authorize new forms of representation without creating new rules of historical practice about what constitutes proper history itself."[13]

This book is not about speculative philosophy of history; that is to say, it does not engage with the question of the "forces" of history, or whether History has an inner meaning or direction independent from the meanings given to it by human beings.[14] But it does engage with historical theory (I use that term as synonymous with what is usually and inappropriately called "analytic philosophy of history"[15]) on two levels. The first is a somewhat pedestrian level—that is not meant pejoratively—of historical method, that is, the practical steps historians take to acquire and to criticize sources, and then to produce a synthetic account or narrative of the past in which these processes are combined and implicitly inform the account. The second is a more "high-level" consideration of methodology, that is to say, theoretical reflections on the nature of method and on the "schools" of history (social, economic, intellectual, cultural, diplomatic, and so on). The aim in this second level of analysis is not simply to consider which practical issues of method best ensure historical rigor, but to step back and ask how historical method per se and particular historical approaches or schools advance our understanding of the Holocaust. These two levels of analysis are described by Jörn Rüsen as "object theory" and "meta-theory"; they distinguish theoretical statements about what happened in the past (such as the changes that people experience over time) from theoretical statements about the nature of historical studies. Rüsen notes that the historian's aim in thinking theoretically should be "to make the principles on which their practical work rests so transparent and conscious that they can carry out their work more effectively. It will enable them to prove, defend, develop, and better their argument in a way which will decisively place their practical work on a higher level than would be the case without this knowledge."[16]

This distinction between "method" and "methodology" is too neatly drawn. In practice, the two blur into one another, because even the most practically-minded guide to method (teaching source criticism to graduate students, for example) necessarily involves some theoretical concepts, whether or not the author or tutor is aware of them or can articulate them. This book should thus be understood as a contribution to historical theory; it aims to show how, in the case of the Holocaust, historical method and methodology come up against severe challenges by virtue of the material under consideration and as a result of the ways in which the Holocaust has widely been understood to impugn many basic tenets of western civilization, including those central to historical scholarship: impartiality, objectivity, progress, clarity of meaning, scholarly rigor. As Friedländer pointed out in his introduction to *Probing the Limits of Representation*, "it is precisely the 'Final Solution' which allows postmodernist thinking to question the validity of any totalizing view of history, of any reference to a definable metadiscourse, thus opening the way for a multiplicity of equally valid approaches."[17] In fact, the Holocaust does not present special difficulties of historical representation—the same epistemological difficulties apply to all historical descriptions. But these difficulties present themselves with especial clarity in the case of the Holocaust. This realization, as Alon Confino notes, "opens up new ways of understanding the Holocaust. It entails a shift in historical sensibility from conceiving of the Holocaust not only in terms of the limits of representation but also—because of generational, professional, interpretative and cultural changes—in terms of the possibilities and promises of historical representation."[18]

So, on the one hand this is a book of historical theory, a consideration of historical method and historical methodology. On the other hand, it is specifically about the Holocaust and how these theoretical issues affect the historical study of it, and vice-versa. What is curious, as I discuss below, is that there has been so much interest in questions of Holocaust representation, but that the vast majority of these studies have been undertaken in the fields of the visual arts, museum studies, film studies or literature.[19] Very few historians have taken up the questions raised by Friedländer's volume, even though the Holocaust, in Rüsen's words, "represents a 'borderline event,' the importance of which consists in its transgression of the level of the subject matter of historical thinking and reaching into the core of the mental procedures of historical thinking itself."[20] Thus, this book aims to revive interest amongst historians in theoretical issues of Holocaust representation, not on the level of speculative philosophy of history but in a way that is hopefully relevant to what historians consider their everyday practice. The book's focus is not explicitly on questions of the status of truth in history or on the limits of representation, but on the possibilities of different methodology and approaches, for example culture, memory, testimony, or ecology, as well as questions raised by comparative genocide studies. To explain what this means, I will first briefly set out what is meant by historical method and then show what effects theoretical discussions of method have on the particular field of Holocaust history.

On Historical Method

"Method makes the historian," claimed Lord Acton, and his precepts for rigorous historical inquiry still form the basis of a historian's training. For Acton the critical method required self-abnegation and the scholar's devotion to time-consuming labor, yet in essence "method is only the reduplication of common sense, and is best acquired by observing its use by the ablest men in every variety of intellectual employment," as he put it in his 1895 inaugural lecture at Cambridge. Correct method in the study of history, far more than erudition, "strengthens, straightens, and extends the mind." Historians today might not choose to argue in terms quite so redolent of dead white bourgeois males, but in reality Acton's statements are not that far removed from what is still the basis of the historical discipline. The tripartite combination of an exhaustive search for relevant material (heuristics), a rigorous process of appraising the material for its use as historical evidence (source critique), and producing a formal written statement that synthesizes this material into a dispassionate, coherent narrative (interpretation) is the procedure that budding historians are expected to master.

And quite reasonably so. Knowing where to look or how to find sources is obviously a *sine qua non* of writing history. Subjecting source material to criticism is also fundamental. Not ignoring sources even though they threaten the validity of one's hypothesis is the acme of professionalism.[21] Popular historians can weave this material into compelling narratives, but good history in the scholarly sense can also mean discussing the evidence in a way that places more emphasis on analysis than story-telling, even if Roger Chartier and Paul Ricoeur are right to stress that "history is always narration, even when it claims to be rid of the narrative" because its "mode of comprehension remains dependent on procedures and operations that assure the emplotment of the actions represented."[22] Still, there might be more to history-writing than this. Historical method is only the starting point, the procedure that distinguishes history from fiction and which provides a community of scholars with basic operating principles on which all can agree. It says nothing about the construction of historical texts and how textual constructions should be interpreted. It cannot explain why a novel that is based on substantial historical research, such as Jonathan Littell's *The Kindly Ones,* can be considered more insightful about Holocaust perpetrators than most of the historical research on the subject.[23] The idea that "[i]n historical representation, we never deal with the past; we deal with historical texts as propositions that replace the past" is one that was not on Acton's agenda.[24] It is the third element of historical method—the construction of the historical text—that requires further elucidation.

Many criticisms of Acton's definition of method were proposed over the twentieth century. Some historians sought to place history on a more scientific footing than even Acton thought possible, from his successor, J. B. Bury, whose 1902 inaugural lecture was titled "The Science of History," to Carl Hempel's notion of the "covering law model," an attempt to provide generalizable, causal models of past human behavior.[25] Others showed that by expanding the repertoire of what constituted an appropriate subject for historiography, traditional source criticism became harder to do and needed to be supplemented by more ingenious methods derived from cognate fields, such as sociology or anthropology, not to mention statistics or climatology. The Annales historians, in particular, with their devotion to the *longue durée* and to *histoire totale*, seriously dented the notion of the historian acting as a neutral conduit for the archival material, even as they too promoted a "scientific" ideal, seeking to remove, at least in the Annales' earlier incarnations, the whiff of narrative and thus of artifice from their writings.[26]

More recently, the criticisms have become even harder to answer. In the wake of structuralism, post-structuralism, and deconstruction, historians started to pay more attention to the contingent nature of their sources, and to the fact that even the most reliable of sources was no more than a surviving trace from the infinite possible number of such remnants. "The illusion of integral reconstitution," writes Veyne hyperbolically but not uninstructively, "comes from the fact that the documents, which provide us with the answers, also dictate the questions to us; in that way they not only leave us in ignorance of many things, but they also leave us ignorant of the fact that we are ignorant."[27] The expansion of the very notion of a "source" first by the Annales historians and then in cultural history, so that historians now write histories of the body, of the emotions, or of sexuality, means that even Veyne's highly critical stance must be updated, for not only what is written down can be a historical source. Besides, what should historians make of events such as genocide, whose monstrousness consists partly in their "destruction of the archive," that is, the attempt to render their occurrence incomprehensible?[28] Perhaps the problem, as Constantin Fasolt writes, was not that too little was being asked of history, but too much: "Expecting history to reach the reality of the past is to allow oneself to be seduced by a mirage arising not from the past but from a historical imagination run amok."[29] The "noble dream" of "writing up" the past *wie es eigentlich gewesen ist* began to recede from historians' realm of expectations.[30] Historians started to resort to "defenses" in order, as they saw it, to "save" history as a discipline from the onslaught of irresponsible relativists.[31]

Foremost among the latter is Dominick LaCapra. An intellectual historian, LaCapra has taken it upon himself to warn historians of the unexpected dangers that lurk in assuming a positivistic (or "common sense") stance towards the past. In particular, since he has turned his focus to the Holocaust, LaCapra has discussed the writing of history in psychoanalytic terms, alerting historians to the problem of transference and counter-transference, especially when dealing with traumatic events. Indeed, the notion that a historian might have an affective relationship with the past is absent from Acton, for whom the historian, with suitable training, was simply a conduit, through whose labours the past revealed itself. For LaCapra, not only must we pay attention to the ways in which historians construct the past—this is now a given of critical historical theory—but we must also take heed of the ways in which events, especially limit events such as the Holocaust, hinder historical construction. Whilst LaCapra's attention to rituals, symbols, language, textuality, trauma, memory, and transference all mean that he—along with Hayden White—presents a "literary challenge" to historiography,[32] it is right to stress that LaCapra presents opposition to history from within the profession, promoting diversity and interdisciplinarity over narrow boundary-drawing and methodological rigidity.[33]

However, none of those theoretical criticisms means that the past the historian writes is not in some way related to what happened, even if it cannot represent the totality of the past and even if language constructs the past rather than opening a window on to it. Otherwise, there would be no difference between history and fiction.[34] History, as Ankersmit notes, is "a continuous experiment with language; an experiment in relating language to the world."[35] And, as the "linguistic turn" made clear, "the fact that there may be different 'languages' for speaking about historical reality is no less an argument in favour of historical relativism than the fact that we can describe the world in English, French, German, or Japanese."[36] There are many ways of representing the same past. Here is where method remains important. What Kevin Passmore describes as "the method of hypothesis formulation and testing—the hypothetic-deductive method—favoured by many equally conventional historians actually combines acceptance of the unlimited interpretative possibilities open to historians with the recognition that all interpretations are not equally valid."[37] What historians now aim to achieve is a "satisfactory incompletion" or "substitute" for the past on the one hand, and the establishment of criteria for judging the success of other historians' interpretations on the other. Acton's dictum about method remains germane, even if the dream of an "ultimate history" has disappeared—that is to say, even if the ends to which that method is put are now conceived differently.

That said, after all the debates about history and theory in the context of postmodernism, it is obvious that Acton's historical method can hardly be accepted unaltered. Some historians may still operate on that basis, in the belief that any consideration of theory distracts them from their "real" work of narrating the past (as opposed to explaining regular and general phenomena, which characterizes the natural sciences). But this is a caricature most likely to appear in the writings of history's detractors. The majority of historians today do pay attention to theoretical questions, of both the "object-theoretical" and "meta-theoretical" sort. Although few historians actively research and write about methodology, that does not mean they operate in the methodological darkness. Source research is presupposed by historical-philosophical theorizing, as Rüsen observes, for otherwise there would be nothing to theorize about.[38] "Postmodernism and narrativism," Ankersmit writes, "thus must be amended in such a way that the historian's intuitive ability to represent a past reality in and by his narrative is respected."[39] In the context of Holocaust history, most historians are acutely aware of the difficulties they face in representing the

Holocaust. They know that the language they (necessarily) use may obscure or occult the past as much as reveal it,[40] even if they might be uncomfortable with Hayden White's assertion that "even the most rigorously objective and determinedly 'clear' and literal language cannot do justice to the Holocaust without recourse to myth, poetry, and 'literary' writing."[41] It is perhaps for that reason that, paradoxically, the field of Holocaust history is dominated by an approach that Lord Acton would more clearly recognize as akin to his own than almost any other area of historical inquiry today. Holocaust history is "self-policed" for methodological consistency and convention, perhaps out of fear of overstepping the bounds of decency or "using" the Holocaust as the subject for inappropriate experimental narrative,[42] perhaps just because much basic factual knowledge still remains to be uncovered. It is for the same reason that more searching questions need to be asked, to make the methodological unease that all Holocaust historians recognize and experience have a greater impact on the historiography of the Holocaust.

It goes without saying that the interpretive questions and analytical frameworks that have dominated Holocaust historiography have changed over time, the most famous being the debate between "intentionalists" and "functionalists" that has given way in the last decade or so to the "return of ideology." These changes do not occur without meta-theoretical reflection on the aims and purposes of historical study or on the most appropriate methods for achieving them, appropriateness being determined by the perspectives and aims of the historians concerned at any given time. Method is intimately related to historiography.[43] For example, Saul Friedländer's many theoretical writings from the 1980s and 1990s helped him to construct the complex narrative of his two-volume *Nazi Germany and the Jews*; Christopher Browning's empirical work on testimonies from the Starachowice labor camp led him to a position in which he challenged, from a strictly empirical standpoint, the traditional reluctance amongst Holocaust historians to use survivor testimony, which they perceive as unreliable.[44] Nevertheless, the history of the Holocaust tends to be written from a traditional understanding of historical methodology, with the result that the field, massive though it is, is methodologically quite staid (on both the levels of methodology described earlier). This in turn means that there is a certain sense of predictability about what is produced, so that even given the changes in focus of the last decades, the overall interpretive framework has changed very little.[45] As Confino says, the interpretive leitmotifs of Holocaust historiography—ideology, race, context and war/radicalization—are no longer sources of historiographical innovation in quite the same way as they once were: "As the Holocaust shocks us less than a generation ago, so the specific rendition of these notions seems to have become less challenging. The historiography will change, as all historiographies do, new approaches will emerge, new interpretations be put forward."[46] It is time to reflect on Holocaust historiography from a methodological point of view. How can the story we tell about the Holocaust be told anew?[47]

On the Holocaust and Historical Methodology

There is a danger when using the Holocaust as the basis for theoretical discussions that the "horror behind the words," as Friedländer put it, might be forgotten. Just as the contributors to *Probing the Limits of Representation* never neglected the real reason behind their inquiries, so I trust that readers will see that the same can be said of the contributors to this volume, both those who deal with questions of method (ways of gathering and assessing sources) and those who discuss methodology (theoretical analyses of method). Besides, if it was true in the early 1990s that the "present memory of Nazism and its crimes is directly influenced by global intellectual shifts intrinsically linked to the questions raised" in Friedländer's volume (Friedländer meant debates about postmodernism), then in the context of ubiquitous representations and official commemorations of the Holocaust that now prevail in the western world, theoretical questions about what we are doing and how we go about representing the Holocaust are no less important now. Indeed, they are more important, not just because "Holocaust consciousness" has become remarkably pervasive, even in countries like Britain and Spain where such awareness lagged well behind other European countries,[48] but because, sadly, much of what passes for Holocaust representation today, in art, film, fiction, education, children's literature, and so on, contributes to a banalization and infantilization of the subject matter and of those who consume it. Nazism and the Holocaust in contemporary culture have gone way beyond the limits that gave rise to Saul Friedländer's fears in the 1980s, when he wrote *Reflections of Nazism*.[49] Today, supposedly with the aim of challenging us to maintain the memory of the Holocaust, we are inundated with Holocaust kitsch, from virtual candle lighting on commemorative websites to exploitative artworks where death camp imagery is employed for its "shock" value.[50] This book is motivated by a wish to think about how historians can respond in innovative but responsible ways to the horror of the Holocaust.

This question is no less relevant today than it was in the heyday of debates over postmodernism, and thus *Probing the Limits of Representation* can itself now be historicized. Those debates have died away to a large extent, but it would be a mistake to conclude, as seems to be implied by the predominance of empirical work, that the historians "won" the debate. Far from it, in fact. First, there are many sorts of historians, and many of the theoretical suppositions of postmodernism (broadly understood) have become part of historians' everyday sensibility, especially cultural and intellectual historians, for whom attending to textual construction and representation is second nature. Second, merely brushing something aside is not the same as having dealt with it head on. But in the case of the historiography of the Holocaust things are more complicated. Debates about postmodernism often turned on the Holocaust because it is "an event at the limits," and both those who favored postmodern approaches and those who saw the need to "defend" history used the Holocaust as a kind of "trump card."[51] Yet among Holocaust historians, as opposed to historical theorists, theory barely intruded, and the research that was done in the years after 1990 was overwhelmingly empirical. This empiricism was facilitated by the huge wave of newly-accessible archival material that emerged from the formerly communist countries of Eastern Europe, and it has revolutionized our understanding of the unfolding of the Holocaust at a local level, especially in Eastern Europe, and the relationships between the networks of perpetrators who carried it out, from the vast RSHA apparatus to the level of local administration.[52] But the fact that theory appeared at best only implicitly was not a sign that the problems raised by Friedländer had gone away, but merely that historians were too busy with new archival material to find time for other matters—in Ankersmit's terms, they were so busy with the first level of *historische Sinnbildung,* the recording of true statements about the past, that they neglected the two other levels of narrative representation (the organization of knowledge, i.e., the true statements about the past) and historical experience.[53]

Thus it seems that there is an inverse correlation between the closeness of an event to "the limits" and the willingness of historians to engage theoretically with it, when the reverse ought to be true: precisely the "events at the limit" should be the ones that engender discussion about how historians do what they do. Following the empirical achievements of the last twenty years, which has seen an extraordinary accumulation of factual detail on the Holocaust, this book's presupposition is that, with major culminating works by Browning, Friedländer, and Longerich now available, as well as the huge changes in perspective engendered by genocide studies, postcolonial studies, and world history, the time has come for a return to theoretical reflection on the nature of Holocaust historiography.[54] Twenty years ago Dominick LaCapra wrote that the study of the Holocaust "may help us to reconsider the requirements of historiography in general."[55] That challenge remains to be taken up. And over a century ago, Lord Acton said that "there is far more fear of drowning than of drought" where historical sources are concerned; today's problem is therefore not one of access to material but of what to do with it and how to make it generate meaning, a particularly thorny problem for a topic—the Holocaust—that fundamentally challenges the very notion of meaning in history, both for those who experienced it and for those of us who seek to try and write its history.

Not everyone sees the need for this sort of inquiry. Donald Bloxham, for example, writes that Holocaust historiography has of late "sustained a standard of sobriety and nuance" that he thinks is lacking in the broader discipline of "Holocaust studies," in which over-production has had a negative impact on quality: "Bolstered by a now well-known cohort of comparatively junior German scholars," Bloxham writes, "as well as longer-established figures like Christopher Browning, Holocaust history is a vibrant field."[56] This claim is easily verified, for high-quality historical research on the Holocaust is being published at a rapid rate, from works on the ghettos to individual country or regional studies, to studies of the looting of Jewish property, among many others that could be cited.[57]

Yet if these studies can be lauded for their historical rigor and sobriety, this is largely because they share a common methodology.[58] They are driven first and foremost by an empiricism that places most of the focus on the first two facets of Acton's method (heuristics and source critique) and far less on the third (interpretation). Historical approaches that seek to investigate aspects of the human past that are less easily proven empirically, such as symbolically-laden ritual violence or "collective memory," are much less common in Holocaust historiography than in other areas of historical study (as the chapters by Finchelstein, Goldberg, and Neumann discuss). This is less the case for American Holocaust scholarship than for German, as Frank Bajohr has noted, commenting on the works of younger German historians:

> Clearly, in Germany, dealing with this subject matter is no way to advance careers. The reason is not simply because the history of the "Third Reich" still triggers defensive reflexes among academics. It also arises from the methodological conservatism of empirical research into Nazism, not infrequently characterized by a morally charged, pernickety concentration on facts, while theoretical foundations—even those of minimal or middling scope—are often frowned upon.[59]

This is not a new problem. In 1947, Columbia literature professor Emery Neff criticized German historians for their excessive devotion to fact-finding, which "had prevented Theodor Mommsen from writing more than one good book and kept Acton from writing one at all."[60] And it is certainly true that the most obvious characteristic of German PhD or *Habilitation* (postdoctoral) dissertations written on the Holocaust—even where they have had a justifiably significant impact on our understanding of the Holocaust, as in some very noteworthy cases—is their massive attention to factual detail at the expense of interpretation. But if German scholarship is the most obvious manifestation of this phenomenon, it is hardly absent from Holocaust history in general.

In other words, while the intersection of Holocaust history and historical theory of the 1980s and early 1990s led many to regard the Holocaust as the harbinger of postmodernism, the latter has not really had much impact on historical research into the Holocaust other than in the feeling of a changed sensibility. The "discipline" of history, in Karyn Ball's sense, remains in place. It is still necessary, according to Ball, to investigate "the nexus of scientific, aesthetic, moral, and rhetorical ideals that scholars in different fields invoke as they defend an 'appropriate' (rigorous and ethical) approach to the Holocaust."

When Ball talks of "disciplining the Holocaust," she refers to "efforts to secure its moral and historical significance for 'us' against potential trivializations over time." For Ball, the logic of "discipline" is shown most clearly in historians' "voluble" reaction to Daniel Goldhagen's *Hitler's Willing Executioners* (1996). Objecting to his *ressentiment,* historians rejected Goldhagen's challenge to their "reliance on logical criteria to define appropriate Holocaust historiography." But Ball regards "Goldhagen's 'undignified' ressentiment as an understandable response to a genocide that destroyed families, communities, and future generations." The vehemence of the historians' response exposes, she thinks, "the depth of academics' investment in the protocol of restraint, which is inextricably bound up with the epistemological idea of rigor that governs professional scholarship as a mode of rational behavior."[61] Indeed, she goes so far as to claim that "Goldhagen's impropriety is a symptom of a posttraumatic anxiety among members of a vulnerable group, the rage of the betrayed minority clamouring at the gates of a self-entitled majority that aided or turned its back on murder. Traumatic events challenge historians to open these gates by divesting themselves of a scientistic equanimity that is barbaric in the face of genocide."[62] Questions of ethics, memory, and experience all inform historical research, along with empiricism. There is no such thing as just "doing history," especially on a topic as politically and emotionally charged as the Holocaust.

Ball's findings are not novel. The impact of, *inter alia,* Hayden White, Frank Ankersmit, Jean-François Lyotard, Jacques Derrida, Berel Lang, Lawrence Langer, Dominick LaCapra, Moishe Postone, Dan Diner and many others has been profound. But their impact has been less on the practice of history than on debates in "Holocaust Studies" on the representation of the Holocaust in mediums such as film, art, and literature. Thus, even if there were many good reasons apart from his impropriety for historians to reject Goldhagen's arguments, Ball's recent book represents a brave attempt to reinvigorate debates about Holocaust history's relationship to historical theory. In philosophy of history, too, debates have been less lively than they were in the 1980s and 1990s. If there is continued interest in the work of White, LaCapra, Ankersmit, et al. amongst philosophers of history, this is not true of historians at large.[63] And among Holocaust historians a feeling seems to prevail that turning one's attention to theoretical matters is a distraction from the "real" work of writing history, somehow a waste of valuable time that could be spent recovering the as-yet unknown facts of the Holocaust. Yet this makes no sense; one cannot have one without the other.

Even away from theory, the repertoire of historical methods remains limited when it comes to the Holocaust, in comparison with other major events. Perhaps the most important exception concerns the historiography of the Holocaust's victims. Since its inception, cultural history—understood less as the study of symbolic meaning-production in the past than as the study of "culture" in a more Arnoldian sense as the most "precious" qualities and characteristics of any society—has informed the history of the Jews under Nazi occupation, especially in Israeli history writing. However, in the anthropologically-inflected sense of attempting to discover the ways in which past actors sought to give meaning to their lives through symbol, ritual, and narrative, the literature is in its infancy, as Alon Confino, Amos Goldberg, and I argue in this book.[64] This attempt to recover the meanings that people in the past gave to their lives and the events around them should not be confused with White's arguments about the historian creating meaning in the present. There is, however, no paradox: cultural history is subject to the same epistemological problems as any other field of history writing, with the historical text acting as a substitute for the past itself, and the recovery of meanings in the past does not mean that historians are not at the same time creating meanings in the present. Equally, just because cultural history involves the search for past meanings—by no means an uncomplicated affair, for the sources are often opaque at best—does not exclude it from the assertion that the fundamental importance of the 'historical operation' is its role in meaning-creation in the present.

Within the broad arena of cultural history, there is one theme that stands out in the literature: memory. Commensurate with the "memory boom" that has been such a striking characteristic of western societies (but not only western) in the last two decades or so, Holocaust historiography has seen a turn to memory as a dominant paradigm.[65] The work of Alon Confino, Peter Fritzsche, Wulf Kansteiner, and others has set up memory as central to understanding the Holocaust, even though, as Confino tellingly notes (in a comment that is of a piece with Bajohr's analysis of German history-writing), there has been no work on German memories during the Third Reich, nothing that would help to connect Nazism to the ways of life of Germans that might help us understand how Nazism as both break and continuity with German mores, norms, and prejudices could have taken over so effectively.[66] Again, the bulk of this work has been done either on the memory of the Holocaust in postwar Europe or the United States—including many very fine historical studies[67]—or is conducted by literary or cultural scholars whose work—on commemoration and artistic carriers of memory[68]—has not permeated into the historical study of the Holocaust itself (that is, explaining the Holocaust as an event rather than analyzing how people responded to it after 1945).[69] The same is true of testimony, as Zoë Waxman indicates. A sophisticated theoretical literature on testimony now exists,[70] but when Saul Friedländer made use of "the voices of the victims" in his two-volume *Nazi Germany and the Jews*, most Holocaust historians considered this to be a major advance. Cultural history has had great impact on historical research in general, but remarkably not on the study of the Holocaust.[71]

The other area that has made some impact on Holocaust history is gender studies. The resistance to asking questions about women and the Holocaust that was so striking in the 1980s and early 1990s has subsided, so that gender has become more or less part of the mainstream. However, the questions that are asked remain somewhat constrained, with debates still centered on the role of women as "carers and sharers" and whether women were better equipped to survive than men. Those who raise questions of "non-standard" female behavior have a harder time getting their voices heard, although it is no longer the case—as with female perpetrators—that we are so shocked by women who do not conform to cultural norms.

But if the shaking of historically-determined female roles has been beneficial, in certain respects it gives rise to more awkward questions. By "unmasking" female behavior that is considered "deviant," do we perhaps engage in an "inadvertent complicity" with sexual perversity? Can it be that, as Ball asks, "a feminist scholarly agenda calling for attention to the gendered and sexual differentiation of historical experiences colludes with this will in sexualizing the untold and therefore 'secret' horrors of the Holocaust"?[72] These sorts of questions are only beginning to be addressed, and until Holocaust historians start to write family histories and to address the role of Jewish masculinity and fatherhood in the Holocaust, will be impossible to answer fully.

Perhaps the most notable development in Holocaust history that directly touches on the concerns of this book is the growth of interest in Holocaust historiography. This is not just a generational matter, now that the grandchildren of the perpetrators and survivors are themselves taking responsibility for writing the history of the events; it is also a question of how to historicize the Holocaust without losing a sense of its moral enormity—returning us to Friedländer's debate with Broszat—and a response to arguments that silence reigned in the postwar period where the Holocaust was concerned. Although one cannot gainsay the difference between the first thirty years after World War II and the following thirty years which saw the gradual rise of "Holocaust consciousness" and the incorporation of Holocaust memory into the official commemorative calendar across the world, it is also correct that the difference is not an absolute one. Early historians of Holocaust, although largely independent and outside the university setting, made significant strides in developing the field, often building on work that had been done before and during the war itself. However, this revival of interest in historiographical concerns is driven more by a desire to get a handle on the massive literature and its sub-disciplines than out of theoretical-methodological concerns.[73] These historiographical studies still reveal the typical historian's tendency to "wrap up" the problem, even when explicit warnings against doing so are provided as part of the nature of the historical text. The Holocaust remains a challenge to historical methodology.

Frank Ankersmit, in an important essay on White, asks at one point: "is not the historical discipline, when considered as a whole, the interior monologue of contemporary Western civilization about a past from which it originated? ... Is historical culture not how our civilization, so to speak, 'writes itself' in the style of the middle voice?" In this sense, our attempt to "write ourselves" by writing history means that "history functions as the mirror of the radically alien in which we can begin to recognize our own cultural identity." Historical reality is then not "a positivist given" but "a permanent challenge to the historical discipline as a whole."[74] The Holocaust is paradigmatic of the challenge within a challenge: it challenges history writing to provide a methodological basis that would do more than merely record facts, and it exemplifies the problematic described by Ankersmit of what sort of civilization we want to "write" for ourselves in a world in which Auschwitz is a reality.

Notes

1. I am very grateful to Donald Bloxham, Alon Confino, Mark Donnelly, Becky Jinks, and Dirk Moses for their comments on an earlier version of this introduction.

2. Hannah Arendt, "Understanding and Politics (The Difficulties of Understanding)," in *Essays in Understanding 1930–1954: Uncollected and Unpublished Works by Hannah Arendt*, ed. Jerome Kohn (New York, 1994), 318. See also Ravit Reichman, "The Myth of Old Forms: On the Unknowable and Representation," in *Theoretical Interpretations of the Holocaust*, ed. Dan Stone (Amsterdam, 2001), 27–53.

3. See Robert Eaglestone, *Postmodernism and Holocaust Denial* (Cambridge, UK, 2001) and, more generally, Barbara Herrnstein Smith, *Belief and Resistance: Dynamics of Contemporary Intellectual Controversy* (Cambridge, MA, 1997), 28–31. Herrnstein Smith's brilliant book is perhaps the best way to understand "constructivist" epistemology.

4. Hayden White, "Historical Emplotment and the Problem of Truth," in *Probing the Limits of Representation: Nazism and the "Final Solution,"* ed. Saul Friedländer (Cambridge, MA, 1992), 37–53.

5. Martin Jay, "Of Plots, Witnesses, and Judgments," in *Probing the Limits of Representation*, ed. Friedländer, 97.

6. As he has maintained since, as, for example, in his exchange with Dirk Moses: A. Dirk Moses, "Hayden White, Traumatic Nationalism, and the Public Role of History"; Hayden White, "The Public Relevance of Historical Studies: A Reply to Dirk Moses," *History and Theory* 44 (2005): 311–22, 333–38.

7. Jay, "Of Plots, Witnesses, and Judgments," 99.

8. Paul Veyne, *Writing History: Essay on Epistemology* (Manchester, 1984).

9. See Wulf Kansteiner, "Mad History Disease Contained: Postmodern Excess Management Advice from the UK," *History and Theory* 39, no. 2 (2000): 218–29.

10. An exception is Alex Callinicos, *Theories and Narratives: Reflections on the Philosophy of History* (Cambridge, 1995).

11. Hayden White, "'Figuring the Nature of the Times Deceased': Literary Theory and Historical Writing," in *The Future of Literary Theory*, ed. Ralph Cohen (New York, 1989), 34–35.

12. Allan Megill, *Historical Knowledge, Historical Error: A Contemporary Guide to Practice* (Chicago, 2007), 186.

13. Robert F. Berkhofer, Jr., *Beyond the Great Story: History as Text and Discourse* (Cambridge, MA, 1995), 283.

14. See Dan Stone, *Constructing the Holocaust: A Study in Historiography* (London, 2003), esp. ch. 1.

15. See Mark Day, *The Philosophy of History: An Introduction* (London, 2008).

16. Jörn Rüsen, *History: Narration-Interpretation-Orientation* (New York, 2005), 78.

17. Friedländer, "Introduction," in *Probing the Limits of Representation*, ed. Friedländer, 5.

18. Alon Confino, "A World Without Jews: Interpreting the Holocaust," *German History* 27, no. 4 (2009): 534.

19. For example, Michael Rothberg, *Traumatic Realism: The Demands of Holocaust Representation* (Minneapolis, 2000); Michael Bernard-Donals and Richard Glejzer, *Between Witness and Testimony: The Holocaust and the Limits of Representation* (Albany, 2001); Paul Eisenstein, *Traumatic Encounters: Holocaust Representation and the Hegelian Subject* (Albany, 2003): Gary Weissman, *Fantasies of Witnessing: Postwar Efforts to Experience the Holocaust* (Ithaca, 2004); Robert Eaglestone, *The Holocaust and the Postmodern* (Oxford, 2004); Brett Ashley Kaplan, *Unwanted Beauty: Aesthetic Pleasure in Holocaust Representation* (Urbana, 2007).

20. Rüsen, *History*, 190. For examples, see Moishe Postone and Eric Santner, eds., *Catastrophe and Meaning: The Holocaust and the Twentieth Century* (Chicago, 2003); Dominick LaCapra, *Representing the Holocaust: History, Theory, Trauma* (Ithaca, 1994); LaCapra, *History and Memory after Auschwitz* (Ithaca, 1998); LaCapra, *Writing History, Writing Trauma* (Baltimore, 2001); Omer Bartov, *Murder in Our Midst: The Holocaust, Industrial Killing, and Representation* (New York, 1996); Bartov, *Mirrors of Destruction: War, Genocide, and Modern Identity* (New York, 2000); Dan Diner, *Beyond the Conceivable: Studies on Germany, Nazism, and the Holocaust* (Berkeley, 2000).

21. Martha Howell and Walter Prevenier, *From Reliable Sources: An Introduction to Historical Methods* (Ithaca, 2001).

22. Roger Chartier, "On the Relation of Philosophy and History," in his *Cultural History: Between Practices and Representations* (Cambridge, 1988), 62.

23. Jonathan Littell, *The Kindly Ones* (London, 2009). On Littell, see Susan Rubin Suleiman, "When the Perpetrator Becomes a Reliable Witness of the Holocaust: On Jonathan Littell's *Les Bienveillantes*," *New German Critique* 106 (2009): 1–19; Jonas Grethlein, "Myths, Morals, and Metafiction in Jonathan Littell's *Les Bienveillantes*," *PMLA* 127, no. 1 (2012): 77–93; cf. Wulf Kansteiner's comments on *The Kindly Ones* in this volume.

24. Robert Braun, "The Banality of Goodness: The Problem of Evil and Good in Representations of the Holocaust," in *The Holocaust in Hungary Fifty Years Later*, ed. Randolph L. Braham and Attila Pók (New York, 1997), 623. Cf. F. R. Ankersmit, "Historical Representation," *History and Theory* 27, no. 3 (1988): 205–28; Ankersmit, "Reply to Professor Zagorin," *History and Theory* 29, no. 3 (1990): 291 ("we can say that the *absence* of the past, that provokes all writing of history, has been compensated for by the *presence* of narrative substances").

25. J. B. Bury, "The Science of History," in *The Varieties of History: From Voltaire to the Present*, ed. Fritz Stern (London, 1970), 210–23; Carl G. Hempel, "Reasons and Covering Laws in Historical Explanation," in *The Philosophy of History*, ed. Patrick Gardiner (Oxford, 1974), 90–105.

26. François Furet, "Beyond the *Annales*," *Journal of Modern History* 55 (1983): 389–410; Lynn Hunt, "French History in the Last Twenty Years: The Rise and Fall of the *Annales* Paradigm," *Journal of Contemporary History* 21 (1986): 209–24; Hans Kellner, "Disorderly Conduct: Braudel's Mediterranean Satire (A Review of Reviews)," in his *Language and Historical Representation: Getting the Story Crooked* (Madison, 1989), 153–87; Paul Ricoeur, *Time and Narrative*, vol. 1 (Chicago, 1984), 207–17. Ricoeur notes that even economic history, as in volume three of Braudel's *History of the Mediterranean*, "lends itself to a plot when an initial term and a final term are chosen, and these are provided by categories other than conjunctural history itself, which, in principle, is endless, unlimited in the strict sense" (214–15).

27. Veyne, *Writing History*, 13.

28. Marc Nichanian, *The Historiographic Perversion* (New York, 2009), 11 ("The genocidal will, in other words, is that which wants to abolish the fact in and through the very act that establishes the fact"); Jean-François Lyotard, *The Differend: Phrases in Dispute* (Manchester, 1988). On the Holocaust as "a negation of narrative frameworks," see Ernst van Alphen, *Caught By History: Holocaust Effects in Contemporary Art, Literature, and Theory* (Stanford, 1997), 53–55.

29. Constantin Fasolt, *The Limits of History* (Chicago, 2004), 40.

30. Peter Novick, *That Noble Dream: The "Objectivity Question" and the American Historical Profession* (Cambridge, 1988).

31. Richard Evans, *In Defence of History* (London, 1997); Joyce Appleby, Lynn Hunt and Margaret Jacob, *Telling the Truth about History* (New York, 1994).

32. Lloyd S. Kramer, "Literature, Criticism, and Historical Imagination: The Literary Challenge of Hayden White and Dominick LaCapra," in *The New Cultural History*, ed. Lynn Hunt (Berkeley, 1989), 97–128; Paul Ricoeur, *Memory, History, Forgetting* (Chicago, 2004), 251–54.

33. Michael S. Roth, "Opposition from Within," *Rethinking History* 8, no. 4 (2004): 531–35.

34. Ann Curthoys and John Docker, *Is History Fiction?* (Sydney, 2006).

35. Frank R. Ankersmit, "Language and Historical Experience," in *Meaning and Representation in History*, ed. Jörn Rüsen (New York, 2006), 149.

36. F. R. Ankersmit, *Historical Representation* (Stanford, 2001), 36.

37. Kevin Passmore, "Poststructuralism and History," in *Writing History: Theory and Practice*, ed. Stefan Berger, Heiko Feldner, and Kevin Passmore (London, 2003), 132–33.

38. Rüsen, *History*, 90.

39. Frank R. Ankersmit, "The Three Levels of '*Sinnbildung*' in Historical Writing," in *Meaning and Representation in History*, ed. Rüsen, 110. Ankersmit's proposal for achieving this goal of transcending "the debate between modernism and postmodernism" is to use the notion of "experience."

40. Gabrielle Spiegel, "History and Post-Modernism," *Past and Present* 135 (1992): 194–208.

41. Hayden White, "Figural Realism in Witness Literature," *Parallax* 10, no. 1 (2004): 118. See also White, "Introduction: Historical Fiction, Fictional History, and Historical Reality," *Rethinking History* 9, nos. 2–3 (2005): 149.

42. Cf. Saul Friedländer, "On the Representation of the Shoah in Present-Day Western Culture," in *Remembering for the Future*, vol. 3, ed. Yehuda Bauer (Oxford, 1989), 3097.

43. Rüsen, *History*, 83.

44. Wulf Kansteiner, "Success, Truth, and Modernism in Holocaust Historiography: Reading Saul Friedländer Thirty-Five Years after the Publication of *Metahistory*," *History and Theory*, Theme Issue 47 (2009): 29–53; Kansteiner's chapter in this volume; Christian Wiese and Paul Betts, eds., *Years of Persecution, Years of Extermination: Saul Friedländer and the Future of Holocaust Studies* (New York, 2010); Christopher R. Browning, *Collected Memories: Holocaust History and Postwar Testimony* (Madison, 2003); Browning, *Remembering Survival: Inside a Nazi Slave-Labor Camp* (New York, 2010).

45. I am aware that this is a gross generalization. See my *Histories of the Holocaust* (Oxford, 2010) for more detailed discussion.

46. Confino, "A World Without Jews," 547.

47. Confino, "A World Without Jews," 556–57. Cf. Berkhofer, *Beyond the Great Story*, 280.

48. Andy Pearce, "The Development of Holocaust Consciousness in Contemporary Britain, 1979–2001," *Holocaust Studies* 14, no. 2 (2008): 71–94.

49. Saul Friedländer, *Reflections of Nazism: An Essay on Kitsch and Death* (New York, 1984); Gavriel D. Rosenfeld, "The Normalization of Memory: Saul Friedländer's *Reflections of Nazism* Twenty Years Later," in *Lessons and Legacies, Vol. VII: The Holocaust in International Perspective*, ed. Dagmar Herzog (Evanston, 2006), 400–10.

50. But cf. Ankersmit, *Historical Representation*, 186–88.

51. See Michael Dintenfass, "Truth's Other: Ethics, the History of the Holocaust, and Historiographical Theory after the Linguistic Turn," *History and Theory* 39, no. 1 (2000): 1–20. Dintenfass writes, "Instead of the theorization of the event that would make evident its qualifications as the litmus test of historiographical theory, we find the invocation of the Holocaust functioning as an incantation with which the adherents of history as faithful reconstruction attempt to ward off the demons of the linguistic turn" (4); and "I find the language with which Appleby *et al.*, Evans, Himmelfarb, and Bartov constitute the Holocaust as the touchstone of postmodernist historiographical theory richly revealing of the repressed moral dimension of historical inquiry"

(5). See also my chapter below and Richard Carter-White, "Auschwitz, Ethics, and Testimony: Exposure to the Disaster," *Environment and Planning D: Society and Space* 27 (2009): 682–99.

52. Stone, *Histories of the Holocaust*, chs. 2 and 3. On the importance of local municipalities, see Wolf Gruner, "The History of the Holocaust: Multiple Actors, Diverse Motives, Contradictory Developments and Disparate (Re)actions," in *Years of Persecution/Years of Extermination*, eds. Wiese and Betts, 323–41.

53. Ankersmit, "The Three Levels of '*Sinnbildung*' in Historical Writing."

54. Christopher R. Browning with Jürgen Matthäus, *The Origins of the Final Solution: The Evolution of Nazi Jewish Policy, September 1939–March 1942* (London, 2004); Saul Friedländer, *The Years of Extermination: Nazi Germany and the Jews 1939–1945* (London, 2007); Peter Longerich, *Holocaust: The Nazi Persecution and Murder of the Jews* (Oxford, 2010); A. Dirk Moses, ed., *Empire, Colony, Genocide: Conquest, Occupation, and Subaltern Resistance in World History* (New York, 2007); Dan Stone, ed., *The Historiography of Genocide* (Houndmills, 2008); Donald Bloxham and A. Dirk Moses, ed., *The Oxford Handbook of Genocide Studies* (Oxford, 2010).

55. Dominick LaCapra, "Representing the Holocaust: Reflections on the Historians' Debate," in *Probing the Limits of Representation,* ed. Friedländer, 110. See also Jörn Rüsen, "Humanism in Response to the Holocaust—Destruction or Innovation?," *Postcolonial Studies* 11, no. 2 (2008): 191–200. Or, as Gil Anidjar puts it, rather more provocatively: "Instead of placing the discipline of history under interrogation—minimally, as a significant actor in the production of the modern (and totalitarian) state—the Holocaust serves to buttress undisturbed notions of history and of historical methods." Anidjar, "Against History," afterword to Nichanian, *The Historiographic Perversion,* 189 n. 80.

56. Donald Bloxham, "Modernity and Genocide," *European History Quarterly* 38, no. 2 (2008): 301.

57. For example: Sara Bender, *The Jews of Białystok During World War II and the Holocaust* (Waltham, 2009); Barbara Epstein, *The Minsk Ghetto, 1941–1943: Jewish Resistance and Soviet Internationalism* (Berkeley, 2008); Samuel D. Kassow, *Who Will Write Our History? Rediscovering a Hidden Archive from the Warsaw Ghetto* (London, 2009); Barbara Engelking and Jacek Leociak, *The Warsaw Ghetto: A Guide to the Perished City* (New Haven, 2009); Martin Dean, *Robbing the Jews: The Confiscation of Jewish Property in the Holocaust, 1933–1945* (Cambridge, UK, 2008); Anton Weiss-Wendt, *Murder Without Hatred: Estonians and the Holocaust* (Syracuse, 2009); Yitzhak Arad, *The Holocaust in the Soviet Union* (Lincoln, 2009); Alan E. Steinweis, *Kristallnacht 1938* (Cambridge, MA, 2009).

58. Cf. Amos Goldberg, "One from Four: On What Jaeckel, Hilberg, and Goldhagen Have in Common and What is Unique about Christopher Browning," *Yalkut Moreshet* 3 (2005): 55–86; Federico Finchelstein, "The Holocaust Canon: Rereading Raul Hilberg," *New German Critique* 96 (2005): 1–47.

59. Frank Bajohr, "Robbery, Ideology, and Realpolitik: Some Critical Remarks," *Yad Vashem Studies* 35, no. 1 (2007): 179–80.

60. Richard T. Vann, "Turning Linguistic: History and Theory and *History and Theory,* 1960–1975," in *A New Philosophy of History*, ed. Frank Ankersmit and Hans Kellner (London, 1995), 42 (citing Neff, *The Poetry of History* (New York, 1947), 193).

61. Karyn Ball, *Disciplining the Holocaust* (Albany, 2008), 8.

62. Ball, *Disciplining the Holocaust,* 43–44.

63. See Frank Ankersmit, Ewa Domańska, and Hans Kellner, eds., *Re-figuring Hayden White* (Stanford, 2009).

64. For a discussion of cultural history in this sense, see Roger Chartier, "Intellectual History and the History of *Mentalités*: A Dual Re-evaluation," in his *Cultural History*, 19–52.

65. See my essays on this theme: "Beyond the Mnemosyne Institute: The Future of Memory after the Age of Commemoration," in *The Future of Memory,* ed. Rick Crownshaw, Jane Kilby, and Antony Rowland (New York, 2010), 17–36; "Genocide and Memory," in *The Oxford Handbook of Genocide Studies,* ed. Bloxham and Moses, 102–19; "Memory Wars in the 'New Europe,'" in *The Oxford Handbook of Postwar European History,* ed. Dan Stone (Oxford, 2012), 714–31.

66. Confino, "A World Without Jews."

67. Jeffrey Herf, *Divided Memory: The Nazi Past in the Two Germanys* (Cambridge, MA, 1997); Robert Moeller, *War Stories: The Search for a Usable Past in the Federal Republic of Germany* (Berkeley, 2001); Peter Reichel, *Politik der Erinnerung: Gedächtnisorte im Streit um die nationalsozialistische Vergangenheit* (Munich, 1995); Habbo Knoch, *Die Tat als Bild: Fotografien des Holocaust in der deutschen Erinnerungskultur* (Hamburg, 2001); Gavriel D. Rosenfeld, *Munich and Memory: Architecture, Monuments, and the Legacy of the Third Reich* (Berkeley, 2000); Alon Confino and Peter Fritzsche, eds., *The Work of Memory: New Directions in the Study of German Society and Culture* (Urbana, 2002); Wulf Kansteiner, *In Pursuit of German Memory: History, Television, and Politics after Auschwitz* (Athens, OH, 2005); Jonathan Huener, *Auschwitz, Poland, and the Politics of Commemoration, 1945–1979* (Athens, OH, 2003); Neil Gregor, *Haunted City: Nuremberg and the Nazi Past* (London, 2008). It is no surprise that many of the leading theorists of memory, especially in relation to mourning and trauma, such as Assmann, Rüsen, and Koselleck, are German or work on German history. See also Burkhard Liebsch, "Trauer als Gewissen der Geschichte?," in *Trauer und Geschichte,* ed. Burkhard Liebsch and Jörn Rüsen (Cologne, 2001), 15–62.

68. Eelco Runia, "Burying the Dead, Creating the Past," *History and Theory* 46 (2007): 313–25; James E. Young, *The Texture of Memory: Holocaust Memorials and Meaning* (New Haven, 1993); Andreas Huyssen, *Twilight Memories: Marking Time in a Culture of Amnesia* (New York, 1995); Ulrich Baer, *Spectral Evidence: The Photography of Trauma* (Cambridge, MA, 2002); Peter Carrier, *Holocaust Monuments and National Memory: France and Germany since 1989* (New York, 2005); Caroline Wiedmer, *The Claims of Memory: Representations of the Holocaust in Contemporary Germany and France* (Ithaca, 1999); and many others.

69. For example: Marianne Hirsch, *Family Frames: Photography, Narrative, and Postmemory* (Cambridge, MA, 1997); Ernst Van Alphen, *Caught By History: Holocaust Effects in Contemporary Art, Literature, and Theory* (Stanford, 1997); David Bathrick, Brad Prager, and Michael D. Richardson, ed., *Visualizing the Holocaust: Documents, Aesthetics, Memory* (Rochester, NY, 2008).

70. Shoshana Felman and Dori Laub, *Testimony: Crises of Witnessing in Literature, Psychoanalysis, and History* (New York, 1992); Lawrence L. Langer, *Holocaust Testimonies. The Ruins of Memory* (New Haven, 1991); Zoë Vania Waxman, *Writing the Holocaust: Identity, Testimony, Representation* (Oxford, 2006); Alexandra Garbarini, *Numbered Days: Diaries and the Holocaust* (New Haven, 2006); Jane Kilby and Antony Rowland, eds., *The Future of Testimony* (London, forthcoming).

71. I privilege cultural history here not because it differs epistemologically from more familiar methodologies, such as political history, but because it does not.

72. Ball, *Disciplining the Holocaust,* 195. Cf. Carolyn J. Dean, *The Fragility of Empathy after the Holocaust* (Ithaca, 2004), esp. ch. 1.

73. Notably: Dan Stone, ed., *The Historiography of the Holocaust* (New York, 2004); Moshe Zimmermann, ed., *On Germans and Jews under the Nazi Regime: Essays by Three Generations of Historians* (Jerusalem, 2006); David Bankier and Dan Michman, eds., *Holocaust Historiography in Context* (Jerusalem, 2008); Peter Hayes and John K. Roth, eds., *Oxford Handbook of Holocaust Studies* (Oxford, 2010). Betts and Wiese, eds., *Years of Persecution/Years of Extermination* is partly devoted to theoretical questions. See also Tom Lawson, *Debates on the Holocaust* (Manchester, 2010), and Jean-Marc Dreyfus and Daniel Langton, eds., *Writing the Holocaust* (London, 2010).

74. F. R. Ankersmit, "Hayden White's Appeal to the Historians," in *Historical Representation,* 259, 261.

Part I
MEMORY AND CULTURE IN THE THIRD REICH

CHAPTER 1

A World Without Jews
Interpreting the Holocaust[1]

ALON CONFINO

History exists only in relation to the questions we pose to it.
—Paul Veyne, *L'inventaire des différences.*
Leçon inaugurale au Collège de France

The recognition of the pastness of the Holocaust is a sort of a novelty in a culture where the presence of the event has been entrenched in the last generation. Recognition of its pastness is not equal to forgetting, nor is it simply a result of the passing of three-score years since 1945. Indeed, it is partly a result of the very intense public and professional preoccupation with the Holocaust, the cumulative effect of which has been to make the event not only an integral part of German, Jewish, and European history, but also into a central moral event in human history. Knowledge is a key to a new understanding. We know infinitely more about the Holocaust today than we did in 1970, 1980, or 1990. The shock of Holocaust representation—think for example of Claude Lanzman's 1985 *Shoah,* Art Spiegelman's 1986 *Maus,* or David Grossman's 1986 *Momik*—has been absorbed and has given way to sombre reflection.[2] The startling revelations of historical studies have made their way into mainstream historiography.[3] The Holocaust shocked and startled because it was so much a part of the present. It still shocks and is still part of the present, but it is also receding into the past. This sense of pastness opens up new ways for understanding and interpreting it.

It is my claim that a period of Holocaust consciousness stretching from the mid-1970s to the present is coming to an end. In this essay, I discuss three interpretative notions that up to now have dominated historians' discussion of

---
Notes for this section begin on page 40.

the Holocaust—racial ideology, radicalization of Nazi policy, and the context of war—and that in my view need to be rethought. The text shows how these notions were used in Holocaust historiography and how their use has been changing. I discuss future avenues of research, but, in particular, I suggest a new direction that builds on these notions and on new historiographical innovations but that diverges from them. I propose to treat the persecution and extermination of the Jews as a problem of culture, a term that is admittedly vague but interpretatively rewarding; that is, narrating the world the Nazis and some Germans built—a Germany, and later a world, without Jews—and what they thought they were engaged in, namely, a necessary battle against their enemy, "the Jew," by placing memories, identities, fantasies, and symbols at the center of the explanation.

The Holocaust is Over

Scholars know how difficult it is to talk about the Holocaust while keeping a sense of historical perspective: that is, keeping at one and the same time the foundational aspect of the Holocaust without making the event into a unique, central point of history. In an attempt to address this difficulty I propose to think of Holocaust consciousness and historiography in tandem with the consciousness and historiography of another foundational event in modern European history, the French Revolution. When, in 1978, François Furet published his essay "The French Revolution is Over," he knew well that in France this ur-event of modern history would on some level never be over. "The Revolution does not simply 'explain' our contemporary history; it is our contemporary history," he wrote. But that, he added, "is worth pondering over."[4] He called for a new interpretation that would go beyond the "revolutionary catechism" influenced by Marxism, beyond the Right-Left political divisions in France, and that would recognize that the passing of time, of memories, and of histories have now enabled a new understanding of 1789. The Holocaust, I would like to suggest, is over in a largely similar way. Of course, the Holocaust is still our contemporary history. Survivors are still alive and their nightmare will never be over as long as they live. The attempt to exterminate the Jews is and will remain a moral signifier of Judeo-Christian civilization. But as the Holocaust now becomes part and parcel of history, memory, and the wider culture, a stage in the process of internalizing it comes to an end.

Following a period of moderate engagement with the Holocaust between 1945 and 1975, Holocaust consciousness from the mid-1970s to the present has been characterized by two simultaneous trends. The first trend, prominent in diverse fields such as history, philosophy, the arts, and literature, has involved a strenuous attempt to acknowledge the Holocaust and to cope with the difficulty of representing it. This trend has required laborious effort and has been distinguished by a high degree of self-conscious reflection, as is evident in such book titles as *Admitting the Holocaust* and *The Limits of Representation*.[5] The second trend, which might appear to stand in opposition to the intense discussion of the limits of Holocaust representation, is manifest in the massive cultural production of the Holocaust in history books, novels, films, plays, comics, and other artistic vehicles. In fact, the two trends are complementary, not contradictory. Historians, contrary to their theoretical trepidations about the limits of narrating the Holocaust, have been at the forefront of this cultural production: a lasting contribution of Holocaust studies has been its detailed recounting of the Holocaust in works that now add up to an immense specialized historiography. The result has been a vast new body of knowledge and a level of understanding and sensitivity that, I contend, anchors the Holocaust in the past in a way that was not previously possible.

The ending of a period in Holocaust consciousness comes into sharp focus when we call to mind Saul Friedländer's 1989 essay "The 'Final Solution': On the Unease in Historical Interpretation."[6] In his doubts about the possibility of producing a historical representation of the Holocaust at all, Friedländer reflected the public and scholarly consciousness of an age. But precisely the development of Holocaust historiography in the last generation makes us see these doubts not as inherent to the event but as reflecting a specific perception bounded in time. As Dan Stone has observed, "it is not that with Auschwitz one encounters special problems of representation but rather that Auschwitz makes especially clear the problem of representation: the fact that there always exists a lacuna between the representation and what is represented."[7] This view opens up new ways of understanding the Holocaust. It entails a shift in historical sensibility from conceiving of the Holocaust not only in terms of the limits of representation but also—because of generational, professional, interpretative, and cultural changes—in terms of the possibilities and promises of historical representation.

A Dominant Interpretative Framework

The historiography of the Holocaust in recent decades, divided as it is among varied fields of research, methods, and languages, has been tremendously rich and complex.[8] But like all historiographical bodies of work, it has given rise to several dominant conceptual categories that have informed, often imperceptibly and across interpretative differences, historians' arguments and use of methods, categories that create boundaries of interpretative common sense. Saul Friedländer's recent *The Years of Extermination* is a sort of a summa of Holocaust research of the last generation and therefore an excellent source for the identification of these categories.[9] The book has been a major scholarly and public event, partly because it represents the apogee of an era of historical understanding of the Holocaust.¹⁰ The Holocaust, according to Friedländer, was determined by "the centrality of ideological-cultural factors as the prime movers of Nazi policies in regard to the Jewish issue, depending of course on circumstances, institutional dynamics, and essentially ... on the evolution of the war.... The anti-Jewish drive became ever more extreme along with the radicalization of the regime's goals and then with the extension of the war. It is in this context that we shall be able to locate the emergence of the 'Final Solution.'"¹¹ This statement represents in a nutshell the main interpretative components currently used to understand the Holocaust: racial ideology, radicalization of Nazi policy, and the context of war.

There has been an agreement among scholars with respect to the explanatory centrality of these categories. To articulate this I use the excellent historiographical summaries by Ulrich Herbert and Ian Kershaw, who do not share my views as to the interpretative consequences of these categories.¹² The context of the war has been viewed as the breeding ground for the extermination. The war in general but especially the war on the Eastern Front, following the German invasion of the Soviet Union on 22 June 1941, was fought as a racial ideological struggle for life or death, whose prime enemies were the Bolsheviks and Jews. The barbarization of war on the Eastern Front, a cumulative result of the scale of the fighting, geographical conditions, and ideological indoctrination, led to killing and extermination.¹³

The notion of the radicalization of racial ideology has been important for capturing the contingency that ran through the making of the Holocaust. The radicalization is no longer understood as a realization of long-term plans, or as inherent in the system, but rather as the outcome of plans for the deportation of the Jews that were always being revised and extended. The scholarly "consensus," writes Kershaw, is "that no single decision brought about the 'Final Solution,' but that a lengthy process of radicalization in the search for a solution to the 'Jewish Question' between spring 1941 and summer 1942—as part of an immense overall resettlement and 'ethnic cleansing' program for central and eastern Europe, vitiated through the failure to defeat the Soviet Union in 1941—was punctuated by several phases of sharp escalation."¹⁴

Perhaps the central innovation of Holocaust scholarship in the last generation has been the emphasis on racial ideology. Previously, Nazi motivations were seen as emanating from long-term antisemitic beliefs, or were excluded altogether by emphasizing impersonal dynamics inherent in the Nazi system of government, whereas now the Holocaust is squarely placed within the context of the regime's overall racial ideology. Vast scholarship has shown that the regime's racial ideology penetrated well beyond a circle of Nazi true believers into all levels of society, be it institutions (the army or the churches), social spheres (cinema, architecture, or sport), or cultural artifacts (ranging from children's board games to the Nuremberg party rallies). This ideology stands in current historiography in self-conscious contrast to the older understanding of

Nazi ideas as a mixture of fuzzy beliefs, vague intentions, or sheer passion and madness.

The combination of the notions of racial ideology, the context of war, and Nazi radicalization has constituted, I argue, the dominant interpretative framework for understanding the Holocaust, a framework that allowed for different interpretative configurations. While the historiography of the Holocaust is too complex to be reduced to these categories, they have dominated, among other concepts, the two leading interpretative schools, intentionalism and functionalism. The crux of each interpretation has depended on different combinations of these factors. Over the years, the two schools have moved closer together. Few scholars subscribe to one school over the other, and most choose their position, explicitly or implicitly, somewhere between the two. If most scholars may not think of themselves as taking a position of either intentionalism or functionalism, it has however been much more challenging to think beyond the categories themselves of racial ideology, the context of war, and radicalization.[15]

Two recent magisterial studies encapsulate the ability of the dominant interpretative framework to produce starkly different interpretations. *The Years of Extermination* commingles intentionalism and functionalism with a tendency towards the former, while at the same time enriching it by crafting a story that provides "both an integrative and an integrated history" of the Holocaust. The narrative focuses on the Jews, without placing this genocide within the Nazis' other exterminations. This narrative is told as a sort of a total history that "penetrates all the nooks and crannies of European space."[16] Friedländer thus crafts an account that integrates much of the large Holocaust research of recent decades; in terms of interpretation, *The Years of Extermination* takes the interpretative framework of the Holocaust onto a larger spatial category, namely Europe, while being located squarely within it. In this sense, *The Years of Extermination* is a monument to a generation of innovative scholarship producing a particular understanding of the Holocaust. And as such, it may also signal its end.

Mark Mazower's *Hitler's Empire,* commingling intentionalism and functionalism with a tendency towards the latter, uses the same framework with different interpretative results: the Final Solution was "driven by Nazi ideology, and by Hitler's personal animus.... [W]hat happened to the Jews of Europe grew out of the circumstances of the war and fluctuated according to its fortunes." But the meaning of the Holocaust is located in its emergence "out of even more ambitious Nazi plans for a racial reorganization of much of eastern Europe.... [T]he Jews constituted only one—albeit the most urgent—of the regime's ethnic targets."[17]

The question is whether we can think of the Holocaust beyond these categories—beyond context and ideology, in particular—finding new narratives that challenge our usual perceptions. Of course, there is nothing wrong with using these categories. They are and will remain central to understanding the Holocaust. But there are three points worth reflecting on. First, one result of the dominance of these categories has been that, in a historiography that is written very close to the documents, the particular characters are different but the libretto is the same, as yet another group or topic (military units, ideological manifestations) is explored within the framework of radicalized Nazi ideology in the context of war. One has a sense of *déjà vu*. It seems that many contributions to the historiography of the Holocaust confirm yet again the well-known thesis of an influential study (the role of the *Wehrmacht* in mass murder, the importance of racial ideology in a given social or professional group) or validate a well-known argument in great detail based on an unused trove of documents. The accumulation of facts in massive studies is accompanied by diminishing interpretative return. We know more of the same things. But what are the new questions we ask about why they happened?

Second, it is interesting that a historiography that is considered to have fierce interpretative debates has actually been in large measure identified by several deep layers of consensus. There is nothing wrong with broad agreements on specific issues of historical explanation as long as this explanation is insightful. The historian is not required to revise at all costs. But broad agreement may inhibit asking new questions, and it thus calls for critical attention. The writing of history is based on the constant historiographical procedure of revision, even if revision is a tangled process that involves generational, professional, and cultural aspects. One task of the historian is to locate and question the dominant set of ideas that are adopted as a given, and that determine which historical questions are asked, which problems are posed, and which connections are made.

Third, the problem with the categories of ideology, context, and radicalization is not that they are wrong, but that they are right in a way that obscures some important elements that made up the Holocaust and the Third Reich. Using them has important consequences in terms of method and interpretation and determines a certain way of telling the story. It is to this topic therefore that we now turn.

Narratives that Challenge Usual Perceptions

Things have begun to change in the last decade or so in ways that have unsettled these categories. Which story of the Holocaust has been told by the narratives of ideology–radicalization–context of war, how has the story changed, and what possible stories lie ahead? My analysis follows the notions of ideology, race, context, and radicalization. It shifts at times from the story of the persecution and extermination of the Jews to the story of the Third Reich, because the two historiographies are inevitably intertwined.

About ideology, the simplest argument is the following: the point is not that ideology is marginal to understanding the Holocaust, but that as a guide for values and beliefs it is insufficient. The historiography is dominated by a hegemonic view of ideology as the organizer and arbiter of motivations in the Third Reich, of mentalities and sensibilities. What else is there left to explain? Scholars' assertion that we need "to take ideology seriously" now has the sound of *déjà vu* based on a historiographical reflex, not on a critical evaluation. I suggest taking ideology seriously by diminishing its explanatory role. A broad, very broad, view of ideology is characteristic of a historiography which designates and labels anything as ideological, from a reflection by Goebbels in his diaries to medical experiments in Auschwitz. Of course, on one level, ideology is everywhere and can explain anything. And yet, if it is everything and everywhere, it explains nothing. If ideology is everything, there is no ideology. It has become such a catch-all notion about motivations in the Third Reich that it is difficult to discriminate between on the one hand, ideology, and on the other, ways to think outside, alongside, against, underneath, and above it.

The focus on ideology has generated valuable attempts to complicate its role in German society and culture. Geoff Eley, responding to Daniel Goldhagen's one-dimensional use of ideology, suggested using an "*extended* understanding of [Nazi] ideology, as being embedded in cultural practices, institutional sites, and social relations."[18] Peter Fritzsche explored ideology, in his brilliant, evocative *Life and Death in the Third Reich,* as a composite of Nazi ideas and the personal process of "becoming a National Socialist, a comrade, a race-minded German." Ideology is not something produced by the regime and imposed from above, but a product of a process shaped also by individuals, who ultimately changed their most intimate beliefs.[19]

And yet the hegemony of ideology as an explanation of the culture, beliefs, and motivation of Germans in the Third Reich is undiminished because while the notion of ideology has been made more complex and differentiated it is often still the framework within which culture, beliefs, and motivation are understood. An extended understanding of ideology may simply add more items to the list of what we understand by the term, while the point is to understand the Third Reich by putting ideology in relation to other forms of thought within German culture. There were many truths in German society beyond ideology, and without them it would have been impossible to understand how the ideology was believed and constructed to begin with. German collective mentalities existed before, during, and after Nazi ideology. "Ideology" cannot exhaust the world of emotions and mentalities that was German culture because Nazi ideology had to interact with different and older collective representations, such as Christianity and nationhood. As a statement about the mental horizon of the Third Reich, ideology seems intellectually undemanding: too cerebral to encompass people's ways of thought in the past. Ideology is part of culture, but it is not the thing itself. It is only one part of the web of symbols and meanings that underlie the way people understand the world and act in it.

In order to explore this it is imperative to center differently the power of racial ideas in the Third Reich. The historiography of the last three decades has documented conclusively that Nazism's historical novelty was its attempt to create a society based on racial biological ideas. This view, which emerged after years during which the meaning of National Socialism was obfuscated under terms such as "fascism" or "totalitarianism," is unassailable. But the interpretative hegemony of race now itself obfuscates ways of understanding life and death in the Third Reich. It often sets race in opposition to other identities, while the issue is how identities existed in relationships of commingling and reciprocal influence. It often severs the racial regime from pre-1933 and post-1945 German history, instead of locating the period within long-term German traditions and forms of beliefs. It often suggests a cohesion and uniformity to racial thought and practice and to Nazi culture and aims, while a much better explanatory metaphor is Nazism as a work in progress. The prevalence of race in the Third Reich, then, is not in question: the question is how to interpret it with respect to Germans' beliefs and actions.

An insightful historiography has shown that race penetrated every aspect of life in Nazi Germany, including those aspects that several decades ago seemed wholly unrevealing about the period. Racial ideology informed the Nazi pursuit of happiness, linked to fulfillment of consumption and travelling pleasures. Even Coca Cola, the sales of which doubled each year between 1933 and 1938 in Germany, was racialized, together with the German landscape, roads, the anti-smoking campaign, and even policies against asbestos-induced lung cancer.[20] Indeed, everything was racialized. On one level, race seems to have been the measure of all things and the source of all beliefs in the Third Reich.

But there is another way to evaluate this evidence. Take the *Heimat* idea, for example. The Nazis appropriated the *Heimat* idea, racializing it for their ideological purposes. It can be argued that here is another example of the hegemony of race. But it can also be interpreted very differently. By 1933, the *Heimat* idea was a historical mentality that had articulated national and local sentiments since 1871. It was perceived as essential to Germanness. Consequently, the main point about the relationship of Nazis to the *Heimat* idea was not that they racialized it. *Heimat* was used for different ideological purposes before and after the Nazis: *Heimatlers* in imperial Germany infused it with nationalism, Nazis with race, East German Communists with socialism, and West Germans with dreams of victimhood, lost territories, and local-democratic renewal. The main point rather is that the Nazis identified their sentiment of nationhood, localness, and political legitimacy with the *Heimat* idea: the revolutionary idea of race was thus built on tradition, and the racialized *Heimat* idea fitted within the boundaries of the *Heimat* genre that existed before and after the Third Reich, as the Nazis articulated their *Heimat* in traditional rhetoric and images.[21] It is not so much race that made sense of *Heimat* in the Third Reich, as the *Heimat* idea that gave meaning to racial sentiments, making them amenable, legitimate, familiar.

Viewed from this perspective, National Socialism enjoyed remarkable stability not simply because of the idea of race, but because the idea of race commingled successfully with other identities of German and European culture, in particular Christianity, nationhood, and consumption and private property. Nazism set itself fundamental limits by being defined by the preservation of these ideas. In 1933 Germans founded the racial state, but this was only the beginning of the process of commingling race with the multitude of other identities in German society. Nazism was a racial civilization that could not exist without, and often fitted quite comfortably with, major ideas of German and European culture. To be sure, there were conflicts between race and other identities. There is nothing new about this: identities coexist in tension. But the point is that they coexisted in tension but without breaking, thus creating a Nazi civilization that was bigger than the sum of its parts. One interesting question about the Third Reich seems to be not about conflicts of identities, but rather about the stability of the regime. The Nazi revolutionary attempt to construct a new society only begs the question, what were the elements that gave stability to this revolutionary project characterized by the absence of serious internal opposition and the presence of loyalty among many Germans? Coercion alone explains too little, and does not give an answer to the motivations and willingness of the great many who exercised it.[22] It is also inconceivable that a body of racial ideas, which was present but not dominant before 1933, was received and internalized so quickly thereafter while successfully marginalizing other important identities. That is not how identities work. In human affairs, even the most radical transformations are maintained by previous memories, beliefs, and habits of mind. If Nazism was supported by Germans it is also because it allowed a person to maintain his or her identity as, for example, a certain kind of Christian, while taking on a new aspect of German identity as a Nazi.[23]

In many respects, this is the direction of some current research. Still, the racial paradigm of ideology and state remains hegemonic. To consider the perspective of Nazi attitudes towards Christianity or towards self-fulfillment is not the same as crafting a narrative of commingled, coexisting identities, where Nazism shaped as much as was shaped by other, long-standing loyalties. With respect to the Holocaust, the claim that the extermination of the Jews was determined by 'the attempt to build a German empire along racial lines' has underplayed a whole set of identities, beliefs, and memories that made Nazi Germany.[24] And this racial-ideological argument has been reinforced by the explanatory focus on the context of the war at the expense of memories and identities of longer chronology, a topic to which we shall now turn.

In terms of understanding the Holocaust, the question is not whether the context of a brutalizing war is important (of course it is), but in what way, and what it explains. There is no doubt of the "catalytic impact of the war itself."[25] In terms of method, in reconstructing the context one describes the circumstances within which something happened, not necessarily why it happened. Neither peer pressure nor wartime brutalization tells us much about sentiments and beliefs that existed before 1939 and that shaped what happened during the war. It is not that the war conditions alone created an exterminatory mindset, but that the years before 1939 created the conditions that made this context possible to begin with. Thinking in association with another short, violent, seismic event, we can recall Furet's observation that "every history of the Revolution must therefore deal not only with the impact of 'circumstances' on the successive political crisis but also, and above all, with the manner in which those 'circumstances' were planned for, prepared, arranged and used in the symbolic universe of the Revolution."[26]

Over-determining the war context severs the extermination from the pre-war culture that made it possible. Chronologically, the Holocaust is narrated now within the context of the war, the years 1933–1945, and often reaching as far back as World War I, but not beyond. There are good reasons for this, but also some issues to ponder over. It is a narrative that reproduces in different form the Nazi narration of modern Germany, with the myth of the Great War, the defeat of 1918, and the role of the Jews. It risks reifying the identity that was most visible in public and ideological discourse, namely, race, and underplaying elements of culture that were less visible or not publicly and consciously admitted by contemporaries. Interpreting the motivation for the extermination by focusing on racial ideology between 1933 and 1945 neglects the symbols and memories that constituted anti-Jewish fantasies, when and how they originated before 1933, and how and why they were received in German society thereafter. This is a history of the Holocaust with pre-1933 cultural antecedents left out. Differently put, the over-determined presence of the context of the war in the interpretation of the Holocaust obscures the importance of the presence of the past in its making.

A sense of continuity that leads to unexpected outcomes is linked to a notion of contingency. In the historiography of the Holocaust the notion of the radicalization of Nazi policy has come in many respects to stand for contingency. How can one understand the persecution and extermination of the Jews, to borrow the words of Roger Chartier on the French Revolution, "as neither pure accidents produced by chance circumstances nor absolute necessities whose moment and modalities were logically inscribed in their very causes?"[27] Is it possible to write an unscripted narrative of the Holocaust given the predominant agency of the Nazis in moving events forward? The notion of contingency is often represented in narratives of the Holocaust by the idea of a dynamic process of radicalization. The assumption is that by describing a process that is dynamic we capture possibilities and unpredictability. But does this capture a sense of contingency? Radicalization and contingency are not interchangeable, and the notion of radicalization in itself does not safeguard against the danger of tautology.

Let us think about this problem by associating it with the work of Furet, who ascribed important meaning to the radicalization of the Revolutionary process: "Each successive political group [the Girondins, Jacobins, etc.] pursued the same objective: to radicalize the Revolution, by making it consistent with its discourse [of pure democracy].... The Terror ... [was] inherent in the ever-escalating rhetoric of the various groups competing for the exclusive right to embody the democratic principle."[28] For Furet, then, the revolutionary dynamic of the Terror was self-propelled, indifferent to the vicissitudes of political changes and human action. The "ever-escalating dialectic of rhetoric" has the same impact on his narrative of the Revolution as the "radicalized dynamic process of racial ideology" has on the narrative of the Holocaust: it is not a guarantee against a narrative of inevitability, but may in fact produce it.

In current Holocaust narratives the function of the idea of radicalization is often rhetorical: it moves the story forward. Historians thus "finesse difficult questions of contingency with their most powerful tool: narrative," as the historian of the American South Edward Ayers observed in a different context.[29] No doubt there was a process of radicalization in the making of the Holocaust, and narratives pay attention to changes of Nazi policies and the actions of Germans. But the danger is that radicalization produces a narrative, if unintentionally, of the inexorable spiral ahead of ideology and war conditions: necessarily forwards, towards ever-extreme conditions and states of mind. The notion of radicalization describes a condition, and in itself explains little. It should not obscure the fact that it was not a cause, but a result; radicalization did not emerge automatically but was deliberately brought into being. The challenge for the historian is to capture not "radicalization," but a sense of the present, at any given time between 1933 and 1945, that could not anticipate the future: "I am reading the first few pages of the Tocqueville [*The Ancien Regime and the French Revolution*], which Frau Schaps gave me in 1924," wrote Victor Klemperer in his diary on 29 September 1939. "No one, not even the most significant and knowledgeable contemporaries, anticipated the course of Revolution. Every page of the book surprises me with analogies to the present."[30] It is difficult to see in what ways the narrative of radicalization can provide new insights into the persecution and extermination of the Jews. Instead, it would be more helpful to use the idea of capturing contingency within dominant structures by focusing on Nazism as a work in progress.

An argument for rethinking the categories of ideology, race, context, and radicalization in the interpretation of the Holocaust is based on the principle that the best research claims to be innovative because it reveals factors previously unobserved that question our usual ideas about the event. In so doing, such research also opens the field for experimentation in terms of method and argument. As the Holocaust shocks us less than a generation ago, so the specific rendition of these notions seems to have become less challenging. The historiography will change, as all historiographies do, new approaches will emerge, and new interpretations will be put forward.

Thinking Ahead

How should Holocaust scholarship proceed from here? Some new directions do follow from the above discussion, and I would like to discuss one that is to my mind especially beneficial. In the short space remaining to this chapter, I cannot possibly claim to be comprehensive; I therefore ask the reader to bear this in mind. Still, I believe that the direction I shall discuss is illuminating to future study of the Holocaust.

I begin by suggesting that a central explanatory problem of the Nazi persecution and extermination of the Jews is no longer to account for what happened—the making of racial ideology, the context of a brutalizing war in search for an empire, and the radicalized, administrative process of extermination—because we now have sufficiently good accounts of these historical realities. Rather, a central problem is to account, in a cultural key, for what the Nazis thought was happening: namely, an apocalyptic battle against their enemy, "The Jew." How and why did Germans construct an imaginary war against a non-existent enemy (one that possessed no army, state, or government) in a war whose essential motivations were not practical (Germans and Jews did not have a conflict over territory, land, resources, borders, or political power, which often characterize cases of ethnic cleansing and genocide) but about identity? This requires us to examine how Germans, in the years following 1933, constructed a moral community based on antisemitic fantasies that made the persecution and extermination of the Jews possible by making them conceivable. This community was not moral, of course, nor were the fantasies based on a truthful description of reality, but it was nonetheless believed by many Germans and therefore was for them real and truthful. For this reason, at this historiographical juncture, I suggest that we view the Holocaust as a problem of culture: the making of and believing in a moral community of fantasies. This racial community was constructed on a set of practices and representations that in spite of their revolutionary meaning were connected by shared images and symbols across 1933 and 1939. The Third Reich was revolutionary, but not as revolutionary as was argued by contemporaries and current historiography: it was a revolution based on continuities. It was a world made by a fusion of German and Nazi identities in a way that linked Germans in the Third Reich to pre-1933 traditions and forms of belief, and where the extermination of 1941 to 1945 was part of the symbolic universe of Germany between 1933 and 1941.

I use "culture" not to signify a magic interpretative wand or a sense of methodological avant-garde. These are false premises and promises. Indeed, it would be retrograde to presume the innovation of "culture" when at present one can refer "to the banality of cultural history and its prevalent commonplaces that may not provide thought provoking impetus."[31] I am interested not in a label, but in understanding. A cultural approach is used here as a shorthand for a diverse body of approaches and methods that in the last generation emphasized the social and the cultural as interpreted in terms of representation, experience, subjectivity, negotiation, agency, shifting relationships, and the importance of memory. The only important thing about applying a body of work to a given historical topic is: does it reveal factors previously unobserved?

Imaginary worlds, fantasies, and memories are not "anything as self-conscious as 'ideology' nor as passive as 'world view,' but rather those characteristic ways of apprehending, evaluating, enjoying, and managing the world," to use Inga Clendinnen's words in her splendid interpretation of the Aztecs. It means to shift our interest from beliefs on the formal level to sensibilities: "the emotional, moral and aesthetic nexus through which thought comes to be expressed in action" and memories come to shape the world. Historians have come to label these characteristics "obscurely and comfortably" as culture.[32] But some recent historiography of the Holocaust is much more comfortable avoiding these sources of enmity against the Jews. Terms such as modernity, industrial killing, state-sponsored extermination, scientific racism, resettlement, university-educated and technocratic true-believers—these are useful in various degrees, but they also convey a world of pragmatism and rationalism for a topic whose core is a leap in human imagination. In terms of voice, they often reflect the way some Nazis, such as the university-educated technocrats, saw themselves and wanted others to see them. The notion of ideology in recent historiography, based on these terms, has partly had the similar effect of neutralizing the issue of fantasies and memories. For a historical topic whose essence is the belief in fantasies, this is quite remarkable.[33]

This comes into sharp focus when we consider the place in the historiography of the Third Reich and the Holocaust of one of the leading interpretative notions in the last generation, namely memory. There is a massive literature on post-1945 German memory and quite a large one on pre-1933, but very little on the memories of Germans during the Third Reich. Of course, there is no obligation to use every historical approach for every period. But one must surely see the dissonance between the current primacy of the notion of memory in German historiography overall and the glaring omission of the period of the Third Reich as a topic of memory study; between the use of diverse approaches to understanding Nazism, such as gender, everyday life, political, military, economic, colonialism and empire, and others, and the overlooking of memory. Explaining this dissonance away is part of the problem, not the solution. In its most innovative rendition, memory studies changed the way historians understand the presence of the past in the life of people by making it into an essential empirical, analytical, and theoretical tool with which to understand social, political, cultural, even economic phenomena that had regularly been seen as determined by a very different set of factors. The high point of memory studies may be over, but the question is not whether memory is fashionable; something can be fashionable, and still be useful. It is rather: has memory contributed to our historical knowledge? And here the answer is no doubt "yes," as memory studies have brought to the fore topics and uncovered knowledge that were simply unknown a generation ago. The insights of memory with respect to the Third Reich are unexplored.

Take the topic of the presence of the past, for example. In the historiography, the sources and images of Nazi enmity against the Jews are overwhelmingly modern. Nazi ideology imagined the Jews as the harbingers of all modern evils, of communism, capitalism, liberalism, atheism, as well as of being the culprits for the German recent past: the defeat in World War I, the revolution of 1918, and the Weimar Republic. This historiographical argument is true, but it seems to me to be only half of the truth. It is too modern a view of the presence of the past, given the prior history of antisemitism. Studies often mention this history as a sort of a background, but not that it might in some way be part of the explanation. But Hitler's view in *Mein Kampf* that "by defending myself against the Jew, I am fighting for the work of the Lord" or in a radio address on 30 January 1942 that the Jews are "the most evil world enemy of all times" cannot be reduced to modernity; they are about the past *tout court*.[34] On 10 November 1938 in Baden Baden, all Jewish men were forced to march through the streets to the synagogue holding a sign reading "God does not forgive us," while in Regensburg the Jews were forced to parade through the town holding a big sign saying "Exodus of the Jews" (*Auszug der Juden*).[35] These rituals of degradation spoke the rhetoric of racial ideology but used the symbols of past relationships between Jews and Christians.

This material virtually calls for memory exploration. The point is not, in case such a clarification is needed, to find causal relations between earlier centuries and the Third Reich; this is not how memory studies operate. Instead, the point is to uncover the mental universe of Germans in the Third Reich constituted by memories, a universe which was at times explicit and at other times hidden and subterranean. Germans in the Third Reich are defined in the historiography in terms of their various attitudes and positions towards the racial ideology, state, and war; we know an enormous amount about that. I suggest defining Germans in terms of their constructed history and memory, with all its oppositions, contradictions, and conflicts. Among other things, Germans were the sum of their representations of the past and the sum of their representations of the Jews. This mode of proceeding is based on evidence, voices of contemporaries, and emotions revealed in public places. The work by Michael Wildt on the symbolic meaning of anti-Jewish public violence in Weimar and

Nazi Germany, and by Dirk Rupnow on memory and history in the Third Reich, are excellent contributions in that direction.[36]

The starting point should be the intentions of the Nazis and the policy of the German state, starting from 30 January 1933: the construction of a Germany, and later a world, without Jews. This perspective captures the general sense of search in the Third Reich for a Germany without Jews while taking cognizance of the different opinions and sentiments of the project, its complexity, probability, and uncertainty. It is similar, if we think again by association, to the construction of the idea of nationhood. The nation has been a work in progress where different ideas of the nation coexisted in relationships of opposition, disagreement, and conflict; and yet, there exists a whole that is greater than the sum of its parts. The idea of a Germany without Jews works in much the same way. Some supported it, some opposed, some were left indifferent, but it was and remained a goal of the Third Reich from the beginning, a whole larger than the sum of Germans' views about the Jews. A narrative of Germany without Jews does not require the notion of radicalization to move the story forward because the assumption is not about the story's final destination (the extermination beginning in 1941), but about its starting point on 30 January 1933, when the German state adopted its anti-Jewish policy. A moral, historical, post-Enlightenment break was made then, not by planning extermination, but by thinking that a German world without Jews could be a reality, somehow. Differently put, it is not Auschwitz that stands at the center of the historian's study of Nazi antisemitism, but the making of a German world without Jews. This world would have been created with or without Auschwitz; it was on the way to being created from 1933.

In a historiography that has admirably and massively documented in the last generation the conditions that made the persecution and extermination possible, exploring the memories that made them possible is a new departure. We can appreciate the claim that I am advancing here by considering it in relation to the most innovative interpretation of the Holocaust in the last decade, namely the view that places it within the history of modern genocides and colonialism. At first sight, this interpretation seems to undermine the argument discussed here that has so far emphasized memories about the Jews but not about other racial enemies of the Nazis. But in fact, exploring the memories about the Jews fits very well with some innovative renditions of the colonial interpretation.

Led by scholars such as Dirk Moses, Dan Stone, and Jürgen Zimmerer, studies of colonial genocides emphasized the combination of settlement, a millennial utopian thinking, security anxieties, and murder among the colonizers. In this respect, Zimmerer claims, "with its central concepts of 'race' and 'space,' the Nazi policy of expansion and annihilation stood firmly in the tradition of European colonialism, a tradition also recognizable in the Nazi genocides."[37] What set the stage for the Nazi genocides were the broken taboos of earlier decades: the Holocaust was thinkable because of the prior German extermination of the Herero in 1904 and the realization that wiping out peoples was a possibility. This interpretation, which has grown in volume and sophistication in recent years, is problematic on several counts (too complex to discuss here), but it has unquestionably brought fresh insights into a Holocaust historiography bogged down in old categories and at times pious moralizing (such as the uniqueness of the extermination). Overall, this approach, together with studies on Nazi occupation and resettlement plans in Eastern Europe, such as the works of Götz Aly, and the contributions of the "race paradigm" discussed above that highlighted the multiplicity of Nazi victims, showed that the Jewish genocide was tied up with a whole set of racial ideas that produced other genocides.[38] The Nazi program of German renewal was future-oriented, and in it Jews were one target among many, if symbolically the most important one. As Mazower put it, the Jews represented the most "urgent" of the regime's racial targets.

It is precisely this issue of symbolic urgency that is fundamental. The enmity against and extermination of the Jews was part of a Nazi universe of racial enemies and exterminations. This only sharpens the question: what was the symbolic urgency against the Jews, and why? Mazower's *Hitler's Empire* is a good example of how this question ultimately remains unanswered. He describes convincingly the construction of Hitler's racial empire in Europe and the persecution of diverse racial enemies, but because his analysis is confined to the racial paradigm it is not clear from the book why the Jews were the most urgent target. (It is an interpretative vicious circle to argue that the Jews were the most urgent racial target because they were the most dangerous racial enemy.)

Ways We Tell the Story

Is the mode of proceeding articulated above, though, not simply a return to an old-fashioned intentionalist argument couched in current historiographical parlance? I do not think so. Indeed, my critique is that this view is trapped within existing established categories about the Holocaust. In as much as intentionalism is a broad term uniting diverse studies (recently, for example, from Goldhagen to Friedländer to Herf) their common denominator is the central role of ideas and ideology in understanding the Holocaust. Reified or modified, intentionalism has meaning only in relation to its explanatory twin, functionalism, and both have meaning only within the specific understanding of their core categories, ideology and context (especially the context of the war) discussed earlier. But what happens when we reject this understanding of ideology and context, when we break down these categories, as suggested in this essay, only to recompose them with different interpretative potential?

This is an invitation to rearrange the story in different ways: our aim is not to capture racial ideology but to map out the memories and identities that made German society; it is not to limit the presence of the past in the Third Reich to the recent past but to explore memories and fantasies of earlier pasts; it is not to conceive of the context of the war as an explanation, but to place it within the culture that preceded and produced it. The overall point is to rethink the interpretative meaning of the core categories not in order to rethink intentionalism and functionalism but in order to jettison this framework altogether. When we link this research avenue with new as well as established views of the Holocaust as a European event, as part of a larger Nazi attempt to reorder European civilization, as linked to other Nazi persecutions and genocides, to colonial imagination and dreams of empire, then, it seems, the use of the term "intentionalism" to describe the mode of proceeding suggested in this chapter appears simply unhelpful, a reflexive use of a familiar term that no longer illuminates the realignment of the categories.

Differently put, the avenue suggested here is born of intentionalism, functionalism, and their interpretative commingling in the last generation; this is its historiographical genealogy. But the overall result of rethinking core categories is to overhaul interpretative consequences and to point to a different set of questions. It is in this relationship of historiographical continuity and change that we can find the meaning of the argument made in this chapter. I would like to unpack this claim by making three points, about culture, memory, and method. The first, about culture, concerns what is familiar in the mode of proceeding proposed in this chapter: I do not claim originality in looking at the Holocaust through the prism of culture, however we define it. This has been done extensively.[39] Concepts of space and anthropology have been used to explore the actual sites of mass murder as well as their landscape and ghettos.[40] Original work, for example by Alexandra Garbarini and Amos Goldberg, has investigated the sense of selfhood of Jewish victims, and explored films, photographs, testimony, and others.[41] Moreover, "cultural history, in its contemporary sense," observed Dan Michman, "has been a highly important component of Holocaust research from its earliest beginnings."[42] These diverse trends, approaches, and studies over a long period of time have remained often unconnected and isolated within their specific sub-discipline of Holocaust research; it is only recently that a discussion has started to take place on how a theoretically mindful cultural history contributes to changes in our understanding of the Holocaust.

The second point, about memory, proposed a new research topic: to explore the memories that made the Third Reich, those images of the past that not only represented the society around it, but shaped it. The final and most important point is about method. The argument of this chapter has not been to add new topics of memory and culture to the existing dominant categories of ideology, race, context, and radicalization that have supported intentionalism and functionalism. It has rather been to have memory and culture reorder these categories and their interpretative potential, looking for different ways to tell the story.

One aim of this avenue of research is to challenge the daunting interpretative gap between the anti-Jewish persecution of the prewar years and the subsequent almost unimaginable total extermination, by exploring those practices and representations that linked them. It is a mainstay in the popular and scholarly understanding of the Holocaust that the total extermination had not been anticipated, that victims and perpetrators alike scarcely believed what was happening. Primo Levi expressed it in one of the twentieth century's most profound short sentences: "Today, at this very moment as I sit writing at the table, I myself am not convinced that these things really happened."[43] The sentiment cannot be denied. At the same time, historians know that all that happens was, in some way, imagined, not literally, not exactly, but it was put in some images and words that made it possible. If we look for Auschwitz in prewar Nazi culture we explain too much and assume causal relations that are bound to confirm this gap. If we emphasize ideology we assume a causal relation that explains too little. Instead, our aim should be to seek patterns of meaning and purpose in a world made of fantasies that made the extermination possible because it was, somehow, imaginable.

★ ★ ★

In 1939, courts ruled that race defilement was not linked to a conscious attempt at seduction or at any physical contact. A Jewish man was convicted of race defilement for simply quickly looking at a young Aryan girl across the street.[44] By 1940, Jews were banned from listening to German music or performing German plays: "any contact," writes Friedländer, "between the German spirit and a Jew, even if the Jew was merely a segregated and passive recipient, soiled and endangered the source itself."[45] In 1942, Jews were no longer allowed to keep pets. The animals had to be killed even if the Jewish owners found non-Jewish friends to take care of them—because the animals were now "Jewish." Eva and Victor Klemperer brought their Jewish cat to the vet on 19 May 1942 to be put to sleep.[46] Are these human affairs best understood by racial ideology? In the context of war? There is a world of meaning that is lost when these views predominate, because the question is not only how these made the Holocaust but what was the ground of culture, memories, feelings, and sensibilities that made them possible to begin with. How and why did these fantasies speak to key elements of life in Germany at the period, and what made them persuasive as ways to experience the world?

Notes

1. This chapter provides the bare bones of an extensive argument first published in *German History* 27, no. 4 (2009): 531–59. I am grateful to the journal for the permission to reprint it.

Earlier versions of this essay were presented at Oxford University and Sussex University; I am indebted to Paul Betts, Jane Caplan, Nick Stargardt and Lyndal Roper for the hospitality and the insightful discussions. At the German Studies Association 2008 I benefited from the comments of Doris Bergen. I am grateful to the participants of these talks for the stimulating discussions. My thinking has been particularly enriched by Dirk Moses, who early on offered a sharp, incisive critique that challenged me to articulate my ideas more clearly; by Amos Goldberg, Allan Megill, Jeffrey Olick, Mark Roseman, Dan Stone, and Maiken Umbach who read earlier drafts of the essay; and by Sophie Rosenfeld who illuminated to me that other foundational past.

2. Art Spiegelman, *Maus: A Survivor's Tale,* vols. 1 and 2 (New York, 1986, 1991). Momik is the first story in David Grossman, *See Under: Love* (New York, 1989).

3. As in, for example, Christopher R. Browning, *Ordinary Men: Reserve Police Battalion 101 and the Final Solution in Poland* (New York, 1992).

4. François Furet, *Interpreting the French Revolution* (Cambridge, 1981), 3. The original title was *La Révolution française est terminée.*

5. Lawrence Langer, *Admitting the Holocaust: Collected Essays* (New York, 1995). Saul Friedländer, *Probing the Limits of Representation: Nazism and the "Final Solution"* (Cambridge, MA, 1992).

6. *History and Memory* 1, no. 2 (1989): 61–76.

7. Dan Stone, *Constructing the Holocaust: A Study in Historiography* (London, 2003), 30.

8. For excellent overviews, see Michael R. Marrus, *The Holocaust in History* (New York, 1987); Ian Kershaw, *The Nazi Dictatorship: Problems and Perspectives of Interpretation,* 4th ed. (London, 2000); Dan Stone, ed., *The Historiography of the Holocaust* (Basingstoke, 2004); and the recent, comprehensive David Bankier and Dan Michman, eds., *Holocaust Historiography in Context: Emergence, Challenges, Polemics and Achievements* (Jerusalem, 2008).

9. Saul Friedländer, *The Years of Extermination: Nazi Germany and the Jews, 1939–1945* (New York, 2007). For an evaluation of the book's masterful narrative, see Alon Confino, "Narrative Form and Historical Sensation: On Saul Friedländer's *The Years of Extermination*," *History and Theory* 48, no. 3 (2009): 199–219.

10. The book won the Pulitzer Prize, the Friedenspreis (Peace Prize) of the Frankfurt Book Fair, and rave reviews.

11. Friedländer, *The Years of Extermination,* xvii, xix.

12. Kershaw, *The Nazi Dictatorship,* ch. 5, and Ulrich Herbert, "Extermination Policy: New Answers and Questions about the History of the 'Holocaust' in German Historiography," in *National Socialist Extermination Policies: Contemporary German Perspectives and Controversies,* ed. Ulrich Herbert (New York, 2000), 1–52. Short histories of the Holocaust are an excellent source to tease out the dominant interpretative ideas because they convey the general consensus without getting into the detailed debates that often obscure it. See the excellent book by Doris Bergen, *War and Genocide: A Concise History of the Holocaust* (Lanham, 2003) that represents accurately the dominant interpretative framework portrayed here. Concerning agreements among Holocaust scholars, Peter Fritzsche begins his recent essay "The Holocaust and the Knowledge of Murder" by saying, "There is a remarkable consensus about the origins of the Holocaust that was not imaginable twenty years ago." *Journal of Modern History* 80 (2008): 594.

13. The work of Omer Bartov is central here. See *The Eastern Front 1941–45: German Troops and the Barbarisation of Warfare* (London, 1985).

14. Kershaw, *The Nazi Dictatorship,* 130.

15. Intentionalism and functionalism continue to structure thinking in a particular way. Studies can be grouped in one or the other camp, or in both. The debate serves as point of departure to evaluate Holocaust historiography in the most recent collections and encyclopedia entries. Michael R. Marrus, "Historiography," in *The Holocaust Encyclopedia,* ed. Walter Laqueur (New Haven, 2001), 279–85. A synthesis between functionalism and intentionalism is portrayed as the main achievement of current historiography. See Omer Bartov, "Introduction," in *The Holocaust: Origins, Implementation, Aftermath,* ed. Bartov (London, 2000). The terms are still important markers of recognition. Bergen defines herself as a "modified intentionalist" in *War and Genocide,*

30, and so too does Jeffrey Herf in *The Jewish Enemy: Nazi Propaganda during World War II and the Holocaust* (London, 2006), vii. Kershaw, *The Nazi Dictatorship*, ch. 5, frames the historiographical discussion around the debate between intentionalists and structuralists, concluding that "neither model offers a wholly satisfactory explanation" (131). Dan Stone recently noted that "it would be a mistake to assume that the fierce debates between intentionalists and functionalists of two decades ago have disappeared altogether," for they are just differently situated in a current "much broader, empirically richer as well as more complex historical context." Dan Stone, "The Holocaust and its Historiography," in *The Historiography of Genocide*, ed. Dan Stone (Basingstoke, 2008), 377–78. The terms change though the meaning remains much the same; thus, Michael Geyer termed the two interpretative camps "the rationalists" and "the idealists," in Konrad Jarausch and Michael Geyer, *Shattered Past: Reconstructing German Histories* (Princeton, 2003), 120–21. There are attempts to go beyond it only to commend several years later the value of this framework. Christopher Browning, "Beyond 'Intentionalism' and 'Functionalism': The Decision for the Final Solution Reconsidered," in Browning, *The Path to Genocide* (Cambridge, 1992), 86–121; Richard Bessel, "Functionalists vs. Intentionalists: The Debate Twenty Years On or Whatever Happened to Functionalism and Intentionalism?," *German Studies Review* 26 (2003): 15–20.

16. Friedländer, *The Years of Extermination*, xv, xix.

17. Mark Mazower, *Hitler's Empire: How the Nazis Ruled Europe* (New York, 2008), 412, 414.

18. Geoff Eley, "Ordinary Germans, Nazism, and Judeocide," in Geoff Eley, ed., *The "Goldhagen Effect": History, Memory, Nazism—Facing the German Past* (Ann Arbor, 2000), 23 (emphasis in original).

19. Peter Fritzsche, *Life and Death in the Third Reich* (Cambridge, MA, 2008).

20. Jeff Schutts, "'Die erfrischende Pause': Marketing Coca Cola in Hitler's Germany," in *Selling Modernity: Advertising in Twentieth-Century Germany*, ed. Pamela Swett, Jonathan Wiesen, and Jonathan Zatlin (Durham, 2007), 151–81; Thomas Zeller, *Driving Germany: The Landscape of the German Autobahn, 1930–1970* (New York, 2007); Thomas Lekan, *Imagining the Nation in Nature: Landscape Preservation and German Identity, 1885–1945* (Cambridge, 2004); Robert Proctor, *The Nazi War on Cancer* (Princeton, 1999).

21. For this argument about the meaning of the *Heimat* idea, see Alon Confino, *Germany as a Culture of Remembrance: Promises and Limits of Writing History* (Chapel Hill, 2006), ch. 5.

22. For the coercion argument, see Richard Evans, "How Willing Were They?," *The New York Review of Books*, 55 (26 June 2008).

23. Philippe Burrin views Nazism as a "newly invented identity," commingling Christian, nationalist, and racist antisemitism, which is "more pertinent than the presence of any racist grid." See his essay *Nazi Anti-Semitism: From Prejudice to the Holocaust* (New York, 2005), 26, 48.

24. Fritzsche, *Life and Death in the Third Reich*, 241.

25. Mazower, *Hitler's Empire*, 11.

26. Furet, *Interpreting the French Revolution*, 63.

27. Roger Chartier, *The Cultural Origins of the French Revolution* (Durham, 1991), 169.

28. Furet, *Interpreting the French Revolution*, 69, 70, 77.

29. Edward Ayers, *What Caused the Civil War?* (New York, 2006).

30. Victor Klemperer, *I Will Bear Witness: A Diary of the Nazi Years* (New York, 1998), 314.

31. See the forum following Dan Stone's "Holocaust Historiography and Cultural History," *Dapim: Studies on the Shoah* 23 (2009): 52–68 (see Stone's chapter in this volume). The citation is from Dominick LaCapra's contribution, "A Response to 'Holocaust Historiography and Cultural History' by Dan Stone," 89–90.

32. Inga Clendinnen, *Aztecs: An Interpretation* (Cambridge, 1991), 2, 5.

33. This builds on the important work of earlier scholars such as Leon Poliakov, *Harvest Of Hate: The Nazi Program for the Destruction of the Jews of Europe* (1951; rev. and expanded ed., New York, 1979). On the writings of George Mosse on race, antisemitism and ideology, see Saul Friedländer, "Mosse's Influence on the Historiography of the Holocaust," in *What History Tells: George L. Mosse and the Culture of Modern Europe*, ed. Stanley Payne, David Sorkin and John Tor-

torice (Madison, 2004), 134–47; Uriel Tal, *Religion, Politics and Ideology in the Third Reich: Selected Essays* (New York, 2004); Dan Diner, *Beyond the Conceivable: Studies on Germany, Nazism, and the Holocaust* (Berkeley, 2000); Burrin, *Nazi Anti-Semitism*; and Friedländer, of course.

34. M. Domarus, *Hitler—Reden and Proklamationen 1932–1945. Kommentiert von einem Zeitgenossen,* vol. 2 (Neustadt/Aisch, 1963), 1828.

35. For Baden-Baden, see Yad Vashem photographic archive, no. 139BO1. For Regensburg, see the website of the Jüdische Gemeinde Regensburg, www.jg-regensburg.de.

36. Michael Wildt, *Volksgemeinschaft als Selbstermächtingung: Gewalt gegen Juden in der deutschen Provinz 1919 bis 1939* (Hamburg, 2007); Dirk Rupnow, *Vernichten und Erinnern: Spuren nationalsozialistischer Gedächnispolitik* (Göttingen, 2005).

37. Jürgen Zimmerer, "Colonialism and the Holocaust: Toward an Archeology of Genocide," in *Genocide and Settler Society: Frontier Violence and Stolen Indigenous Children in Australian History,* ed. A. Dirk Moses (New York, 2004), 67. See also A. Dirk Moses and Dan Stone, eds., *Colonialism and Genocide* (London, 2007); Stone, "The Holocaust and Its Historiography," esp. his discussion of "Holocaust and/as genocide," 387–91; Stone, *Histories of the Holocaust* (Oxford, 2010), ch. 5.

38. Götz Aly, *Final Solution: Nazi Population Policy and the Murder of the European Jews* (London, 1999). On Nazism's other victims and their link to the Holocaust, see Henry Friedlander, *The Origins of Nazi Genocide: From Euthanasia to the Final Solution* (Chapel Hill, 1995).

39. Wendy Lower, "A Response to Dan Stone's 'Holocaust Historiography and Cultural History,'" *Dapim: Studies on the Shoah* 23 (2009): 84.

40. Omer Bartov, *Erased: Vanishing Traces of Jewish Galicia in Present Day Ukraine* (Princeton, 2007).

41. Alexandra Garbarini, *Numbered Days: Diaries and the Holocaust* (New Haven, 2006); Amos Goldberg, "If this is a Man: The Image of Man in Autobiographical and Historical Writing During and After the Holocaust," *Yad Vashem Studies* 33 (2005): 381–429.

42. Dan Michman, "Introducing More 'Cultural History' into the Study of the Holocaust. A Response to Dan Stone," *Dapim: Studies on the Shoah* 23 (2009): 72.

43. Primo Levi, *Survival in Auschwitz* (New York, 1996), 103.

44. Patricia Szobar, "Telling Sexual Stories in the Nazi Courts of Law: Race Defilement in Germany, 1933 to 1945," *Journal of the History of Sexuality* 11 (2002): 160.

45. Friedländer, *The Years of Extermination,* 98.

46. Fritzsche, *Life and Death in the Third Reich,* 239. For a full elaboration of the arguments of this chapter, see my *Foundational Pasts: The Holocaust as Historical Understanding* (New York, 2012).

CHAPTER 2

Holocaust Historiography and Cultural History[1]

DAN STONE

Culture is when mothers who are holding their babies in their arms are excused from digging their own graves before being shot.
—Romain Gary, *The Dance of Genghis Cohn*

In a recent paper, Peter Burke, Britain's leading proponent of cultural history, reflected on the problems that had arisen as a result of cultural history's success.[2] These, according to Burke, are five in number, though naturally they overlap.

The first is the very success of cultural history: its ubiquity tends towards the disintegration of the discipline. If cultural history is so widely practiced, then the question is no longer how to convince people of the validity of its claims or how to persuade people to engage with it, but "what is *not* cultural history?" The second is the idea that cultural history constitutes a "turn" in historical thought. Where we have had linguistic, visual, bodily, material, narrative, and performative turns, now we must add a "cultural historical turn" to the list. The implication, presumably, is that if there is a "turn" there will sooner or later be a "turn against." Cultural history is obviously, in Burke's eyes, too valuable to be so subject to the whims of intellectual fashion. The third problem is a related one, that of pluralism. By this Burke means the problem of determining the field. Diversity is a good thing, but at what point does it become disunity and incoherence? The fourth relates to the fear that the historical arena will be dominated by cultural history with the resulting loss of other forms of explanation. If cultural history becomes the dominant paradigm for historians, what will become of economic or political forms of explaining the past? Here Burke signals a fear of reductionism, but where practitioners of cultural history

Notes for this section begin on page 56.

might have levelled that accusation against, say, political historians, in the past, now Burke fears that the charge might apply to cultural historians. Finally, and somewhat surprisingly—though related to the issue of reductionism—Burke suggested that the cultural constructivism inherent in cultural history carries the danger that it might lead historians to embrace extreme voluntarism, leaving no place for social facts.

These are serious problems, suggesting that it may be time to take stock of what cultural history has achieved and where it might be heading in the future. In this chapter I use the example of historiography of the Holocaust in order to respond to Burke's challenge and to offer some thoughts on the as yet unfulfilled promises, as well as the limits of cultural history. In order to do so meaningfully, I will start with some thoughts on how to define cultural history.

According to Burke, cultural history is the writing of history from a symbolic point of view, a rather vague definition that is meant to suggest both its strong and weak points. Cultural history, so Burke says, encourages the writing of history with proper emphasis on the various ways of being human.

What does this mean? Surely all history deals with various ways of being human? Clearly, we need to consider what Burke means by "writing history from a symbolic point of view."[3] The use of the term "symbolic" suggests that cultural history takes much of its inspiration from anthropology, especially from American, symbolic anthropology, which seeks to explain culture as a set of shared meanings. The work of Clifford Geertz, Victor Turner and David Schneider, especially, aims to resist scientism or positivism and to emphasise cultural particularism.[4] Examining rituals and symbols, the anthropologist sets out to decode symbols that are key to a particular group and thus to provide detailed meaning. Historians have for the last thirty years or so been attracted to this approach, not only because it suggests a way of interpreting past societies through previously unused sources but because it suggests a reinterpretation of the past, re-describing well-known facts or events in ways that are new but nevertheless recognizably historical: "thick description," Geertz's watchword, is an immediately comprehensible idea for a historian.[5]

In cultural history, the historian's narrative or analysis is based on interpreting symbols, that is to say, aspects of a society that stand for something else and that provide focal points for the functioning of and, hence, understanding of that society. Although more recently, anthropologists have complicated this picture by suggesting that the scholarly text is also part of symbolic discourse, or by claiming that much of culture is inaccessible to language, the stress on the symbolic has been responsible for some of the most innovative work in history over the last few decades, especially history of the medieval and early-modern periods.

Cultural history is different from intellectual history because it does not only situate texts in their ideological or social context. It is different from the history of cultural production (whether elite, such as opera, or popular, such as food) because it does not trace changes in their production or content. As Moshe Rosman writes, in cultural history:

> The historian reads texts and other historical sources and artefacts not so much as discursive expositions, but rather like an anthropologist studying live behavior. By doing so, the historian seeks both to discover the ways in which people in the society in question construed meaning, and to develop a catalogue of the fundamental concepts that mediated interpretation of reality and ordered experience for them. Cultural history might be summed up as "a history of meaning and feelings broadly defined, as embedded in expressive practices widely observed."[6]

And vitally, especially if this methodology seems to be divorced from "real life," cultural history seeks to show how meanings in society are made manifest in power relations, for example, as expressed in gender, racial, or class relations. "Culture," as Miri Rubin puts it, "was the site where relations of power could very readily be discerned."[7] This approach can and usually does involve the study of texts, but also of ritual, memory and other forms of social practice. Most significant of all, it focuses on the body—of the individual in different communities and in relation to the state. Cultural history seeks, as Rubin puts it, "to read symbols in clusters of meaning, in contexts of use, in cases of meaningful practice, through texts and the artefacts of varying genres and texture."[8] As I will explain later, then, in the context of the Holocaust, cultural history means more than the study of Nazi ideology.

Carolyn Dean has written of Michael Rothberg's book, *Traumatic Realism*, that its method renders "the incommensurability of historical knowledge and its representation a permanent dimension of that history."[9] This articulation also captures to some extent the aim of cultural history: to understand the past in the manner of all historical endeavor (hence "realism"), but doing so through a self-reflexive awareness that access to the past is always mediated through the historian's own "informed subjectivity, human and intellectual capacities for categorization, system-building and empathy" and the "wishes, pain, hope and desire" that the historian brings to the past.[10]

Considering the various ways of being human, writing the history of the Holocaust presents a special challenge: the "inhumanity" of the perpetrator, as the oft-used and inappropriate platitude has it (inappropriate not because the perpetrators' actions were not horrendous but because they reveal an unwelcome aspect of the human condition) is one problem, and the multiple experiences of the victims another. It is possible, though sadly rare, to try and combine perpetrator and victim history in a single narrative, as has been done in the most accomplished fashion by Saul Friedländer in his recently completed two volume *Nazi Germany and the Jews*.[11] But doing so does not necessarily entail writing cultural history. Indeed, most historians of the Holocaust would find the de-emphasis on political history intolerable, even those writing, say, about music in the ghettos: one has to understand the circumstances in which the victims found themselves and this necessitates political history of a sort. So too did the judicial requirements of the Nuremberg, Frankfurt, and other trials that were so important in the early development of Holocaust historiography.[12] The key point here is that although Jews were not simply passive victims, as an older stereotype had it, their fate was ultimately out of their hands. As the minutes from the Białystok *Judenrat* (Jewish council) record, in an important corrective to those who regard the *Judenräte* (Jewish councils) as complicit in the Jews' destruction, "We are a state without finances, without budgets, without gold reserves.... The decisions will not after all be made by the *Judenrat*, nor by the Executive Board. The Germans will settle things."[13] The question of agency, or the lack of it, that is central here suggests that political history, with its stress on power relations, rather than cultural history, provides the most appropriate way of understanding the position of the Jews under Nazi rule. Thus the first thing we note in this context is that Burke's claim about the all-pervasiveness of cultural history is not true of Holocaust historiography. Since this is no longer the marginal branch of historiography that it was just two decades ago, it is worth considering why cultural history—as opposed to the historical study of culture—has as yet failed to have any significant influence on historians of the Holocaust.

Rather than proceed on a negative note, however, we should perhaps start by acknowledging, indeed welcoming, the impressive impact that cultural history has had on the history of World War II, for example in the recent volume *Surviving Hitler and Mussolini,* edited by Robert Gildea, et al.[14] This approach marks a welcome addition to the historiography, which remains otherwise dominated by military history. We should say the same for the war's aftermath, about which we now have a plethora of studies devoted to post-war memory, consumerism, gender, the body, and so on, in the context of the emerging Cold War.[15] Most significantly, cultural history has had a major impact on the writing of modern German history. In *Pain and Prosperity,* a volume edited by Paul Betts and Greg Eghigian, modern German history is reinterpreted through the symbolic lenses of pain, memory, modernity, childbirth, sacrifice, prosperity, scarcity, and nostalgia. In *The Work of Memory,* edited by Alon Confino and Peter Fritzsche, modern German memory is analyzed, not through memorials and other *lieux de mémoire,* as has become customary in memory studies, but through power relations in society, for example, the role of industrialists, medicine, and literature.[16] A noticeably burgeoning area of German cultural history is landscape and environmental history, with works by David Blackbourn, Thomas Lekan, Frank Uekoetter, and others—notably from cultural geography—on conservation, forestry, and the symbolic role of landscape.[17] The current mass of works on post-war consumerism and, especially on gender, are also largely outgrowths of cultural history.

Alon Confino writes that "the goal is to write a history of twentieth-century Germany whereby the disciplinary techniques of the state and the making of the self interact."[18] This is a statement that can only have been made at the end of a long development of cultural history, such that its exponents feel confident in its achievements and can see the merits of bringing it into a relationship with political history. Confino is an exemplary practitioner of the genre, with his analyses of local symbolism, especially his studies of Württemberg, of the idea of *Heimat*, and of tourism, and the ways in which they interact with national narratives. This goes beyond merely juxtaposing the history of sensibilities or emotions with the history of the state, but involves bringing cultural history into the heart of modern German history, in a way vindicating Peter Burke's claim about the centrality of the genre.

But to what extent has cultural history influenced writing of the history of the Holocaust? They are not exactly the same thing, but the postmodernist turn is deeply indebted to developments in Holocaust historiography, and contributions such as Saul Friedländer's *Probing the Limits of Representation* (1992)—which includes Hayden White's much-discussed essay "Historical Emplotment and the Problem of Truth"—are also contributions to wider debates about the nature of history writing, which is why Keith Jenkins includes several excerpts from the book in his *Postmodern History Reader*.[19] Furthermore, it is very striking that within debates about theory, the Holocaust is often appealed to as a definitive test case.

For example, in an article attacking what he sees as the dying legacy of postmodern philosophy of history, Perez Zagorin implies that he is driving the nail into the coffin by noting an apparent inability of the postmodernists to respond to Holocaust deniers:

> Historians of the Holocaust in particular have been disquieted by the assertion that historical facts are products of discourse, not true evidence of an antecedent reality, and that past events may be emplotted in any way a historian might choose. As [Roger] Chartier has noted, there seems to be no basis under [Hayden] White's view for invoking the facts of the historical record to refute the rewriting of history in revisionist narratives which allege that the Holocaust is a myth invented by Zionist propaganda and that the death camps and the gas chambers never existed.[20]

From the opposite point of view, it has been argued that historical relativism need not lead to helplessness in the face of Holocaust deniers:

> Another important example of historians' commitment to the quest for a single, best interpretation is the debate about how to textualize the enormity of the Holocaust perpetrated by the Nazis' "Final Solution".... As these searches for the best Great Story of the Holocaust—whether focused on intentions or on Germanness, Europeanness, and humanness—demonstrate, acknowledged facts are not enough to guarantee a single best interpretation. To admit such interpretive diversity, however, is not to endorse the so-called revisionist denial of the acknowledged historical facts. Rather, it shows that these facts can be admitted and still not provide a definitive (con)textualization of the set of events colligated by the term [Holocaust].[21]

These are just a few examples of the kind of statement with which most students of philosophy of history will be familiar, and can easily be multiplied. Rather than do so here, I want just to note the curious fact that whilst the Holocaust has often been the argument of last resort in theoretical debates about postmodernism, representation, or cultural history, the history of the Holocaust in the narrow sense appears to be quite resistant to such ideas. It is this disjunction that I want to account for here, and to show how cultural history is finally and valuably starting to make inroads into how the history of the Holocaust is written.

First, then, we should pause to reconsider what it is that cultural history seeks to do. Even granting that it has become central to the discipline, as Burke argues, how much of what passes for cultural history actually conforms to some of its basic assumptions? Anne Kane, in a useful article published in *History and Theory,* makes some basic methodological statements about cultural history that are worth bearing in mind. Students of "culture" are familiar with the debates amongst theorists of cultural history as to whether culture counts as structure or practice, as well as with older debates about what is actually meant by "culture," from the sense, now usually regarded as elitist, proposed by Matthew Arnold, that culture constitutes the finer aspects of a society, its art, music, and literature, to the supposedly postmodern notion that culture is everything that makes up a society, a position often associated with Clifford Geertz and self-reflexive anthropology. Kane writes that instead of the "culture as structure / culture as practice" conundrum, we should place more emphasis on the "recursivity of meaning, agency and structure—or more specifically, the mutual transformation of social structure, social action, and cultural systems—in historical transformation."[22] This statement appears to be saying that instead of a synchronic analysis of culture, à la Lévi-Strauss,[23] we should see culture historically, and think about its role in historical transformation, which to a historian seems eminently sensible. One thinks here of Marshall Sahlins's claim, in *Islands of History,* that the combination of event and structure *is* history, an argument that allows for the transformation of culture to take place, but within certain parameters defined by what a culture can and cannot comprehend.[24] This ties in with Kane's comments that "the foundation underlying the reciprocity of social action, social structuring, and the reproduction and transformation of cultural systems, is meaning construction, the process of using cultural models to make sense of experience" and that "meaning structure and meaning construction together form the basis for cultural explanation in historical processes." The best way to uncover meaning in cultural models, Kane asserts, is "to study the 'active' component of culture structures, namely narrative," because narratives are where cultural meanings are metaphorically embodied, are the first place people turn for interpreting experience, and are thus "configurations of meaning, through which an individual and/or community comes to understand itself."[25] In order to study the Holocaust through the lens of cultural history, then, we would want to examine how meaning construction, understood through the narratives that individuals and groups understand themselves, both shaped and was transformed by the event of the genocide.

On this basis, one's initial suspicion might well be that very few aspects of Holocaust historiography can be seen as cultural history. First of all, on a somewhat emotional level, if cultural history seeks to explain the transformation of meaning, how can it respond to an event that is often said to be fundamentally meaningless, or that shatters all established methodologies, as thinkers as diverse as Hannah Arendt and Jean-François Lyotard have suggested? But even if we bracket off this discussion—which takes us into the realms of aesthetics and ethics—if cultural history seeks "to make social and economic structures become utterly malleable entities in the web of signs and symbols" such that it would "end the longstanding subjugation of history to the material side of life," as Ernst Breisach understands it,[26] can Holocaust historiography be considered cultural history? How many historical studies of the Holocaust could be considered to "share a distrust or at least a distaste for histories of a linear type," another of cultural history's characteristics, according to Breisach?[27] Still, despite this obvious lack of fit, I will suggest in what follows that although Holocaust historiography shows that Peter Burke's claim about the ubiquity of cultural history does not apply in all cases, nevertheless there are areas of the discipline where cultural history methods have been quite influential. In general, this influence has increased the more historians of the Holocaust turn away from the dominant, structuralist interpretation of the 1980s and 1990s and toward a renewed emphasis on what, for the moment, I will designate with the shorthand "ideology."

Before proceeding further, however, it is important to note that this emphasis on ideology does not mean a return to a naive intentionalism. As put forward by historians such as Lucy Dawidowicz, intentionalism argues not merely that the Holocaust was the logical outcome of antisemitism but that Hitler and the Nazi elite had a plan to kill the Jews long before it was realized, as early, in some versions of the argument, as 1919 or 1925. Nor does it necessarily support (though it need not stand in contradiction to the findings of) a "modified intentionalism" as represented by, for example, Philippe Burrin or Jeffrey Herf.[28] These historians recognize that there was in fact no preconceived plan to murder Europe's Jews and that the decision-making process was ad hoc and reactive, but they place these structuralist claims in a framework of overarching antisemitism within the Third Reich, so that antisemitic ideology—understood almost as an agent in its own right—was ultimately the driving force of the Holocaust. This modified intentionalism, then, has the tendency to be not very modified at all. Cultural history differs from the structuralist approach because it places a strong emphasis on the world of ideas, symbols and narratives. And it differs from intentionalism because it is not an argument concerned primarily with reconstructing the chronology of the decision-making process for the "Final Solution," but a way of understanding the world of meanings that allowed the idea of the "Final Solution" to emerge as an option for the Third Reich's leaders. Equally, where the history of the Holocaust's victims is concerned, cultural history permits not just a reconstruction of the experiences of the Jews, but a way of trying to understand how their experiences were given meaning, or, as one might expect, were opaque to meaning-production.[29]

Let us take some examples, all of which draw upon what can be seen in the broadest sense as an anthropological sensibility, to try and grapple with the nature of Nazism and the occurrence of the Holocaust, an occurrence which, taking Kane strictly at her word, might be considered to be incomprehensible since its victims had no culturally-accepted narratives through which they could make sense of what was happening. (Although there are some who argue to the contrary, the majority of scholars consider it a paradox that throughout the persecution, the Jewish victims used established narratives to try and provide meaning for what was happening, with the result that they all fell short of the task, even if many diarists and chroniclers did formulate penetrating insights into Nazism's hatred of the Jews.[30])

A good example is the work that has been done to try and understand the nature of Nazism. There is of course a risk in such study, in that one has to share a mental space with the thing one is studying, but it is a necessary risk, as some brave—and very disparate—thinkers such as Aurel Kolnai, Georges Bataille, and R. G. Collingwood understood in the 1930s.[31] From the point of view of cultural history, the Nazi self-description of "thinking with the blood" could not be more symbolic. Here we see what Kane means by the transformation of narratives that contain symbolic meanings with regard to how the world should be interpreted. With its critiques of Weimar degeneracy, materialism, and rationalism, Nazism overturned established narratives and replaced them with mythical narratives of authentic, Teutonic belonging based on racial homogeneity, the struggle against "the Jew," and the creation of the *Volksgemeinschaft*. It is no doubt true, as those who have protested against the so-called "voluntaristic turn" in the historiography of the Third Reich have stressed (most notably Richard Evans), that most Germans were not ideologically committed and that their everyday lives were taken up with mundane matters such as obtaining food and shelter. Yet, bearing in mind Charles Maier's important comment that "[w]hat are morally significant are the few institutions that were murderous, not the normal aspects of running a society,"[32] it is worth remembering that what recent scholarship has shown is, first, that the institutions that were "murderous" were more numerous than historians have long thought, and second, that even if not outright conspiracy theorists, most Germans during the Hitler years subscribed more or less willingly to the dictates of the regime, that is, allowed themselves to be *gleichgeschaltet* ("co-ordinated").[33]

The "return of ideology" in Holocaust historiography, then, represents a general trend away from the 1980s' structuralist consensus that was reliant on a social science approach and a turn toward symbolic, anthropological modes of thinking. As already indicated above, "return of ideology" is meant not as an attempt to rehabilitate a simplistic Goldhagen-type mono-causal approach,[34] but rather as detailed empirical research into the role played by the professions and academic disciplines, from anthropologists to astrophysicists (and even, belatedly, historians); antisemitic research institutes; military education programmes; wartime propaganda; Nazi ethics; the "ideological roots of Nazism" in religion, *völkisch* thought, and so on; the Hitler Youth; and the social make-up of perpetrator agencies such as the SD (*Sicherheitsdienst*, security service of the Nazi Party) and SS agencies like the WVHA (*Wirtschafts-verwaltungshauptamt*, the Economics Administration Main Office), RSHA (*Reichssicherheitshauptamt*, the Reich Security Main Office, the SS's umbrella organization) and the RuSHA (*Rasse- und Siedlungshauptamt*, the Race and Resettlement Office).[35]

Most of what I have discussed so far concerns cultural interpretations of Nazism and of the Third Reich's agencies and institutions. When it comes to turning our attention to the murder process itself, the task becomes harder. It has become a truism that no matter how sophisticated the historian's approach and no matter how subtle the historian's writing, "an opaqueness remains at the very core of the historical understanding and interpretation of what happened," as Friedländer notes[36]; rightly so, we might add. But that is not meant in the quasi-mystical way used by thinkers as diverse as Elie Wiesel and Maurice Blanchot. Rather, I mean that no single historical approach will take us to the heart of the matter, and that here we reach the limits of cultural history in theory and methodology, for how can a historical method devoted to explicating meaning be applied to account for the opacity of meaning?[37] Nevertheless, I would argue that here, the real contribution of cultural history to Holocaust history is only just beginning to be made. The most significant contribution to this emerging approach, which stands on the shoulders of giants but which seeks to turn away from the focus on the politics of decision-making that remains the mainstay of the literature, is that made, unsurprisingly, by a scholar who has already established himself as one of the foremost practitioners of German cultural history: Alon Confino. In an article in *History & Memory* in 2005, Confino set out what promises to be a major line of investigation into the cultural assumptions underpinning the Holocaust.

Confino's argument is clearly and provocatively laid out, beginning with this assertion:

> [W]e cannot understand why the Nazis persecuted and exterminated the Jews unless we are ready to explore ... Nazi fantasies, hallucinations, and imagination. The campaign against the Jews was based on and motivated by fantasies about the Jews as the eternal and mortal enemy of humanity, and about the historic need to either exterminate the Jews or perish.[38]

This is a claim that is of a piece with the "return of ideology" that I have outlined, and it is also one, as Confino recognizes, that accords with a commonsense understanding of the Holocaust; that is, that it must have been motivated by hatred of Jews (not, it is important to stress, by any means an uncontested claim in the historiography). It breaks with the rational approach signaled implicitly in much functionalist scholarship and especially in the scholarship of those who see the Holocaust as primarily driven by economic factors, such as Götz Aly.[39] Confino builds on Saul Friedländer's notion of "redemptive antisemitism" and on George Mosse's pioneering work from the 1960s onwards.[40] But he notes, quite rightly, that by comparison with the explosion of cultural history in German history, many of Mosse's ideas about sexuality, symbolism, myth and racism have not been integrated into Holocaust history: "It is as if debates in Holocaust historiography are isolated from major methodological trends in the historiography of German society and culture," he writes.[41] This is an argument that I put forward in my book *Constructing the Holocaust* (2003)—that the extermination of the Jews should be approached not through the lens of rational calculus, decision-making procedures or bureaucracy, but through that of non-pragmatic, redemptive fantasies, the latter of which do

> not necessitate the existence of a plan to murder the Jews, a canard which has long exercised Holocaust historiography. Rather, the role of fantasy bound up in the idea of redemption through murder is sufficient to account for the desire to murder the Jews without requiring that historians find a signed document setting out such a plan.... This is a significant step in a field of historiography which has traditionally been reluctant to deviate from the archival material left by the Nazis, and signals a new desire to take ideas in the past seriously.[42]

Confino's point accords with Kane's argument about what cultural history is, in that he seeks to show that Nazi ideology transformed German culture, so that even if, as he notes, ideology does not represent reality and experience in a straightforward way, yet "an element in Nazi anti-Semitism that should be interpreted as the history of representations, memory and symbolic meanings" does provide insights into how Nazi culture functioned.[43]

Where Confino is most forthright is in his claim that his cultural historical approach offers something that traditional methodologies cannot:

> Ultimately, all those who attempt to understand the Holocaust as caused by institutional and policymaking processes inherent in the Nazi system of government, by the inner logic of National Socialist policies geared toward resettlement and expansion, or by the need to solve immediate local pragmatic problems (such as food problems)—that is, all attempts that fundamentally underplay the beliefs and values embedded in the acts of the perpetrators—are bound to end in an interpretative cul-de-sac.[44]

In my opinion, the benefits of cultural history complement rather than supersede other historical approaches—as I have argued elsewhere, only a multiplicity of narratives and approaches can hope to represent the Holocaust[45]—but

Confino is nevertheless right to say that cultural history, with its emphasis on fantasy, violence and Nazi narratives of meaning construction, takes us closer to understanding the all-elusive "why?" than do studies of day-by-day decision-making, no matter how detailed.

Other keywords that have recently come to the fore in Holocaust historiography include: violence, blood ritual, sacrifice, and fantasy. While study of the impact of eugenics and racial science remains important, Confino is right when he says that "[t]he description of biological racism as represented in sober and objective language seems insufficient to account for a topic whose essence was inner demons and hallucinations."[46] A quick glance at the writings of the Nazis' favorite race theorists, Hans F. K. Günther, Houston Stewart Chamberlain and others, proves this to be true, as does the fact that ultimately, the regime fell out with many of the race scientists, as their awkward academic hair-splitting meant that they often contradicted the basic racial propaganda messages of the Third Reich.[47] Even the writings of scientists such as Eugen Fischer or Otmar von Verschuer, though they generally steer clear of the mystical statements found in Günther and Chamberlain, take as their premise ideas about race that cannot be proven scientifically. As the race-philosopher Ernst Krieck put it:

> For real spiritual life does not exit in a vacuum, nor in a professor's study, nor through ignoring natural reality, but precisely through what Thomas Mann in his destructive work called the *Politisierung des Geistes*.... Only the conquest of the spirit by the force of the regime, of policy, and also by physical force will set the spirit in its real place, which is in civilizations and not in spiritual abstract culture. The purpose of the spirit is to serve the race, the state, and, as Alfred Bäumler said, the spirit is to be encompassed in the totality of racialism (*Arteigenheit, Artgleichheit*).... [T]he time for humanism and liberalism has passed and ... nowadays blood and race are the place upon which man attains a consciousness of himself and thus freedom. Race and blood are unavoidable primeval forces with primeval power (*Urzwang*), and in accepting the yoke of these forces man is liberated from enslavement to reason, logic, and other sterile forms of the human spirit.[48]

Or, even more explicitly:

> The scientific system of Eugen Fischer, according to which hereditary characteristics should be considered the motive force of history, is the key to understanding the value of the individual. And there are scientists in the world rising to disagree with the possibility of proving the existence of race scientifically. However we have learned from Chamberlain's and especially from the Führer's teachings that the verification of the existence of race, and perhaps of existence in general, does not require artificial scientific tools.... The fact of the existence of race is not doubtful, because man carries it in his heart, his spirit, his soul, or because man wants race to become a fact.[49]

This passage reminds us that Confino is building on the works of earlier scholars, notably Tal, Mosse, Léon Poliakov, Norman Cohn, and Joshua Trachtenberg, whose writings sought to show that the "deep psychology"—for want of a better term—of the Holocaust is to be found not in the perpetrators' own emphasis on their rationality and professionalism, but in their "fantasies about the Jews," which are bound up with and inseparable from the sober, technical and professional language of science and modernity.[50] Whilst such works focus on antisemitic stereotypes and traditions, especially in Germany, they do not do so under the rubric of "cultural history"; the difference between them and today's studies is that these earlier works are essentially contributions to the "intentionalist" understanding of Hitler's and the Nazis' world view, and that recent research, as I have indicated, focuses on German society and culture more broadly.

Can any of this be seen as according with cultural historical practices such as micro-history, with its emphasis on the local and unique, and its distrust of overarching, unifying narratives? Perhaps, but historians have not yet really attempted it, perhaps for fear of entering too deeply into the Nazi mindset on the one hand, and for fear of stepping away from the mainstream and appearing to focus on non-measurable factors, on the other. In Holocaust historiography, where a cultural historical approach is most needed, it is striking that the historiography has remained far more traditional than in most other fields of history—and this despite the massive literature.

There are some exceptions to this claim. Much Israeli historiography, from the early post-war period onwards, has focused on Jewish religious behaviour with regard to the question of *kiddush hahayim* (sanctification of life) versus *kiddush hashem* (sanctification of the Lord) for example; on Nazi vocabulary and linguistics, and on Jewish reactions to persecution.[51] Many local studies—published in all the languages of Europe and beyond—continue to appear in large numbers, dealing with matters of resistance and complicity, rescue and collaboration, as well as religious issues. But these studies are to some extent isolated from the mainstream of what Robert Berkhofer would call the "great story" (or grand narrative) of the Holocaust.[52] And none of these studies is conceptualized in terms of cultural history, however, even if their concerns are close to the approach being advocated here. Even accounting for Wendy Lower's list of topics—interethnic violence, rescue, resistance, testimony, memorialisation, fascism—and the impact of interdisciplinary or comparative work in literary studies, postcolonial studies or genocide studies, it is, I think, too soon to say that "the broader field of Holocaust studies may be changing its position from being a caboose on the cultural train to a locomotive."[53] Were that the case, then pleas for cultural history along the lines of those made recently by Moshe Rosman in the context of Jewish history or by Amos Goldberg in this volume would not be necessary.[54]

One final area that is linked to the emergence of cultural history but which is too large to be encompassed by it and which therefore requires separate treatment, is the theme of memory in Holocaust studies. For Confino, memory and cultural history are more or less synonymous and in this sense the main contributions to Holocaust memory have also been contributions to wider debates, in a manner similar to that made by studies of the question of representation as discussed above. Indeed, here historians have long been at the forefront of research, as in the work in German history of Confino, Peter Fritzsche, Rudy Koshar, Gavriel Rosenfeld, Paul Betts, and others. But it must be said that although much of the work on Holocaust memory has been influential in memory studies more generally, it has largely been undertaken, not by historians but by literary scholars, sociologists, and philosophers. The writings of Saul Friedländer, Dominick LaCapra, Barbie Zelizer, Geoffrey Hartman, Marianne Hirsch, and many others has been extremely influential, but even the few historians in that list have non-standard research interests and are unusually open to theory, especially trauma theory.[55] In Germany one could even argue that two distinct scholarly enterprises have developed, one dealing with the empirical history of the Holocaust, one focusing on the aftermath and representation of the Shoah, and that the two barely interact.

Conclusion

In his remarkable analysis of Nazism, *Germany Jekyll and Hyde,* published in exile in 1940 and recently republished, Sebastian Haffner argued that it does not suffice to historicise Hitler; to try and understand him, as so many Allied propagandists did, as part of a German tradition,

> to tabulate Hitler, as it were, in the History of Ideas and degrade him to an historical episode is a hopeless undertaking, and can only lead to perilous miscalculations. Much more progress towards an accurate estimation of the man can be made if one takes exactly the opposite course and considers German and European history as a part of Hitler's private life.[56]

Here is an insight that is central to a cultural history approach: rather than seek to provide economic, social, military, or other factors that provide a meaningful context for understanding the way in which the Holocaust unfolded, we should instead willingly suspend our disbelief and assume for the moment that the Nazis meant what they said, that they created reality to fit in with their belief system and not vice-versa. Only in this way can the Holocaust become comprehensible—as the outcome of a German narrative through which the perpetrators made sense of the world. This is also the reason why the victims could not make sense of events while they were occurring and why they, their descendants, and, in recent years, the community at large, have struggled to make sense of them too.

Notes

1. Romain Gary, *The Dance of Genghis Cohn* (Harmondsworth, 1978), 53. My thanks to Alon Confino and Amos Goldberg for providing close readings of earlier drafts of this piece, which was first published in *Dapim: Studies on the Shoah,* 23 (2009): 52–68, with responses by

Dan Michman, Carolyn J. Dean, Wendy Lower, Federico Finchelstein, and Dominick LaCapra, 69–93. I have revised the article for this volume to take into account their valuable comments, and cite their responses using the formula: "surname, *Dapim*" (e.g., LaCapra, *Dapim*).

2. Peter Burke, "Strengths and Weaknesses of Cultural History, 1980–2006," paper presented at the Philosophy of History Seminar, Institute for Historical Research, University of London, 1 March 2007.

3. For a discussion, see Lynn Hunt, "Introduction: History, Culture, and Text," in *The New Cultural History*, ed. Lynn Hunt (Berkeley, 1989), 12.

4. I am greatly indebted here to, and borrow some formulations from Jonathan Spencer, "Symbolic Anthropology," in *Encyclopedia of Social and Cultural Anthropology*, ed. Alan Barnard and Jonathan Spencer (London, 2002), 535–39.

5. Clifford Geertz, "Thick Description: Toward an Interpretive Theory of Culture," in *The Interpretation of Cultures: Selected Essays* (London, 1993 [1973]), 3–30. Indeed, as Dominick LaCapra notes (*Dapim*, 89), "thick description" is "all-too-easily assimilated by historians as an analogue (if not simply a synonym) of context" and can therefore be used "to ward off other levels of analysis … as well as forms of critical self-reflection."

6. Moshe Rosman, *How Jewish is Jewish History?* (Oxford, 2007), 131 (cited in Michman, *Dapim*, 71). Rosman is citing Jean-Christophe Agnew, *Worlds Apart: The Market and the Theatre in Anglo-American Thought, 1550–1750* (Cambridge, 1986), xii.

7. Miri Rubin, "What is Cultural History Now?" in *What is History Now?* ed. David Cannadine (Basingstoke, 2002), 84.

8. Ibid., 85.

9. Carolyn J. Dean, "History and Holocaust Representation," *History and Theory* 41, no. 2 (2002): 247. The article is a review of Michael Rothberg, *Traumatic Realism: The Demands of Holocaust Representation* (Minneapolis, 2000).

10. Rubin, "What is Cultural History Now?," 81.

11. Saul Friedländer, *Nazi Germany and the Jews: The Years of Persecution 1933-39* (London, 1997); Friedländer, *Nazi Germany and the Jews 1939–1945: The Years of Extermination* (New York, 2007). For discussion, see Christian Wiese and Paul Betts, eds., *Years of Persecution, Years of Extermination: Saul Friedländer and the Future of Holocaust Studies* (New York, 2010).

12. Lower, *Dapim*, 83–84.

13. From the minute book of the Białystok *Judenrat*, 2 November 1941, in *A Holocaust Reader*, ed. Lucy S. Dawidowicz, (West Orange, NJ, 1976), 278, 282–83.

14. Robert Gildea, Olivier Wieviorka and Annette Waring, eds., *Surviving Hitler and Mussolini: Daily Life in Occupied Europe* (Oxford, 2006).

15. Among many others, see for example István Deák, Jan T. Gross, and Tony Judt, eds., *The Politics of Retribution in Europe: World War II and its Aftermath* (Princeton, 2000); Richard Bessel and Dirk Schumann, eds., *Life after Death: Approaches to a Cultural and Social History of Europe During the 1940s and 1950s* (Cambridge, 2003); Hanna Schissler, ed., *The Miracle Years: A Cultural History of West Germany, 1949–1968* (Princeton, 2001); Uli Linke, *German Bodies: Race and Representation after Hitler* (New York, 1999).

16. Paul Betts and Greg Eghigian, eds., *Pain and Prosperity: Reconsidering Twentieth-Century German History* (Stanford, 2003); Alon Confino, Paul Betts, and Dirk Schumann, eds., *Between Mass Death and Individual Loss: The Place of the Dead in Twentieth-Century Germany* (New York, 2008); Alon Confino and Peter Fritzsche, eds., *The Work of Memory: New Directions in the Study of German Society and Culture* (Urbana, 2002). See also Konrad H. Jarausch and Michael Geyer, *Shattered Past: Reconstructing German Histories* (Princeton, 2003), and Frank Biess, Mark Roseman, and Hanna Schissler, eds., *Conflict, Catastrophe, and Continuity: Essays on Modern German History* (New York, 2007).

17. Axel Goodbody, ed., *The Culture of German Environmentalism: Anxieties, Visions, Realities* (New York, 2002); Thomas Lekan, *Imagining the Nation in Nature: Landscape Preservation and German Identity, 1885–1945* (Cambridge, MA, 2004); Franz-Josef Brüggemeier, Mark Cioc, and Thomas Zeller, eds., *How Green were the Nazis? Nature, Environment and Nation in the Third Reich*

(Athens, OH, 2005); Thomas Lekan and Thomas Zeller, eds., *Germany's Nature: Cultural Landscapes and Environmental History* (New Brunswick, NJ, 2005); David Blackbourn, *The Conquest of Nature: Water, Landscape and the Making of Modern Germany* (New York, 2006); Frank Uekoetter, *The Green and the Brown: A History of Conservation in Nazi Germany* (Cambridge, 2006). For a useful overview see David Motadel, "The German Nature Conservation Movement in the Twentieth Century," *Journal of Contemporary History* 43, no. 1 (2008): 137–53. The work of Karen E. Till exemplifies the cultural geographers' work on this subject; see especially *The New Berlin: Memory, Politics, Place* (Minneapolis, 2005).

18. Alon Confino, *Germany as a Culture of Remembrance: Promises and Limits of Writing History* (Chapel Hill, 2006), 212.

19. Saul Friedländer, ed., *Probing the Limits of Representation: Nazism and the "Final Solution"* (Cambridge, MA, 1992); Keith Jenkins, ed. *The Postmodern History Reader* (London, 1997).

20. Perez Zagorin, "History, the Referent, and Narrative: Reflections on Postmodernism Now," *History and Theory* 38, no. 1 (1999): 19–20. See also Berel Lang, "Is It Possible to Misrepresent the Holocaust?" *History and Theory* 34, no. 1 (1995): 84–89, for a similar argument.

21. Robert J. Berkhofer, Jr., *Beyond the Great Story: History as Text and Discourse* (Cambridge, MA, 1995), 49. This point of view stands in direct opposition to that of Chris Lorenz, who writes that "[a]s soon as the 'fragmentation' of historiography leads to—and is legitimated by—epistemological scepticism, a healthy pluralism has given way to an unhealthy relativism." See "Comparative Historiography: Problems and Perspectives," *History and Theory* 38, no. 1 (1999): 25. See also Lorenz's comments at the end of his "Model Murderers: Afterthoughts on the Goldhagen Method and History," *Rethinking History* 6, no. 2 (2002): 146. For some of the best considerations of historical narration in relation to the Holocaust, see Dan Diner, *Beyond the Conceivable: Studies on Germany, Nazism, and the Holocaust* (Berkeley, 2000).

22. Anne Kane, "Reconstructing Culture in Historical Explanation: Narratives as Cultural Structure and Practice," *History and Theory* 39, no. 3 (2000): 311.

23. See Kamala Visweswaran, "The Interventions of Culture: Claude Lévi-Strauss, Race, and the Critique of Historical Time," in *Race and Racism in Continental Philosophy*, ed. Robert Bernasconi with Sybol Cook (Bloomington, 2003), 227–48.

24. Marshall Sahlins, *Islands of History* (Chicago, 1985), especially 155 ("culture is precisely the organization of the current situation in the terms of a past").

25. Kane, "Reconstructing Culture," 312, 314, 315.

26. Ernst Breisach, *On the Future of History: The Postmodernist Challenge and its Aftermath* (Chicago, 2003), 144.

27. Ibid., 148.

28. Philippe Burrin, *Nazi Anti-Semitism: From Prejudice to the Holocaust*, trans. Janet Lloyd (New York, 2005); Jeffrey Herf, *The Jewish Enemy: Nazi Propaganda During World War II and the Holocaust* (Cambridge, MA, 2006).

29. For further discussion, with a wide range of examples, see Dan Stone, *Histories of the Holocaust* (Oxford, 2010), ch. 6.

30. Cf. David G. Roskies, *Against the Apocalypse: Responses to Catastrophe in Modern Jewish Culture* (Cambridge, MA, 1984); Roskies, *The Jewish Search for a Usable Past* (Bloomington, 1999).

31. Dan Stone, *Responses to Nazism in Britain 1933-1939: Before War and Holocaust* (London, 2003), 17–44; Stone, "Anti-fascist Europe Comes to Britain: Theorising Fascism as a Contribution to Defeating it," in *Varieties of Anti-Fascism: Britain in the Inter-war Period*, ed. Nigel Copsey and Andrzej Olechnowicz (London, 2010), 183–201.

32. Charles S. Maier, *The Unmasterable Past: History, Holocaust, and German National Identity* (Cambridge, MA, 1988), 96.

33. See, among many studies, Aurel Kolnai, *The War Against the West* (London, 1938); Eric Voegelin, *Hitler and the Germans*, trans. and ed. Detlev Clemens and Brendan Purcell (Columbia, 1999); Sebastian Haffner, *Germany Jekyll and Hyde*, trans. Wilfrid David (London, 2005 [1940]); Fred Weinstein, *The Dynamics of Nazism: Leadership, Ideology, and the Holocaust* (New York, 1980);

Peter Longerich, *"Davon haben wir nichts gewusst!" Die Deutschen und die Judenverfolgung 1933–1945* (Munich, 2006); Peter Fritzsche, *Life and Death in the Third Reich* (Cambridge, MA, 2008). And, for an excellent discussion of the need for a history of German memory during the Third Reich, see Alon Confino's chapter in this volume.

34. See Daniel J. Goldhagen, *Hitler's Willing Executioners: Ordinary Germans and the Holocaust* (London, 1996). Apart from those who engaged in debate with Goldhagen (Christopher Browning, Ruth Bettina Birn, Norman Finkelstein), the best analysis of Goldhagen's book and the debate that it spawned is A. Dirk Moses, "Structure and Agency in the Holocaust: Daniel J. Goldhagen and His Critics," *History and Theory* 37, no. 2 (1998): 194–219. In Israel, where "intentionalism" was simply common sense, Goldhagen's book met with a lukewarm response in comparison with the reception it received elsewhere, especially in Germany and the United States.

35. See, for example, Alan Steinweis, *Studying the Jew: Scholarly Antisemitism in Nazi Germany* (Cambridge, MA, 2006); Dirk Rupnow, "Racializing Historiography: Anti-Jewish Scholarship in the Third Reich," *Patterns of Prejudice* 42, no. 1 (2008): 27–59; Isabel Heinemann, *Rasse, Siedlung, deutsches Blut: Das Rasse- und Siedlungshauptamt der SS und die rassenpolitische Neuordnung Europas* (Göttingen, 2003); Michael H. Kater, *Das "Ahnenerbe" der SS 1935–1945: Ein Beitrag zur Kulturpolitik des Dritten Reiches* (Munich, 2006); Kater, *Doctors Under Hitler* (Chapel Hill, 2000 [1989]); Kater, *Hitler Youth* (Cambridge, MA, 2004); Michael Wildt, *Generation der Unbedingten: Das Führungskorps des Reichssicherheitshauptamtes* (Hamburg, 2002); Michael Thad Allen, *The Business of Genocide: The SS, Slave Labor, and the Concentration Camps* (Chapel Hill, 2002); Ute Deichmann, *Biologists Under Hitler,* trans. Thomas Dunlap (Cambridge, MA, 1996); Margit Szöllösi-Janze, ed., *Science in the Third Reich* (Oxford, 2001); Jürgen Matthäus et al., *Ausbildungsziel Judenmord? "Weltanschauliche Erziehung" von SS, Polizei und Waffen-SS im Rahmen der "Endlösung"* (Frankfurt/M, 2003). On historians see Nicholas Berg, *Der Holocaust und die westdeutschen Historiker: Erforschung und Erinnerung* (Göttingen, 2003); Ingo Haar, *Historiker im Nationalsozialismus: Die deutschen Geschichtswissenschaft und der "Volkstumskampf" im Osten* (Göttingen, 2000); Winfried Schulze and Otto Gerhard Oexle, eds., *Deutsche Historiker im Nationalsozialismus* (Frankfurt/M., 1999); Götz Aly, *Macht Geist Wahn: Kontinuitäten deutschen Denkens* (Berlin, 1997); Peter Schöttler, *Geschichtsschreibung als Legitimationswissenschaft 1918–1945* (Frankfurt/M., 1997). For an excellent discussion see Konrad Jarausch, "Unasked Questions: The Controversy about Nazi Collaboration among German Historians," in *Lessons and Legacies, VI: New Currents in Holocaust Research,* ed. Jeffrey Diefendorf (Evanston, 2004), 190–208.

36. Saul Friedländer, "The 'Final Solution': On the Unease in Historical Interpretation," in *History, Memory, and the Extermination of the Jews of Europe* (Bloomington, 1993), 103.

37. Dean, *Dapim,* 77–78.

38. Alon Confino, "Fantasies about the Jews: Cultural Reflections on the Holocaust," *History & Memory* 17, nos. 1–2 (2005): 297.

39. See especially Götz Aly, *Hitlers Volksstaat: Raub, Rassenkrieg und nationaler Sozialismus* (Frankfurt/M, 2005). For more subtle statements about the significance of economic motivations, especially theft, in the murder of the Jews, see Jonathan Petropoulos, "The Nazi Kleptocracy: Reflections on Avarice and the Holocaust," and Frank Bajohr, "Cliques, Corruption, and Organized Self-Pity: The Nazi Movement and the Property of the Jews," both in *Lessons and Legacies, VII: The Holocaust in International Perspective,* ed. Dagmar Herzog (Evanston, 2006), 29–38 and 39–49; Frank Bajohr, "Robbery, Ideology, and Realpolitik: Some Critical Remarks," *Yad Vashem Studies* 35, no. 1 (2007): 179–91.

40. Friedländer, *Nazi Germany and the Jews;* George L. Mosse, *The Crisis of German Ideology: Intellectual Origins of the Third Reich* (New York, 1964); Mosse, *Nazi Culture: Intellectual, Cultural and Social Life in the Third Reich* (New York, 1966); Mosse, *Germans and Jews: The Right, the Left, and the Search for a "Third Force" in Pre-Nazi Germany* (London, 1971); Mosse, *Masses and Man: Nationalist and Fascist Perceptions of Reality* (Detroit, 1987).

41. Confino, "Fantasies," 305.

42. Dan Stone, *Constructing the Holocaust: A Study in Historiography* (London, 2003), 164 (cited in Confino, "Fantasies," 307).

43. Confino, "Fantasies," 309.
44. Ibid., 302.
45. Stone, *Histories of the Holocaust.*
46. Confino, "Fantasies," 310.
47. See Christopher M. Hutton, *Race and the Third Reich: Linguistics, Racial Anthropology and Genetics in the Dialectic of Volk* (Cambridge, 2005), especially 139 ("there was never any question of the Party and state authorities yielding their final authority in such matters to purely scholarly criteria.... The regime increasingly sought to keep academic and scholarly discussion of race separate from race propaganda in the public sphere").
48. Ernst Krieck, "Die Intellektuellen und das Dritte Reich," 1938 lecture (cited in Uriel Tal, "Violence and the Jew in Nazi Ideology," in *Religion, Politics and Ideology in the Third Reich: Selected Essays* (London, 2004), 6–7).
49. Ibid, 9. On the distinction in Verschuer's work between "scientific" and "antisemitic" studies, see Eric Ehrenreich, "Otmar von Verschuer and the 'Scientific' Legitimization of Nazi Anti-Jewish Policy," *Holocaust and Genocide Studies* 21, no. 1 (2007): 55–72.
50. Léon Poliakov, *Harvest of Hate* (London, 1956); Poliakov, *The Aryan Myth: A History of Racist and Nationalist Ideas in Europe*, trans. Edmund Howard (London, 1974); Norman Cohn, *Warrant for Genocide: The Myth of the Jewish World Conspiracy and the Protocols of the Elders of Zion* (London, 1967); Cohn, *The Pursuit of the Millennium: Revolutionary Millenarians and Mystical Anarchists of the Middle Ages* (London, 1970 [1957]); Cohn, *Europe's Inner Demons* (London, 1975); Joshua Trachtenberg, *The Devil and the Jews: The Medieval Conception of the Jew and its Relation to Modern Anti-Semitism* (Philadelphia, 1983 [1943]).
51. Michman, *Dapim*, 73–74.
52. Berkhofer, *Beyond the Great Story.*
53. Lower, *Dapim*, 84–86.
54. Rosman, *How Jewish is Jewish History?*, ch. 5. By that comment, I do not mean to say that Holocaust history is a sub-field of Jewish history. See David Engel, *Historians of the Jews and the Holocaust* (Stanford, 2010), and my review of that book on H-Judaic online discussion forum (April 2010).
55. For a broad-brush discussion of this literature, see my "Beyond the Mnemosyne Institute: The Future of Memory after the Age of Commemoration," in *The Future of Memory*, ed. Richard Crownshaw, Jane Kilby, and Antony Rowland (New York, 2010), 17–36. An interesting article that brings trauma theory to bear on Holocaust historiography is Amos Goldberg, "Trauma, Narrative, and Two Forms of Death," *Literature and Medicine* 25, no. 1 (2006): 122–41.
56. Haffner, *Germany Jekyll and Hyde*, 5.

CHAPTER 3

The Invisible Crime
Nazi Politics of Memory and Postwar Representation of the Holocaust

DIRK RUPNOW

Questions of representation are at the core of scholarly engagement with the Holocaust. The term "Holocaust" has become globally established as a signifier of genocidal crimes, but in its own way it is problematic as a term to signify the complex historical events of the mass crimes against Jewry that were initiated by Germans and Austrians and committed with and by their collaborators all across Europe.[1] As soon as the Nazi crimes began coming to light, the discussion started on what kind of language and imagery was adequate and, most importantly, was able to convey the multifaceted and extreme experiences of the many victims suffering from exclusion, persecution, deprivation, expulsion, deportation, ghettoization, and culminating in systematic mass murder at execution sites and specifically designed killing centers; and what kind of explanation was adequate to shed light on the perpetrators' actions and motives without exculpating them and blurring their guilt and responsibility. The victims, when confronted with the destruction of their culture and their life, had already grappled with those challenges of representation that we still face today.[2]

I will first analyze the Nazi perpetrators' politics of memory and representation, and their deliberate planning and construction of the crimes before I discuss their influence on the postwar cultures of memory, including historiography. I will concentrate on the discourse of unrepresentability and its effects for our understanding of the historical events. Many of our representations and concepts—for example, the focus on the gas chambers as the quintessential sites of the crime—tend to obscure the act and the actors, thus still conforming to

Notes for this section begin on page 75.

their intentions. This has become especially visible in the German and Austrian debates around the exhibition on crimes committed by the German Army in World War II (the so-called *Wehrmachtsausstellung,* 1995) that focused on mass shootings instead and thus on a huge number of "ordinary men" as immediate killers instead of a small group of rather faceless perpetrators. Another case in point is the recent debate on Georges Didi-Huberman's work on the Auschwitz *Sonderkommando* photographs, drawing attention to the documents of the victims and their efforts to represent the crimes and make them visible—in contrast to the documentary tradition of the perpetrators that still dominates our memory.

The Nazi Politics of Memory

Discourses on the Holocaust and on memory have often aroused the suspicion that the Nazi perpetrators not only planned the physical annihilation of the Jews but also wanted to erase them "from history and memory."[3] The Roman practice of *damnatio memoriae,* whereby statues of a person found to be an enemy of the state were destroyed and the name removed from inscriptions and coins might be seen as the model for this practice. The stereotypical, albeit understandable, characterization of Jews as the "people of history" with privileged access to remembrance and memory seems to make the intent of total destruction that transcends the physical act even more plausible. Thus, terms such as "memorycide" and "mnemocide" were coined in order to modify and strengthen the term "genocide."[4]

Especially with the rise of memory as a research paradigm in the humanities and social sciences, the allegation of memorycide seems to be above all an attempt to represent a contemporary construction of, and justification for, the uniqueness of the Holocaust—unlike previous arguments using the number of victims or the "industrial" way of killing. If one wants to retain the special status of the Holocaust in times when the significance and importance of memory and remembrance have become clear and have moved to the center of interest, it seems that focusing on a targeted policy of forgetting that transcends even the physical annihilation of the Jews is the solution to a scholarly unproductive comparison and contrasting of the numbers of victims. At the same time, in a period where determination of identity is often carried out by pointing to one's status as victim, the image of a victimized memory—that has itself become a victim—is the best legitimization for this new central concept in cultural studies.

Beyond that, the assumed project of memorycide offers a negative foil for the duty to remember and for the dedication of museums, memorials, and monuments. The duty to remember thus is not only derived from the mass murder but above all from its particular character as a double homicide, which was directed both at the people and the memory of them. By mirroring it, the allegation of memorycide justifies the statement that remembrance of the crimes is a necessary precondition for the prevention of comparable crimes. The ritualized commemoration of the persecution of the Jews and their mass murder, the rhetoric of not-forgetting ultimately assumes that the committed crimes cannot be repeated as long as they are remembered. Destruction and forgetting on the one hand and remembrance and justice on the other hand are usually seen as not simply arbitrarily linked but as inseparable in their character.

The deliberate actions to erase the evidence of the mass murder at the end of the Third Reich offer factual points of reference and models for the claim of memorycide: the exhumations and the burning of the dead bodies carried out by *Aktion 1005* beginning in 1942 under the leadership of SS-Standard Leader Paul Blobel at the main sites of the murders, as well as the destruction of documents by German authorities at the end of the war in obedience to an order from the Reich's interior ministry.[5] Traces of the racist politics of extermination were not supposed to fall into the hands of the allied forces owing to their incriminating nature. Heinrich Himmler's so-called Posen speech, which he gave on 4 October 1943 to an audience of SS group leaders, has often been cited as evidence of the regime's memorycidal intentions. A section from this speech about the mass murder of Jews and the allegedly untarnished "propriety" (*Anständigkeit*) of the SS men who supposedly remained untouched after the murders is often used as a quote in this context: "This is a glorious chapter in our history that has never been written and that never will be."[6]

Rarely mentioned in the scholarly literature is another Himmler speech given only two days later at the same place, this time to a gathering of *Reichs-* and *Gauleiter*. This speech explicitly but even more ambivalently deals with the problems of secrecy and historical transmission in regard to the "final solution of the Jewish question." "The hard decision had to be made," Himmler stated, "to let this people [the Jews] disappear from this earth.... One can consider at a much later time whether the German people should be told more about this. I think it is better that we—we as a whole—have carried this for our people, have carried the responsibility (the responsibility for a deed, not just for an idea); and then we will carry this secret to our graves."[7]

The question of remembrance or forgetting was, of course, becoming more and more virulent while the "final solution" was progressing. Kurt Gerstein (who, as an expert on hygiene in the *Waffen-SS,* witnessed gassings at Bełżec and Treblinka and was complicit in providing Zyklon B for the mass murders) reports that in August 1942 the following exchange is said to have taken place in Lublin among Hitler, Himmler, and his friend and confidant Odilo Globocnik, who was the leader of the SS and the police in Lublin and the head of *Aktion Reinhard*. Also included in the conversation was Dr. Herbert Linden of the interior ministry, who was involved in conducting the euthanasia program:

> [T]he *Ministerialrat* Dr. Herbert Linden then asked "Mr. Globocnik, do you consider it right and fair to bury the corpses instead of burning them? A generation could follow us that does not understand this!" Globocnik replies, "Sirs, if we are ever succeeded by a generation that is so weak and lily-livered as to not understand our great task, then, admittedly, National Socialism has existed entirely in vain. On the contrary, I am of the opinion that we should install bronze plates that document that we had the courage to carry out this big and necessary project." The *Führer* answers, "Right, Globocnik, I indeed share your view."[8]

Even if this was only a fleeting idea, a boast, an invention of Globocnik's (Globocnik is said to be the one to have told the exchange to Gerstein only a few days later), or an imprecise memory or invention of Gerstein's (Hitler never visited a concentration or extermination camp like Majdanek), the ambivalence of the perpetrators' situation becomes clear. For Himmler, the architect and organizer of the "final solution," who vacillates between the self-glorification of the perpetrators and secrecy, the need for secretiveness wins out, which only confirms and underlines the elite character of the SS. In contrast, Globocnik demands a calculated form of remembrance of an act that the perpetrators interpret as heroic. The commemoration is only possible in a delayed and hidden manner because the criminal character of the actions seems to be obvious even to the perpetrators. An open and direct representation, however, is only delayed and not entirely avoided out of concern for secrecy.

In the statements by Himmler and Globocnik, the victims do not play any visible role at first, but their ongoing representation is also necessary and virtually decisive for the perpetrators in order to re-shape the crime as a historical necessity.[9] The murder of millions of people not only leaves traces but a blank position that is difficult to ignore. A forgetting by decree after such a crime has to be considered impossible. It can, of course, remain unexplained, but no art of forgetting can guarantee that the act of forgetting will be successful. This is true for the deed itself as well as for the victims. The attempt to seize control of memory and representation thus appears both more effective and more perfidious at the same time.

Many scholars direct their attention to the last phase of the war—to the perpetrators, who already realized that they would lose the war. The approaching armies of the Allies were understandably not supposed to find any evidence of the mass crimes. Accordingly, the works on the Holocaust and memory have dealt above all with—as has the research on genocide—the traumatic consequences of the mass murders and the process of coming to terms with them, the postwar cultures, and politics of memory. The cultures and politics of memory in the Third Reich, the nature and function of memory in the very context of persecution and genocide, have—beyond the generalized hypothesis of an orchestrated memorycide—received hardly any attention.[10]

In fact, the perpetrators themselves were the first to produce calculated representations of their own crimes, not exclusively for reasons of camouflage but to save the perpetrators from an immediate confrontation with their own crimes: with complex and highly ambivalent heroic narratives like those found in Heinrich Himmler's speeches and a neutralizing language concealing reality but enabling the crimes in the first place; with photographic and filmed documentation of daily antisemitism and anti-Jewish persecution, of deportations and mass-shootings, of the crushing of the Warsaw Ghetto uprising as well as the selection and extermination process in Auschwitz-Birkenau after the arrival of a transport. In particular the framing and setting of the actual extermination process from mass shootings in the occupied Soviet Union and executions in mobile gas vans to the installation of gas chambers at specific killing centers in the East is full of considerations about visibility and non-visibility.

At the same time, parallel to the genocide of the European Jews and the construction and representation of the crime as a necessary and heroic deed, the perpetrators again preserved the history and culture of their victims 1) in photographs and films, shot for example in the Warsaw Ghetto, and partly used in propaganda pictures like Fritz Hippler's *Der ewige Jude* (The Eternal Jew, 1940) to prepare the public in Germany and in the occupied countries for a radical "solution of the Jewish question." Originally the filming was fueled by the need to document, just in time, what the filmmakers themselves were about to destroy; 2) in museums like the *Jüdisches Zentralmuseum* (Jewish Central Museum) in the synagogues of Prague's old Jewish quarter, operated by Jewish specialists but supervised by the Security Service (SD) of the SS, more specifically the *Zentralstelle für jüdische Auswanderung* (Central Office for Jewish Emigration, later the *Zentralamt zur Regelung der Judenfrage in Böhmen und Mähren* (Central Office for the Regulation of the Jewish Question in Bohemia and Moravia)),the Prague outpost of Eichmann's "Jewish Affairs" section in the Reich Security Main Office in Berlin. The museum absorbed systematically the ritual objects of the communities in the Protectorate when their inhabitants were deported; and 3) scholarly research on Jewish history and culture, the so-called *Erforschung der Judenfrage* (research on the Jewish question) or in shorthand *Judenforschung* (research on Jews), conducted at specifically established research institutions and universities. The non-Jewish academics pursuing this kind of anti-Jewish Jewish Studies confiscated the entire field—material resources and even the body of knowledge and expertise from Jewish scholars and institutions all over Europe: history became the leading discipline in the field of Nazi *Judenforschung* because, with the "final solution" on the agenda, a historicization of the "Jewish question" seemed both possible and necessary. Studies of the history of antisemitism could serve Nazi anti-Jewish policies by retroactively constructing a tradition and therewith a legitimization. The anti-Jewish scholars even conducted research on the currently ongoing anti-Jewish politics in the Third Reich, thereby already inscribing them into history.[11]

All these projects oscillate between looting, humiliation, and destruction on the one hand, and preservation on the other. Even Himmler, who wanted to preserve the process of extermination at best as an esoteric secret knowledge of the SS, supported the anatomist August Hirt at the *Reichsuniversität* Strassburg in establishing a collection of Jewish skulls for scientific examination. Himmler thus contributed to the conservation of the putative enemy beyond its physical destruction—the extreme case of a trophy collection and the conservation efforts of the Third Reich, which at least indirectly would have pointed to the mass murder and therefore would have contradicted the effort to conceal it.

This, however, easily evokes a concept of a calculated, coordinated, and centrally planned Nazi politics of memory. This assumption is just as impossible to prove as that of a planned memorycide and as misleading as the myth of a monolithic "Hitler state." It underestimates the initiative of different agencies and actors within the Third Reich, the competition within the system, the role of pragmatic and situational considerations and specific local conditions, and finally the momentum within the entire process of expulsion, deportation, looting, and mass murder. There was never a consistent and uniform or even an articulated Nazi politics of memory, and never was an attempt made to institutionalize or coordinate it. It remains highly ambivalent, oscillating between visibility and non-visibility, between telling and silencing. Representations of the crime and representations of the victims cannot in every case be distinguished from each other. Moreover, if one wants to reconstruct a Nazi politics of memory it is only possible to arrive at fragments and traces that will partly contradict each other to a certain degree—because of the incompleteness of the events.

But while the Jews were denounced as superfluous and useless, killed at the execution sites and murdered in the camps, they had to be preserved as "the Others." Even though the victims were removed from the present reality—that is, murdered—they had to remain present and visible within the bipolar Nazi ideology. The concept "*judenfrei*" (free of Jews), the Nazi term to designate the completion of the "final solution" in a certain area, makes that clear; it is the absence that is described and thereby kept present; the erasure/murder remains visible. A German Reich and a Europe free of Jews under National Socialist rule would have meant a constant present absence of the Jews.

Only the expropriation of the memory of the victims would have represented the climax of their humiliation and the completion of their annihilation. The attempt to seize hold of memory, to determine it, has to appear more perfidious and more effective than the pointless attempt of a deliberate forgetting. The complementary phenomenon to physical annihilation does not have to be the act of forgetting but rather the act of remembering, of preserving and constructing very specific narratives while silencing others. The "final solution" would not have been completed until even the memory and representation of the victims had been hegemonically defined by the perpetrators. To be sure: in contrast to today, it would have been a dead and affirmative memory without any living and dissenting counterpart, without any challenge, competition, or provocation, and—most importantly—without an authentic voice of the victims and without their perspective on the crimes. The Jews were supposed to be only "dead" history written by their murderers.

Referring to projects like the Prague museum, some scholars misleadingly talked about a "final solution of remembrance." We, on the other hand, have to speak of the attempt to bring about an "Aryanization" of memory, a further conservation and instrumentalization for the purposes of the National Socialist ideology. From the start, "Aryanization" meant the expropriation and appropriation of Jewish property, its transfer into non-Jewish hands, and the expulsion of Jews from business and public life. This double strategy was consequently pursued until the end. Not only did the perpetrators appropriate the material assets of their victims but they tried to exploit the memory of the victims to their own advantage.

The Nazi politics of representation and memory cannot be seen as a marginal area, for it leads directly into the center of expulsion, deportation, looting, and mass murder—the dynamic of the Holocaust as well as the intentions and self-images of the perpetrators. The Nazis attempted to influence and control contemporary and later images of their crimes and their victims. The perpetrators tried to establish their own structure of memory and representation which would have determined our contemporary attitude toward the crimes—their future—and that in fact extends into our present-day reality and affects it although they could not meet their objective—win the war and complete the annihilation of the Jewish people. Within this framework memory and representation must be understood both as strategies for managing the past and as plans for designing the future.

The Ambivalence of Postwar Memories

In a victorious Germany, contrary to the common assumption of a memorycide, a variety of "comic emplotments" about the disappearance of the Jews might have circulated,[12] Jewish museums and research about the victims (still understood as enemies) might have existed, and memorials might have remembered the German crimes (perceived as heroic deeds)—exactly as happened after the defeat, although of course with opposite signs. The ambivalences of postwar memories and remembrance of the Holocaust seem only to reflect the ambivalent actions of the perpetrators, documenting their crimes and obliterating their traces; narrating the mass murders as morally justified and heroic deeds and knowing about their criminal character; telling and at the same time silencing and denying.

With the name of the location of the biggest complex of concentration, forced labor, and extermination camps within the Nazi empire, "Auschwitz," the supposedly industrial method of killing became the emblem of the Nazi genocide.[13] The gas chamber was highlighted as the specific and quintessential killing technique of the Holocaust. (That is also reflected in the Holocaust deniers' focus on the gas chamber.) What happened inside is not only not visible but is considered to be unrepresentable and incomprehensible. The gas chamber is literally a "black box," a hermetically closed room that renders a view of the scene inside impossible.[14] (Therefore, a glance through the spyhole in the door and a look inside became an obsession in the popular imagination at the same time, played out, for example, in the TV miniseries "Holocaust" as well as in Steven Spielberg's "Schindler's List" and other motion pictures.) Furthermore, the invisibility of the killing in the gas chamber provided an argument for the general unrepresentable character of the mass murder although "only" 60 percent of the six million murdered Jews were killed in the gas chambers of the different killing centers.[15] The actual and different practices of killing vanished behind the enormous number of victims—and the walls of the gas chambers. This *Bilderverbot* (image ban) was also widely observed in historical scholarship, especially in post-Nazi societies: Visual representations and descriptions of the crimes were equally absent. The omission could be comprehensibly justified by reference to the self-protection of the researching scholar and an understandable inability to bear the details; it could also be argued that the silence and invisibility derived from compassion for the victims and a conscious effort to avoid obscene voyeurism and lurid depictions—in any case it has prevented a confrontation with the actual violence and has concealed the concrete practice of the crimes.

In all media and formats the center of the crime is blocked out. Instead of the crime itself, usually its results were shown: photos of piles of corpses that the Allied forces found when they liberated the camps. Those pictures, presented to the Germans right after the war as proof of the crimes and their own complicity and often linked to Christian iconographic traditions, could easily be integrated into the postwar cultural-pictorial memory as "icons of destruction." However, they did not show an image of the crime but eliminated from view the everyday practice of killing and getting killed.[16] With the image of the suffering victims they communicated the fact that a crime had happened but did not make explicit its specific character. The impression was rather that the victims mainly starved to death.

Where something is described and visible, the impression of representation and visibility needs to be contradicted with ritualized phrases, calling the Holocaust "unrepresentable" and "incomprehensible," as if what was visible and describable would not be adequate. The heated discussions around the so-called *Wehrmacht* exhibition in Germany and Austria (1995) and (partly) Daniel J. Goldhagen's *Hitler's Willing Executioners* (1996) can only be understood against the background of that particular tradition. The scandal in both cases was the pitiless transgression of a tacitly established and generally accepted threshold—with the presentation of images of the war of extermination in the East in the one case, and detailed descriptions of massacres in the other.

The direct and immediate killings in the mass shootings have been eclipsed and forgotten for a long time. Eastern Europe was the theater for those events—no less systematically than the operations of the killing centers. So the conditions of the Cold War might have had their part in downplaying them. In Germany and Austria the exhibition *Vernichtungskrieg: Verbrechen der Wehrmacht 1941-1944* (War of Extermination: Crimes of the German Army), organized by the privately funded Hamburg Institute for Social Research, confronted the audience and in the end both of the post-Nazi societies with the unfiltered brutal reality of the war in the East, with crimes against the civilian population, humiliations, executions, pogroms, and mass shootings.[17] The public debate on the exhibition was a dispute over the character of the war in the East, the complicity of German and Austrian society with the mass crimes of the Nazi regime, and the participation of the German Army and with it of large parts of the German and Austrian population in the politics of extermination. In particular, the many photographs on display allowed a hitherto commonly avoided visibility of the crimes and the perpetrators, a view of average husbands, sons, fathers, and grandfathers at their everyday work of archaic killing. The photographs shot by the soldiers themselves, who obviously were predominantly in accord with the pictured procedures, were turned into instruments of accusation and enlightenment, contrary to their original intention.

This does not mean that the crimes and their outcome were not present in the postwar societies of the perpetrators. Even one of the first German motion pictures after the war, Wolfgang Staudte's *Die Mörder sind unter uns* (*The Murderers Are among Us,* 1946) broached the issue of the coexistence of a successful suppression of the past as a precondition for reconstruction and re-advancement on the one hand, and a mental blockade as a result of experiences with violence during the war on the other hand. How is it possible to talk about suppression, forgetting, and silence in the plain sense for the postwar societies when in 1960 in Nuremberg a former member of a reserve police battalion apologizes to the chief of police and the mayor for a parking violation by referring to an intestinal sickness contracted while participating in mass shootings in Russia—although he maintained that he never shot anyone himself.[18] Nevertheless, the perpetrators were very successful in facilitating a mainly non-traumatic everyday life for the German and Austrian post-Holocaust societies, without depressive and mentally dysfunctional demobilized servicemen, without sites of crimes and mass graves in their own countries, apart from the concentration camps that tell a different story than the specific killing sites and centers—all this just by situating the killing operations in the East, at the border or outside of the *Reich,* and with a specific politics of memory and representation and a deliberate construction of the crimes.

"Auschwitz" as the dominating symbol with the "black box" of the gas chamber at its center produces a misleading image of the Holocaust as an anonymous and almost hygienic process. In fact, the development of the Nazi politics of extermination is also a history of designing killing techniques to spare the mass murderer: from the shootings to the mobile gas vans to stationary gas chambers. The intention was to relieve and unburden the immediate perpetrators. Especially Himmler was worried about the people who executed the crimes and the possible consequences of a brutalization of the participants in mass shootings in the eyes of the entire German society. The gas chamber provided not only an efficient way of killing; by means of the hermetically closed room and the intermediary technique, the perpetrators could dissociate themselves from their crimes. The unavoidable work of disposing of the corpses was in any case the responsibility of Jewish prisoners in the so-called *Sonderkommandos,* and the wage they received for carrying out their forced duties was ultimately their own execution.

Even as a postwar symbol of the Holocaust the gas chambers made possible a partial repression of the mass murder and could function as an alibi for ordinary Germans and Austrians. After all, the crime took place a long way away and was not accessible to public view; not only was it impossible to see and know, but no one killed directly—it was therefore a crime without a criminal, a murder without a perpetrator. The gas chamber fulfilled its function even in postwar memory: it represented a pictureless and unimaginable crime without any persons immediately involved, and it operated more as a blank position and blind spot ("black box") than an actual image of what had happened. The postwar images and concepts of the deed and the actors still conform in a very peculiar way to the intentions of the Nazi perpetrators.

The entanglement of visibility and invisibility, of showing and disguising, of telling and silencing, is manifested in Stanisław Mucha's iconic photograph of the Auschwitz-Birkenau gatehouse (1945). Contrary to the common assumption, the picture shows the gatehouse from inside the camp, not from the outside; the tracks do not come together from all parts of Europe as is usually assumed but are split at the inside ramp that was only built for the transports from Hungary in spring 1944 to guarantee a more efficient extermination process. The photograph epitomizes paradigmatically the discourse of invisibility. Neither the crime nor perpetrators and victims are visible. The location of the Holocaust is a place seemingly not of this world—far away and totally different. Moreover, the strict central perspective pictures the assumption of a monolithic Nazi system in which anonymous structures are held to account but individuals are exculpated. The genocide remains invisible and unreal.[19] The gatehouse and with it "Auschwitz" function as a coulisse with nothing behind it. Therefore it makes no difference from which side it is seen. (Interestingly enough, the same "ambiguity" and blankness were used in the making of Steven Spielberg's motion picture *Schindler's List*. Since he was not allowed to shoot inside Birkenau but wanted to use the authentic site as background scenery, he filmed the disembarkation of a transport outside, in front of the gatehouse, simulating what it would be like inside.)

After the war, most of the self-manifestations of the Nazi perpetrators were used without hesitation and without reflecting the problems and ambivalences intrinsically tied to it. In the different cultures of remembrance they were even used to commemorate the victims. The best-known example might be the so-called "Auschwitz Album": Some of the photographs it contains are virtually omnipresent in our pictorial-cultural memory. But they were shot by two SS men of the camp's "Identification Service," presumably to document the efficiency of the extermination process during the time of maximum activity at Birkenau when the Hungarian transports were arriving. But the implications of this original intention for its totally reversed postwar usage have been rarely reflected.[20] Another case in point is the so-called "Stroop Album" documenting the brutal suppression of the Warsaw Ghetto uprising in April/May 1943. The commander of the German forces that liquidated the Ghetto prepared it as an official report and souvenir for Heinrich Himmler and his immediate superior, Friedrich Krüger, the Senior SS and Police Leader in the General-Government that the Germans created to administer occupied Poland. It is known especially for the widely used photograph of a young boy held at gunpoint.[21] Even the photographs used in the German Army's crimes exhibition inescapably perpetuate the perspective of the perpetrators and also the humiliation of the victims. In general, in German-speaking research the documents and information of the (former) perpetrators were used as the main base for historical reconstruction, especially since these individuals were quite talkative after the lost war—expecting they could at least influence the perception and representation of their crimes. In the Historical Division of the US Army, 328 German Army officers under the direction of former Colonel General Franz Halder could create the myth of the "clean" *Wehrmacht* that would dominate postwar memory for decades; they may have been prisoners of war, but precisely for this reason they had a favorable working environment with privileged access to the files.[22] In contrast to the majority of the surviving victims, they all had the advantage of speaking the same language as the German and Austrian population.

From a specific media theoretical vantage point, the French art historian and philosopher Georges Didi-Huberman recently reminded us how essential it is to provide space and attentiveness for documents left behind by the victims, to disseminate them, and to let them speak. He points concretely to photographs clandestinely taken at the risk of their lives by members of the Jewish *Sonderkommando* in Auschwitz-Birkenau—as an act of resistance, to document the crimes they suffered. A total of three pictures (the camera slipped on a fourth one and shows only the tree tops) show women waiting outside the gas chambers and the burning of corpses after the gassing (which had to be carried out outside the crematoria because they were temporarily overloaded during the murder of the Hungarian Jews in summer 1944).[23] They are the only remaining photographs from the killing process in Auschwitz-Birkenau that were not shot and commissioned by the perpetrators. However, Didi-Huberman's thesis produced a major dispute when it appeared. The French culture of remembrance, under the influence of Claude Lanzmann and his cinematic masterpiece (1985), is still focused on the gas chambers as quasi-sacred spaces and as a pictureless "Shoah." Under these conditions, Didi-Huberman's plea for a detailed look at the testimony of the victims was denounced as voyeuristic, revisionist, and even antisemitic although it was above all the victims who had an interest in making the crimes visible, representable, and also comprehensible as an indictment of their torturers and murderers and to preserve the memory of their own fate.

The tradition of the victims is still often unnoticed. Survivors of the gas chamber who could bear witness, of course, do not exist. In this respect it remains effectively a "black box"; nobody can attest to it from the inside. Nonetheless it is not correct that the victims left no sources that document the crimes. Even in plain view of the gas chambers and in the crematoria of Auschwitz-Birkenau, members of the Jewish *Sonderkommando* kept records and successfully tried to pass them on although they, too, were killed in the end. They not only described the deportations, the arrival of the transports and the gassings, including their own employment; they also recorded the history of the places the victims came from.[24] In the underground, in the ghettos, and at many other places during the Holocaust, the victims tried to document their culture and their fate. The best-known and most impressive example might be the "Oneg Shabbat" archives from the Warsaw Ghetto, created by the Polish historian Emmanuel Ringelblum and his numerous co-workers.[25] Also from the war of extermination in the East, from the humiliations, pogroms, and mass shootings, accounts of victims and survivors exist apart from the perpetrators' documents.[26] Those sources are always a corrective to abstract concepts and appeasing phrases. They enshrine the shock of the actual experience at the time; they evoke perturbation and enforce a "dwelling on horrors" (Hannah Arendt) that are both indispensable for any insight into the events of the Holocaust but that have no place in our routines of remembrance and "concern" (*Betroffenheit*).[27]

Phrases and concepts of unrepresentability und incomprehensibility are easily at hand. But in fact, there is no fundamental difference between the problems involved in depicting and representing the Nazi genocide or everyday life in the Middle Ages, the horrors of the Thirty Year's War or of World War I, neither in historiography nor in literature.[28] After all, the Holocaust was by no means a natural disaster as ritualized phrases and concepts in this context often suggest, but was deliberately put into practice by Germans, Austrians, and their collaborators and therefore is explicable as all human undertakings are explicable—as hard and demanding as this might be (above all to accept the outcome). The essential difference lies exclusively in the meaning and relevance of the event for our societies. This is why historiographical or also artistic representations are often considered to be inadequate and deficient. The narrativity of historiography and the fictionality of literature seem to be precarious while an attempt at historiogaphic sobriety and mere factography appears to be superficial.[29] To say that the Holocaust is unrepresentable and incomprehensible might, in fact, be an articulation of the disappointment that no specific language and no different kind of representation for the Holocaust exists.

Confronting Continuities

The ritually and routinely claimed unrepresentability and incomprehensibility stand vis-à-vis a veritable flood of images, descriptions, and interpretations—without the possibility of mutual reconciliation. A final representation and description of the Nazi crimes that might be universally satisfactory and redemptive in every respect might never exist and may be impossible. But the accent on unrepresentability and incomprehensibility can easily acquire a relieving and exculpating momentum.[30] Neither the overemphasis on representational and interpretational problems, nor the simplification of highly complex developments and contexts can do justice to the historical events and their relevance for us in the present day and age. The obsessive focusing on the problems of representation and comprehension simply blocks any understanding and any account of the history. An unease (Saul Friedlander) will remain. But without making an effort at understanding prejudice, persecution, expulsion, deportation, and systematic mass murder and their aftermath, without making an effort at narrating the crimes of the perpetrators and the experiences of the victims, the perspective and the intentions of the Nazis gain a new life.

German crimes during World War II have strongly called into question the possibility of remembrance, representation, and reconstruction. Remembrance is not difficult because the crimes are unrepresentable or because the Nazis attempted to eradicate the spirit that makes remembrance possible but also because of the perpetrators' politics of memory and representation. However, they do not influence things to a degree that would prevent evading it. This is a decisive difference from the politics of extermination and its inescapable consequences. But it usually goes unnoticed how the Nazi politics of memory and representation sustainably influence and work themselves into our concepts and interpretations.

Our postwar imagery of the Holocaust is largely dominated by the perpetrators. Despite the current interest in survivor testimonies in the "era of the witness" (Annette Wieviorka) it should not be forgotten that most of the victims' voices and with them their perspective and experiences were silenced by the genocide.[31] The radical impossibility of testimony and the continuing forgetting of the witnesses and their perspective are integral parts of the Holocaust and unfortunately also its aftermath.[32]

The question of the degree to which the postwar cultures and politics of memory and representation unconsciously continue the perspective and tradition of the perpetrators refers to a complex and highly delicate context, one that transcends the so-called "zero hour" of 1945 that is usually seen as the beginning of any memory and representation. Especially in Holocaust remembrance, memory is usually associated with justice and restitution; remembrance alone is already claimed as a satisfactory answer to the Holocaust. Continuities within the ranks of officials and personnel are largely known by now, even if they may not be considered with all their consequences. But the continuities on other levels have aroused little or no attention.[33] Especially for memory and representation, for the imagery and concepts of history no "zero hour" and no clear breaks exist. The allegedly essential connection between annihilation and forgetting on the one hand and memory/remembrance and justice/compensation on the other hand—one of the fundamental principles of our memorial culture—is, in fact, unmasked as a (maybe convenient) misapprehension. History is not necessarily written by the victors on the battlefields—or it might not always be so clear who prevailed beyond the battlefields of history.

Unfortunately, the discourses about the events of the Holocaust on the one hand, and about their aftermath and representations on the other, are increasingly drifting apart so that more and more, two completely separate areas of scholarship have evolved with hardly any real communication between them. But in fact, there can be no discussion of postwar representation of the Holocaust without a look at the actual crimes, their conceptualization, and the construction of a certain image of the victims by the perpetrators. Neither does it make sense to examine the crimes and end with the year 1945, as was often the case in earlier scholarship and sometimes still is, without considering the aftermath, namely, questions of representation and interpretation. One cannot be understood without the other. This is not an argument for an epistemologically naïve realism suggesting that there can be just one inevitable or adequate image of a historical event in memory. But this, on the other hand, does not mean that memory and representation are not influenced and affected by certain historical conditions. Representation was part of the crime—and a crime in itself. Therefore, the crime remains part of the representation. Our landscape of memory has a predecessor in the perpetrators' politics of memory and representation and thus has to grapple with it, regardless of whether that happens transparently and consciously. The postwar history of coming to terms with the mass crimes of Nazism is thus not merely "the second history" of Nazism; rather it is its own second history—the second history of the representation of the crimes.[34]

This reminds us of the heterogeneity and fragmentation of what we simply call "the Holocaust" or "Shoah" as if it were a monolithic and elementary event. It is, of course, bound together by the antisemitic intention and the will to murder all Jews in a very compact time-frame. But it happened in different settings, with different procedures employed by the Germans, different reactions on the part of the local populations, different kinds and degrees of complicity, collaboration, and resistance, dealing with very different historical starting positions, different kinds of Jewish populations with different backgrounds and different degrees of assimilation and integration—and therefore different results for the postwar situation, as well as for memory and remembrance.

Thus it seems essential to bring both perspectives together: one focusing on the historical events and the other on the aftermath, memory, representation, and interpretation. Only in this way can what has often been lamented as an "intellectual kitschification" of the memory discourse be prevented.[35] If—aside from an ethics of memory—an ethics of representation exists, it might include the duty not to follow unconsciously the intentions of the perpetrators in the representation of their crimes. Since representation is always governed by a multilayered interplay of visibility and non-visibility, we need to be aware of what we—sometimes necessarily, sometimes not—blot out and forget when we reconstruct history, remember, and represent.[36] This should also be part of an "integrated history" that not only includes the different perspectives on the historical events but also "history and memory" reflected in the presence of commentary.[37] It is important not because the Nazis planned a memorycide, a total annihilation of memory beyond the physical murder of masses of human beings, but precisely because they actually intended a complex construction and preservation of memory with totally controlled images of their crimes and victims.

Notes

1. For the antisemitic legacy of the term "Holocaust," dating back to the Middle Ages, see Giorgio Agamben, *Was von Auschwitz bleibt. Das Archiv und der Zeuge* (Frankfurt/M, 2003), 27. Beside that, the original denotation from ancient times as a sacrifice—an animal wholly burnt—has obviously inappropriate aspects. On the other hand, especially in post-Nazi societies the competing term "Shoah" with its Hebrew origin (meaning "calamity," or "catastrophe," and also "destruction") can be an easy but inappropriate way of identification with the victims.

2. See, for example, Joseph Kermish, ed., *To Live with Honor and to Die with Honor: Selected Documents from the Warsaw Ghetto Underground Archives "O.S." (Oneg Shabbath)* (Jerusalem, 1986), 2–24, 703–08.

3. Cf. Jean-François Lyotard, *Heidegger und „die Juden"* (Vienna, 1988), 35–36; James I. Freed, "Das United States Holocaust Memorial Museum," in *Mahnmale des Holocaust: Motive, Rituale und Stätten des Gedenkens,* ed. James E. Young (Munich, 1994), 63–77, here 69; J. E. Young, *Beschreiben des Holocaust* (Frankfurt/M, 1997), 293–94; Detlef Hoffmann, "Das Gedächtnis der Dinge," in *Das Gedächtnis der Dinge. KZ-Relikte und Denkmäler 1945–1995,* ed. Detlef Hoffmann (Frankfurt/M, 1998), 12.

4. Cf. Christoph Münz, *Geschichtstheologie und jüdisches Gedächtnis nach Auschwitz: Über den Versuch, den Schrecken der Geschichte zu bannen* (Frankfurt/M, 1994), 21 (*Gedächtnozid*); Harald Weinrich, *Lethe. Kunst und Kritik des Vergessens,* 3rd ed. (Munich, 2000), 232 (*Gedächtnismord, Memorizid*); Aleida Assmann, *Erinnerungsräume. Formen und Wandlungen des kulturellen Gedächtnisses* (Munich, 1999), 336 (*Mnemozid*).

5. Cf. Hans-Stephan Brather, "Aktenvernichtung durch deutsche Dienststellen beim Zusammenbruch des Faschismus," *Archivmitteilungen* 8, no. 4 (1958): 115–17; Shmuel Spector, "Aktion 1005—Effacing the Murder of Millions," *Holocaust and Genocide Studies* 5, no. 2 (1990): 157–73; Jens Hoffmann, *„Das kann man nicht erzählen"—„Aktion 1005": Wie die Nazis die Spuren ihrer Massenmorde in Osteuropa beseitigten* (Hamburg, 2008).

6. Heinrich Himmler, "Rede vor SS-Gruppenführern in Posen, 4.10.1943," in *IMT,* PS-1919, 64–6. See also Bundesarchiv Berlin, NS 19/4010. Beside this official, written version that was used at the Nuremberg Major War Criminals Trial and that is usually cited exists an audio recording of the whole speech. In that document preserved in the German Broadcast Archives in Frankfurt am Main (76 U 3374-76/1), Himmler says only: "… and this is a glorious chapter that has never been mentioned and that never will be." Himmler usually used notes for his speeches; transliterations were made after the audio recordings and thereafter revised by him. See Richard Breitman, *Himmler Himmler. Der Architekt der „Endlösung"* (Zurich, 2000), 343, 424 n. 50.

7. Bradley F. Smith and Agnes F. Peterson, eds., *Heinrich Himmler. Geheimreden 1933 bis 1945 und andere Ansprachen* (Frankfurt/M, 1974), 170–72.

8. Hans Rothfels, "Augenzeugenbericht zu den Massenvergasungen. Dokumentation," *Vierteljahreshefte für Zeitgeschichte* 1 (1953): 189. On Gerstein see Saul Friedländer, *Kurt Gerstein: The Ambiguity of Good* (New York, 1969); Pierre Joffroy, *Der Spion Gottes. Die Passion des Kurt Gerstein* (Stuttgart, 1972).

9. During the war, Franz Neumann assumed in his work about the structure and the practice of National Socialism that the value of antisemitism for domestic politics would never allow a "complete annihilation of the Jews": "The enemy cannot and may not disappear; he constantly has to be available as the scapegoat for all the ills that the socio-political system produces." F. Neumann, *Behemoth. Struktur und Praxis des Nationalsozialismus* (Frankfurt/M, 1984), 163. About the same time, Emmanuel Ringelblum wrote down the same idea in the Warsaw Ghetto: "If all the Jews were cleared out of Warsaw and out of the Government General as a whole, They would lose the Jewish argument. It would be hard for Them then to attribute all their difficulties and failures to the Jews. The Jews have to remain, in keeping with the proverb: 'God grant that all your teeth fall out, except one to give you a toothache!'" E. Ringelblum, *Notes from the Warsaw Ghetto,* ed. Jacob Sloan (New York, 1958), 325. Later scholars like Erich Goldhagen came to a similar conclusion: "By murdering the Jews the National Socialists destroyed their instrument for power. Instead of preserving the scapegoat they slaughtered it." E. Goldhagen, "Weltanschauung und Endlösung. Zum Antisemitismus der nationalsozialistischen Führungsschicht," *Vierteljahreshefte für Zeitgeschichte* 24 (1976): 393.

10. Cf. Alon Confino, "Fantasies abouth the Jews. Cultural Reflections on the Holocaust," *History and Memory* 17, nos. 1–2 (2005): 315; Confino, "A World without Jews: Interpreting the Holocaust," *German History* 27, no. 4 (2009): 545-46, 552. See also Kai Struve, „Ritual und Gewalt—Die Pogrome des Sommers 1941," in *Synchrone Welten. Zeiträume jüdischer Geschichte,* ed. Dan Diner (Göttingen, 2005), 225–50 (which tries to uncover and analyze the different "time levels" and memories involved in the emergence of the pogroms in occupied Poland).

11. For the reconstruction of a Nazi politics of memory, see Dirk Rupnow, "Racializing Historiography: Anti-Jewish Scholarship in the Third Reich," *Patterns of Prejudice* 42, no. 1 (2008): 27–59; Rupnow, *Vernichten und Erinnern. Spuren nationalsozialistischer Gedächtnispolitik* (Göttingen, 2005); Rupnow, *Aporien des Gedenkens. Reflexionen über "Holocaust" und Erinnerung* (Freiburg i.Br, 2006); Rupnow, "'Ihr müßt sein, auch wenn Ihr nicht mehr seid': The Jewish Central Museum in Prague and Historical Memory in the Third Reich," *Holocaust and Genocide Studies* 16, no. 1 (2002): 23–53; Rupnow, *Täter-Gedächtnis-Opfer. Das „Jüdische Zentralmuseum" in Prag 1942–1945* (Vienna, 2000).

12. Cf. Saul Friedländer, "Introduction," in *Probing the Limits of Representation: Nazism and the "Final Solution,"* ed. Saul Friedländer (Cambridge, MA, 1992), 10; see also Hayden White, "Historical Emplotment and the Problem of Truth," in Friedländer, *Probing the Limits,* 37–53.

13. Cf. Norbert Frei, "Auschwitz und Holocaust. Begriff und Historiographie," in *Holocaust: Die Grenzen des Verstehens. Eine Debatte über die Besetzung der Geschichte,* ed. Hanno Loewy (Reinbek b. Hamburg, 1992), 101–09.

14. For the "black box" concept in the context of the Holocaust, see Dan Diner, "Zwischen Aporie und Apologie. Über Grenzen der Historisierbarkeit des Nationalsozialismus," in *Ist der Nationalsozialismus Geschichte? Zu Historisierung und Historikerstreit*, ed. Dan Diner (Frankfurt/M, 1987), 62–73; Gertrud Koch, "Der Engel des Vergessens und die Black Box der Faktizität. Zur Gedächtniskonstruktion in Claude Lanzmanns Film *Shoah*," in *Die Einstellung ist die Einstellung. Visuelle Konstruktionen des Judentums*, ed. Gertrud Koch (Frankfurt/M, 1992), 155–69. For the "black box" concept in the theory of photography, see Vilém Flusser, *Für eine Philosophie der Fotografie*, 6th ed. (Göttingen, 1992), 65. See also the description of the camera as a "magic box" in Susan Sontag, *Über Fotografie* (Frankfurt/M, 1999), 55. Opposed to the description as "black box" or "camera obscura" is Roland Barthes, *Die helle Kammer: Bemerkungen zur Photographie* (Frankfurt/M, 1989), 117.

15. Cf. Ulrich Herbert, "Vernichtungspolitik. Neue Antworten und Fragen zur Geschichte des 'Holocaust,'" in *Nationalsozialistische Vernichtungspolitik 1939–1945: Neue Forschungen und Kontroversen*, ed. Ulrich Herbert (Frankfurt/M, 1998), 57.

16. Cf. Cornelia Brink, *Ikonen der Vernichtung. Öffentlicher Gebrauch von Fotografien aus nationalsozialistischen Konzentrationslagern nach 1945* (Berlin, 1998), 240.

17. See Hannes Heer, Walter Manoschek, Alexander Pollak, and Ruth Wodak, eds., *The Discursive Construction of History. Remembering the Wehrmacht's War of Annihilation* (Basingstoke, 2008).

18. Cf. Jim G. Tobias, *„Ihr Gewissen war rein; sie haben es nie benutzt": Die Verbrechen der Polizeikompanie Nürnberg* (Nuremberg, 2005), 5. See also Svenja Goltermann, *Die Gesellschaft der Überlebenden: Deutsche Kriegsheimkehrer und ihre Gewalterfahrungen im Zweiten Weltkrieg*, 2nd ed. (Stuttgart, 2009).

19. See Christoph Hamann, *Visual History und Geschichtsdidaktik: Bildkompetenz in der historisch-politischen Bildung* (Herbolzheim, 2007), 92–106.

20. See *The Auschwitz Album: The Story of a Transport*, ed. Israel Gutman and Bella Gutterman (Jerusalem, 2002).

21. See *„Es gibt keinen jüdischen Wohnbezirk in Warschau mehr!": Stroop-Bericht (IMT, Exhibit USA 275, 1061-PS)* (Darmstadt, 1960).

22. Cf. Charles B. Burdick, "Vom Schwert zur Feder. Deutsche Kriegsgefangene im Dienst der Vorbereitung der amerikanischen Kriegsgeschichtsschreibung über den Zweiten Weltkrieg. Die organisatorische Entwicklung der Operational History (German) Section," *Militärgeschichtliche Mitteilungen* 10, no. 2 (1971): 69–80; Bernd Wegner, "Erschriebene Siege. Franz Halder, "die 'Historical Division' und die Rekonstruktion des Zweiten Weltkrieges im Geiste des deutschen Generalstabes," in *Politischer Wandel, organisierte Gewalt und nationale Sicherheit. Beiträge zur neueren Geschichte Deutschlands und Frankreichs*, ed. Ernst Willi Hansen, Gerhard Schreiber, and B. Wegner (Munich, 1995), 287–302.

23. Cf. Georges Didi-Huberman, *Bilder trotz allem* (Munich, 2007). See also Clément Chéroux, ed., *Mémoire des camps. Photographies des camps de concentration et d'extermination nazis (1933–1999)* (Paris, 2001); Dan Stone, "The Sonderkommando Photographs," *Jewish Social Studies* 7, no. 3 (2001): 132–48.

24. See *Inmitten des grauenvollen Verbrechens. Handschriften von Mitgliedern des Sonderkommandos* (Oświęcim, 1996), and also Nathan Cohen, "The Diaries of the Sonderkommando," in *Anatomy of the Auschwitz Death Camp*, ed. Yisrael Gutman and Michael Berenbaum (Bloomington, 1994), 522–34.

25. See Kermish, ed., *To Live with Honor and To Die with Honor!*; E. Ringelblum, *Notes from the Warsaw Ghetto*. See also Samuel D. Kassow, *Who Will Write Our History? Emmanuel Ringelblum, the Warsaw Ghetto, and the Oyneg Shabbes Archive* (Bloomington, 2007).

26. See Wassili Grossmann and Ilja Ehrenburg, *Das Schwarzbuch. Der Genozid an den sowjetischen Juden* (Reinbek b. Hamburg, 1994); Joshua Rubenstein and Ilya Altman, eds., *The Unknown Black Book. The Holocaust in the German-Occupied Soviet Territories* (Bloomington, 2008).

27. Cf. Hannah Arendt, *Elemente und Ursprünge totaler Herrschaft. Antisemitismus, Imperialismus, totale Herrschaft*, 7th ed. (Munich, 2000), 912. See also Harald Welzer, *Verweilen beim Grauen. Essays zum wissenschaftlichen Umgang mit dem Holocaust* (Tübingen, 1997).

28. Cf. Dan Stone, *Constructing the Holocaust: A Study in Historiography* (London, 2003), 30.

29. Cf. Jacques Ranciére, "Are Some Things Unrepresentable?," in *The Future of the Image* (London, 2009), 126–29.

30. Cf. Primo Levi, *Die Untergegangenen und die Geretteten* (Munich, 1990), 7; Saul Friedländer, *Kitsch und Tod. Der Widerschein des Nazismus* (Frankfurt a/M, 1997), 108–09; G. Agamben, *Was von Auschwitz bleibt*, 136–37.

31. Cf. Peter Fritzsche, *Life and Death in the Third Reich* (Cambridge, MA, 2008), 146, 153–54.

32. Cf. Shoshana Felman, "The Return of the Voice: Claude Lanzmann's Shoah," in Shoshana Felman and Dori Laub, *Testimony: Crises of Witnessing in Literature, Psychoanalysis, and History* (New York, 1992), 204–83.

33. See, for example, the recent evaluations of continuities in race thinking and racial distinctions beyond the defeat of the Third Reich and its genocidal European empire in Rita Chin, Heide Fehrenbach, Geoff Eley, and Atina Grossmann, *After the Nazi Racial State: Difference and Democracy in Europe* (Ann Arbor, 2009).

34. Cf. Peter Reichel, *Vergangenheitsbewältigung in Deutschland. Die Auseinandersetzung mit der NS-Diktatur von 1945 bis heute* (Munich, 2001), 199.

35. Cf. Karl-Heinz Bohrer, *Ekstasen der Zeit. Augenblick, Gegenwart, Erinnerung* (Munich, 2003), 11.

36. Cf. J. Rancière, "Are Some Things Unrepresentable?," 113–14.

37. Cf. Saul Friedländer, "Trauma, Memory, and Transference," in *Holocaust Remembrance: The Shapes of Memory*, ed. Geoffrey H. Hartman (Oxford, 1994), 252–63; Saul Friedländer, *Den Holocaust beschreiben. Auf dem Weg zu einer integrierten Geschichte* (Göttingen, 2007).

CHAPTER 4

The History of the Jews in the Ghettos
A Cultural Perspective[1]

AMOS GOLDBERG

In his chapter in this volume, Dan Stone argues that despite the fact that cultural history has proved both a popular and fertile paradigm within the historical discipline, it has not staked much ground for itself in the study of the Holocaust.[2] Following in the footsteps of Alon Confino, Claudia Koonz, Dominick LaCapra, and others,[3] Stone is mostly concerned with the study of the "perpetrators." To understand Nazism, the Holocaust and the "final solution," he says, it is imperative to return to the research of Nazi ideology, which must be treated with the utmost seriousness. But the research directions and the methodology of this renewed research program need to be more anthropologically oriented, drawing on concepts such as ritual, collective, fantasy, scapegoating mechanisms, carnivalesque excess, "thinking with the blood," etc. Such inquiries will be better equipped to explain the world of symbolism, desires, and collective fantasies at the root of Nazi ideology and the genocide perpetrated by the Germans. They will be capable of illuminating several of the most disturbing questions in the study of the final solution—especially in respect to the "why" and not only to the "how" of the event.

Stone is quite right. Ever since the 1970s and 1980s, cultural history has become an important branch of historical research, especially of the late medieval period, the Renaissance, and the early modern period. Although cultural history in itself can boast a rather lengthy and impressive history, dating from the end of the nineteenth century and the first half of the twentieth century—names such as Jakob Burkhardt, Johann Huizinga, Aby Warburg, the Annales school headed by Marc Bloch and Lucien Febvre come to mind—this field has

Notes for this section begin on page 96.

enjoyed an unprecedented efflorescence in the past two or three decades.[4] According to a statistical study carried out by the cultural historian Robert Darnton some fifteen years ago, cultural history has become one of the most central fields—if not the most central subfield—of history in the United States, which has usurped the position of social history.[5] At the same time it appears that this perspective is almost entirely absent from Holocaust historiography.

So much is true in respect to the "perpetrators," but what about the "victims?"[6] It seems as though a great deal has been written about the religious, cultural, literary, communal, and spiritual life of the Jews during the Holocaust. A number of comprehensive studies have even been devoted *exclusively* to the description of these dimensions of life in the ghettos, such as Esther Farbstein's book about religious life during the Holocaust,[7] Shirli Gilbert's book about music in the Holocaust,[8] David Roskies' and Yechiel Szeintuch's (and many others') studies of the literary activity in the ghettos, or even the study by landscape architect Kenneth Helphand about ghetto gardens,[9] as well as many more significant contributions.

Is this cultural history, however? Or indeed, what is cultural history, and how should it be written in the context under discussion? Moshe Rosman has already reminded us in the context of Jewish history that cultural history is not interested in the products of creative forces within a particular group, but in the *meanings* these forces and products convey.[10] Or in other words, cultural history is not concerned with describing cultural and religious institutions or their products, but rather in the mechanism of meaning-making within a certain society, or in what Peter Burke sees as the common basis of all branches of cultural history: "dealing with the symbolic and its interpretation."[11] What, then, can the methodology of cultural history contribute to the study of the history of the Jews in the Holocaust?

A comprehensive discussion of these questions is quite beyond the scope of the present article, but here I nevertheless seek to offer a sort of preamble to the issue. First, I shall survey a number of central approaches to the study of Jews and to the uses of contemporaneous Jewish sources. My intention is to sketch out the gaps and absences left open by these approaches. As an alternative, I shall propose an outline of a research agenda which I generally associate with the broad field of "cultural history."

As a point of departure I shall make reference to Saul Friedländer's recent book, *The Years of Extermination: Nazi Germany and the Jews, 1939–1945*,[12] which met with the kind of enthusiastic reception afforded to few works of nonfiction. A transcontinental consensus of scholarly voices, representing a range of historiographical schools, appeared in scores and perhaps hundreds of book reviews, essays, and articles in the printed press and in scholarly journals that were virtually unanimous in their praise of this book.[13] Nearly all reviewers remarked with passion and enthusiasm on the incorporation of "the Jewish voice"[14] into writing which they named "integrative."

As a matter of fact, Friedländer himself stressed in a number of interviews that his intention had been to integrate the "voice of the victims" into a history that appears to have forgotten them. For example, in an interview for *Die Zeit* on 8 March 2007, when asked in what sense his book was distinguished from earlier works on the Holocaust, such as Raul Hilberg's monumental study, *The Destruction of the European Jews,* Friedländer answered: "I tried to write a comprehensive history of the Holocaust which would not only bring to bear a broad perspective on all of Europe, but in which the voices of the victims (*Stimmen der Opfer*) would be heard more powerfully than they have been hitherto."[15]

In the introduction, Friedländer explains this decision. First, he explains, these voices "are like lightning flashes that illuminate parts of the landscape: they confirm intuitions; they warn us against the ease of vague generalizations. Sometimes they just repeat the known with an unmatched forcefulness."[16] However, beyond this, these voices also have another role, which undermines the inherent structural purpose of the historical narrative: "An individual voice suddenly arising in the course of an ordinary historical narrative of events ... can pierce the (most involuntary) smugness of scholarly detachment and 'objectivity,'" Friedländer writes, and continues: "The goal of historical knowledge is to domesticate disbelief, to explain it away. In this book I wish to offer a thorough historical study of the extermination of the Jews of Europe without eliminating or domesticating that initial sense of disbelief."[17]

Thus Friedländer attempts to integrate within the context of an historical monograph the theoretical considerations he had developed in the past in connection with the notions of trauma, excess, and other psychoanalytic concepts. Whether this attempt is successful or not will remain an open question.[18]

Anyhow, in order to better understand the use of Jewish sources by Friedländer, I wish to pause for a moment to consider the admittedly rather overused metaphor of "voice," with which Friedländer refers to the Jewish sources he so extensively quotes. This metaphor suggests that while the murderers have history and a narrative—however cruel and extreme it might be—the victims in essence have voices. These voices and experiences of individuals pierce holes in the narrative and wish to de-automize its reading. But as such, the Jewish sources lack a synthetic and analytical framework. They simply exist—giving presence within the narrative to the raw experience of the Jews who were sucked into the vortex of catastrophe, and thus endowing the narrative with a kind of aesthetic, which seems to tend to the melodramatic. As the historian Shulamit Volkov commented, in a sympathetic tone, "We are perhaps used to the fact that works of art that deal with Holocaust, and especially films, shock us, or bring us to tears. Here is a history book that does the same.... [T]he style is dry and matter of fact. The tears flow of their own accord."[19]

Thus, we can conclude that this use of Jewish sources is aesthetic, as in a work of art, but also epistemological in the sense that it preserves the sense of disbelief, which, in Friedländer's words, "disrupts" the sense of understanding created by the historical narrative that unfolds events and explains them.[20] Another aspect which should be stressed is that in this book the Jews are, first and foremost, individuals. I will return to this point shortly.

The approach described above is very different from the dry and matter-of-fact approach of scholars—in particular German- and English-speaking historians—who conduct research on the final solution. In their sizable published works, these researchers for the most part *almost utterly ignore* Jewish sources and Jewish perspectives. One reason for this is these scholars' inability to read the relevant sources in their original languages. More significantly, however, they are chiefly interested in causal history that explains how the Nazi policy toward the Jews developed: in this respect, Jews scarcely played a role.

This tendency of ignoring the Jewish perspective continued until the late nineties of the previous century and stimulated an incisive critique from many Jewish historians. Most recently, Omer Bartov described his visits to the great German universities in the late 1990s: "These classes were ably taught by distinguished scholars ... but everything the students read and wrote had to do with the German perpetrators; not a single reading concerned the victims— not one testimony, one memoir, one historical reconstruction of Jewish life or death from a Jewish perspective."[21]

This state of affairs began to change in the late 1990s. Awareness of the problematic elision of the point of view of the victims has led to the creation of a new body of work by researchers, who began to deal with Jewish sources. Thus for example, Götz Aly was able to reconstruct the short biography of the child Marion Samuel who was murdered in Auschwitz in 1943,[22] and Raul Hilberg made use of Jewish texts in a few of his later works.[23] Until now, such works were seen as embellishments and additions to the main body of significant research by historians who dealt with the murderers, which almost completely avoided examination of Jewish sources. However, this trend has come of age with the publication in 2010 of Christopher Browning's study *Remembering Survival*,[24] which is devoted to the reconstruction of the history of a single labor camp—Starachowice. This study relies almost exclusively on 292 testimonies of Jewish survivors, collected between 1945 and 2008.[25] The study parallels, almost like a mirror image, his famous book about reserve police battalion 101, which, as is well known, was based on later court testimonies.[26] In both cases an attempt is made to implement the technique of micro-history in order to reconstruct the story of one small yet significant locus of Holocaust history. In both cases the sources are post-factum testimonies—in the former case by the victims and in the latter case by the perpetrators.

In Browning's study the Jews are not "voices" that give expression to experiences, but primarily victims of Nazi persecution struggling for their survival; their testimonies are historical sources for the maximal reliable reconstruction of the history of one place—the Starachowice labor camp—and of the modes of life and the struggle for survival in that site. In contrast to their treatment by Friedländer, the sources in Browning's study fulfill no aesthetic or epistemological role. In many senses this type of micro-historical research can be called *synecdochic* research, which attempts by means of micro-history to provide answers to some of the most significant historical questions. In the case of *Ordinary Men* the question was obvious: what led the actual "doers" to participate in the murder? But in his new book Browning seeks, albeit less directly, to answer a different question: what were the conditions that made survival in the labor camp possible?

It is notable that Browning does not perceive Jews as a national or cultural community, but rather as a group of victims struggling jointly and separately for their survival and for the survival of each of the group's members. This is markedly different from the way Jews are perceived in the Israeli school of Holocaust historical research.

Whereas Friedländer's approach is very different from that of English-speaking and German historians, it is also very distinct from the Israeli school of Holocaust research. The above notwithstanding, Friedländer's intentionalist tendency and his firm position that views antisemitic ideology in its particular Nazi form of "redemptive anti-Semitism"[27] as the chief cause of the Holocaust are indeed in keeping with the dominant spirit of what has been called the Israeli school of Holocaust research.[28] His radical critique of the Pope and of the Catholic Church, which appears as a leitmotif in his book, matches the tenor of this school of research as well. However, Friedländer's historical outlook also differs from the latter approach in a number of significant ways, especially in respect to the issue of writing about Jews.

The Israeli school of Holocaust research crystallized during the 1970s and 1980s, and as Dan Michman has pointed out, Yehuda Bauer, Yisrael Gutman, and others were considered its founders.[29] This school's research responds to a large extent to Philip Friedman's early appeal in 1957, during a lecture at the World Congress of Jewish Studies: "What we need is a history of the Jewish people during the period of the Nazi rule in which the central role is to be played by The Jewish People, not only as the victim of a tragedy, but also as the bearer of a communal existence with all the manifold and numerous aspects involved. In short: our approach must be definitely 'Judeo-centric' as opposed to 'Nazi-centric,' which it has been so far."[30]

This tradition is concerned with the Jews as historical agents in their own right and it differs from Friedländer's approach in two senses. First, it does not view the Jews as mere individuals. Rather, as Dan Michman has repeatedly pointed out: in alignment with the Jerusalem school of Jewish studies,[31] this school views the Jews as a *national collective*.[32] Furthermore, in contrast to Friedländer's integrative approach, this tradition of writing does not focus on the *experience* of the victims, but rather on the attempt to reconstruct the history of the Jews, above all, from an *institutional perspective*.[33]

The most comprehensive conceptual summary of this approach has been formulated by Yehuda Bauer himself in his book *Rethinking the Holocaust*.[34] In this work, Bauer discusses the problem of the character of the history of the Jews in this era in two chapters which he considers his major interpretive contribution. For the purpose of our present discussion I wish here to closely examine one of the dimensions Bauer emphasizes in his treatment. The key terms of Bauer's historiography, according to his own affirmation, are "resistance," "response," "reaction," and "*amida*."

In the original English edition of the book, Bauer claims that the concept of *amida* is difficult to translate into a foreign language. The term, he says, connotes both armed and unarmed resistance, but also the smuggling of food, cultural, religious, educational, and political activity as well as other types of action, aimed at bolstering the personal and collective capacities for survival.[35]

The development of this historiography is tied, of course, to the accusatory claims emanating from many different quarters—academic, political, and others—that Jews during the Holocaust era were led to their deaths "as sheep to the slaughter."[36]

The Israeli school, on the other hand, as Yisrael Gutman has also pointed out, sought to present the Jews in both the individual and the collective sense as having resisted Nazi persecution as long as even the most meager means were available to them to do so, including actual armed resistance. As a consequence, the concept of resistance was sweepingly expanded to include almost any organized or even private act that enabled or supported Jewish existence during this era.[37] As such, Israeli historiography constituted the Jewish historical subject—both on the collective and individual plane—as an active agent, as the owner of his or her own history, whose own interiority or mental, cultural, religious, communal, and ethical self, continued to stand strong and invincible.[38] The Jews, therefore, are a proud historical agent whose interiority cannot be crushed or even undermined.

The achievements of this school of historiography were extremely significant, and the writing it produced is of course inestimably more complex and multifaceted than I am able to convey here. But nonetheless it appears to me that the principles I have enumerated so far adequately represent the contours of this school of thought and the writing informed by it up until the end of the 1990s, and in particular through its deployment of the concepts of resistance, reaction, and *amida* as the capstone of all its historiographic endeavors.[39]

What this historiography frequently seems to have missed, however, are central aspects of Jewish daily experience as expressed in writing from the period—experiences of despair, shame, truncation, fundamental upheaval of the self, tremendous anxiety about the future, mourning and terror, radical disorientation, helplessness, unraveling of everyday habits—or *habitus*, as Bourdieu would have called it—and more. All of these experiences, which vividly and tremulously populate every scrap of paper written during that era, are scarcely reflected at all in this historiography, and certainly have not been made into an object of historical research. One reason for this, among others, is, as I have argued, that the dominant perspective has been one of institutional history.

It is precisely these aspects which are so central to the narrative offered by Friedländer, who is not beholden to the premises of Israeli historiography, from which he distinguishes himself already at the beginning of his book. In contradistinction to the premise of the unity of Jewish history as national history,[40] Friedländer states: "no obvious common denominator fitted the maze of parties, associations, groups and some nine million individuals ... who nonetheless considered themselves Jews (or were considered as such)."[41] In Friedländer's book, as we already asserted and from a very liberal point of view,[42] Jews are first and foremost individuals. Moreover, whereas Israeli historiography seeks to emphasize dimensions of Jewish solidarity (despite critical awareness to contrary phenomena as well)—be this the solidarity of Jews who came under Nazi occupation, or the solidarity of Europe's Jews and Jews in Palestine, the United States, or elsewhere—Friedländer emphasizes precisely the contrary.[43]

He summarizes his position most unequivocally: "One of the striking aspects of the dramatically changing Jewish condition appears to be the ongoing disintegration of overall Jewish solidarity—insofar as it ever existed."[44]

To the above three historiographical approaches should be added a fourth, which the literary and cultural critic Alan Mintz has designated the "constructivist" approach in the study of Jewish texts, especially in respect to texts stemming from the period of the Holocaust.[45] This approach, with focal points in the United States but also represented in Israel and Poland, asserts that the only correct interpretation of a text is that which emerges first and foremost from within the cultural context in which it was written. The proponents of this approach tend to focus chiefly on Eastern European Jewish cultural expression, seeking, for example to read ghetto journals chiefly (if not exclusively) in the cultural context of Eastern European Jewry in the pre-war era, and with reference to the richness of Jewish culture embedded in the Jewish languages of that time—Yiddish and Hebrew. This reading emphasizes aspects of the cultural-linguistic collective; its key word is "continuity," for this approach aims to examine continuities and discontinuities of language, symbols, ideological identities, poetic elements, and institutional activities. Most of the researchers identified with this school of thought are cultural and literary scholars, although recently a fascinating historical monograph—written from the same cultural perspective—has been published by Samuel Kassow about Emmanuel Ringelblum and the monumental project of the Oneg Shabbat archives, which the latter undertook in the Warsaw Ghetto.[46] This work convincingly elucidates how Ringelblum's phenomenal activity in the different spheres of life in the Warsaw ghetto grew out of the conceptual, ideological, social, and cultural world he inhabited in the pre-Holocaust era, and argues that his actions can receive their proper historical meaning only when read against this particular background. However, by emphasizing the notions of continuity, this approach, like that of Israeli historiography, does not always give a full account, so it would seem, of the fundamental upheavals, disruptions, and the disintegration embodied in the texts with which it is concerned.[47]

Indeed, some of this writing already verges on what I am calling "cultural history," but only partially, as I will explain shortly. The type of history to which I am referring is also contiguous with what the historical literature often defines as "everyday life"—a sphere to which certain monographs about the Jews in the Holocaust era frequently dedicate several chapters.[48] However, despite its proximity to the topics dealt with in contexts such as those just cited, the cultural history of the Jews in the ghettos, as I understand it, should not be limited to these subjects of "everyday life."[49]

What then is cultural history? As defined by Lynn Hunt, "The deciphering of meaning, rather than the inference of causal laws of explanation is taken to be the central task of cultural history."[50] This kind of history, when applied to the history of the Jews in the ghettos, seeks then to analyze and decipher in depth the production of social and cultural meaning. It is history that does not focus on empirical reality, but rather on the reality of consciousness and the modes of its production via collective institutions. And if this perspective is brought to bear on the Holocaust era, the same kind of analytic should be applied also to the collapse or radical transformation of such institutions and their capacity to produce meaning.

Beyond the fact that this historiographical stance opens up new series of historical questions, it also comes back, so I argue, with a more sophisticated tool kit, to address the questions that troubled a great many Holocaust-era writers, and to the themes that intensely animate their writing—questions and themes from which the other approaches which I described somehow tend to distance themselves. For the large number of texts written by Jews during the Holocaust, and chiefly those written in the ghettos, convey a sense of duality in regard to Jewish life. On the one hand, life in the ghettos displayed a type of continuity, even in the geographical and urban sense. Many of those who lived in the ghettos did not even have to change their place of residence, and many of those who were forced to move relocated to familiar areas of the city in which they had lived for many years (this of course is not true of the many refugees who came into the large ghettos). Many of the ghettos, certainly the large ones, functioned as a type of "urban" environment in which remnants of previous life as well as the institutions of civilization continued to exist, even at the most mundane levels, such as in the payment of electricity bills and municipal taxes in Warsaw. On the other hand, this life was completely overturned and was saturated with terrible distress, drastic changes in everyday realities, the near utter devastation of most of life's institutions, hunger, terror, pain, despair, mourning, loss, rage, amazement, worry, uncertainty, and an overwhelming presence of death. All of these experiences are extremely salient in these texts.

They form the basic matrix of those texts, and these are the issues with which cultural history must contend.

Moreover, the point I wish to make here is that this research-orientation which focuses on "meaning production"—what we would designate today as questions of cultural history—made its initial appearance and indeed presented its most fascinating insights in the writing of the first generation of observers who wrote reflectively about those events.

I am referring here to the writings of Jewish writers who experienced the Holocaust, members of the intelligentsia, most of whom had an academic education, and some of whom were professional academics, in Eastern, Central and Western Europe, and who wrote during the war-era (many of them were murdered) or during the first years after the war. These texts, which are not easy to classify—whether as proto-research, testimony, or ethnographic records—are chiefly concerned with issues of consciousness and culture; in them, the writers turn, each coming from his or her own political, spiritual, academic, and intellectual orientation, to the examination of the social psychological and cultural existence of the Jews under Nazi rule. These writers produced the very first analytic and reflective texts about Jews in the Holocaust era, and to my mind theirs are the most interesting texts that survived that era. The central concerns of these texts are matters of culture—not in the sense of cultural institutions and the activity of such institutions, but rather in the sense of the mechanisms through which victims produced meaning and the nature of the consciousness they developed within the difficult circumstances into which they were thrown. I wish to point out three methodological channels suggested by these texts, and to shortly point to the vast potential they embody in attempting to understand the world of the Jews during the Holocaust. The three channels are: social psychology; ethnography and anthropological history; and the study of language, speech, and discourse.

Social Psychology: Rumors as a Case Study

In 1947, Emil Utitz published a short book in Slovakian which was translated a year later into German under the Title *Psychologie des Lebens im Konzentrationslager Theresienstadt*[51]—a psychology of life in the Theresienstadt concentration camp. Utitz, who was born in Prague in 1883, studied philosophy and psychology and specialized in aesthetics. Although he converted to Christianity at a young age, Utitz belonged to a circle of Czech Jewish intellectuals and was friendly with Max Brod, Franz Kafka, and Hugo Bergman. He was a teacher at the University of Halle and then in Prague. In July 1942 he was sent to Theresienstadt, where he was put in charge of the library. Like Leo Baeck, he gave memorable public lectures in the ghetto, on topics related to culture and the humanities. After the liberation he returned to Prague to teach at the university, and passed away in Jena in 1956. In the course of his academic career he wrote several important books, especially in the field of aesthetics.

Early in the book, Utitz justifies writing it (and this is in the year 1947), in spite of the fact that, as he asserts: "so much has already been written about the concentration camps in general and about Theresienstadt in particular."[52] Nevertheless, he submits that he has a unique perspective to offer: "Due to my profession as a psychologist and philosopher," he explains, and based on his three-year experience as an inmate in Theresientstadt, he is capable of providing an account of several matters which should be of scientific interest. Utitz viewed Theresienstadt as a sort of "experiment" on human social life, which possibly had never before been conducted, and, which he hoped "would never again take place." The study is therefore a kind of scientific meditation on his personal experiences, through which he seeks to understand fundamental themes of the social psychology of the ghetto's residents.[53] The book offers observations concerning a number of issues, but here I wish to focus on the topic of rumors in the ghetto.

Rumors, Utitz explains, were the only means for transmitting information from the outside world concerning critical issues such as the war's progress, the fate of the Jews, and the expected date of liberation; these matters indeed comprised the main *content* of the rumors. However, their *meaning* for ghetto residents was utterly different. Although frequently containing a kernel of truth, the rumors were ultimately grotesque inventions and exaggerations, as Utitz put it. As such, they possessed scarcely any news value, and everyone was aware of this fact. Yet, for the most part, the rumors fulfilled an intra-social psychological function—to strengthen the hope and belief which had become moral imperatives in the ghetto, for only hope and belief enabled people to bear the intolerable difficulties of ghetto life. Rumors staked out a battlefield between the optimists who inspired hope and the pessimists who threw a pall of gloom over things; as such the rumors instituted a new ethics. "You who are not a believer," Utitz quotes an optimist accusing a pessimist in the summer of 1942, in regard to the latter's doubts about the rumor that the Reich's collapse was nigh, and would come to pass before the winter—"you are a bad person!"[54] To believe the comforting rumors was a moral imperative in the eyes of many, whereas to doubt them was perceived as sin.

However, this ethics of illusion which depended upon and promoted auspicious rumors was so pervasive that many people cut themselves off from reality completely and thus even endangered themselves. Some people, and no small number of them, Utitz reports, sold their warm clothes in the summer because they believed in the near defeat of the Nazis, which was expected to occur before winter. The price paid for this illusion was sometimes unbearable.[55] These issues lead Utitz to analyze the culture of nostalgia, illusion, and delusion that existed in Theresienstadt, its modes of expression, and the mechanisms that activated it. Such mechanisms were a product of a collective mood that sought in any way possible to evade the life-realities of the insufferable present and to escape into a glowing future of imminent German defeat or else to nostalgically recollect a lost Eden as a source of inspiration for the future. In the absence of any such past, some people simply invented one. Thus for example Utitz describes the common tendency among Theresienstadt inmates to upgrade their pre-war profession. All of the petty shop owners became successful merchants in their stories, and a distributor for a small publishing house presented himself as a professor at the Sorbonne.

Indeed, a number of phenomena surrounding the rumors and the delusional mode of the thought which variously characterized many ghetto societies depending on various circumstances are abundantly documented in contemporaneous sources. As such, they merit comprehensive and in-depth inquiry from the perspectives of social psychology, folklore, and linguistic studies, as for example Marc Bloch and Paul Fussell applied to the study of World War I.[56]

Such a research project would examine the modes of public communication within the ghettos against the background of the intensely modern culture of communication, discussion, and debate which various Jewish publics had been cultivating before the war in the large cities of Europe. This culture of communication was based, especially in Eastern Europe, on an extremely alert and vibrant public sphere, which consisted of hundreds of newspapers and journals as well as political and cultural institutions and discussion platforms, both official and popular, ranging from the café and social or political club to trans-national Jewish organizations. These modern institutions of communication and discussion in the public sphere practically ceased to exist within the ghettos and were replaced by the welter of rumors that served as the dominant mode of mass communication. Research oriented to these issues was pioneered by Alexandra Garbarini, in one of the chapters of her book about diaries written by Jews during the Holocaust period.[57] However, this can be counted merely as a preliminary endeavor, for the topic of rumors appears innumerable times in Jewish writing of the period, and indicates precisely the direction which Utitz outlines. Or, as Chaim Kaplan of Warsaw put it already at the end of 1939: "These are the workings of the sick imagination of a despised people, which has nothing in its world but imagination. The miserable masses are waiting for a miracle. Such Messianism finds fertile ground, because every nonsensical fact is eagerly listened to. Common sense has evaporated. Rationality and a sense of reality have evaporated." The nature of this double bind is summarized by Chaim Kaplan again on 2 September 1941 in his poetic formulation: "Woe to the people that lives in illusion—and happy is the people that lives in illusion, without its fanciful illusions it would be lost."[58] This is the kind of dual consciousness that characterizes addicts who know that their addiction is based on a harmful illusion, yet, it is an illusion which they cannot at the same time avoid consuming.

Indeed, the incipient research about the collective consciousness of illusion was begun soon after the war, and not only by Emil Utitz. Nahman Blumenthal, for example, viewed this form of consciousness as a way of coping with a state of helplessness. In one of his early essays he deals with what he calls "magical thinking" which in his opinion characterized Jewish consciousness in the ghettos—the idea that by acting or imagining the Jews could influence a reality which was in fact totally controlled by the Germans.[59]

In the foregoing passages I have outlined only one possible theme that invites the incorporation of social psychology into research concerning the world of the Jews. Indeed, any serious and comprehensive study would have to examine this issue diachronically in a number of locales, under varying conditions, and in different contexts. However, the theme itself emerges powerfully in the earliest reflective texts, which I suggest should be revisited, and it eloquently illustrates the gist of my argument.

Ethnography and Anthropological History: The Dead and the Living

As Boaz Cohen and Roni Stauber have pointed out,[60] in the early days of Israeli historiography of the Holocaust, which dealt primarily with the history of the Jews, a fundamental struggle took place between a group of historians and documentarians, most of whom were survivors, and professional historians from the Hebrew University, members of the Jerusalem school of Jewish history, which we described above. The latter group was at the time chiefly interested in addressing the issue of antisemitism and the perception of the Holocaust within the continuum of Jewish history in modern Europe. The former group, however, most of whom were educated in broad and diverse fields, including history, literature, philosophy, psychology, etc., chose, as Boaz Cohen puts it, to confront the terrible trauma they had experienced and to understand all aspects of ghetto society—social, cultural, and psychological. This was in part a dispute between different cultural groups, but it was also a methodological dispute, as Cohen writes: "The disharmony was abetted by the differences in the scholarly approach. The survivor-historians drew on the typical folk-history outlook of East European Jews, while Dinur's students drew on the German scholarly perspective that was typical of the Hebrew University."[61]

The survivor historians to whom I am broadly referring here include the circle of researchers and documentarians who gathered at The Ghetto Fighters' Museum and at Yad Vashem during the 1940s and 1950s, such as Nahman Blumenthal, mentioned above, Rachel Auerbach, Yosef Kermisch, Nathan Eck, but also Samuel Gringauz, who was the most prominent intellectual figure in the deportee camps, and who later immigrated to the United States.[62] In many respects, their writing and the topics they focused on were a continuation of the work of the ethnographic-oriented Ghetto documentarians. Their kind of writing was influenced both directly and indirectly, wittingly or unwittingly by the YIVO tradition of ethnographic documentation "from below"—the tradition that had developed in Eastern Europe as part of the creation of a collective Jewish ethnic consciousness at the end of the nineteenth century and the beginning of the twentieth.[63] In fact, among these early survivor historians were a number who wrote ethnographic-style diaries during the Holocaust itself, such as Rachel Auerbach who was one of the central figures active in the clandestine Warsaw Ghetto Oneg Shabbat archives. Auerbach had received no formal education as a professional historian, but was trained rather in philosophy, psychology, and literature, and as Samuel Kassow has remarked, was deeply attached to popular folklore.[64] Indeed, her essays from the Holocaust era and the post-Holocaust era both have an ethnographic character, accompanied by a profound psychological appreciation of the human spirit and of the nature of society.

The central problematic around which this sort of writing revolves can be described most fittingly with the words of the diarist Yosef Zelkowicz (who was murdered) of Łódź:

> It is not only the external form of life that has changed in the ghetto.... It is not only the clothing that has come to look tattered and the faces to wear masks of death, *but the entire Jewish trend of thought has been totally transformed* under the pressure of the ghetto.... The ghetto ... has swiftly obliterated the boundaries between sanctity and indignity, just as it obliterated the boundaries between mine and yours, permitted and forbidden, fair and unfair.[65]

Ways of thinking, basic cultural classifications, and nearly every cultural symbol—all were radically transformed within ghetto society. This is what Zelkowicz perceived and these are the drastic changes he sought, like many other ethnographic diarists in the ghetto, to capture through his documentary writing.

One example of a realm affected by such transformation in the Warsaw Ghetto was the relationship between the dead and the living—a subject dealt with by all the ethnographic writers without exception. The background is well known.

When the ghetto was first sealed off in November 1940, the first wave of typhoid fever among Warsaw's Jews waned. But in the spring of 1941, in wake of the waves of refugees who entered the ghetto; the crowding, hunger, and lack of sanitation; and the scarce means of immunization and medical treatment, a new violent strain of typhus broke out which began to subside only toward the spring of 1942. The epidemic along with hunger decimated many lives, especially among the refugees and the ghetto's poor. It is estimated that some 20 percent of the ghetto population died as a result of hunger and diseases.[66] The dying and the dead lay about in the streets, and the funerary societies could not adequately cope with a reality that fundamentally changed the relations between the dead and the living—a relationship which every culture manages by means of coping mechanisms, the purpose of which, according to Van Gennep, is to enable the passage and radical separation between the two realms.[67] This was especially true of Eastern European Jewish society, in which, as Avriel Bar Levav has noted, the care that was taken to distinguish between the corpses of the dead, which were perceived as impure, and between sanctified life, as well as the practice of funerary rites and mourning periods, was comprehensive and radical.[68]

Some twelve private companies, which sprouted up quickly in the ghetto as a response to this reality,[69] were in charge of conducting funerals and burials in the ghetto. The largest company was owned by Motel Pinkiert, who was given the name "king of the corpses."[70] The company had its major branch on Grzybowska Street, but also had a few secondary branches around the ghetto. From time to time it published an advertisement in the German-auhorized Jewish newspaper in the Generalgouvernement, Gazeta. But only a few families could afford a private funeral. Most of the dead, especially those who died on the streets, were collected every morning. The bodies were piled up in a sort of storeroom for corpses and disposed of without any ceremony in mass graves.

As Hunt argues, anthropologists and historians of an anthropological orientation will generally discover rites everywhere.[71] The question that arises in connection with the ghetto is reversed. What happens to a society that places a heavy emphasis on elaborate and strict rites, when, although still functioning somehow as a society, it is compelled by circumstances that strip it of practically all of its ritual capital? This pertains to the most basic rites of passage such as funerals, in which the taboo separation between the dead and the living is utterly undone. If, as Mary Douglas has written, one of the important roles of ritual and of taboo—pertinent also certainly to burial ceremonies and purity/impurity practices connected with the dead—is to organize a chaotic reality into comprehensible schemes that create social cohesion,[72] then the unraveling of these schemes to a great extent causes the meaning of reality to fall apart and social cohesion to dissolve. This is precisely what the ethnographers of the Holocaust and post-Holocaust era, such as Rachel Auerbach,[73] write about. And as Jacek Leociak has already argued, the reality of mass death in the ghetto obscures the most basic classifications of culture and the ways in which Jewish tradition has dealt with them.[74]

Some people attempted to combat this state of affairs. Thus for example, in March 1942, a group of rabbis established the *halvayat hamet* funerary society, which included the Rabbi of Strikov and the Rabbi of Alexander, who also sent a memo to Czerniaków in which, horrified, they warned against the desecration of the dead and the living in the ghetto, in utter opposition to Jewish tradition: "The sight of corpses in the street stupefies the basic sense of humanity." As a consequence they proposed assisting the poor with burial arrangements and collecting the dead as quickly as possible from the public areas.[75] However, reality was ultimately more formidable than any action that might have been taken. Numerous testimonies exist concerning the effect of this reality on the psyches of ghetto residents. The issue was very much on the minds of the ghetto chroniclers, and Janusz Korczak, for example, wrote of the children who played in the streets and ignored a corpse lying nearby,[76] while Ringelblum wrote of children playing with the corpse itself.[77]

If among other things, burial rites are meant to affirm social cohesion, Chaim Kaplan points to the inverse process occurring in the Warsaw Ghetto: desensitization with respect to the dead dissolves social cohesion or is a symptom of that dissolution. On 4 January 1942 he wrote as follows:

> Walk out into the Ghetto streets … and you will find the casualties of hunger and cold lying stretched out across the pavement lifeless. Thousand of people, including the religious and ultraorthodox, and if on the Sabbath, wrapped in their prayer shawls with their *humashim* [prayer books] tucked under their arms, walk past the deceased, while their hearts do not as much as stir. Only a sense of nausea arises in them as if they had walked by a foul corpse of a dog or of a cat.… [H]earts have hardened and become cruel, as if we had become beasts of prey, collaborators with the accursed Nazism which has turned us into unworthy of the name human, as so we have become in our eyes.… [O]ur hearts are full of bitterness, and our faces display misanthropy.… [M]ore than [Nazism] has damaged the body of [Polish Jewry,] it has damaged its soul.[78]

Study of Language and Discourse

A third direction to which Jewish ethnographers and the researchers of the first generation after the Holocaust turned was the study of language. Among these was Victor Klemperer, whose wartime diaries are replete with the professional observations of a philologist. His 1947 book, *LTI,* collects these observations and serves as a sort of reflective linguistic testimonial of the way in which the German language changed during the Nazi era, especially among the Germans, but also among the Jews.[79]

Klemperer's interest in Nazi language arose out of the tradition of *Völkerpsychologie* whose origins lie in the middle of the nineteenth century. This philosophical-anthropological approach, identified chiefly with Moritz Lazarus and Heymann Steinthal, Jewish intellectuals who were active in Germany during the nineteenth century, was crucially shaped by Herder's philosophy of language, which viewed language as the central medium through which the spirit of a people is manifested. Language therefore is crucial to the interpretation of this spirit; it possesses an unconscious independence which embodies the truth of the speaker, of the era, and of the culture in which it is spoken.[80]

Among those who investigated the German language of the Nazi era were Shaul Asch, George Steiner, Hannah Arendt, and Nahman Blumenthal. Blumenthal, however, went even further and thoroughly examined the changes that Yiddish underwent in his fascinating and comprehensive work titled *Verter un vertelekh von der Hurban tekufa* (Words and proverbs from the period of the Holocaust).[81] The impulse for writing this work arose after Blumenthal had returned in the middle of 1944 to the liberated regions of eastern Poland, where he met simple Jews, and, as he writes, was astounded to discover that "I could barely understand their language, so great were the changes that had taken place during the short period of my three year absence."[82] Like many of his essays and studies, here too, Blumenthal's research arises out of the YIVO approach to studying Jewish folklore and folkways.

These two traditions of linguistic research, the first stemming from the school of central European nationalism and the second erected on the foundations of YIVO's study of Eastern European Jewish folklore, came together in the fascinating and tragic writing project, the "Encyclopedia of the Łódź Ghetto." This project was carried out during the final period of the ghetto's existence by Jewish Zionist intellectuals from Central Europe, such as Oskar Rosenfeld of Prague and Vienna and Oskar Singer of Prague who had been deported to the Łódź ghetto, and by members of the Eastern European intelligentsia, such Yosef Zelkowicz, Henrik Naftalin, Yerahmiel Brieman, and others. This fascinating text has not yet received the attention and analysis it deserves. Written in three languages, German, Yiddish, and Polish, it is actually a lexicon of the Łódź ghetto. It includes, for example, alongside articles on the identification and characterization of eight types of cigarettes, entries devoted to various characters in the ghetto, the institutions that had been renewed in it, new turns of phrase, slang, and more.

One of the initiators of the project was, as noted above, Oskar Rosenfeld, who explained in a diary entry on 1 December 1943 the importance of the encyclopedia by noting, "[T]he language is a more reliable witness and source of truth than other, material artifacts."[83] Thus, for example, he concludes from the initial analysis of ghetto language, "Intellectual needs are pressed together in a narrow frame. They require only a few words, concepts or word associations." This led him to conclude further, "A collection of these linguistic and word treasures forms part of the cultural history of the ghetto."[84]

The study of the Jews' languages and discourses during the Holocaust, viewed against the background of Jewish languages in the pre-Holocaust era, is still awaiting a massive scholarly work that will undertake the task of better understanding the social and cultural consciousness of the victims.

Summary

At the end of World War II, *New York Times* correspondent Anne O'Hare McCormack astutely observed that the catastrophe brought on by the war could not only be measured materially or in terms of human life: "There has never been such destruction, *such disintegration of the structure of life,*" she asserted.[85] And if this is true of all of Europe, it is all the more valid in reference to the Jews who were imprisoned in the ghettos. Oskar Rosenfeld of the Łódź Ghetto was very well aware of these dissolutions of the structure of life—the transformations it underwent—and in the diary entry quoted above he wrote the following: "The change of social, intellectual and economic functions brought with it a change in the most commonplace conceptions. Concepts that until then were understood unambiguously everywhere among Europeans underwent a *complete transformation.*"[86]

This is the first point I wish to stress in this summary. In contrast to the notions of continuity, resistance, and *"amida"* on the one hand, or the concepts of voice, experience, and horrific disbelief on the other, I believe that the concept of transformation must be posited as a key concept in the writing of the cultural history of the Jews in the Holocaust era.

In so arguing, I am following, in a sense, the path of Hannah Arendt, who in her book *The Origins of Totalitarianism* wrote: "What totalitarian ideologies therefore aim at is not the transformation of the outside world or the revolutionizing transmutation of society but the *transformation of human nature itself.*"[87]

Another premise embedded in Rosenfeld's above quoted text is that such transformation occurs not only on the surface of things, but at the deep level of the fundamental concepts that constitute culture—concepts that modern Europeans, Jews included, take for granted. It is only in reference to such concepts that one can understand the transformation the ghetto prisoners underwent. In contemporary terms, one can speak of a transformation of "deep categories" that inform the "world views" as Aron Gurevich, the historian of the medieval period,[88] called them, or the "episteme" as Foucault called it, or "habitus" in Bourdieu's terms. Although they differ from one another, all of these theoretical constructs share a common feature. They all signify fundamental deep structures on the basis of which a culture is organized. This is the locus of the crisis and transformation of which Rosenfeld writes. This is the direction which the cultural history of the Jews in this era should be pursuing.

As I already noted, research into the matrix of victim "consciousness," based on rudimentary sources, has already been developing over the last decade in several directions. My own research, together with that of Alexandra Garbarini, Shirli Gilbert, Jacek Leociak, and others,[89] is indicative of this trend, which appears to have the potential to yield fascinating results with respect to understanding "the victim."

If these methodologies of studying the victim gain momentum, the ensuing studies will, in my opinion, be capable of providing insight into the question that the historiographic trends I have surveyed have failed to answer: how is it possible to write the history of *helplessness*, without sliding into heroization on the one hand, or obscuring the magnitude of the crisis on the other, but also without it becoming a sanctified and melodramatic icon? Such a research paradigm would adopt the statement articulated by anthropologist Linda Green (who deals with much less extreme circumstances of terror) as the basis for its inquiry:

> Gradually I came to realize that terror's power, its matter of factness, is exactly about doubting one's own perception of reality. The routinization of terror is what fuels its power. Such routinization allows people to live in a chronic state of fear with a façade of normalcy, while that terror, at the same time permeates and shreds the social fabric.[90]

It is precisely the incorporation of a cultural history perspective centered on the notion of transformation into the historical research of the Jews during the Holocaust era which will enable an in-depth consideration, conceptualization, and analysis of the radical and excessive aspects of the victim's experience. In so doing, this perspective can move beyond melodramatic images of the Jewish victim which have become commonplace in museums and albums the world over, as fulfillment of the all-embracing imperative of "listening to the victim's voice," a slogan which has almost become kitsch.[91] It would also enable scholars to track the processes of dissolution caused by extreme situations of occupation, oppression, and discrimination and thus enable the comparative study of other situations of oppression.

On the other hand, such a history will not reduce the perspective of the victim to raw "voices" and "experiences" alone, as Friedländer does. It would propose methodologies for a thorough and careful examination of the texts written by Jews during the Holocaust era, not only in order to provide a sense of horrific disbelief, but also by proposing a conceptualization that would enable a better understanding of the components of which this horrific disbelief is made. Such an investigation would re-engage the questions that so urgently preoccupied many of the first reflective writers who wrote during the Holocaust era and immediately after it, before the passage of time, apologetics, and the trends of glorifying and sacralizing the victims became dominant in public consciousness and historiography,[92] allowing such questions to be evaded.

Notes

1. I wish to dedicate this chapter to the memory of Professor David Bankier, who might not have agreed with all of its assertions, but who, I would like to believe, might have been pleased with it.

2. Originally published as Dan Stone, "Holocaust Historiography and Cultural History," *Dapim* 23 (2009): 52–68. See also the scholarly forum in the same publication, featuring responses from Dominick LaCapra, Federico Finchelstein, Carolyn J. Dean, Dan Michman, Wendy Lower, and Amos Goldberg (ibid., 69–93).

3. See Claudia Koonz, *The Nazi Conscience* (Cambridge, MA, 2003) and Alon Confino, "Fantasies about the Jews: Cultural Reflections on the Holocaust," *History & Memory* 17 (2005): 297; Dominick LaCapra, *Writing History Writing Trauma* (Baltimore, 2001), esp. ch. 5; and in a slightly different context, Enzo Traverso, *The Origins of Nazi Violence* (New York, 2003). See also Dan Michman, *The Emergence of the Jewish Ghettos during the Holocaust* (New York, 2010).

4. Peter Burke, *What is Cultural History?* (Cambridge, UK, 2008).

5. Robert Darnton, *The Kiss of Lamourette: Reflections in Cultural History* (New York, 1989), 191–218.

6. See Dan Michman, "Introducing more 'Cultural History' into the Study of the Holocaust: A Response to Dan Stone," *Dapim* 23 (2009): 69–75.

7. Esther Farbstein, *Hidden In Thunder: Perspectives on Faith, Halachah and Leadership during the Holocaust* (Jerusalem, 2007).

8. Shirli Gilbert, *Music in the Holocaust: Confronting Life in the Nazi Ghettos and Camps* (Oxford, 2005).

9. Kenneth I. Helphand, *Defiant Gardens: Making Gardens in Wartime* (San Antonio, 2006), 60–105.

10. Moshe Rosman, *How Jewish is Jewish History?* (Oxford, 2009), 131–32.

11. Burke, *What is Cultural History?*, 3. See also David Chaney, *The Cultural Turn* (London, 1994).

12. Saul Friedländer, *The Years of Extermination: Nazi Germany and the Jews, 1939–1945* (New York, 2007).

13. An exception is the essay by Daniel Goldhagen, "The War Years," *Washington Post* (13 May 2007). For a thorough theoretical, historiographic and critical discussion of the book, see Wulf Kansteiner, "Success, Truth, and Modernism in Holocaust Historiography: Reading Saul Friedländer Thirty-Five Years after the Publication of Metahistory," *History and Theory* 47 (2009): 25–53; and the forum published in *History and Theory* 48, no. 3 (2009), including responses from Alon Confino, "Narrative Form and Historical Sensation: On Saul Friedländer's The Years of Extermination," 199–219; Amos Goldberg, "The Victim's Voice and Melodramatic Aesthetics in History," 220–37; and Christopher Browning, "Evocation, Analysis, and the 'Crisis of Liberalism,'" 238–47. See also Dominick LaCapra, "Historical and Literary Approaches to the 'Final Solution': Saul Friedländer and Jonathan Littell," *History and Theory* 50, no. 1 (2011): 71–97.

14. See for example Ulrich Herbert, "Die Stimmen der Opfer," *Suddeutsche Zeitung* (29 September 2006); Klaus-Dietmar Henke, "Die Stimmen der Opfer," *Frankfurter Allgemeine Zeitung* (4 October 2006).

15. "Brandstifter Hitler: Ein Gespräch mit dem Historiker Saul Friedländer über seine große Geschichte des Holocaust," *Die Zeit* (8 March 2007).

16. Friedländer, *The Years of Extermination,* xxv.

17. Ibid., xxvi.

18. For a discussion of this question see the scholarly forum, note 12, and especially the author's and Alon Confino's remarks, as well as the discussion of the first volume of Friedländer's book that treats the first years of the Nazi era before the war broke out. Saul Friedländer *Nazi Germany and the Jews 1933–1939: The Years of Persecution* (New York, 1997). See Dan Stone, *Constructing the Holocaust: A Study in Historiography* (London, 2003), 161–64. For a different assessment, see Carolyn J. Dean, "Minimalism and Victim Testimony," *History and Theory* 49 (2010), 85–99.

19. Shulamit Volkov, "The Holocaust from Every Side," *Haaretz Book Review* (14 October 2009 [in Hebrew]). I am grateful to Prof. Idith Zertal, who brought this quotation to my attention.

20. Friedländer, *Years of Extermination,* xxvi.

21. Omer Bartov, *Erased: Vanishing Traces of Jewish Galicia in Present-Day Ukraine* (Princeton, 2007), xi–xii.

22. Götz Aly, *Into the Tunnel: The Brief Life of Marion Samuel 1931–1943* (New York, 2007).

23. For example Raul Hilberg, *Perpetrators, Victims, Bystanders* (New York, 2007), and Raul Hilberg, *Sources of Holocaust Research: An Analysis* (Chicago, 2001). It is simultaneously important to remember that Hilberg was the editor of the translation into English of the diary of Adam Czerniaków, the head of the Warsaw *Judenrat*.

24. Christopher Browning, *Remembering Survival: Inside a Nazi Slave Labor Camp* (New York, 2010).

25. See also very similarly in Daniel Blatman, *The Death Marches: The Final Phase of Nazi Genocide* (Cambridge, MA, 2010).

26. Christopher Browning, *Ordinary Men: Reserve Police Battalion 101 and the Final Solution in Poland* (New York, 1992).

27. Friedländer, *Nazi Germany*, ch. 3.

28. As stated above, Israeli research rarely dealt with the "murderers," but chiefly with the "victims." However, when it did concern itself with the murderers, its focus was frequently on examining the antisemitic component of Nazi ideology as a dominant element for understanding the final solution. See, for example David Bankier's voluminous writings about the topic of antisemitism in German public opinion, among the Nazi leadership, in opposition circles, and more. For another example, see Yaacov Lozowick, *Hitler's Bureaucrats: The Nazi Security Police and the Banality of Evil* (London, 2002). And see the original and interesting linguistic study by Michman, *The Emergence of the Jewish Ghettos*.

29. For a characterization of this research school, see Dan Michman, "Is There an Israeli School of Holocaust Research? The Holocaust and the study of Antisemitism in the State of Israel," *Zion* 74 (2010): 219–43 [in Hebrew]; Michman, *Holocaust Historiography: A Jewish Perspective* (London, 2003).

30. Philip Friedman, "Problems of Research on the European Jewish Catastrophe," in *The Catastrophe of European Jewry*, ed. Yisrael Gutman and Livia Rothkirchen (Jerusalem, 1976), 643.

31. On this school in Jewish historiography, see David Myers, *Re-Inventing the Jewish Past: European Jewish Intellectuals and the Zionist Return to History* (New York, 1995).

32. See, for example, Dan Michman, "One Theme, Multiple Voices. The Role of Linguistic Cultures in Holocaust Research," in *The Holocaust: The Unique and the Universal: Essays Presented in Honor of Yehuda Bauer*, ed. Shmuel Almog et al. (Jerusalem, 2001), 8–37 (in Hebrew).

33. This school's central journal is *Yad Vashem Studies*, but *Yalkut Moreshet* and *Dapim*, journals which began to appear in English recently, are also identified with this school.

34. Yehuda Bauer, *Rethinking the Holocaust* (New Haven, 2001).

35. Ibid., 120.

36. On this issue see the extensive treatment in David Engel, *Historians of the Jews and the Holocaust* (Stanford, 2010), ch. 3. For an extended discussion of Engel's book, see Guy Miron, "Bridging the Divide: Holocaust Research vs. Jewish History Research—Problems and Challenges," *Yad Vashem Studies* 38, no. 2 (2010): 155–93.

37. See, for example, the article "Resistance," in the *Encyclopedia of the Holocaust*, ed. Israel Gutman (Jerusalem, 1990), 1265–72, which is representative of this school.

38. See, for example, Israel Gutman, *Struggle in Darkness* (Tel-Aviv, 1985), 81 [in Hebrew].

39. In this context, see the critique by Gilbert, *Music in the Holocaust*, esp. 1–20; and Amos Goldberg, "If This Is a Man: The Image of Man in Autobiographical and Historical Writing during and after the Holocaust," *Yad Vashem Studies* 33 (2005): 381–429.

40. For the significance of this premise in the context of Holocaust research, see Otto Dov Kulka, "The 'Reichsvereinigung' of the Jews in Germany 1938/9–1943," in *Patterns of Jewish Leadership in Nazi Europe 1933–1945*, ed. Yisrael Gutman and Cynthia J. Haft (Jerusalem, 1979), 45–58. See also David Engel's comments explaining the antagonism of the Jerusalem school toward Hilberg, because, among other things, his arguments "violated the fundamental principle of Jewish historiography upon which Dinur [one of the founders of the Jerusalem School] and his followers insisted—the historical unity and continuity of the Jewish people." *Historians of the Jews*, 140.

41. Friedländer, *The Years of Extermination*, 5.

42. Christopher Browning, "Evocation, Analysis, and the 'Crisis of Liberalism.'"

43. See, for example, in various contexts, Friedländer, *The Years of Extermination*, 458, 623, 528. Historian David Cesarani has also commented on this topic in "'Integrative and Integrated History': A Sweeping History of the Shoah Rooted in Everyday Life—and Death," *Yad Vashem Studies* 36, no. 1 (2008): 271–77.

44. Friedländer, *The Years of Extermination*, 192.

45. Alan Mintz, *Popular Culture and the Shaping of Holocaust Memory in America* (Seattle, 2001), 36–84.

46. Samuel D. Kassow, *Who Will Write Our History? Emmanuel Ringelblum, the Warsaw Ghetto, and the Oyneg Shabes Archive* (Bloomington, 2007).

47. A different approach is that of the Israeli literary and cultural scholar, Yechiel Szeintuch. See, for example, Yechiel Szeintuch, *Isaiah Spiegel—Yiddish Narrative Prose from the Lodz Ghetto* (Jerusalem, 1995), 7–92 [in Hebrew].

48. See, for example, Michal Unger, *Łódź: the Last Ghetto in Poland* (Jerusalem, 2005), 343–89 [in Hebrew]; Yisrael Gutman, *The Jews of Warsaw, 1939-1943: Ghetto, Underground, Revolt* (Bloomington, 1982), 107–16; Renée Poznanski, *Jews in France during World War II* (Hanover, 2001).

49. For a similar discussion, which arrives at similar conclusions regarding the future of the field in the framework of cultural history, see Miron, "Bridging the Divide."

50. Lynn Hunt, "Introduction: History, Culture, and Text," in *The New Cultural History*, ed. Hunt (Berkeley, 1989), 12.

51. Emil Utitz, *Psychologie des Lebens im Konzentrationslager Theresienstadt* (Vienna, 1948). I wish to thank Dr. Nitzan Lebovic for drawing my attention to this fascinating study.

52. Utitz, *Psychologie*, 5.

53. In this, his writing is reminiscent of that of Bruno Bettelheim and Viktor Frankl, although he does not attempt to establish a psychological theory, but only to analyze ghetto life from the perspective of social psychology.

54. Utitz, *Psychologie*, 17.

55. Ibid., 19–20.

56. Marc Bloch, *The Historian's Craft* (Manchester, 1967); Paul Fussell, *The Great War and Modern Memory* (New York, 1975); Jean Noël Kapferer, *Rumors: Uses, Interpretations, and Images* (New Brunswick, 1990).

57. Alexandra Garbarini, *Numbered Days: Diaries and the Holocaust* (New Haven, 2006), ch. 2.

58. The Moreshet Archive, D.2.470.

59. Nahman Blumenthal, "Magical Thinking in the Era of Nazi Occupation," *Yad Vashem Studies* 5 (1963): 175–86 [in Hebrew].

60. Roni Stauber, The *Holocaust in Israeli Public Debate in the 1950s: Ideology and Memory* (London, 2007); Boaz Cohen, "The Birth Pangs of Holocaust Research in Israel," *Yad Vashem Studies* 33 (2005): 203–43.

61. Cohen, "The Birth Pangs," 208.

62. Samuel Gringauz, "The Ghetto as an Experiment of Jewish Social Organization (Three Years of Kovno Ghetto)," *Jewish Social Studies* 11 (1949): 3–20; Samuel Gringauz, "Some Methodological Problems in the Study of the Ghetto," *Jewish Social Studies* 12 (1950): 65–72. For a biographical consideration of Gringauz, see the extensive discussion in Zeev W. Mankowitz, *Life Between Memory and Hope: The Survivors of the Holocaust in Occupied Germany* (New York, 2002).

63. On this tradition and its relationship to diary writing during the Holocaust, see Samuel Kassow, "Vilna and Warsaw, Two Ghetto Diaries: Herman Kruk and Emmanuel Ringelblum," in *Holocaust Chronicles: Individualizing the Holocaust through Diaries and Other Contemporaneous Personal Accounts*, ed. Moses Shapiro (Hoboken, 1999), 171–216.

64. Samuel Kassow, "Oyerbach Rokhl," in *The Yivo Encyclopedia of Jews in Eastern Europe*, vol. 2 (New Haven, 2008), 1301–02.

65. Yosef Zelkowicz, *In Those Terrible Days: Notes from the Lodz Ghetto*, ed. Michal Unger (Jerusalem, 2002), 139–41 (emphasis added).

66. Gutman, *The Jews of Warsaw*.

67. Arnold van Gennep, "The Rites of Passage," in *Death, Mourning and Burial: A Cross-Cultural Reader*, ed. Antonius C.G.M. Robben (Malden, MA, 2004), 213–23. See also Phyllis Palgi and Henry Abramovitch, "Death: A Cross-Cultural Perspective," *Annual Reviews in Anthropology* 13 (1984): 385–417.

68. Avriel Bar-Levav, "Death and the Dead," *The Yivo Encyclopedia*, vol. 1, 396–99.

69. Barbara Engelking and Jacek Leociak, *The Warsaw Ghetto: A Guide to the Perished City* (New Haven, 2009), 473.

70. Emmanuel Ringelblum, *Notes from the Warsaw Ghetto: The Journal of Emmanuel Ringelblum* (Jerusalem, 1983), 245.

71. Hunt, "Introduction," 13.

72. Mary Douglas, *Purity and Danger: An Analysis of the Concept of Pollution and Taboo* (London, 2002 [1966]).

73. Rachel Auerbach, *In the Streets of Warsaw 1939–1943* (Tel Aviv, 1954) [in Hebrew].

74. Jacek Leociak, *Text in Face of Destruction: Accounts from the Warsaw Ghetto Reconsidered* (Warsaw, 2004), 169–207.

75. Engelking and Leociak, *The Warsaw Ghetto*, 651.

76. Janusz Korczak, *The Warsaw Ghetto Memoirs of Janusz Korczak* (Washington, 1978), 43.

77. Ringelblum, *Notes from the Warsaw Ghetto*, 283.

78. The Moreshet Archive, D.2.470.

79. Victor Klemperer, *LTI* (Leipzig, 1975 [1947]).

80. Matti Bunzl, "*Völkerpsychologie* and German-Jewish Emancipation," in *Worldly Provincialism: German Anthropology in the Age of Empire*, ed. H. Glenn Penny and Matti Bunzl (Ann Arbor, 2003), 47–85. See also Ingrid Belke, "Einleitung," in *Moritz Lazarus und Heymann Steinthal: Die Begründer der Völkerpsychologie in ihren Briefen*, ed. Ingrid Belke (Tübingen, 1971).

81. Nahman Blumenthal, *Verter un vertelekh von der Hurban tekufa* (Tel Aviv, 1981), 7 [in Yiddish].

82. Nahman Blumenthal, ed., "A Valuable Document—The Encyclopedia of the Lodz Ghetto," *Newsletter of the Bet Lohami Ha-Gettaot* 7 (1954): 10–17; 8 (1955): 18–21; 9–10 (1955): 32–35; 11–12 (1955): 28–32; 14–15 (1956): 63–72 [in Hebrew]. See also Robert Kogler and Andrea Löw, "The Encyclopedia of the Lodz Ghetto," in *Kwartalnik Historii Żydów* 206 (2003): 195–208. I wish to thank Yonatan Kanonich for this reference.

83. Oskar Rosenfeld, *In the Beginning Was the Ghetto* (Evanston, 2002), 231.

84. Ibid., 230.

85. Quoted in Tony Judt, *Postwar: A History of Europe since 1945* (New York, 2005), 13 (emphasis added).

86. Rosenfeld, *In the Beginning*, 229 (emphasis added).

87. Hannah Arendt, *The Origins of Totalitarianism* (New York, 1979), 438–39 (emphasis added), 458, and throughout the chapter, 437–79. See also the discussion of the transformation of historical consciousness in the chapters dealing with the *Judenrat*, in Dan Diner, *Beyond the Conceivable: Studies on Germany, Nazism, and the Holocaust* (Berkeley, 2000). For a critique of Arendt's view of this issue, see Michal Aharony, "Hannah Arendt and the Idea of Total Domination," *Holocaust and Genocide Studies* 24, no. 2 (2010): 193–224.

88. Aaron J. Gurjewitsch, *Das Weltbild des mittelalterlichen Menschen* (Munich, 1996).

89. Garbarini, *Numbered Days*; Leociak, *Text in Face of Destruction*. See also Engelking and Leociak, *The Warsaw Ghetto*.

90. Linda Green, "Fear as a Way of Life," in *Genocide: An Anthropological Reader*, ed. Alexander Laban Hinton (Oxford, 2002), 311.

91. On this issue, see Goldberg, "The Victim's Voice." For an excellent summary of the ethical stance toward the witness, see Michal Givoni, *Witnessing in Action: Ethics and Politics in Humanitarians without Borders*, PhD thesis, Tel Aviv University, 2008, esp. ch. 1. See also Didier Fassin and Richard Rechtman, *The Empire of Trauma: An Inquiry into the Condition of Victimhood* (Princeton, 2009).

92. On the construction of the victim as a "martyr," see Paola Traverso's brilliant analysis of Klemperer's diary and its reception in Germany: Paola Traverso, "Victor Klemperers Deutschlandbild," *Tel Aviver Jahrbuch für deutsche Geschichte* 26 (1997): 307–44.

CHAPTER 5

National Socialism, Holocaust, and Ecology

BOAZ NEUMANN

We hope that the time will come one day when it will no longer be necessary to speak about National Socialism, but that it will be the very air that we breathe!
—Joseph Goebbels, *Reden 1932–1939*

The 1990s saw the emergence of a new and surprising research field, establishing a link between the Nazi and ecological movements. Historians began considering whether the Nazi Party, movement, and regime were actually ecological, not to say green. One of the first milestones was *Blood and Soil: Richard Walther Darré and Hitler's "Green Party"* (1985) by the historian Anna Bramwell, who argued that a green wing can be identified in the Nazi movement, including those she calls "Green Nazis." Bramwell concentrated on the figure of Walther Darré, Minister of Food and Agriculture in Hitler's government, and the Weltanschauung focusing on the principles of *Blut und Boden* (blood and soil). According to Bramwell, Darré was the head of the Nazi Party's "green" wing which influenced central figures such as Hitler and Himmler. She called Darré "green" because during the Third Reich period he promoted organic farming and supported methane gas plants and suitable machinery for small farms, preferring horse-drawn ploughs to combine harvesters. Darré was interested in the dangers of erosion, a topic which he also investigated.[1] The 1990s saw the publication of a flood of studies on the subject. One of the prominent books was titled *How Green Were the Nazis?* (2005).[2] It would thus appear that a positive answer to the question has already been provided.

Notes for this section begin on page 121.

In this chapter I will discuss the issue of a possible link between the Nazi and ecological movements (Part 1), focusing on the historical, historiographical, and methodological implications for Holocaust studies. I will consider whether the Holocaust can indeed be considered not only as an ideological, political, socioeconomic, ethnic and racial project, but also as an ecological *project* (Part 2), and even as an ecological *event* (Part 3). Moreover, I will argue that with regard to the issue of the Holocaust and ecology, "ecologism" can function for historians not only as a historical characteristic of the Holocaust, but also as a methodology in and for Holocaust studies.

Nazism and Ecologism

In July 1935, the German government under Adolf Hitler enacted the Reich Nature Protection Law.[3] Unlike previous similar legislation, this time the legislation was federal in nature, rather than a local bylaw or regulation. The Reich Nature Protection Law was of unprecedented scope. Its purpose was "the protection and fostering of our indigenous nature in all its manifestations"—flora and non-huntable fauna, natural monuments and their surroundings, nature reserves and other parts of the open countryside, whose preservation is in the general interest on the grounds of their rareness, beauty, or special nature or because of their importance to science, habitat, forestry, or hunting. The law further stipulated that it was prohibited to remove, damage, or change a registered natural monument without permission. The same applies to its protected surroundings. The law also defined the mechanism for defining Reich nature reserves and to this end gave the state the right to expropriate the requisite areas. It further stipulated that no legal remedy would be available to those likely to be injured by it, such as where land was confiscated or some right denied. In order to apply the law, the Reich Nature Protection Office was set up. Those who transgressed the law ran the risk of being fined or sent to jail for up to two years. Britain did not reach such a legislative level until after World War II, and France not until the 1960s.[4]

The Reich Nature Protection Law was only one of the Nazis' ecological or green legislative triumphs. There were also other laws and regulations that, for example, protected fauna and forests, attempts to enact federal legislation to prevent air pollution, and more. The Nazis reduced and forbade the slaughter of unstunned animals, hunting and experiments on animals, promoted programs for studying and providing training in the animal protection field, and so on.[5] The related legislation was typified by its great detail. Thus the Animal Protection Law of 24 November 1933 forbade such activities as releasing tamed animals into the wild, using animals in public amusements, the use of blinders on horses, cockfights, bullfights, clipping the ears of dogs, and more. The law specifically stipulated that animals were to be protected not for the sake of human beings but "for their own sakes."⁶ On 14 January 1936, the government enacted the Law on the Slaughter and Holding of Fish and Cold-Blooded Animals. According to this piece of legislation, lobsters and other crustaceans were to be killed by placing them in water that had already been brought to the boil, making their death swift and sure.⁷

Were the Nazis really ecologically minded, really "green"? We must first and foremost examine the historical context. In contemporary terms, the answer will be negative. Until the 1960s and 1970s, ecological and green ideas were almost ignored, not to say unknown. They certainly had almost no impact on political and social interests, let alone economic ones, and undoubtedly did not supersede them. Not until the economic growth in the West from the end of World War II until the mid-1970s did the background and basis for turning ecological and green ideas into an effective agenda come about for the first time in this part of the world. This took place against the background of social challenges to the authority of state and establishment, the civil rights movement, the rise of the second wave of the feminist movement, and so on. It was not until the 1960s that "planet earth" became part of the political, social, and economic agenda. Only then did genuine ecological and green movements, organizations, and parties appear, in other words ones which even subordinated political, social, and economic interests to ecological and green ones. And only then did universalist, globalist views of nature and the environment appear. In 1969, the Friends of the Earth organization was set up in the United States, followed in 1971 by Greenpeace. The first green party in history was New Zealand's Values Party, formed from local citizens groups in 1972.⁸ It goes without saying that nowhere in the Nazi Party's platform, in *Mein Kampf*, or in any other Nazi programmatic text would we find anything that today could be referred to as an ecological or green agenda. And in the historical context, such an agenda is, as I have argued, based on a preference for the ecological and green over political, socioeconomic interests, and, in the Nazi case, definitely ethnic and racial ones, too.

Nevertheless, we are unable to solve the issue by concluding that the Nazis were certainly not ecological and green. After all, there definitely was both ecological and green legislation, as well as practice in the same vein. I would contend that it would be a mistake for us to judge using notions of the 1960s and 1970s a phenomenon from a number of decades earlier. Such an approach would be a historical anachronism. Nevertheless, henceforth the discussion will have to be sensitive to this historical context. It may therefore be asserted that while the Nazis were not green and ecological in terms of the green and ecological agenda of the last third of the twentieth century, it may well be the case that they were in the "ecological" and "green" terms of the first half of the twentieth century. Henceforth, therefore, I will write the adjectives "ecological" and "green" in quotation marks when they are used in the context of our discussion of Nazism, in order to remind us of the historical context.

It may be said, therefore, that Nazi legislation and practice were "ecological" and "green" to a certain extent. That being the case, did the Nazis deserve to be called "ecological" and "green"? One possibility is to understand Nazi "ecological" and "green" legislation and practice and Nazi "greenness" as a chance matter, one having no substantial link with this content. In fact, from the beginning of the twentieth century, many in Germany—individuals, pressure groups, and environmentalist associations—tried to promote legislation along the lines enacted by the Nazis. One example was the *Deutscher Bund Heimatschutz* (Homeland Protection Association of Germany), established in 1904.[9] There were also various local successes. However, they all failed in their efforts to enact legislation on a federal level. The most bitter disappointment occurred during the Weimar Republic, which was perceived as, and to a large extent was in fact, politically impotent. In this sense, the institution of the Third Reich was an excellent opportunity to promise "ecological" and "green" legislation on the federal level. However, this legislation did not necessarily come about because the Nazi regime had an "ecological" and "green" Weltanschauung, but rather because it was a dictatorial regime. In such regimes, it is easier to "move things along" than in liberal parliamentary systems such as the Weimar Republic. From this point of view, the link between the German "ecological" and "green" movement and the Nazi regime may be seen as the outcome of opportunism by the former. The Nazis, following this narrative, were not "ecological" and "green," but simply totalitarian.

However, it takes two to tango. Without cooperation from the Nazi government and establishment, "ecological" and "green" legislation would not have been able to come about. Here it may be argued that the Nazis for their part were interested in and promoted such legislation, not necessarily because of their interest in this agenda, but, for example, for purely propaganda purposes. "Ecological" and "green" legislation was also a way of consolidating the new regime's position as it sought legitimization among its political partners and public opinion. Following this explanation, the Nazis were not "ecological" and "green," but simply opportunistic.

Even if we argue that the Nazi Party, movement, and regime were not "ecological" and "green," in other words not standard bearers for this kind of an agenda overpowering political and economic interests, as a movement with right-wing, conservative, and extreme nationalist characteristics, it was also sensitive and open to "ecological" and "green" ideas as part of an outlook seeking to safeguard and conserve the German *Heimat,* or homeland—German nature, land, and scenery. The stress here is of course on preserving national natural resources and in no way whatsoever on preserving nature on an international level. And when one thinks about it, what modern nationalist movement has not sanctified the nation's soil and scenery as an external expression of the *Volksgeist?* We should remember in this context that politically the modern ecological idea originates from the conservative Right, a point to which I will return later.¹⁰ The Left did not espouse these ideas because it put its faith in industrialization and the principles of progress. The Nazi movement and the "ecological" and "green" movement shared not only an interest in conserving the country's natural resources, its soil, and its scenery, but also in other ideological components such as the urgent need for national regeneration, the idealization of the farming class, a belief in a Greater Germany and the principles of the *Volksgemeinschaft* (people's community), and fierce anticommunism. A certain degree of antisemitism was also not absent from German environmentalist circles.¹¹ Following this narrative the Nazis were not "ecological" and "green," but conservative and nationalistic.

Whether or not the Nazis were "ecological" and "green" is perhaps actually irrelevant to the outcome. First of all because even if this legislation was implemented—and of course this was not always the case—something got lost between the letter of the law and its application. Studies of the Reich Nature Protection Law, for example, found that bureaucratic and budgetary problems made it impossible to apply the provisions, whether in part or in full. Even when the law was implemented, it did not actually bring about the desired environmental change, and instead had only a superficial effect. Instead of changing the environment's ecological status, those who applied the law made do with sporadically removing aesthetic nuisances only, rather than tackling the cause of water pollution, for example.¹² In the case of air pollution, the actual legislation was never put into practice.¹³

Evaluated by the final outcome, the Nazi regime was destructive to the environment. The Four-Year Plan, announced in 1936, was designed to make the German economy autarkic and pave the way to war. This plan, in combination with arms-development programs that had already begun, as well as plans to reinvigorate the economy by means of what was known as the "battle for production," made a mockery out of all efforts to protect the environment against over-exploitation of resources and systematic destruction. Section 6 of the Reich Nature Protection Law stated explicitly that nature conservation was not to impair the use of areas that exclusively or predominantly serve the needs of the armed forces, major public highways, maritime and inland navigation, or vital economic concerns.

Moreover, what weight is to be ascribed to the legislation and the application of "ecological" and "green" principles in light of the environmental catastrophes brought about by the Nazis in World War II? A "green" and "ecological" movement and regime do not undertake a systematic "scorched earth" policy, including ruining the lives of tens of millions, and murdering and exterminating millions more. The Nazis were undoubtedly far more ideological than "ecological," far more "brown" than "green," and more than "brown" and "green" they were "bloody" all over.

Is an argument about the Nazis' "ecologism" anecdotal at best, not to say negligible? Ultimately, is this argument nothing but an upshot of contemporary interest in ecology blowing up something marginal during the Nazi period out of all proportion? Historically speaking, studies of the "ecological" and "green" components of Nazism offer us a topic and research area unknown until the 1980s and 1990s. In historiographical terms, we have here a contribution that places the Nazi phenomenon within the history of the ecological and green movement in the twentieth century, given, of course, the correct historical context to this discussion. From the methodological point of view, however, I do not think this debate makes a meaningful contribution to the study of Nazism and the Holocaust. The methodology applied is often traditional. For example, authors examine the links between the two movements on the social, ideological, and establishment-functional levels, while making a distinction between intent, action, and outcome, and so on

The Holocaust as an Ecological Project

I am unfamiliar with a single historian who unreservedly contends that the Holocaust generally, and, in particular, its final stages as they occurred in the East from 1941–1942 on may be described, explained, and understood as an ecological project. The closest thing to such a contention is that of historian David Blackbourn, who in his book on the conquest of nature in modern Germany asks: "Was there some kind of perverse connection between genocide and ecological sensitivity that made Nazis eager to save the wetlands and the forests while they planned the destruction of fellow humans who lived in them?"[14] According to Blackbourn, the possible connection between Nazi "ecological sensitivity" and genocide is primarily instrumental. In order to bring about their desired ecology in the form of Lebensraum in the East, the Nazis used Slav and Jewish slave labor, for example, in order to deal with the marshlands. In such places their victims could be worked to exhaustion or beyond. This was also the case at Auschwitz, established on the marshes of Upper Silesia. Primo Levi, quoted by Blackbourn, wrote that Auschwitz was the "ultimate drainage point of the German Universe," thereby managing to express the thinking of his murderers: from their point of view, "drainage" was both a metaphor and a concrete reality.[15] Blackbourn identifies another possible link between Nazi "ecological sensitivity" and genocide, which is also basically instrumental. Professionals from a variety of disciplines were involved in the policy of creating *Lebensraum* in the East, including environmental design and conservation experts. Among other things they operated in such fields as conservation areas, planting, afforestation, agriculture, and soil erosion.[16] Being involved in creating Lebensraum in the East, they also participated—directly or indirectly—in the genocide that took place in this part of the world.

Blackbourn was right about the possible link between Nazi "ecological sensitivity" and genocide, but in my view he did not go far enough, beyond the instrumental ties between the two phenomena. My understanding is that Nazi ecology cannot be subsumed as "ecological sensitivity" alone, but is an expression of a Weltanschauung, a way of looking at the world. As I shall show, nor is this a "perverse" connection between ecology and the Holocaust, but a fundamental, even mandatory one. Furthermore, in the Holocaust I would not only identify an ecological project, but would also see ecologism itself as a methodology that can be used in Holocaust studies.

In order to enable us to use "ecology" both as a historical characteristic of the Holocaust and as a methodology in Holocaust studies, we must go beyond the discussion presented in the first part of this paper, limited to examining the link between the ecological and Nazi movements in the historical context of the twentieth century. I will, therefore, now go back to the nineteenth century and the original meaning of the term "ecology," as coined in 1866 by the biologist and zoologist Ernst Haeckel: "By ecology, we mean the whole science of the relations of the organism to the environment, including, in the broad sense, all the 'conditions of life.'"[17] Haeckel, it should be remembered, was one of the authors of racist theory in the second half of the nineteenth century, supported the Spartan outlook of undertaking a physical examination and selection of newborns, and further advocated the killing of the handicapped and sick.[18]

In addition to the historical interpretations of the Holocaust as an ideological, political, socioeconomic, ethnic, and racial project, I thus suggest describing, explaining and understanding the Holocaust as an ecological project in the original sense of the notion as defined by Haeckel: a project based on a Weltanschauung and practice operating where the organism is bound up with the environment, a project relating to "conditions of life."

The Nazi Weltanschauung was undoubtedly obsessive about the relationship between the organism in general, and the human organism specifically, and their environment. And Nazi practice was primarily designed to bring about ecological order in this complex of relationships—to leave some human beings in their environment, "to return" others to their environment, and "to remove" yet others from their environment. Through these three operations, according to the Nazi Weltanschauung, the relationship between the organism and its environment would be restored to its optimum condition, because the relationship between the human organism and its environment was viewed by Nazis as two-way—humans influencing their environment and their environment influencing them. This is illustrated by the following description of the relationship between the two. It is a typical Nazi argument, advanced in a document issued by the Reichsführer SS, SS-Head Office, and entitled *Racial Policy* (1943):

> Just as a plant or an animal only develops fully in an environment favorable to it, so man too [the Nordic race] first needs a natural environment to guarantee his growth and development. Inferior races make do with the space given them by nature, but from the very beginning the creative Nordic race has shaped its natural

environment to suit its natural abilities, so that the German land today in all its parts bears the imprint of the Nordic man.... The existence of a *Volk* depends on its having sufficient space for its natural growth, because otherwise it must wilt like a plant that lacks soil, air, and light. As a race of farmers and warriors, in order to fully develop its natural abilities, the Nordic race in particular needs sufficient space in which to live and which it can shape to suit its nature.[19]

This Nazi Weltanschauung contains no innovations. It draws on many different traditions—German romanticism, the back-to-nature movement, Social Darwinism, geopolitics, the politics of *Lebensraum,* and more. However, pragmatically speaking, the question of whether there was anything new in the Nazi environmental views, or alternatively whether this was a direct continuation, an aberration, or a complete distortion of these traditions, is irrelevant to what is under discussion here.

The Nazi Weltanschauung was based on a dual, complementary movement of creating Lebensraum for "the worthy," while destroying the *Lebensraum* of the "unworthy," and first and foremost of the Jews. In the case of the Jew, the Other, the process of ecological shaping—involving the relationship between the organism and its environment and affecting "conditions of life"—is absolutely clear. Nazi urban space in the shape of the New German City could not have come about without the Jews being confined to the urban space they deserved—the ghetto. The political and social space of the Nazi "agora"—the mass meeting and the stadium—could not have taken place without removing Jews to the political and social space that they deserved—the camp. The Nazi ethnic-biological-racist space of the Lebensraum in the East could not have existed without the extermination of the Jew in the space of the camp—the extermination camp.[20] This process was not arbitrary, and was based inter alia on ecological insights. Any space allocated to a *Reichsdeutscher* or *Volksdeutscher* (Reich or ethnic Germans) or a Jew was so allocated because it was environmentally suitable for them. When Himmler wanted to justify cramming the Jews into the ghettos, he argued that this step was taken because a crowded, congested, and chaotic urban space suited them, since "[t]he Jew always has catacombs, passages, channels. This is an ancient system. He is an ancient nomad."[21]

In practice, the Holocaust took place in the Lebensraum areas in the East. The Nazi plan was based on settling the *Volksdeutsche* in these areas, on Germanizing the local populations, on the spiritual, economic and physical enslavement, transfer or extermination of populations. This policy was based on the *Generalplan Ost* (General Plan East), which was officially formulated for the first time in 1940–1941 and underwent a number of transformations in the wake of the changing circumstances resulting from the war. The plan laid down a new and revolutionary spatial order. With regard to the Slavs and Jews, who made up some 30 to 40 million people defined as "racial undesirables," the plan stated that they were to be deported and in part exterminated (*Ausrottung*). A second group who numbered in the millions, people of German descent—*Volksdeutsche,* Dutch, Norwegians and others—was supposed to settle the occupied territories, particularly rural areas. A third group comprising an estimated 14 million Slavs was intended to remain where they were and act as forced laborers.[22] A document issued by the Reich Security Main Office in December 1942 defined four categories and practices for dealing with the population in the East: co-existence with racially and ethnically equal *Volk* groups; *Umvolkung* (assimilation) of an alien *Volkstum* in the German *Volkstum*; a *räumliche Verdrängung* (spatial expulsion) of an alien *Volkstum*; and the physical *Vernichtung* (extermination) of the alien *Volkstum* which was "undesired" in the power sphere of the German Reich.[23]

The working hypothesis of these programs was primarily ecological and sought to adjust the inanimate, flora, fauna, and human aspects of the environment. The structure of the "areas that had come home to the Reich" was based primarily on housing developments involving the countryside and farms designed to make these *Gaue* or administrative districts "home" to an ever greater number of German people. Right from the outset, "exemplary attention" was devoted to constructing farms and housing developments in the new Reich—a significant starting point for the broad and sweeping goal of establishing a "German cultural countryside" in the "new territory in the East."[24]

In December 1942 Heinrich Himmler issued an order about shaping the landscape in the incorporated Eastern Territories, designed to adapt them to the *Volksdeutsche* presence there. These territories, he asserted, had been spoiled by the local populations. As he put it, broad swathes of the countryside in the incorporated Eastern Territories "have been neglected, laid waste and despoiled 'by the cultural incompetence of alien *Volkstum.*'"[25] According to Himmler, the *Volksdeutsche* had a particularly harmonious relationship with nature and their surroundings. This was the source of one of the major guidelines regarding expansion into this area, relating to its ecology. "Hence if the new living areas are to become home to the settlers, it will be absolutely vital that developments in the countryside be planned and shaped in a way that is close to nature. This is one of the bases for strengthening German *Volkstum.*"[26]

Himmler's view was that such matters as removing an alien population from the *Lebensraum* in the East, not to mention its elimination, constitute a key element in influencing its ecology. This was not, however, enough. "Hence it is not sufficient to settle our *Volkstum* in these areas and exclude foreign *Volkstum*. Rather, these areas must be shaped in accordance with their character so that the Germanic person will feel at home, will settle there and be prepared to love and defend this, his new home."[27] Only in an area which has ecological value can a *Volksdeutsche* exist and develop. The development and shaping of the race's creative forces can only be influenced by an appropriate environment. The "green nature of a rural environment" has a large number of diverse purposes: it makes it easier to defend and launch an attack from a particular area. It also improves general economic farming circumstances; in particular it is the basis for promoting plant and animal habitats in both woodland and open country, to protect and enhance the topsoil and so on. In conclusion, Himmler observes: "The face of the countryside should be the most beautiful and valuable expression of the *Volks- und Raumgemeinschaft* (ethnic and spatial community)."[28] This document also specifies the actions needed in order to adapt the *Lebensraum* in the East to its stated purpose, from dealing with flora and fauna, through how to construct roads and streets, villages and towns, to industrial areas. All of this was laid down in parallel to the demand that populations deserving of expulsion and elimination be dealt with accordingly.

The Holocaust thus inescapably became part of an ecological project that, in addition to dealing with the inanimate, flora, and fauna, also had to deal with the human element. From the Nazi ecological point of view, the creation of an environment also comprises a human ecology in the shape of murdering human beings. It is of interest in this context to note an additional ecological possibility that was brought up at the time—the enclosing of the Jews in a special reserve known, inevitably, as the "*Judenreservat.*"[29]

In the Nazis' Weltanschauung, the Jew—the Other—was perceived not only as a "problem" in ideological, political, socioeconomic, ethnic, racial, and other terms, but also specifically as an environmental and ecological problem, as a genuine "ecological hazard." In Nazi eyes, the Jew was considered a soiled and soiling figure, contaminated and contaminating. The Jew lived in *Schmutz* (filth), and was himself *schmutzig* (filthy).[30] The Jew was considered the "embodiment of the ugly and the filthy."[31] In the well-known Nazi collection of stories for children *Der Giftpilz* (*The Poison Mushroom*) (1938), we find all the stereotypes and clichés about the Jew in this context. The Jew is presented as having "filthy" ears.[32] He himself is a "poison mushroom."[33] The Jew's being is fundamentally adverse to nature, and the writer bases his argument on an alleged quotation from the Talmud: "There is no lower occupation than farming. Commerce is far more bearable."[34] The text then continues: "The Gentiles are created to serve the Jews. They must plow, sow, weed, dig, reap, bundle, sort and grind. The Jews are created to find everything ready."[35] In this collection of stories, the Jews are depicted as torturers, cruel beings who murder animals—unless they themselves are portrayed as animals of the most loathsome kind, such as rats.[36] Acting in this way also gives them great pleasure. Below a picture describing Jews killing a cow is the following text: "The animal falls to the ground again. It dies slowly. But the Jews stand around and laugh about it."[37]

For the Nazis, the Jews' capitalist, commercial, urban, intellectual, rootless, parasitic way of life makes them the embodiment of a threat to German nature: for example, a threat to the German forests.[38] They are perceived as people who are at the very bottom of the natural hierarchy, or even outside it, and hence as parasites living at the expense of nature or as entities that live in an unnatural and anti-natural fashion respectively.[39] The dichotomy between the Jew and (German) nature, between Jewish existence and natural existence, is demonstrated in the view that the Jew has no territory and hence is not involved in, does not wish to be involved in, and is unable to be involved in, what Adolf Hitler and many others identified as the most basic process in history—the struggle for life and self-preservation fought through the struggle for soil and *Lebensraum*. As a being lacking all ties to concrete territory, the Jew is an ahistorical element in history and hence can be removed, especially by the Nazis who were so obsessive in their attempts to achieve Lebensraum.[40] Carl Schmitt roundly condemned the Versailles Treaty, arguing that its authors had failed to recognize the concept of "natural borders" and instead created a text that contained only "positivistic" formulations based on arbitrary decisions regarding borders.[41] This positivistic western view of "*Entterritorialisierung*" or deterritorialization is, in his view, manifestly influenced by "Jewish thinking": "The special features of Jewish existence result in this absence of any natural ties with the tangible ground."[42]

The classic Nazi position on the issue of the relationship between the Jew and the environment and nature may be found in a 1939 article titled "Jews and nature conservation," published in *Naturschutzparke,* the journal of the Conservation Associations. The article was apparently written by the chairman of the association, Heinrich Wilckens. In it the Jew is described as having no homeland and no ties with the land. The central argument is that only somebody who loves the land where he or she was born, and only somebody who "feels at one with it" can grasp the idea of nature conservation. Which is the very reason why the Jew must be obstructed:

> Since he sought to subjugate the world as he wanders restlessly, he has never gained an innermost relationship to the earth on which he lived as a parasite. The ground and earth lack meaning for him unless he can turn them into movables. Land has no significance for him, but its mortgage does; an animal has no significance, but its market value does.... Judaism and German nature are irreconcilable concepts. And only after warding off the final remnants of Jewish subversive spirit can we entirely understand the great thought of nature conservation as well.[43]

Sociologist Zygmunt Bauman suggested seeing in the Holocaust an expression of gardening practice, focusing above all on distinguishing between cultivated plants and weeds. Tending to the former and removing the latter are actually one and the same action. Hence weeding is not destructive, but creative.[44] The Nazis definitely acted as gardeners tending to the Lebensraum as if it was their garden. Not without reason was the Jew viewed by them as an "*Unkraut*" (weed), an "*Ungeziefer*" (pest, vermin), to be eradicated.[45] When the Nazis tried to explain and justify such radical actions as eliminating those with hereditary diseases, promoting those clans whose ethnic background was considered valuable, and keeping their blood clean, they drew their justification from the world of flora and fauna. Here is a typical Nazi argument, in an attempt to explain the law of selection on the basis of observations of plant life:

> Our natural forest is sustained by self-reproduction. Seeds fall from the parent tree onto the forest floor. Numerous saplings develop. And here the struggle for existence begins. Some of the young plants grow up above their neighbors like a "master stratum," striving to achieve the sunlight. According to the law of combat, those that remain behind in the shadow of the "big ones" are condemned to a miserable existence. And furthermore, one day the forester appears with his cleaver and cleans things out. The trees that have grown best are allowed to survive, but he fells the others. In this way he speeds up the eradication of those which are not sufficiently viable. Those that are left now have all the light, space, and food, and can develop fully. Once the old generation disappears, the elite of the young trees will constitute the new forest.[46]

In addition, the process of creating *Lebensraum* involved soil specialists, foresters, botanists, and plant geneticists.[47] Two outstanding figures in this area were landscape and garden architects and designers Alwin Seifert and Heinrich Friedrich Wiepking-Jürgensmann. In the biographical encyclopedia *Who's Who of Munich Cultural Life* (1937), Seifert is referred to as a passionate gardener, and the entry says that through his work "all of Germany has become his garden."[48] Seifert was the most prominent environmentalist in Nazi Germany and was awarded the title of *Reichslandschaftsanwalt* (Reich landscape advocate). Among other things, he was a leading adviser for the landscaping of the autobahn.[49] Wiepking-Jürgensmann was far more influential than Seifert in all matters relating to landscape design in the Eastern occupied territories. At the end of 1939, shortly after the invasion of Poland, Wiepking-Jürgensmann published an article in which he envisaged the advent of "a golden age for the German landscape and garden designer that will surpass everything that even the most enthusiastic among us had previously dreamed."[50] Wiepking-Jürgensmann, who in 1934 was appointed professor and director of the Institute for Garden Design at the Agricultural College of Berlin, not only envisaged the future but also participated in bringing it about. He was Himmler's special appointee for landscape design and served as the main SS adviser on matters relating to the landscaping of the "East," including on the planning and design of the landscape at Auschwitz. Max Fischer, one of his graduate students, wrote a master's thesis in 1943 on planning for the new city of Auschwitz.[51]

And it is in the extermination camp that Nazi human ecology will assume its most extreme, final form. There the Nazi ecological imperative—to make Germany "judenrein"—will be implemented in full. It is no coincidence that both the murderers and the victims gave Auschwitz a name defining it as a place for disposing of waste material—*anus mundi*, the "anal orifice of the world."[52]

I will now focus the discussion on two constitutive technologies of the extermination camp which made it possible to *concentrate* and *murder* people in it—barbed wire fences and Zyklon B gas respectively. I will seek to show that both of these can be read on the basis of a longer, wider-ranging history of establishing and forging an "ecology of modernity." I have borrowed this term from historian Reviel Netz's *Barbed Wire: An Ecology of Modernity* (2004), a history of barbed wire.⁵³ Barbed wire was invented in the United States in 1874 in order to cope with the Great Plains. It was originally intended to prevent the free movement of cattle. Although barbed wire came about as a technology intended for a very specific purpose, it very soon became clear—primarily because it could be used on a large scale, very quickly, and at low cost—that it would change the eternal order of things, by bringing about what Netz calls "an ecology of modernity." Barbed wire made possible the colonization of vast areas, something that had been impossible under the previous system of control points in the classical colonization process. For the first time and without precedent, barbed wire made it possible to define open spaces on an almost immediate basis.

Netz identifies three historical stages in the development of modern ecology based on barbed wire. The first was that of *expansion,* which began in North America. As indicated above, during this stage the main use of barbed wire was the rapid colonization of open spaces. The second stage was one of *confrontation,* with barbed wire acting as a means of defense in warfare. This stage reached its acme in an entire generation which literally "barbed-wired" itself to death in the trenches of World War I. The third and final stage was that of *containment*, with barbed wire serving as a means of incarcerating people.

The history of barbed wire started with the fencing in of cattle. However, this very quickly moved on to people—insurgents in colonies (in South Africa in the British case, and in German South-West Africa, today's Namibia, in the German case), prisoners-of-war and foreign civilians (in World War I in all the belligerent countries), or the state's own citizens (mainly in the USSR). This wretched history also continued on to the Nazi concentration and death camps. However, in the Nazi death camps they were no longer incarcerated as human beings—as insurgents, as POWs, as civilians, as criminals, as homo faber. Now, as in the case of the Jew, they were incarcerated as a biological organism. To some extent this is the closing of a historical circle—a history that began with the fencing in of animals and moved on to human beings, coming full circle with the fencing in of human beings as if they were animals. The Nazi extermination camp was not a human compound but a biological one, and I will go on immediately to argue that it was also an ecological site. This was a site where man was reduced to an organism per se. Many camp inmates testified about themselves that they actually underwent a metamorphosis into animals—they lived like animals, felt like animals, were treated as animals are treated. Primo Levi even went so far as to argue that one of the expressions of this metamorphosis was the scarcity of acts of suicide at the camp. He and his fellow inmates in Auschwitz "lived precisely like enslaved animals that sometimes let themselves die but do not kill themselves."⁵⁴

The site defined by barbed wire affected people through their environment. The barbed wire distanced politics and violence from the body, to continue the Foucauldian line of thought,⁵⁵ producing a new, modern environment and ecology by redefining the relationship between the human organism and its environment. With barbed wire the environment itself became a means of control, monitoring and applying violence. In addition, barbed wire also brought about a new environment, a new ecology on the immediate, experiential level of the person who was fenced in. Barbed wire became an integral, constitutive part of the "nature" and "scenery" of the Holocaust. Abel Herzberg, who was incarcerated in Bergen-Belsen, wrote in his diary: "Around this camp, surrounded by barbed wire and sentries, are more barriers. More sentries with loaded rifles and accompanied by guard dogs."[56] And so, "wherever you stand or go there is barbed wire."[57] Similarly, Kalman Gochman, incarcerated in a ghetto, wrote: "Around the new area of the ghetto there shot up high posts, connected by barbed wire, arrogantly dividing the length and breadth of the streets. At 'sensitive' locations they added high walls of boards so that people outside could not see what was going on inside and in order to make it harder to leave the ghetto.... All of this gives the impression of a large cage for animals."[58] "Suddenly," Gochman writes when he reached Auschwitz,

> you enter an area flooded with dazzling lights, there are high concrete poles, some of them with curved tops, arranged in incredibly straight lines, and on each pole there is a strong light. In the corner there stands out a pole which is four times thicker than the other ones. The poles are interconnected by means of thick high-voltage electrical cables. There is another row of smaller poles connected by barbed wire, parallel to the row of these poles. Between the two rows of poles are coils of barbed wire. All of this gives an impression of a shut-in, isolated fortress.[59]

The limits of the barbed wire were indeed the limits of the prisoners' world.

Psychologist Bruno Bettelheim also reached a fascinating conclusion in terms of how barbed wire impacted the environment in the Third Reich. He argued that the perceptual situation of the camp inmate and that of the free German in Nazi Germany were the same. The camp, as he put it, was not limited to the fenced-off site, nor to all the camps. In Bettelheim's thinking, the camp comprised the whole of Germany. In Nazi Germany, both the incarcerated prisoner and the ostensibly free German were, in fact, in a single enormous camp that no one could escape from. Bettelheim even took his argument to greater extremes, remarking that the only place in Nazi Germany where politics could still be talked about freely was the camp![60] Bettelheim's conclusion is to some extent reinforced by the perceptions of ordinary Germans. The fact is every German might have found him or herself being thrown into a camp sooner or later. Dreams, for example, show this. One case involved a German physician who dreamed that SA men surrounded the hospital where he worked with barbed wire. In another dream he found himself incarcerated in a concentration camp.[61] Thus barbed wire does not have an inside and an outside. Although it is intended to fence off those who are "inside," in a society with so many barbed wire fences, to some extent those who are "outside" these fences start running into them and to a considerable extent start feeling that they too are fenced in.

The extermination camp is not only a camp, in other words a closed, fenced-off site, but also an extermination facility. And the killing technique in the extermination camps was primarily gas-based. Here too we can identify in the use of gas a modern technology which, instead of affecting the victim through his body, did so through the environment or its ecology, in this case by means of polluting or poisoning the air. And in the case of Auschwitz and Majdanek—the most highly industrialized and sophisticated camps in the Nazis' network of camps—we can identify an additional environmental, ecological aspect through the use of Zyklon B, related to its original purpose. (It must be stressed that Zyklon B was used at other extermination and concentration camps but not in the same quantities nor with the same industrial quality as at these two camps.)

Zyklon B was invented in the early 1920s for *Schädlingsbekämpfung* (pest control) purposes. The original Zyklon—subsequently called Zyklon A—was patented in 1920 by Degesch (*Deutsche Gesellschaft für Schädlingsbekämpfung* or German Pest Control Company). For a variety of reasons, one of which was the postwar ban imposed on Germany on using this substance, its other version—Zyklon B—was developed a few years later. In the 1920s and early 1930s, the lethal gas was used mainly for disinfecting closed spaces such as ships, boxcars, hospitals, and hotels. During World War II, Zyklon B was primarily used for the fumigation of military quarters, supplies, uniforms, vehicles, rolling stock, and vessels. During the war it was also used for civilian purposes in the framework of *Schädlingsbekämpfung* programs to disinfect the clothing and belongings of populations such as foreign workers brought to Germany, or new German settlers in the East. Zyklon B was additionally used for disinfecting industrial and agricultural installations and storehouses and milling installations. In addition to the Wehrmacht and various civilian authorities, another large-scale, important, and key customer for the toxic gas was the SS, which also needed it to disinfect closed facilities, primarily in light of the dramatic growth in the number and size of the camps. The most attractive products the SS acquired from Degesch were the so-called circulation chambers that disinfected clothing with warm air and Zyklon B. The Auschwitz authorities ordered 19 of these, although they were never installed at the camp. Such circulation chambers were installed at other camps, such as Sachsenhausen. Both the Wehrmacht and the SS were primarily frightened of typhus outbreaks. According to estimates, just one percent of the poisonous gas was used during World War II to murder by asphyxiation around one million people, overwhelmingly Jewish, mainly at the Auschwitz and Majdanek extermination camps.[62]

The Nazis undoubtedly saw the extermination of the Jews as part of the practice of *Schädlingsbekämpfung*. Proof of this is provided by the very idea of deliberately using a disinfectant agent to murder them, technically based on similar procedures, the use of "for disinfection" signs, and misleading victims moments before their death that they were about to undergo "disinfection."

The argument that the transition from murder by shooting the victims, as in the case of the Einsatzgruppen, and murder using carbon monoxide in gas trucks and the "primitive" extermination camps, to murder by means of Zyklon B occurred for humane reasons—according to the Nazis, the use of Zyklon B prevents the victim from suffering—shows that from their viewpoint, this was not a question of punishment or causing pain, but was rather a disinfection and decontamination procedure.[63] Here is Höss's description of the procedure:

> Death occurred in the crammed full cells immediately after the gas was thrown in. Only a brief choking outcry and it was all over.... I must admit openly that the gassings had a calming effect on me, since in the near future the mass annihilation of the Jews was to begin.... Now we [Eichmann and Höss] had discovered the gas and the procedure. I was always horrified of death by firing squads, especially when I thought of the huge numbers of women and children who would have to be killed.... Now I was at ease. We were all saved from these bloodbaths, and the victims would be spared until the last moment.[64]

We must not forget that the Nazis always identified the Jew as *Schädling,* and hence as requiring disinfection to prevent the outbreak of epidemics. It was not without reason that the disinfection of the Jews was, among other things, called "*Entseuchung*" (decontamination).[65] And for the Nazis, there were no metaphors when it came to the Jews.[66]

The gas-chamber technology enabled the Nazis to switch over to murder, based on creating a lethal environment/ecology. Inside the gas chamber the Jew was deprived of his "*Lebensraum*" in the most straightforward and immediate sense of the word—he was deprived of air to breathe. Depriving the Jew of "*Lebensraum*" was thus a decisive condition for bringing about Nazi *Lebensraum*. What was exterminated in the gas chamber was not only human life but first and foremost the environment, the ecology, that made life possible in the first place.[67]

Barbed wire and Zyklon B—two modern technologies originating in the attempt to control and master the environment and nature (cattle and pests), two technologies that would ultimately be applied to human beings as well (as if they were livestock and vermin)—these two technologies murdered people through the environment. Barbed wire and Zyklon B came together in Nazi Germany to produce the ecology of the Holocaust.

Auschwitz, "Capital of the Holocaust,"[68] is the complete embodiment of the Nazi ecological revolution—a lethal combination of producing Nazi *Lebensraum* by eradicating Jewish "*Lebensraum*." Auschwitz, as described by the historian Sybille Steinbacher, was a *Musterstadt* (model town) where this ecology was put into practice. The decisive moment in the history of turning Auschwitz into a "model town" based on practices of resettlement, Germanization, servitude, ethnic cleansing, and extermination came in the spring of 1941, on the day when it was decided that the IG Farben plant should be constructed nearby. Henceforth, processes of industrialization, urban improvement, and population restructuring would be bound up with processes of concentration, exploitation of the labor force, mass murder, and extermination.

In order to put its plans into practice on the spot, the Nazi government offered incentives and benefits, primarily economic, to all Germans—especially those with the requisite skills—and their families, to get them to move to live in the town. In April 1941 a start was made on cleansing it of its Jewish residents. They were to be replaced by new German settlers. None of Auschwitz's new founders and residents really cared that there was a camp around the corner. The plans, some of which were realized, included the construction of 1,600 apartments measuring 60 to 90 square meters, as well as single-family houses and maisonettes with vegetable gardens and garages. For New Year 1942, the chief director of the rebuilding of Auschwitz, architect Hans Stosberg, was able to send out greeting cards reading: "Birth of the new German town of Auschwitz."[69]

Auschwitz was intended to become a "model town" of the German *Volksgemeinschaft*. It was based on dividing the town into cell-shaped districts with monumental community buildings, parade grounds, showpiece buildings, and Party assembly rooms, an imposing avenue. Whole satellite towns and new districts were planned, twelve schools, six kindergartens, 20 playing-fields, green spaces, and several additional stadiums with swimming pools and playing fields. As part of the plan, the Jewish quarter was intended to be obliterated. A party building with a hotel, a cinema, and a restaurant was to be erected on the ruins of the Jewish cemetery. The Nazis used gravestones for road building. The "model town" was completed with the labor of the camp next to it.

Thus Auschwitz demonstrably became an experimental site for the establishment of a "model town," and for town and country planning. As described by Steinbacher, Auschwitz was characterized by "a pioneering spirit, a belief in the future" of all those new settlers who wanted to plant "German culture" in this location.[70] The same spirit also characterized the activities of garden designers, landscape architects, and botanists, who turned Auschwitz into an experimental site with the encouragement and support of Himmler, who urged the development of recycling refuse and sewage, for biological waste processing, and the growth of plant cultures and technical innovations in the use of slurry and composting.[71]

At the villa of the camp commandant, Rudolf Höss, located on the edge of Auschwitz I and about 145 meters from the camp's gas chamber and the crematorium, was a garden tended by his family and two Polish prisoner-gardeners. Höss's wife, Hedwig, used to grow exquisite flowers in the garden and hothouses. She also ordered seeds and young plants from elsewhere. Höss describes the garden as a "flowery paradise." According to one report, strawberries were sometimes planted there in earth fertilized with human ashes.[72]

To conclude this part of the chapter, here are a number of anecdotes that appear in the memoirs written by Rudolf Höss, who constantly emphasized the many difficulties he encountered in his work as the Auschwitz camp commandant, inter alia, the strenuous and arduous work required of him and the need to deal with particularly painful situations and sights. Moreover, Höss was shocked by the behavior of the Jews—the members of the *Sonderkommando* who collaborated with the murderers in putting to death members of their own people by preparing them for destruction, deceiving them and calming them; the Jewish women who knew or at least guessed their fate and nevertheless played with, amused, and calmed their children and babies before they were murdered.[73] And how did Höss cope with all of these difficulties? One way was by viewing himself as carrying out orders: "I had received an order; I had to carry it out."[74] Alternatively, he cut himself off from his surroundings: "I saw only my work, my duty. All human feelings were pushed aside."[75] Sometimes he drank alcohol which, he said, "put me into a happy mood."[76]

However, Höss also had another, "more natural" way of coping with the difficulties he had to deal with: "When something upset me very much and it was impossible for me to go home to my family, I would climb onto my horse and ride until I chased the horrible pictures away. I often went into the horse stables during the night, and there found peace among my darlings."[77] The "horrible pictures" to which he refers, let us not forget, were composed of the "mass murder" that he was compelled "to coldly watch ... without any regard for the doubts which uprooted my deepest inner feelings." Höss goes on to testify that his family had a "deep love for farming and especially for animals": "Every Sunday I had to drive with them across all the fields, walk them through the stables, and we could never skip visiting the dog kennels. Their greatest love was for our two horses and our colt. The prisoners who worked in the household were always dragging in some animal the children kept in the garden. Turtles, martens, cats, or lizards; there was always something new and interesting in the garden."[78] And what, indeed, could be more therapeutic when dealing with "unnatural" people and situations than returning to nature?

In contrast to what I suggested in the first section of the chapter—which examined the links between the Nazi movement and ecological movement—"ecology" is no longer just a historical phenomenon here but a methodology for studying Nazism and the Holocaust. On the other hand, the choice to engage both phenomena from an ecological perspective and to argue that the Holocaust was an ecological project is not arbitrary at all. Other methodologies, Marxism, for example, observe Nazism and the Holocaust from a critical perspective. They are critical in the sense that their vantage point is located outside the historical phenomenon under examination. In the case of Marxist interpretations of Nazism, one must always remember that, at the end of the day, Nazi Weltanschauung was itself not Marxist! The ecological methodology hence should be regarded alongside other, more traditional methodologies, which include the German *Sonderweg*, non-Marxist theories of Fascism, and bio-politics. It is another methodology for researching Nazism and the Holocaust in phenomenological fashion, that is, one that aims to reveal them as they manifested themselves. More than striving to explain (*erklären*) Nazism and the Holocaust, the ecological methodology aims at understanding (*verstehen*) them in and through their own terms.

The Holocaust as an Ecological Event

I would like to propose another way of conceptualizing the relationship between the Holocaust and ecology. A way that has no link to the historical connections between the "ecological," "green" movement and the Nazi movement, as I proposed in the first part of this chapter. A way that also does not begin with Ernst Haeckel's coining of the concept "ecology" in the 1860s, finding the "ecological" dimensions according to Haeckel in the Nazi policy of *Lebensraum* and extermination.

The path I am proposing here begins with the etymological source of the notion of "eco-logy," which is a combination of the Greek words "oikos" and "logia." The word "oikos" means "house," "dwelling place," or "habitation." An eco-logical policy in this sense means making the world become a "house," "dwelling place," "habitation."[79]

According to Hannah Arendt's well-known and important remark, the Nazis determined in their Weltanschauung "who should and who should not *inhabit* the world."[80] I believe that the profound meaning of this argument can be revealed through its eco-logical meaning in the original etymological sense of the concept. That being the case, the Nazis sought not only to exterminate the Jew politically, socially, racially, biologically. They did not only strive to incarcerate him, remove him, kill him, destroy him. What Arendt means here—and this is the reading I propose—is not only to remove the Jew from the world, but to strip him of the human ability to be-in-the-world. To strip the Jew of what her teacher, Martin Heidegger, would have defined as the ability to *dasein*. And Arendt cannot be understood without Heidegger.

Had Heidegger not remained so silent about the Holocaust[81] and had he made up his mind to say something about it, what he would have said, I believe, would have been in the spirit embodied in Arendt's argument. (It is worth noting that the only time Heidegger mentioned the Holocaust he did so in a technological-ecological context. According to him, agriculture as a motorized food-industry is equivalent to manufacturing corpses in gas chambers and extermination camps.[82]) Heidegger, who at a certain stage went over to the Nazis and was entranced by them, saw "man" as a dwelling creature. When Heidegger argues about the human ability to *dasein,* or to be-in-the-world, he does not mean that "man" is in the world like an object is in a container, for example, like water is in a glass. According to Heidegger, a "man" by being-in-the-world opens up a "place," "makes a room," in which a world appears.

Only "man" has the ability to *be*, and by his *being* all the rest can *be*. Or as Heidegger's commentator, Magda King, put it: "When there is man, the 'there is …' happens; man's factical existence (his being-there) discloses thereness, as the thereness of himself, the thereness of world, and the thereness of being within the world."[83]

Continuing Arendt's general idea, then, what I would call Nazi "eco-logism" did not seek to determine only "who should and who should not *live* in the world." Perhaps Nazi *bio*-logism did try to determine this. Nazi *eco*-logism sought to decide "who should and who should not *inhabit* the world." Hence, the Nazis not only deprived the Jews of their bio-logical ability "to live." They deprived them of far more—they deprived the Jews of their ability "to be." They deprived the Jews of their "there is."

The Holocaust is not only an ecological *project* in which the Jews deserved to be eliminated because they were an "ecological nuisance" in the Nazi ecology, as I proposed in the second part of this chapter. The Holocaust can also be understood as an eco-logical *event* which not only eliminated Jews from the world, but also deprived them of the world as "oikos," that is as "house," "dwelling place," "habitation."

This eco-logical negation was most immediately expressed in the eradication of the Jewish body as if it had never been and would never be. *Sonderkommando* member Shlomo Dragon, a prisoner at Auschwitz, testified that the ashes of the victims' bodies were taken in trucks from the pits near the crematorium to the River Soła. As the ashes were transferred to the river by the *Sonderkommando* personnel, the ground between the trucks and the river was covered with clothing to prevent any residual ash settling on the dirt. When the transfer of the ashes from the trucks to the river was completed, the clothing was shaken into the river.[84]

Isabella Leitner, another Auschwitz prisoner, wrote: "Life denied us the grace of a grave. Just a grave for my mother, my sister, my other sister. Just a grave to bring flowers to…. I crave so a small piece of earth, a testimony that I too had a mother, that this planet is mine too…. *You beast! Give me the body, that frail little body. I want to bury it.*"[85] In Leitner's last words, what must be noted is how she mourns not only the loss of her family, and not only the loss of her loved ones' bodies, but also the eco-logical loss of the "planet."

Understanding the Holocaust as an eco-logical event, I would contend, opens up a new methodological vista in studying the Holocaust (and genocide as a whole). This vista does not posit that the act of murder is an ideological, political, socioeconomic, ethnic, racial, or similar matter only. The victim, accordingly, is no longer simply a victim of ideology, of politics, of socioeconomic status, of ethnic-racial affiliation, and so on. Rather, the Holocaust is also ecocide—the eco-logical murder of man and world alike.

The French philosopher Jean-François Lyotard wrote in the early 1980s that Auschwitz was an earthquake that destroyed the instruments which measured it. Ever since then, he continued, we have been trying to repair those broken devices and construct new ones. In this chapter I have sought to show that "ecologism" can function as an instrument for historians in taking measure of Auschwitz—as a historical theme (Part 1), a methodology (Part 2), and, in certain respects, as an ontology (Part 3).

Notes

1. Anna Bramwell, *Blood and Soil: Richard Walther Darré and Hitler's "Green Party"* (Bourne End, UK, 1985), 171–80.

2. Franz-Josef Brüggemeier, Mark Cioc, and Thomas Zeller, eds. *How Green Were the Nazis? Nature, Environment, and Nation in the Third Reich* (Athens, 2005).

3. "Reichsnaturschutzgesetz," *Reichsgesetzblatt* 68 (1 July 1935), 821.

4. Charles E. Closmann, "Legalizing a *Volksgemeinschaft*: Nazi Germany's Reich Nature Protection Law of 1935," in *How Green Were the Nazis?*, ed. Brüggemeier, Cioc, and Zeller, 21–22.

5. Boria Sax, *Animals in the Third Reich: Pets, Scapegoats, and the Holocaust* (New York, 2000), 110–23, 175–82.

6. Ibid., 111, 113.

7. Ibid., 114.

8. John Robert McNeill, *Something New Under the Sun: An Environmental History of the Twentieth-Century World* (New York, 2000), 325–56; Philip W. Sutton, *Nature, Environment and Society* (Houndmills, 2004), 41–50.

9. John Alexander Williams, *Turning to Nature in Germany: Hiking, Nudism, and Conservation, 1900–1940* (Stanford, 2007), 223–29.

10. Oliver Geden, *Rechte Ökologie: Umweltschutz zwischen Emanzipation und Faschismus* (Berlin, 1996).

11. Friedemann Schmoll, "Die Verteidigung organischer Ordnungen: Naturschutz und Antisemitismus zwischen Kaiserreich und Nationalsozialismus," in *Naturschutz und Nationalsozialismus*, ed. Joachim Radkau and Franz Uekötter (Frankfurt/M, 2003), 169–82.

12. Thomas Lekan, "'It Shall Be the Whole Landscape!' The Reich Nature Protection Law and Regional Planning in the Third Reich," in *How Green Were the Nazis?*, ed. Brüggemeier, Cioc, and Zeller, 90–94.

13. Frank Uekötter, "Polycentrism in Full Swing: Air Pollution Control in Nazi Germany," in *How Green Were the Nazis?*, ed. Brüggemeier, Cioc, and Zeller, 101–28.

14. David Blackbourn, *The Conquest of Nature: Water, Landscape, and the Making of Modern Germany* (New York, 2006), 279.

15. Ibid., 274–75.

16. Ibid., 289–93.

17. Quoted from Gregory J. Cooper, *The Science of the Struggle for Existence: On the Foundations of Ecology* (Cambridge, 2003), 5.

18. Michael Burleigh and Wolfgang Wippermann, *The Racial State: Germany 1933–1945* (Cambridge, 1991), 3–31.

19. Der Reichsführer SS, SS-Hauptamt, *Rassenpolitik* (Berlin, 1943), 21–22.

20. Boaz Neumann, *Die Weltanschauung des Nazismus: Raum, Körper, Sprache* (Göttingen, 2010).

21. Heinrich Himmler, "Rede vor Generalen in Sonthofen [21.6.1944]," in Heinrich Himmler, *Geheimreden 1933 bis 1945 und andere Ansprachen* (Frankfurt am Main, 1974), 205.

22. Czesław Madajczyk, "Vom 'Generalplan Ost' zum 'Generalsiedlungsplan,'" in *Der "Generalplan Ost": Hauptlinien der nationalsozialistischen Planungs- und Vernichtungspolitik*, ed. Mechtild Rössler and Sabine Schleiermacher (Berlin, 1993), 16–17.

23. Hans Ehlich, "Die Behandlung des fremden Volkstums [10/11.12.1942]," in Der "Generalplan Ost," ed. Rössler and Schleiermacher, 49.

24. *Das Bauen im neuen Reich* (Bayreuth, 1943), vol. 2, 7.

25. Heinrich Himmler, "Allgemeine Anordnung Nr. 20/VI/42 über die Gestaltung der Landschaft in den eingegliederten Ostgebieten [21.12.1942]," in Erhard Mäding, *Regeln für die Gestaltung der Landschaft: Einführung in die Allgemeine Anordnung Nr. 20/VI/42 des Reichsführers SS, Reichskommissars für die Festigung deutschen Volkstums* (Berlin, 1943), 51.

26. Ibid.

27. Ibid.

28. Ibid.

29. Hans Frank, *Das Diensttagebuch des deutschen Generalgouverneurs in Polen, 1939–1945* (Stuttgart, 1975), 131, 146; Dieter Pohl, "The Murder of Jews in the General Government," in *National Socialist Extermination Policies: Contemporary German Perspectives and Controversies*, ed. Ulrich Herbert (New York, 2000), 84–85.

30. See, for example, *Der Jude als Weltparasit* (Munich, 1943–1944), 10.

31. Ernst Hiemer, *Der Pudelmopsdackelpinscher und andere besinnliche Erzählungen* (Nuremberg, 1940), 95.

32. Ernst Hiemer, *Der Giftpilz: Ein Stürmerbuch für Jung und Alt, Erzählungen* (Nuremberg, 1938), 14.

33. Ibid., 6–8.

34. Ibid., 18.

35. Ibid.

36. Sax, *Animals in the Third Reich*, 56–63, 159.

37. Hiemer, *Der Giftpilz*, 38.

38. Thomas Lekan and Thomas Zeller, eds., *Germany's Nature: Cultural Landscapes and Environmental History* (New Brunswick, 2005), 68–70, 197–98; Schmoll, "Die Verteidigung organischer Ordnungen," 174–75, 179, 181–82.

39. Robert A. Pois, *National Socialism and the Religion of Nature* (London, 1986), 117–36.

40. Adolf Hitler, *Mein Kampf* (Munich, 1939), 165, 331; Eberhard Jäckel, *Hitler's World View: A Blueprint for Power* (Cambridge, MA, 1981), 101–07.

41. Carl Schmitt, *Völkerrechtliche Großraumordnung mit Interventionsverbot für raumfremde Mächte: Ein Beitrag zum Reichsbegriff im Völkerrecht* (Berlin, 1941, 1939), 5–7.

42. Ibid., 7.

43. Quoted from Schmoll, "Die Verteidigung organischer Ordnungen," 181–82.

44. Zygmunt Bauman, *Modernity and the Holocaust* (Ithaca, 2001), 18, 91–92.

45. Pois, *National Socialism and the Religion of Nature*, 123.

46. Karl Bareth and Alfred Vogel, *Erblehre und Rassenkunde für die Grunde- und Hauptschule* (Bühl-Baden, 1937), 83–84.

47. Blackbourn, *The Conquest of Nature*, 288, 290.

48. Quoted from Thomas Zeller, "Molding the Landscape of Nazi Environmentalism: Alwin Seifert and the Third Reich," in *How Green Were the Nazis?*, ed. Brüggemeier, Cioc, and Zeller, 147.

49. Ibid., 152, 158–59.

50. Quoted from Joachim Wolschke-Bulmahn, "Violence as the Basis of National Socialist Landscape Planning in the 'Annexed Eastern Areas,'" in *How Green Were the Nazis?*, ed. Brüggemeier, Cioc, and Zeller, 246–47.

51. Ibid., 250; Sybille Steinbacher, *Auschwitz: A History* (London, 2005), 75.

52. Wiesław Kielar, *Anus Mundi: 1,500 Days in Auschwitz Birkenau* (New York, 1980); Johann Kremer, entry for 5 September 1942, in Johann Paul Kremer, "Tagebuch" [1940–1945], in *Auschwitz in den Augen der SS: Rudolf Höß, Pery Broad, Johann Paul Kremer* (Oświęcim, 1997), 154.

53. Reviel Netz, *Barbed Wire: An Ecology of Modernity* (Middletown, CT, 2004).

54. Primo Levi, *The Drowned and the Saved* (New York, 1988), 76.

55. Michel Foucault, *Discipline and Punish: The Birth of the Prison* (New York, 1995).
56. Abel J. Herzberg, *Between Two Streams: A Diary From Bergen-Belsen* (London, 1997), 12, entry for 14 August 1944.
57. Ibid., 16.
58. Kalman Gochman, *Class Reunion* (n.p., 1989), 36 [in Hebrew].
59. Ibid., 85–86 [in Hebrew].
60. Bruno Bettelheim, *The Informed Heart: Autonomy in a Mass Age* (Glencoe, IL, 1960), 282–83.
61. Charlotte Beradt, *The Third Reich of Dreams: The Nightmares of a Nation, 1933–1939* (Wellingborough, UK, 1985), 62–64, 93–108.
62. Peter Hayes, *From Cooperation to Complicity: Degussa in the Third Reich* (Cambridge, 2004), 272–300; Jürgen Kalthoff and Martin Werner, *Die Händler des Zyklon B: Tesch & Stabenow: Eine Firmengeschichte zwischen Hamburg und Auschwitz* (Hamburg, 1998).
63. Rudolph Höss, *Death Dealer: The Memoirs of the SS Kommandant at Auschwitz* (New York, 1996), 28–31, 34, 42–45, 155–64, 263–65.
64. Ibid., 156, 157.
65. C. J. Wells, *German: A Linguistic History to 1945* (Oxford, 2003), 417.
66. Boaz Neumann, "The Phenomenology of the German People's Body (*Volkskörper*) and the Extermination of the Jewish Body," *New German Critique* 106 (2009): 149–81.
67. Cf. Peter Sloterdijk, *Sphären: Plurale Sphärologie* (Frankfurt/M, 2004), vol. 3: *Schäume*, 89–260.
68. Peter Hayes, "Auschwitz, Capital of the Holocaust," *Holocaust and Genocide Studies* 17, no. 2 (2003): 330–50.
69. Steinbacher, *Auschwitz*, 68.
70. Ibid., 74.
71. Ibid., 6–78.
72. Hartmut Ziesing, "A Flowery Paradise in Auschwitz: The Garden of the Kommandant of Auschwitz, Rudolf Höß," *Centropa* 4, no. 2 (2004): 142–46.
73. Höss, *Death Dealer*, 158–59.
74. Ibid., 153.
75. Ibid., 124.
76. Ibid.
77. Ibid., 163.
78. Ibid., 164.
79. *Online Etymology Dictionary* (http://www.etymonline.com/); *Oxford English Dictionary* (http://dictionary.oed.com/).
80. Hannah Arendt, *Eichmann in Jerusalem: A Report on the Banality of Evil* (New York, 1963), 256 (emphasis added).
81. Berel Lang, *Heidegger's Silence* (Ithaca, 1996).
82. Martin Heidegger, "Das Ge-Stell" [1949], in Martin Heidegger, *Bremer und Freiburger Vorträge*, vol. 79 (Frankfurt/M, 1994), 27.
83. Magda King, *A Guide to Heidegger's Being and Time* (Albany, 2001), 48.
84. Shlomo Dragon, in Gideon Greif, *Wir weinten tränenlos … Augenzeugenberichte der jüdischen "Sonderkommandos" in Auschwitz* (Cologne, 1995), 69–70.
85. Isabella Leitner, *Fragments of Isabella: A Memoir of Auschwitz* (New York, 1978), 23, 24.

Part II

TESTIMONY AND COMMEMORATION

CHAPTER 6

Bearing Witness
Theological Roots of a New Secular Morality

SAMUEL MOYN

In the last few decades, the imperative of witnessing has exploded as a powerful secular norm, connecting what was at first a confined idiom of moral response to the Holocaust to a much larger set of political transformations. The figure whom Avishai Margalit influentially labels the "moral witness" has become a central touchstone of contemporary ethical life.[1] In fact, it is now looking as if the cultural practice of "bearing witness to atrocity," or even to lesser forms of human evil, is one of the most disseminated and migratory outcomes of Holocaust memory. It may even have become a dominant framework of response not simply to historical victimhood but also to instability and injustice in current affairs, as local and global audiences before whom victimhood is displayed take on the role of witnesses, too.

In this last way, it recently seeped into the very highest of high politics. When Iranians entered the streets after a stolen election, U.S. President Barack Obama explained the role of outsiders. Invoking, as he often does, Martin Luther King, Jr.'s promise that the arc of the universe, though long, bends towards justice, Obama continued: "Right now, we are bearing witness to the Iranian peoples' belief in that truth, and we will continue to bear witness."[2] No American president had used such rhetoric before. It was a striking illustration of how far witnessing has become as a morally persuasive stance in the world.

Whence witnessing? This chapter is mostly a reflection on this still unanswered question, for the normative status of witnessing—including its uses for historical practice—is self-evidently bound up with the origins of its authority as a moral paradigm. After a long period of complimentary treatments of witnessing, is it time to take a more impartial stance on the sheer priority of

---

Notes for this section begin on page 140.

witnessing today? Has its unquestioned hegemony as an expectation and norm been based on an incomplete understanding of where the witness came from and why he or she matters so much now? What are the contemporary political implications of the rise of a testimonial culture, and should historians—who have incorporated the drive to witness as fundamentally as anyone else—take more critical distance on witnessing than they have so far? In what follows, I suggest that much more attention needs to be given to, and work done on, the long theological incubation of the notions of witnessing and testimony, without which their contemporary relevance for history and law are both hard to understand and impossible to evaluate.

Frameworks of Witnessing

The literature on Holocaust testimony—which set the basis for the contemporary explosion of witnessing—is by itself large and growing, as epitomized by Annette Wieviorka's outstanding study of "the era of the witness."[3] Rather than taking Holocaust testimony as a given, however, I want to reflect in what follows on some of the cultural preconditions of and catalysts for the contemporary salience of witnessing as a meaningful ethical practice. For the place of witnessing in American and European cultural history where it originated remains perplexing.

That historical trauma by itself precipitated witnessing as a cultural reflex is not convincing. It was not simply a "natural" response to the Holocaust that then became generalized. Jay Winter contends that an ethics of witnessing is already visible at least as early as the response to the Great War, laying emphasis on Jean Norton Cru's fascinating interwar exercises in literary analysis of front memoirs, *Témoins* (1929) and *Du témoignage* (1931). Those books, Winter says, prove the early emergence of the otherwise contemporary figure of the witness.[4] The argument is unintentionally revealing. The roots of witnessing are placed in some earlier catastrophe, as if it had to be a natural response to one or another episode of mass violence. Yet Cru's forgotten books actually prove that World War I did not prompt any general cultural transformation along contemporary lines, nor indeed did World War II for a long time. Beyond its occasional role as a personal imperative, witnessing as a cultural phenomenon at the heart of ethical responses to violence seems to be an invention of recent date.

The reasons for the delay may in some individual cases have been due to trauma, but—as Peter Novick has argued for the more general contours of American Holocaust memory—more is needed to make up an adequate general explanation for the escalating and migratory features of contemporary witnessing.[5] The contemporary surge of testimony is a constructed event with a cultural logic, one not due to eternal psychic features of human beings alone. After all, the explosion of Holocaust commemoration has now led even earlier events to be rescripted in memory so that they give rise to representative demands they did not generate on their own, including a search for an ethical culture of witnesses.

One approach to the puzzle is to consider various frameworks of witnessing in Western culture and whether they are the likely sources of the general transformation. Of the three main frameworks, law and history are now the most prominent and most frequently discussed. (It is on these domains that Wieviorka focuses in her study for example.) It turns out, however, that they have been far more affected by this larger explosion of witnessing than they have affected it, as a few interesting examples show. Indeed, in both domains one of the most fascinating dimensions of the rise of witnessing is that it forces what one might call an overthrown epistemological style back into relevance.

In history as well as in law, witnessing is a way of knowing that had to be *overcome* for the enterprises to assume their characteristic modern forms—at least until recently. Ancient history relied much more fundamentally on witnesses than modern history does, for principled reasons; as Amos Funkenstein pointed out, the "conviction that the eyewitness was the best historian" pervaded ancient and medieval sensibilities, until its modern fall, due to the new awareness that witnesses were captive to a subjective point of view that historical "objectivity" would surmount.[6] Similarly, one of the epistemological hallmarks of modern law is the insight that modes of establishing the truth that skirt subjectivity—notably physical evidence—are the most reliable kind. Much of modern evidence law, for example, is built on the goal of locating the conditions under which frequently unreliable witnesses can nonetheless be made of use, when no superior forms of proof are available.

Yet now, witnessing is central to both realms when trauma is involved. To be sure, the chronologies through which it became central to them is different. Moral witnessing in legal responses to catastrophe has grown even since David Ben Gurion's politically motivated decision to stage Adolf Eichmann's trial, and Gideon Hausner's choice to make survivors central in it (very much unlike at Nuremberg, where only two witnesses to crimes against the Jews appeared in ten months, in adjudication based fundamentally on written documentation). Consider now, in contrast, Eric Stover's recent book, *The Witnesses,* which in a somewhat uncritical way catalogs and champions the inclusion of witnesses of atrocity in recent international criminal tribunal proceedings.[7] The specific roots of this current imperative run by way of accountability protocols pioneered in the pursuit of "transitional justice" in the aftermath of Latin American authoritarianism and, more recently, in the South African search for "truth and reconciliation."[8] When transitional justice as an ethical and political program crystallized at a landmark Aspen Institute conference in 1989, philosopher Thomas Nagel summed up the imperative of such programs as not "knowledge" but "acknowledgment," and witnesses have proven central to legal or quasi-legal processes called upon to play a far different role than simply assisting in the determination of what happened.[9] If nothing about the internal epistemological requirements of criminal adjudication accounts for the contemporary prominence of witnessing, then presumably some external explanation is needed.

In history, Raul Hilberg famously spurned witnesses in his classic account of the Holocaust published precisely as the Eichmann trial unfolded.[10] His argument seemed convincing until Daniel Jonah Goldhagen's book, with its angry criticism that "historians of the Holocaust and of Nazism ... rarely, if ever, listen to the voices of the dead Jews speaking to us through their surviving diaries or to the voices of Jewish survivors recounting the manner of their treatment."[11] In more respectable form, such claims are now central to Holocaust historiography, as recent studies by Saul Friedländer especially, but also by Marion Kaplan and many others, show clearly.[12] Goldhagen explicitly appealed to witnesses because they provided evidence of a phenomenon he cared about—perpetrator emotion—that other sources could not. In an interview with *Dissent* on the conclusion of his authoritative new history, however, Friedländer was very clear that witnessing matters *in spite* of the epistemological limitations that had led historians as a profession to marginalize witnessing before. "I wanted to write an integrated history," Friedländer says. "Business-as-usual history flattens the interpretation of mass extermination. But the voices of the victims—their lack of understanding, their despair, their powerful eloquence or their helpless clumsiness—these can shake our well-protected representation of events. They can stop us in our tracks. They can restore our initial sense of disbelief, before knowledge rushes in to smother it."[13] As in law, history seems to be affected by a cultural demand originating outside its own precincts, not least if its basic purpose is telling what happened. For history, too, the role of witnesses is not so much—or not at all, for Friedländer!—to build "knowledge" but to prompt "acknowledgment."

Strikingly, historians of diverse episodes of pain and suffering now not only include witnesses, but sometimes think of themselves as witnesses: In his recent book about the American Civil War, *Upon the Altar of the Nation,* for example, Harry Stout says he is doing a moral kind of history: "One bears witness to the past," he writes, "with all possible integrity and disinterestedness for the sake of the present and the future."[14] This migratory quality of witnessing is one of its most noteworthy features. Barack Obama now provides by far the most high-profile example: after his first invocations, he returned to the concept in accepting the Nobel peace prize, saying that his role was to "bear witness" to the dignity of victims of human rights abuse. In the broad field of legal accountability, James Dawes's recent presentation of human rights interviewers—not simply the victims they seek out—as the ones who bear witness is matched by the self-understanding of historians who take a somewhat self-reverential attitude toward their role in reconstructing a traumatic past.[15] A transformation of the role of witnessing in legal and historical frameworks that had previously done away with it begs some explanation or other.

That All Men Might Believe

But there is a third main framework for witnessing, besides law and history, that Westerners have always cultivated, one strikingly neglected in most accounts, including Wieviorka's. It is the *theological* or *religious* model for witnessing. Contemporary, so-called "moral" witnesses are not simply religious witnesses, but I want to suggest that as a historical matter, a culturally specific theory of religious witnessing may have provided the most relevant framework for the early intelligibility of the idiom and the meaningfulness of the practices. Drawing on Margalit's notion of the moral witness, Winter remarks that such figures are "storytellers of a special kind," not witnesses "in the religious sense, pointing out someone prepared to affirm her faith by dying for it."[16] The question, however, is whether religious witnessing mattered in the origins of moral witnessing, not whether they are identical figures. And while dying for faith certainly is a central element in religious witnessing (in Greek, martyr means witness), there is much more to religious frameworks for witnessing over Western history.

The post-Holocaust construction of witnessing, in other words, presupposed a rich antique past. Of course, the Bible introduces early legal systems in which witnesses have roles. But far more frequent is the concept of witnessing supernatural events and realities. Who or even what can be a witness, and what of, need not detain this discussion. There are Hebraic examples of what sounds like witnessing, notably in the Book of Job, including the refrain of the lone survivor later made famous by Herman Melville: "I only am escaped to tell thee." But whatever the status of these early examples, the New Testament makes witnessing far more central than before, especially in the Gospel of John: Jesus, John says, "came for a witness, to bear witness of the Light, that all men through him might believe" (John 1:7).

From very early on, in Western culture, witnessing is about not just the truth in history and law, but a supernatural truth of theological dimensions. Just as clearly, religious meanings seeped in the West into the very meaning of witnessing and related words for doing so, like the word "to testify." Again, John: "Verily, verily, I say unto thee, We speak that we do know, and testify that we have seen; and ye receive not our witness" (3:11). One might also posit a theological residue in the mere linguistic difference between the secular idea of being a witness (in a trial or as a historical source) and the religious idea of "bearing witness." That this latter notion is the one that has become pervasive in cultural and political understandings of responding to historical trauma is thus highly significant.

And in Jesus's case, of course, witnessing occurs in and through suffering. Already in the Hebrew Bible, to be sure, the suffering of the Jews matters in part because it allows them to be part of God's plan for them—but not because they are witnesses. Job is an individual whose faith is tested, and he certainly suffers; but Jewish sources do not authorize any inference that Jews *collectively* suffer so that they can witness as a people the higher truth. By contrast, just as it made the theological basis of witnesses close to the heart of the whole idea, so Christianity began to treat Jews collectively as witnesses.

St. Augustine founded the central tradition of Christian theology of Jewish persistence in world history, in which God's original chosen people are assigned the role of witnesses to or bystanders of a history they do not and cannot fulfill. Suffering played a central role in Augustine's witness theology. For Augustine, the monitory and testimonial role of the Jews explained why Christians should not want their predecessors to disappear, for they provide in their blindness the positive role of bearing witness to the truth of Christianity and its supersession of their law. As Jeremy Cohen has shown in his monumental book *The Living Letters of the Law*, this idea provided the framework through which Christian civilization understood Jews for nearly two millennia, and indeed until recently. Debate revolves around whether, in his famous reinterpretation of the command in Psalm 59:19 to "slay them not, but scatter them in your might, lest your people forget their law," Augustine pioneered a protective theology, or in effect laid the groundwork for episodic, even cyclical, and theologically authorized violence. Certainly, he was read in the latter way: suffering witnesses needed to be ritually produced before they could play their testimonial role.[17]

Now, by themselves, these sorts of considerations could be called "deep background." They remedy the skewed attention to legal and historical notions of witnessing by recalling a potentially different source for contemporary discourse, saturated as it is by more metaphysical notions of witnessing than law or history ever featured. Yet this deep background would be uninteresting, without some complementary story about its availability and relevance at the specific moment of the origins of contemporary witnessing, and Holocaust witnessing in particular. And without gainsaying the importance of many other media of transmission and moments of cultural transformation of witnessing prior to the postwar era—including a longstanding Protestant tradition from Martin Luther to Martin Luther King, Jr. in which testimony and suffering were powerfully intertwined, or Jewish thinker Franz Rosenzweig's rendition of the Augustinian image of Jews as monitory and testimonial—it seems probable that the key intellectual and political context of that availability and relevance when it mattered was the Cold War ideology of Judeo-Christianity.

The homeland of Holocaust memory in its most original and classic forms was the Cold War "West," not elsewhere, even if it globalized later. And the more one looks, the more that fact matters in trying to come to grips with the unprecedented public moratorium on Jew-hatred, as well as in the creation of positive enterprises of reconciliation with Jews, that occurred in precisely this era. "Without the mobilization of Christian guilt and the transmission that it assured," Pierre Nora has proposed of Holocaust representation generally, "it is hard to understand how a memory about Jews alone could have had such an echo."[18] This has to be right, with the qualification that Christian guilt may not have been the central factor, since much Christian writing about the Holocaust in the early days assumed that Christianity was not deeply implicated in the events, and indeed now stood with Judaism as a key bulwark against paganism in both its past Nazi and present Soviet versions. In this era, to put it differently, the terms of the novel creation of Judeo-Christianity were fundamentally defined by the presentation of a pluralism of religions as the heart of Western civilization against godless secularism. Of course, this transnational construction was no easy task, since it involved treating other, frequently supersessionist or even antagonistic models of Christian Jewish relations as aberrant, downplaying the fact they had dominated in the past, including in the recent World War II past. Indeed, it meant renovating the traditional meaning of the Augustinian script so that the injunction to "slay them not" was not potentially another form of violence but cross-faith understanding and faith-based alliance.[19] It was in this endeavor, I want to propose tentatively, that the ancient notion of the Jews as suffering witnesses for the truth of Christianity provided the basis for Judeo-Christian reconciliation in what were still profoundly Christian terms.

Jewish Witnesses and Cold War Christians

As a promissory note for a more thorough genealogical account that would capture both the pre-Cold War transformations of witnessing in the broad field of Jewish-Christian relations, as well as the local particularities in the transnational invention of Judeo-Christianity (of which Holocaust memory may at first have been a minor feature), let me concentrate here on the French case. It may be worth noting, after all, that as elsewhere in the creation of world cultural and literary phenomena, Paris has a singular place in the rise of Holocaust memory.[20] And to concentrate on two episodes with their epicenters there—the creation of Elie Wiesel's *Night* and the Holocaust controversy called the "Treblinka affair" to which I have recently devoted a book-length investigation—makes obvious the prominent Christianization of the Holocaust in the years it achieved unprecedented visibility.[21]

Simply because it established what became the international paradigm of the suffering Jewish witness, Wiesel's *Night* is a useful starting point. In a prominent essay, Naomi Seidman emphasized the differences between the original Yiddish version (1956) of Wiesel's book and the French edition (1958) that made its author archetypical. Seidman powerfully shows how the translation process, and especially the role of the crucial intercessor François Mauriac, created "two survivors … , a Yiddish and a French—or perhaps we should say one survivor who speaks to a Jewish audience and one whose first reader is a French Catholic." But because her own emphasis is on the "Jewish rage" lost in translation, Seidman does not sufficiently bring out what was constructed and contingent in the French Catholic interest in the Jewish experience she is otherwise intent to emphasize. True, the translation process did help make the Holocaust, as Seidman says, "harmless for Catholic pieties and French loyalties." But Mauriac's interest was not that of "existentialist religion," as Seidman puts it, even as she notices that in Mauriac's preface to *Night* the novelist does defend a version of his faith in which the "historical animosity between Christian and Jew" vanishes, as if it had never been. Not existentialist religion, but a new Judeo-Christianity in which old hostilities disappeared in the name of new imperatives, is what drove Mauriac historically.[22]

Though he invoked it in his preface to *Night*, Mauriac definitely did not invent his main trope: that the persecution of Jews, far from being an activity Christians should support or sponsor, ought to be seen as a persecution of religion analogous to Jesus's passion and in fact part of its continuing scandal. Instead, Mauriac often acknowledged his debt to fellow French Catholic Jacques Maritain, who drew on various sources to pioneer such a theory as early as the late 1930s. In the years after World War II, Maritain tirelessly repeated this approach to a newly coalescing Judeo-Christian audience, joining more obscure Christians who were pioneering the project of Jewish-Christian understanding.

Their hard work and authentic belief show that there is no way to deny the place of theological insight in their vision of the tragic mistake of antisemitism to which they saw their fellow Christians as prone. But it is also clear that the attack on Christian contempt originated and then exploded in concrete sociohistorical contexts. "Jews and Christians are persecuted together and by the same enemies; Christians because they are faithful to Christ, and Jews because they gave Christ to the world," Maritain argued in 1944. "There are innumerable other victims, that's true, but the Jews are the first ones, and it is them only whom people want to exterminate from the face of the earth as a race and as a people. Nor is it only a question of justice and natural law that is raised here, and requires that the truth be cried from all rooftops. It is our God who is attacked too, it is Him who is humiliated, targeted, insulted, and spit upon by antisemitic persecution. For now on Christ does not separate but unites Jews and Christians."[23] It was on these grounds that antisemitism could be understood as worst because it reenacted the Passion, as a guilty world stood by and continued to do so.

What such a theory allowed in Mauriac's interpretation of *Night* is an interpretation of Jews as witnesses to human evil, and Christians as fellow, or second-order, witnesses—who at the same time understand the Jewish passion more deeply because its true meaning is the Christian Passion. Migratory witnessing from Jews to Christians—one of the earliest instances of what Froma Zeitlin calls "vicarious witnessing," to describe second-generation interest in Holocaust experiences—is clearly part of early Christian views.[24]

A similar instance of Judeo-Christian witnessing is to be found scant years later in the Treblinka affair of 1966, in which Mauriac was also involved. In this case, he had help, for Jean-François Steiner—the child of a Holocaust victim who sparked the controversy when he published a controversial book on the Treblinka camp—developed a theory of Jewish witnessing with surprising public ramifications. For Steiner, the drama of the Holocaust was epitomized by the revolt of the Jews of the Treblinka *Sonderkommando* on August 2, 1943—which, Steiner opined, followed from their slow recognition of a need to be witnesses to human evil for the world. It was, for Steiner, a religious imperative, but also one that also encompassed the secular Jews involved in the revolt due to ethnic osmosis or historical memory. Unlike the Warsaw revolt, which was doomed, the Treblinka revolt, for Steiner, returned Jews to their need to survive in the face of extermination in order to record what had happened.

In propounding his theory, through a vivid narrative of the camp, Steiner hoped to make himself the mouthpiece of actual witnesses whose testimonies he gathered and whom he interviewed himself; yet the results of his enterprise—as the angry but neglected responses of Treblinka survivors to his account showed—vividly illustrates how a culturally constructed *theory* of witnessing can sometimes work to screen out the self-understanding of actual witnesses of atrocity. The migration of witnessing, in this case, outraged the original witnesses themselves.[25] But however idiosyncratic, Steiner's theory was what made it so appealing to Christian readers, beginning with Mauriac himself.

Extending his prior interpretations of the genocide, Mauriac attempted to find the principle that would make its recognition compatible with the Cold War Christian philosophy of culture and politics that he advocated. Mauriac struggled to understand the suffering witnessing of the Jews in the Holocaust as an event in a sacramental history intelligible within his own Christian faith. Just as in his reading of Wiesel, the suffering of the Jews in Mauriac's interpretation of Steiner's book became analogous to the suffering of Christ, tragedies reflecting human sinfulness, but also portending Christian redemption. *Treblinka*'s ending, Mauriac stated, narrated "the exit of the Jews from hell," but this exit remained reversible so long as redemption remained in the future. "May Israel itself not lose faith in its election, in this choice that glorifies and crucifies it forever," Mauriac wrote, recommending the spirit in which to read the book he analyzed. In his emphasis on the Jews' mission in history, Mauriac maintained, Steiner had precociously and inadvertently made the insight that his people are "a people of preachers." Mauriac knew, unlike Steiner, that what they preached transcended their own understanding and actually anticipated Christianity and the return of its redeemer. And this anticipation recalled Christians to their own role. They had not been bystanders, let alone perpetrators, but were now vicarious witnesses. "What *Treblinka* reveals to us," Mauriac explained, "in a manner that gives us the strength and the courage to relive in thought what these men, women, and children suffered, is Israel's mission, which is to remind the West the abomination of which it was the witness and thus the accomplice, and to forbid it from forgetting it."[26]

Similar interpretations were available throughout the Christian press, which on balance welcomed Steiner's enterprise with the most warmth of any category of respondents, including the secular left and Jewish venues, notably the Yiddish press whose audience overlapped best with victim communities. Famous Christian resistance figure Edmond Michelet testified in the review of Steiner's book in *Le Monde* that "Treblinka (which was a new discovery for me) confirms my conviction that [Jacques] Maritain was right, that there exists a 'mystery of Israel.' ... The people of the stiff neck remain an incomparable model of the best and the worst for the world of *goyim*."[27] Even Jews could adopt this interpretation, as Pierre Vidal-Naquet—whom *Treblinka* helped discover the Holocaust that would play so significant a role in his scholarly activities thereafter—testified. "It is only in returning to their function as *witnesses*, the role in which the medieval church had thought to imprison them," Vidal-Naquet wrote in *Le Monde* after the controversy heated up, "only in wanting to make themselves witnesses of horror in the world and to play Israel's role among the nations that the Jews of Treblinka found the strength to survive."[28] As another Christian writer agreed, Steiner had unveiled the innate barbarism of human beings without God's promise of universal peace—that "the most religious and lucid of Israel's members at Treblinka wanted themselves to be the instrument of this implacable news, and therefore the suffering servant, the prophet crucified because of his message."[29]

Saul Friedländer's Witnessing

The recent completion of Friedländer's *magnum opus* on the Holocaust provides a convenient and exemplary landmark to pose the question of whether historians have adopted a fetish of witnessing too uncritically. For in spite of the author's sketchy comments on witnessing in his books and interviews, the rapidly—and generally deserved—canonization of *Nazi Germany and the Jews* as the central Holocaust history of the present time necessarily makes it the primary site of inquiry into the promises a Holocaust historiography founded on witnessing. Its status also invites special kind of critical scrutiny, however, and not least for the almost mystical character of its reliance on witnessing. Even in his own recent celebration of the book as a high modernist historical masterpiece that achieves a "truth beyond epistemology" due to its incorporation of witnessing, Friedländer's student Wulf Kansteiner has worried that critics may have treated it in too laudatory a fashion. Kansteiner is right when he worries about the immediate elevation of *Nazi Germany and the Jews* "to the status of a historical monument that is unworthy of historiographical squabble."[30]

But the possible lines of critical response to Friedländer are various. One is to emphasize the gap between principle and practice.[31] The most provocative of responses to Friedländer's book in this vein comes from Holocaust historian Christopher Browning, whose reliance on testimony in his own works is equally pronounced but is radically different in motivation. For Browning, one infers, much less is at stake than for Kansteiner in Friedländer's usage of witnesses, hardly a sophisticated modernist achievement than the mere supplement of analysis with "evocation" that even the most positivist of historians acknowledge as valuable concessions to readability and devices of scene setting. For Browning, the historiographical incorporation of witnessing is not a "post-epistemological" breakthrough (whatever that might mean) but simply another tool to make the past more vivid.[32]

Of course, Browning does acknowledge that the turn to victim voices is Friedländer's "most significant methodological innovation." But he suggests that those voices are perhaps most valuable when they serve as building blocks of historical argument about the events—notably the much discussed character of Jewish response to persecution. Browning is convincing that, often enough, Friedländer's own practical usage of witnesses is in fact to establish or buttress the factual account he has developed through other sources. This reclamation of Friedländer's witnessing for ordinary history, however, could end up seriously damaging its claims to pathbreaking novelty. If the main achievement of Friedländer's turn to witness sources were ultimately—and in spite of his own self-interpretation—to reinforce analytical conclusions typically or potentially based on other evidence, it is not clear what "methodological innovation" the venture could boast.[33]

In any event, whatever Friedländer's own practice, the principles he is credited with invoking matter in their own right. What of Friedländer's professed goal of invoking witnesses to avoid domestication and sustain disbelief? This goal is closer to Friedländer's heart, and very different from mere "evocation." Alon Confino and Amos Goldberg converge in emphasizing that shock is Friedländer's principal aim in turning to witnesses in his texts. Goldberg, however, suggests that the passage of many years since the surge of this imperative—the era of the witness has gone on a long time now—has itself domesticated Holocaust disbelief as an almost ritualistic trope. Much as, in the classic analyses of the Frankfurt school, the most aesthetically challenging and politically promising formal innovations could end up serving the culture industry, so the device of listening to witnesses for the sake of avoiding complacency becomes a wholly banal and expectable—indeed, complacent—move.

Goldberg's most significant worry about Friedländer's witnessing, however, is different than a critique of the timeless risk of aestheticist routinization.

"There are no essential elements within the 'victims' voices' that in themselves cause disbelief," Goldberg maintains, "and ...whether they do so is always dependent on cultural factors."[34] Put differently, Friedländer's fetish of the witness is the outcome of specific historical traditions he himself does not place under historical scrutiny. But then a story about the domestication of witnessing is arguably not as crucial as what made it culturally "believable" and important in the first place. If witnesses have become an aesthetic pleasure—rather than the source of empathic unsettlement that Friedländer and other critics like Dominick LaCapra describe as the central quarry of writing about the Holocaust and other traumatic events—it is because they were constructed in such a way as to prompt a culturally intelligible "disbelief" from the start. It simply became more and more familiar through repetition.

If so, theoretical debates around Friedländer's accomplishment force further study of the cultural construction of history in the postwar age. To be sure, a further reason for the canonization of *Nazi Germany and the Jews* is that Friedländer is himself a witness turned historian. Kansteiner persuasively contends that "it would be foolish to suggest that Friedländer's emphasis on eyewitness testimony and his insistence on a certain measure of inexplicability in Holocaust history are unrelated to his personal experience as a victim."[35] All the same, it would be equally foolish to ignore that Friedländer's emphasis on testimony, far from following from his particular life history alone, is simply the most prominent instance of a pervasive historiographical trend. After all, Friedländer's own early works of Holocaust history were not obviously marked by any imperative of witness incorporation. To say so is to insist that the current historiographical debate about the place of witnesses in Holocaust or any other kind of history-writing is impossible to separate from—or even to treat as a proxy for—a larger cultural analysis of a thoroughgoing ethical and political transformation of which "the witness" is the beneficiary.

Mythology and History

If the starting point for the explosion of witnessing is its inherited canons—its historical, judicial, and theological frameworks of intelligibility—then much more attention has to be given to the last than has been done so far at what may have been a crucial moment in the origins of a contemporary testimonial culture. In emphasizing religious witnessing, this chapter provides a tentative account; even were religious sources of witnessing powerful enough, including in the origins of Holocaust witnessing, to be worth further exploration, there would still be their "secularization" to explain. And indeed, the Cold War formation of Holocaust witnessing, in spite of its often religious surfaces, already represented a kind of secular improvisation on Christian themes: even then, that is, witnessing blended religious tropes and secular and highly contingent ideological purposes. Whatever else they are, contemporary moral witnesses are therefore hardly a simple residue of a Christian culture, and I wouldn't want to suggest otherwise.

It would be deeply implausible, even in thinking about the early years of Holocaust memory, to posit a single, Christian source of the meaningfulness of witnessing. Another obvious framework is the history of psychology, and notably the theory of trauma. As Ruth Leys has documented in her intellectual genealogy, and as Didier Fassin and Roland Rechtman have more recently extended in their contemporary ethnography of "the condition of victimhood," trauma and confession have long had dense conceptual links to each other. And they still do. Yet in part because of its comparative novelty, the discourse of witnessing trauma itself needs to be placed in the interplay of older conceptions of witnessing which long antedated it: history, law, and theology. Without gainsaying both the historical and legal intersection with discourses of trauma, it seems hard to deny the obvious relevance of the theological framework of "bearing witness" to the origins of twentieth-century conceptions of "bearing witness to atrocity."[36]

Whatever account of the secularization of the originally Christian trope were to be offered, it might have to acknowledge that the secularization did not always end up complete. Without some such story, it is hard to know what to make, for example, of theorist Giorgio Agamben's vehement rejection of the notion of "the Holocaust" on grounds of its Christian sources, as if similar considerations might not bear on his own attitude towards witnesses, especially given his Pauline interpretation of the "saving remnant" they are supposed to compose.[37] And even in cases in which witnessing has departed very far in its ethical implications from its original Christian framework, the latter's formative power may have left a legacy. In any event, without the public salience at a particular moment of a Christian theology of Jewish witnessing, no such attempted secularization could have occurred in the first place. The beginnings of the era of the witness depended not simply on the figure of the Jewish witness, in sum, but on a Christian theology that originally scripted that role.

Taking the Christian or "Judeo-Christian" sources of witnessing seriously, for their historical importance as well as for their contemporary resonances, matters not least because of the political outcomes its rise as a secular imperative promotes. In a pioneering and neglected article almost twenty years ago, Martin S. Jaffee argued that "the discourse of Jewish-Christian solidarity in response to the Holocaust calls into being one set of relationships [but] also acts powerfully to preclude other relationships and drowns out other possible discourses that might properly emerge from reflection on the Holocaust." Very provocatively, Jaffee worried that "the myth of the sacrifice of the innocent Christ, whose degradation and death are for all humanity and whose victory transfigures human possibility" provided the lens through which Christians were able to accommodate themselves to Jews and acknowledge the crimes committed against them. Doing so, it ruled out other bases of reconciliation.[38]

Jaffee's emphasis did not fall on witnessing in particular. But he was right that Christian and "Judeo-Christian" grids for interpreting Jewish victimhood require a second look most of all because they may fit with a variety of specific politics that draw on religious myth as an alternative to secular justification. One, which Jaffee himself most clearly emphasized, is the international politics of the Jewish people. But in the years since he wrote, witnessing has infiltrated the politics of a discipline like history, as well as the politics of law, slowly displacing other, prior forms of international morality with a promise to provide global knowledge and acknowledgment, or even the reconciliation of enemy groups based on testimony and expiation.[39] The migration of witnessing has served, even further, to provide observers of tragedy, from historians looking into the past to politicians and publics looking across the world, with a somewhat narcissistic account of their own normative stance and role. But whether for historians, lawyers, or presidents, perhaps "fantasies of witnessing" need not forever rule out other, perhaps better, and certainly less self-reverential ways of relating to both past and present.

Notes

1. Avishai Margalit, *The Ethics of Memory* (Cambridge, MA, 2002).
2. Barack Obama, "Statement from the President on Iran," June 20, 2009. He had introduced this idea in an interview with Harry Smith of CBS News the day before. And he returned to it three days later in a statement on Iran, distributed in Persian translation. The source for all quotations is http://www.whitehouse.gov. One of the most significant aspects of the later Egyptian uprisings has been Obama's decision to drop these earlier stands for more activist solidarity with dissidents around the world.
3. Annette Wieviorka, *The Era of the Witness,* trans. Jared Stark (Ithaca, 2006). See such works as Lawrence Langer, *Holocaust Testimony: The Ruins of Memory* (New Haven, 1991); Shoshana Felman and Dori Laub, *Testimony: Crises of Witnessing in Literature, Psychoanalysis, and History* (New York, 1992); Zoë Vania Waxman, *Writing the Holocaust: Identity, Testimony, Representation* (Oxford, 2006); and Berel Lang, *Philosophical Witnessing: The Holocaust as Presence* (Waltham, MA, 2009).
4. Jay Winter, *Remembering War: The Great War Between Memory and History in the Twentieth Century* (New Haven, 2006) (discussing Jean Norton Cru, *Témoins: essai d'analyse et de critique des souvenirs de combattants édités en français de 1915 à 1928* (Paris, 1929), and Cru, *Du témoignage* (Paris, 1931)).
5. Peter Novick, *The Holocaust in American Life* (New York, 1999).
6. Amos Funkenstein, *Perceptions of Jewish History* (Berkeley, 1993), 34; François Hartog, "Le témoin et l'historien," in *Évidences de l'histoire: Ce que voient les historiens* (Paris, 2005).
7. Eric Stover, *The Witnesses: War Crimes and the Promise of Justice in the Hague* (Philadelphia, 2005).
8. See, for example, Mark Sanders, *Ambiguities of Witnessing: Law and Literature in the Time of a Truth Commission* (Stanford, 2007).
9. See Lawrence Weschler, *A Miracle, a Universe: Settling Accounts with Torturers* (New York, 1990), 4.

10. Cf. Christopher R. Browning, *Collected Memories: Holocaust Memory and Postwar Testimony* (Madison, 2003).

11. Daniel Jonah Goldhagen, "Motives, Causes, and Alibis: A Reply to My Critics," *New Republic,* 23 December 1996. For another historian in search of Holocaust-like witnesses in a different locale, to allow factual reconstruction but also to promote public memory and reconciliation, see Caroline Elkins, *Imperial Reckoning: The Untold Story of Britain's Gulag in Kenya* (New York, 2005).

12. Saul Friedländer, *Nazi Germany and the Jews,* 2 vols. (New York, 1997–2007); Marion A. Kaplan, *Between Dignity and Despair: Jewish Life in Nazi Germany* (New York, 1998). See also the exemplary study by Friedländer's student Alexandra Garbarini, *Numbered Days: Diaries and the Holocaust* (New Haven, 2006).

13. Jon Wiener, "History as Obligation: An Interview with Friedlander," *Dissent* (web), July 5, 2007, http://dissentmagazine.org/online.php?id=29.

14. Harry S. Stout, *Upon the Altar of the Nation: A Moral History of the Civil War* (New York, 2006), xii.

15. James Dawes, *That the World May Know: Bearing Witness to Atrocity* (Cambridge, MA, 2007).

16. Winter, *Remembering War,* 238–39 (discussing Margalit's book).

17. Jeremy Cohen, *The Living Letters of the Law: Ideas of the Jew in Medieval Christianity* (Berkeley, 1999); Paula Fredriksen, *Augustine and the Jews: A Christian Defense of Jews and Judaism* (New York, 2008); Cohen, "Revisiting Augustine's Doctrine of Jewish Witness" (review of Fredriksen), *Journal of Religion* 89, no. 4 (2009): 564–78; David Nirenberg, "Slay Them Not" (review of Fredriksen), *New Republic,* 18 March 2009.

18. Pierre Nora, "Mémoire et identité juives dans la France contemporaine," *Le Débat* 131 (September–October 2004): 24.

19. The rapidly evolving literature on the invention of Judeo-Christianity currently concentrates on the United States, showing prewar roots and Cold War crystallization. See, for example, Arthur A. Cohen, *The Myth of the Judeo-Christian Tradition* (New York, 1969); Katherine Healon Gaston, "The Genesis of America's Judeo-Christian Moment: Secularism, Totalitarianism, and the Redefinition of Democracy," PhD diss., University of California-Berkeley, 2008.

20. See Pascale Casanova, *The World Republic of Letters,* trans. M. B. DeBevoise (Cambridge, MA, 2005).

21. Samuel Moyn, *A Holocaust Controversy: The Treblinka Affair in Postwar France* (Waltham, MA, 2005).

22. Naomi Seidman, "Elie Wiesel and the Scandal of Jewish Rage," *Jewish Social Studies,* n.s. 3, no. 1 (1996): 8, 16, 12; cf. Nathan Bracher, *Through the Past Darkly: History and Memory in François Mauriac's "Bloc-Notes"* (Washington, 2004).

23. Jacques Maritain, "La passion d'Israël" (1944), reprinted in *Le mystère d'Israël et autres essais* (Paris, 1965), 203–04.

24. See Froma I. Zeitlin, "The Vicarious Witness: Belated Memory and Authorial Presence in Recent Holocaust Literature," *History & Memory* 10, no. 2 (1998): 5–42; see also Gary Weissman, *Fantasies of Witnessing: Postwar Efforts to Experience the Holocaust* (Ithaca, 2004).

25. See Moyn, *A Holocaust Controversy,* ch. 5.

26. François Mauriac, "Bloc-Notes," in *Le Figaro littéraire,* 5 May 1966, reprinted in Mauriac, *Bloc-Notes,* 5 vols. (Paris, 1993), vol. 4, 255–58.

27. Edmond Michelet, "Treblinka," *Le Monde,* 2 April 1966.

28. Pierre Vidal-Naquet, "Treblinka et l'honneur des juifs," *Le Monde,* 2 May 1966.

29. Bruno Ribes, "Les témoins de Treblinka," *Études* (June 1966): 782.

30. Wulf Kansteiner, "Success, Truth, and Modernism in Holocaust Historiography: Reading Saul Friedländer Thirty-Five Years after the Publication of *Metahistory*," *History & Theory* 47 (2009): 49.

31. For such a response to Friedländer's first installment in his two-volume work, see Dan Stone, *Constructing the Holocaust: A Study in Historiography* (London, 2003), 161–64.

32. Christopher R. Browning, "Evocation, Analysis, and the 'Crisis of Liberalism,'" *History and Theory* 48 (2009): 238–47. I owe Ethan Kleinberg for discussion of Friedländer's practice.

33. Ibid., 244. Unlike Friedländer, Browning views survivor testimony as a crucial source for history; his interpretation of Friedländer seeks the analytical elements of Friedländer's book, while his own new reconstruction of a slave labor camp based almost entirely on testimony treats it essentially as useful historical evidence. Cf. Browning, *Remembering Survival: Inside a Nazi Slave-Labor Camp* (New York, 2010), and my review in "Ordinary Memory," *Jewish Review of Books* 1 (Spring 2010).

34. Alon Confino, "Narrative Form and Historical Sensation: On Saul Friedländer's *The Years of Extermination*," and Amos Goldberg, "The Victim's Voice and Melodramatic Aesthetics in History," both in *History & Theory* 48 (2009), citation at 229.

35. Kansteiner, "Success," 51.

36. Ruth Leys, *Trauma: A Genealogy* (Baltimore, 2000); Didier Fassin and Richard Rechtman, *The Empire of Trauma: An Inquiry into the Condition of Victimhood*, trans. Rachel Gomme (Princeton, 2009); cf. Thomas W. Laqueur, "We Are All Victims Now," *London Review of Books*, 8 July 2010. For a fascinating study of medical reckoning with Holocaust survivors in France, see Michael Dorland, *Cadaverland: Inventing a Pathology of Catastrophe for Holocaust Survival* (Waltham, MA, 2009).

37. Giorgio Agamben, *Remnants of Auschwitz: The Witness and the Archive*, trans. Daniel Heller-Roazen (New York, 2001).

38. Martin S. Jaffee, "The Victim-Community in Myth and History: Holocaust Ritual, the Question of Palestine, and the Rhetoric of Christian Witness," *Journal of Ecumenical Studies* 28, no. 2 (1991): 228, 233.

39. Consider the forum in the *American Historical Review* 114, no. 4 (2009) on "truth and reconciliation in history."

CHAPTER 7

Transcending History?
Methodological Problems in Holocaust Testimony

ZOË WAXMAN

Auschwitz cannot be explained. ... [T]he Holocaust transcends history.
— Elie Wiesel, *Against Silence: The Voice and Vision of Elie Wiesel*

Survivors of the Shoah such as the 1986 Nobel Peace Prize winner Elie Wiesel insist that the Holocaust is "a mystery begotten by the dead."[1] As such, he believes that Holocaust testimony should be placed outside mainstream historical inquiry and instead interpreted in solely spiritual or wholly religious terms. For Wiesel, the diaries and other writings produced in the ghettos and concentration camps of Eastern Europe as well as the memoirs of survivors represent an important form of spiritual resistance against the attempted annihilation of the Jewish people. By contrast, historians wish to transform these "sacred" testimonies into historical documents and sources of information.[2] This is problematic, for, as Raul Hilberg, one of the foremost historians of the Holocaust, has noted: "In their accounts, survivors generally leave out the setting of their experiences, such as specific localities or the names and positions of persons they encountered."[3] In this chapter I will suggest that a variety of interpretative tools need to be employed in order to engage with testimony in any effective sense. For example, it is necessary to explore both the mechanics of testimony—language, motivation, and tradition—as well as its social, political, and historical context. The challenge is to find a way of working with testimony that unlocks it from the hermetically sealed, very specific literary genre it has been placed in, in a respectful manner that manages to also retain its specific qualities.

The nature of the debate is nicely illustrated in the attack made by David Patterson, a scholar of Jewish studies, on the historian James Young. In his

---

Notes for this section begin on page 154.

Writing and Rewriting the Holocaust, Young argues that we need to take proper account of the subjective nature of personal testimony. This, for Patterson, is simply sacrilege. He, like Wiesel, views the literature of the Holocaust in spiritual terms and regards the treatment of testimonies as sources or historical information (places, names, dates, etc.) as part of a damaging process of regarding "eyewitness accounts ... as data and not as the outcries of Jewish souls that might implicate us in any way."[4] He argues that Young "fabricates a distance between ourselves and the diaries by reducing them not only to documents, evidence, and sources of information but to *problematic* documents, evidence, and sources of information."[5] It is not, of course, Young's intention to reduce diaries "to *problematic* documents," but rather to point out that "the reasons for which diarists wrote and the focus of their witness inescapably regulate, and at times restrict, the diarist's record.... In addition to time and place, the diarists' very language, tradition, and world view played crucial roles in the making of their literary witness."[6] In other words, Young is arguing that we need to look at the individual motivations and concerns behind the recording of testimony rather than treat it as sacred text.

Indeed, whilst the quasi-spiritual approach to testimony advocated by Elie Wiesel and David Patterson may yield important insights, it also often means that the social historical climate shaping testimony and the individual motivations of those who produce testimony are left unexplored. The literary critic George Steiner goes so far as to argue that the sacred nature of Holocaust testimonies implies that all we can do is simply repeat them word for word:

> These books and the documents that have survived are not for "review." Not unless "review" signifies, as perhaps it should in these instances, a "seeing-again," over and over. As in some Borges fable, the only complete decent "review" of the Warsaw Diary or of Elie Wiesel's *Night* would be to re-copy the book, line by line, pausing at the names of the dead and the names of the children as the orthodox scribe pauses, when recopying the Bible, at the hallowed name of god. Until we know many of the words by *heart* (knowledge deeper than mind) and could repeat a few at the break of morning to remind ourselves that we live after, that the end of the day may bring "inhuman trial or a remembrance stronger than death."[7]

Although this attitude to testimony might provide us with a vivid glimpse of the terrible experiences the witnesses suffered, it actually ignores the agency of the victims—their language, tradition, politics, identity, motivation—and therefore cannot tell us anything more about the history of the Holocaust, or the individual men and women who lived through it. Furthermore, such a reverential attitude to testimony overlooks the fact that the events being narrated, however appalling, were enacted by human beings on other human beings. As such, it is unhelpful to situate the Holocaust in a place beyond analysis. As Inga Clendinnen succinctly puts it: "Human history being what it is, there has been a lot of beastliness about."[8]

Given this culture of deference or awe—and the controversy that surrounds the use of Holocaust testimony—it is not surprising that historians have been reluctant to engage seriously with it, if indeed they have used it at all. When they have been forced to use it—for example, in the absence of alternative documentary evidence—they have tended to be highly instrumental, simply mining the material for evidence, illustration, or just background color. The result of this is further to dilute the significance of testimony. Once again—although for very different reasons—no account is taken of the authors' intentions or the specific category of their writing. In his recent and magisterial work *The Years of Extermination: Nazi Germany and the Jews 1939–1945*, Saul Friedländer insists that we must go beyond "a recounting of German policies, decisions, and measures,"[9] to understand the experiences of the victims. Nevertheless he could be rightly accused by Patterson of mining the material for data rather than using it to explore the specific logic of testimony.[10] More strikingly still, Martin Gilbert's innovative work *The Holocaust: The Jewish Tragedy*, a narrative history of the Holocaust based mainly on primary sources and interviews with survivors, while structured by testimony, offers very little analysis of the sources on which it relies. This allows him to making sweeping statements such as: "Simply to survive was a victory of the human spirit."[11] Such a comment is neither borne out by the testimonies he uses, nor indeed does it offer anything like an analysis of the experiences their writers underwent. It is simply banal. And, in fact, much comment on testimony is reducible either to moralising or to the merely instrumental.

Against these two positions—the quasi-spiritual and the instrumental models of engagement with testimony—this chapter will argue that, if taken seriously, testimony can retain both its privileged or "special" status whilst also being regarded as an important source of historical information. Whilst it might to a certain extent be true that the Nazi concentration camps are ultimately "ineffable,"[12] to use Primo Levi's term, testimony *does* hold the potential to take us forward in our understanding of the Holocaust. Wiesel is not asking that we distance ourselves from the terrible events of the Holocaust, but rather that we exercise some humility when studying it and take testimony seriously.[13] Indeed, each testimony—whether coming from those who did not survive, or from those writing after the war far removed from the events they are narrating—has the potential to tell us something more about the world that was lost and the suffering and destruction which befell the Jews of Europe.

Testimony was written before, during, and after the Holocaust.[14] For some historians, only testimony written during the Holocaust is worthy of serious consideration. Raul Hilberg, who fled from Vienna in 1939 and was the author of the seminal three-volume work *The Destruction of the European Jews*,[15] is one of these writers: "I have read countless accounts of survivors. I looked for the missing links in my jigsaw puzzle. I tried to glimpse the Jewish community. I searched for the dead. Most often, however, I had to remind myself that what I most wanted from them they could not give me, no matter how much they said."[16] The historian Lucy Dawidowicz goes even further: "The transcribed testimonies I have examined have been full of errors in dates, names of participants, and places, and there are evident misunderstandings of the events themselves. To the unwary reader, some of the accounts can be more hazard than help."[17] Likewise, David Roskies, working in the field of Jewish literature, argues that the diaries and other Jewish documents produced during the Holocaust should be seen as a distinct category of writing and be read in a different way: "Because of their insistence on the knowability of the destruction," he declares, they "require a separate hermeneutics."[18]

There is much which commends itself in this argument.[19] Clearly, the diary of Dawid Sierakowiak, a young school boy in the Łódź ghetto, needs to be understood in very different terms from the post-war writings of Primo Levi, an Italian scientist, who had come to intellectual maturity before the war and survived Auschwitz to find his home and family intact.[20] Sierakowiak was starving to death as he painfully recorded his diary entries, and as the war develops the reader is made all too aware of the gradual degradation of his physical and mental being. Despite his young age he realized that "[t]here is no way out. It seems that we shall be buried here."[21] Four months after making his last diary entry on 15 April 1943, he died, aged sixteen years, of tuberculosis, starvation, and exhaustion—or "ghetto disease" as it was commonly known. In contrast, Levi, although immeasurably altered by his wartime experiences, was nevertheless unable completely to recapture the grinding monotony of the suffering prisoner of Auschwitz. For example, he writes: "The hardest thing to capture was precisely the boredom ... every single day the same."[22]

Nonetheless, while it is important to distinguish the writing produced during the Holocaust as a distinct literary genre, I would argue against placing—as Roskies would suggest—the diary of Sierakowiak into a "closed canon of wartime writings,"[23] outside of mainstream historical inquiry. Sierakowiak, who started writing his diary in June 1939, shortly before his fifteenth birthday, clearly wanted to leave a vivid picture of the suffering he and his community were forced to endure. He did not shy away from the moral dilemmas living in such extremity necessarily produced, but tried his best to record as true a picture as possible. His diary, recorded in tightly written script in five notebooks was discovered by accident after the war. It is important not to overlook the fact that witnesses such as Sierakowiak did not intend their writings to be a "closed canon": in addition to wanting to leave a record of their own, and in particular, their families' existence, they also wanted to provide a basis for future historical research.[24] This was, for example, clearly the motivation for Załman Gradowski, an observant Jew from Suwałki (on the border of Lithuania and Poland), who was unlucky enough to serve in the *Sonderkommando* (special detachment) unit of prisoners forced to work in the crematoria at Auschwitz-

Birkenau. He wrote in a text buried in the pits of human ashes, and discovered after the war, that he wanted "to immortalize the dear, beloved names of those, for whom, at this moment, I cannot even expend a tear."[25] He was also realistic enough to realize that "it may be that these, the lines I am now writing, will be the sole witnesses to what was my life."[26]

Roskies is right to insist that the significance of the writings produced during the Holocaust is not limited to the simple conveying of information. Sierakowiak and Gradowski were indeed writing from within the abyss—although this does not mean that we need to adopt the analysis wholeheartedly. They were not professional historians and were inevitably—constrained by their circumstances—writing on the basis of limited information. Nonetheless Gradowski in particular was very aware that he was consciously defying the Nazis not only by leaving evidence of his existence, but also by bearing witness to the destruction of European Jewry.[27] He was not alone. A surprising number of Jews both in the ghettos of Eastern Europe and in the deportation and death camps committed themselves to writing down what they saw and experienced in an effort to meet this aim. As Emmanuel Ringelblum, the young social historian responsible for the establishment of *Oneg Shabbat* (Sabbath Celebrants), the underground archive in the Warsaw Ghetto, wrote: "The drive to write down one's memoirs is powerful.... [E]ven young people in labor camps do it."[28] He estimated that in the Warsaw Ghetto alone, hundreds of Jews kept diaries, most of which were either lost or destroyed along with the Jews of Warsaw following the mass deportations to Treblinka on 22 July 1942.[29] Chaim Aron Kaplan, an Orthodox Jew, ardent Zionist, and Hebrew teacher, was one such individual driven to record his suffering. Although he had long kept a diary before the war started, he described his need to continue it amidst the misery of the Warsaw Ghetto as "a flame imprisoned in my bones, burning within me, screaming: Record."[30] The final entry of his diary, dated 4 August 1942, asks: "If my life ends—what will become of my diary?"[31] Shortly before he met his death in the gas chambers of Treblinka, he gave his diary, recorded in perfectly written Hebrew, in more than a dozen small notebooks, to a Polish friend to smuggle out of the ghetto. The books were discovered after the war in a kerosene can and are preserved in archives in Israel and Poland.

As we read the texts of these men and women—for a number of women have left testimony—we are seeped with the knowledge that they like the vast majority of the authors who wrote in the ghettos and concentrations camps, did not survive. More than this, we are reminded that the vast majority of the victims never wrote anything at all. Each text which survived the Holocaust did so against almost overwhelming odds. Heinrich Himmler, addressing a group of SS officers at Poznan in October 1943, declared that the murder of the Jews was to be "an unwritten and never to be written page of glory in our history."[32] The Nazis would be the ones to tell the world about the Jews and Jewish history, for example in the museum they had planned in Prague. The theologian Isabel Wollaston calls it "A War against Memory,"[33] and Shoshana Felman and Dori Laub "an event without a witness."[34] It was not enough therefore to find the strength to record what was happening in circumstances that largely militated against the writing of testimony; the authors also had to ensure that their writings would outlive them. Shortly before burying the archives of *Oneg Shabbat,* eighteen-year-old Nachum Grzywacz expressed his ultimately futile wish that: "I would like to live to the moment when the treasure is dug out and the whole truth proclaimed.... But we certainly will not live to see it."[35] Likewise Zalman Gradowski wrote: "Dear finder, search everywhere, in every inch of soil. Tons of documents are buried under it, mine and those of other prisoners, which will throw light on everything that was happening here. It was we, the Kommando workers, who expressly have strewn them all over the terrain, as many as we could, so that the world would find material traces of the millions of murdered people. We ourselves have lost hope of being able to live to see the moment of liberation."[36] Not only the words that were written but our knowledge of the context of their writing, preservation, and discovery envelop each text with their different layers of meaning.

It is all but impossible to make meaningful generalizations about these testimonies. Each one, reflecting the diversity of human experience, is unique. They are written by both men and women, the old and, those—like Dawid Sierakowiak—who were children during the war. Some were educated, some religious, some both, and some neither. Not only was each ghetto and every concentration camp very different, but ghettos and camps went through dramatic changes in themselves. Reflecting the progression of anti-Jewish policy, conditions were divergent and subject to constant change. Thus every witness experienced his or her own ghetto or concentration camp and did so from a very particular perspective. Not only this, but many witnesses never experienced a concentration camp but survived by hiding (either with false Aryan papers or without); most were alone, but some like Anne Frank were with family members. However, it is through their words that the six million faceless victims become individual men, women, and children, and we are made to see that they are not creatures from a different planet, but human beings with the same sensibilities as ourselves.

The difficulty for historians is that they do not necessarily want to focus on the minutiae of individual experience. Rather their concern is generally how to represent commonalities of experience—hence the tendency to mine individual testimonies for data rather than to focus on the idiosyncrasies of individual experience.[37] The problem with this approach is that stories that do not conform to appropriate expectations are all too often either ignored or confined to the margins or footnotes of history.[38] The result of which is that the Jews are all too often represented as a homogenous, interchangeable mass rather than as distinct individuals. The challenge is to build on the techniques of micro-history and its focus on first-hand experience to find a means of creating a clearer picture of the events of the Holocaust in a manner that does not threaten to erase the identity of the victims. By the same token, the problem for those who would spiritualize the Holocaust is that these individual stories often included details—of cruelty, despair, violence, and human frailty—which challenge empty moralising. Here again, the task is to be able to listen attentively to different voices and differing experiences of hundreds—even thousands—of individuals.

This challenge is still more striking for those who wish to use the testimony written after the end of the war. Inevitably shaped by hindsight, by forgetting, and by the needs of the present, it poses particular problems for the historian. Unlike the testimonies of those who—like Sierakowiak and Gradowski—tragically never survived to see liberation, survivors' memories are subject to the constraints of memory and should not carry expectation of pure, immediate experience. Not only are survivors' memories "indissolubly woven into the present,"[39] meaning that interpretations of the past are inextricably mediated by current concerns, but as Hilberg has rightly highlighted, memory is necessarily imperfect. As Primo Levi has written: "At a distance of thirty years I find it difficult to reconstruct the sort of human being that corresponded, in November 1944, to my name or, better, to my number: 174517."[40] In a similar vein the survivor Bert Lewyn felt compelled to explain in his memoir that without consulting his ex-wife, a fellow survivor, "many important details would have been overlooked."[41] Even more problematic are the errors in the memories of survivors. It is unsurprising that these are of great concern to historians—see for example the comments of Hilberg and Dawidowicz cited above.

One of the most famous examples of such an error has been described by the survivor and psychoanalyst Dori Laub. At a conference on Holocaust education, the videotaped testimony of a woman who witnessed the *Sonderkommando* uprising at Birkenau was shown. She describes how: "All of a sudden … we saw four chimneys going up in flames, exploding. The flames shot into the sky, people were running. It was unbelievable."[42] As only one chimney was blown up, the testimony provoked considerable debate among the historians present who claimed that the major inaccuracy called into question the veracity of the women's testimony in general: "Historically, only one chimney was blown up, not all four. Since the memory of the testifying woman turned out to be, in this way, fallible, one could not accept—nor give credence to—her whole account of the events. It was utterly important to remain accurate, lest the revisionists in history discredit everything."[43] However, Laub urges that rather than rejecting the woman's testimony we rethink our understanding of the nature of historical truth. Not only was "[o]ne chimney blown up in Auschwitz … as incredible as four,"[44] but we need to understand that testimony cannot provide all the answers—or the type of answers sought by Hilberg and Dawidowicz who, frustrated by what they see as the limitations of testimony, turn instead to the more thorough Nazi documentation.[45] Even more recently the historian Christopher Browning has noted that in his study of the testimonies of Jews from the Starachowice slave labor camp, he found numerous contradictions regarding chronology, the identity of different people, and the course of events.[46] What victim testimony can do, however, as Laub recognizes, is supply meaning. This was understood by Chaim Kaplan who was aware that while imprisoned in the Warsaw Ghetto he was unable to "know all the facts,"[47] but he nevertheless could stay true to the essence of the suffering: "But for the sake of truthfulness, I do not require individual facts, but rather manifestations of the fruits of a great many facts that leave their impression on the people's opinions, on their mood and morale. And I can guarantee the factualness of these manifestations because I dwell among my people and behold their misery and their soul's torments."[48] As James Young argues, "in the final analysis, no document can be more historically authentic than that embodying the victims' grasp of events at the time."[49]

Donald Bloxham and Tony Kushner are thus entirely right to argue that in order to appreciate the significance of survivor testimony, we need to place it within the wider context of the survivors' lives. In other words, survivors cannot be treated as separate from their testimony. Nonetheless, there can be problems with even this approach. By focusing on the limitations of testimony—arguing that "getting to grips with survivor testimony is less a question of asking what it can tell us of the experiences recalled than of the way those experiences have been processed"[50]—they unwittingly reproduce the convictions of earlier historians such as Hilberg and Dawidowicz that Jewish testimony can actually tell us very little in terms of concrete information. They do not allow for the possibility that testimony can in fact provide important information regarding the details of the Nazi genocide. Thus Kushner, in a highly perceptive and incisive critique of the use of Jewish Holocaust testimony, is undoubtedly right to insist that scholars "have to take such testimony seriously, as revealing its own internal dynamics, which might mean revealing its strong mythologies and contradictions—the real nature of any life story."[51] But he fails to also point out that testimony can uncover details of historical experience which might otherwise remain unknown. Instead, Kushner is interested in what he refers to as "complex layers of memories."[52] For him—for example—the historian Mark Roseman's account of the life of the German Jewish survivor Marianne Ellenbogen is primarily important because of the way it reveals what is a stake in the construction of a life narrative.[53] True enough, Roseman's work does provide a glimpse into the problems of using personal testimony to reconstruct past events—in this case after a period of fifty years. Perhaps unsurprisingly Roseman found that "compared with sources from the Nazi and post-war periods, a number of important differences and discrepancies emerged."[54] However, the study is significant for more than that. It also provides specific—and otherwise unobtainable—evidence of how it was possible to survive the Holocaust in hiding.

One way of resolving this tension—between those who would deny the objective truth of testimony and those who object to any suggestion of its subjectivity; between those who would sacralize testimony and those who would simply mine it for data—is to ask why testimony has been written at all. A multiplicity of motives inspired those enduring the Holocaust to write. A similarly diverse range of reasons has prompted survivors after the event. The focus of this chapter is on the written narrative, which is a particular form of the representation of experience—mediated through a life, through time (the journey back and forth between past, present, and future), and through text. In other words, the presentation of memory through the written narrative is a particular way of finding meaning and organizing experience: an attempt to make sense of a life. Survivors for example, are all too aware that while they survived, millions of others did not. This can result in feelings of guilt. As Primo Levi has so famously remarked: "The worst survived, that is, the fittest; the best all died."[55] Bruno Bettelheim, who survived Buchenwald and Dachau, elaborates: "One cannot survive the concentration camp without feeling guilty that one was so incredibly lucky when millions perished, many of them in front of one' eyes. ... In the camps one was forced, day after day, for years, to watch the destruction of others, feeling—against one's better judgment—that one should have intervened, feeling guilty for having often felt glad that it was not oneself who perished."[56] Considering the implications for memory, Levi has perceptively remarked: "a person who has been wounded tends to block out the memory so as not to renew the pain; the person who has inflicted the wound pushes the memory deep down, to be rid of it, to alleviate the feeling of guilt."[57] Rather than being seen as a way of making what is absent present, the testimonies of survivors should be understood as an active dialogue between past and present. It is important that they should not be read as snapshots of events independent of the person bearing witness; we need both to consider the limitations of memory, as well as take into account factors such as witnesses' personal attempts to memorialize the dead, make sense of painful experiences, and guide future generations in their attempts to understand the Nazi genocide.

While Primo Levi, who began making notes even before liberation, writes: "those memories burned so intensely inside me that I felt compelled to write as soon as I returned to Italy,"[58] other survivors felt unable to address their painful memories until considerably later.[59] For many, it was not until they had lived in their adopted countries for many years and reached a certain level of financial and emotional stability that they felt able to return to the past. Although survivors writing more than half a century after the end of the war will often add little that is factually new to our knowledge and understanding of the Holocaust, they do importantly remind us that the events of the past cannot be confined to a chapter of history but are real events where real people suffered and died—and, perhaps even more significantly, they continue to have reverberations in the present.[60] For survivors the past is not past and liberation did not necessarily put an end to their suffering.[61] Bertha Ferderber-Salz writes, "Pictures from the past and the images of the people I loved are always with me. It is not natural to live constantly in the past, but I cannot do otherwise."[62] Both the diaries of those who did not survive and the memoirs of survivors perform a similar function: they make what would otherwise be unimaginable imaginable by attempting to make us understand what it meant to live under Nazi occupation and its effects on the individual, the family, community, education, religion, and culture. The survivor Gisela Perl expresses this very well when she writes in her memoir that her task is not just to honor the six million Jewish victims but somehow to attempt to tell their stories. She writes, "Those six million dead are so many terrible, heartbreaking stories.... Every one of them represents not only the second of death, however horrible that is, but an entire, colourful exciting human life, a past, and what is more, a future."[63]

Only a handful of the diaries and other writings that survived the war have been published in their entirety in their original languages; the rest remain in archives in Poland, Israel, and America. Much of the literature is written in Yiddish (the main language of the Jewish victims), Hebrew, Polish, Romanian, Hungarian, Russian, Italian, Dutch, and French and, as such, is inaccessible to many English-speaking historians. In contrast, the memoirs of survivors—together with their diaries, novels, and documentary reports—form an ever-increasing literary corpus. While some spring from the emotional impulse of the survivor to testify, others find their origin in the post-war trials and the demands for survivors to testify against the German trials.[64] Survivor memoirs are in many ways more accessible than contemporary sources as survivors have often chosen to write of their experiences in an adopted language—for example, in English—for, as Andrea Reiter suggests, "the adopted foreign language demonstrates that a new life has really literally begun in the author's consciousness."[65] While, in one sense, neither the diaries of the victims nor the memoirs of survivors can be viewed as history in the strictest sense, for both are inevitably made up of subjective observations[66] and cannot offer analytical accounts of the history of the Holocaust, each testimony nevertheless constitutes an important historical document, for they all contribute to what we know about the Holocaust and the destruction of Jewish life.

The function of testimony does not end there. This is an age in which we seem particularly obsessed by personal experience—as Geoffrey Hartman observes, we live in an "era of testimony":[67] a world of biographical excesses in the form of tell-all talk shows and confessional literature.[68] This is a world where individual experience is at a premium and testimonies of the Holocaust are scanned for "moral" messages. However, while this might seem a recent development, in fact as early as 1967 Wiesel asked:

> Why don't we claim it [the Holocaust] as a glorious chapter in our eternal history? After all, it did change man and his world—well, it did not change man,

but it did change the world. It is still the greatest event in our times. Why then are we ashamed of it? In its power it even influenced language. Negro quarters are called ghettos; Hiroshima is explained by Auschwitz; Vietnam is described in terms which were used one generation ago. Everything today revolves around our Holocaust experience. Why then do we face it with such ambiguity? Perhaps this should be the task of Jewish educators and philosophers: to reopen the event as a source of pride, to take it back into our history.[69]

The inference is that the only response to the Holocaust is one of deference or awe. Wiesel appears to be suggesting that suffering can draw out moral sensibilities. This claim is not uncommon. Terrence Des Pres, who in 1976 produced the first in-depth study of the psychology of Holocaust survivors, wrote that testimonies carry an important moral message: "for survivors the struggle to live—merely surviving—is rooted in, and a manifestation of, the form-conferring potency of life itself."[70] While this may no doubt to some extent be true—although it is equally true that suffering is often a far from ennobling experience—such a stance is problematic for the historian. Indeed, arguing against attempts to find universal significance in the Holocaust, historians such as Saul Friedländer have stated that the enormity of the event makes all efforts to extract universal meaning redundant.[71] Instead he wants us to focus on the specific nature of the Holocaust. This is also the case of course for Wiesel, although for him what is specific about the Holocaust is its essential mystery. While Wiesel has dedicated his life to writing about the Holocaust—as if by doing so he might come closer to its meaning—he is at the same time fearful that the very act of writing translates the mystical into the familiar and thereby erodes the essential incomprehensibility of the Holocaust. This fear is echoed by the literary critic and Holocaust scholar Lawrence Langer who argues: "The universe of dying that was Auschwitz yearns for a language purified of the taint of normality."[72]

Wiesel is more than aware that he is one voice amongst many. Today survivors are still coming forward to tell their stories. Not only they, but their children and even their children's children want to add their perspectives to the now enormous literature bearing witness to the Holocaust. Since the 1980s and 1990s the success of Hollywood films such as Steven Spielberg's Oscar-winning *Schindler's List* (1993), the establishment of audiovisual archives,[73] the growth of "Holocaust tourism," and the proliferation of Holocaust memorial museums, exhibitions, monuments, and conferences have fueled the demand for the testimonies of survivors and contributed to the commodification of testimony.[74] As Wieviorka points out, testimonies are no longer confined to archives, but have become almost ubiquitous in their abundance.[75] Furthermore, the identity of the survivor as one who survived the ghettos or concentration camps has become diluted in recent years to include not only those who survived the ghettos and concentration camps but also those who survived the war in hiding and also, perhaps more contentiously, members of the *Kindertransport*.[76] Wiesel is not alone when he worries that the Holocaust has become a "desanctified theme, or if you prefer, a theme robbed of its passion, its mystery."[77]

The problem is that the Holocaust has become an event either so sacred that it defies comprehension or so ordinary that it means everything to everyone. The challenge is to somehow repair the difficult space between the mystification of the Holocaust and its place in historical understanding; to transcend the gap between the semi-mystical and instrumental views of Holocaust testimony which have dominated the field thus far. Not only is this project valuable for historians and for all who want to learn about the reality of the Holocaust and the lives of those who lived through it and died in it. It is also what many of those who left testimony call on us to do. This is what witnesses such as Sierakowiak, Kaplan, and Gradowski were calling for—for the people of the free world not only to read what they had to say, but to be shaken by it to such an extent that we are forced to revaluate all that we think we know.

Notes

1. Elie Wiesel, *One Generation After,* trans. Lily Edelman and Elie Wiesel (New York, 1970), 43.
2. On the theme of Holocaust testimony as sacred text, see Isabel Wollaston, "'Memory and Monument': Holocaust Testimony as Sacred Text," in *The Sociology of Sacred Texts,* ed. Jon Davies and Isabel Wollaston (Sheffield, 1993), 37–44.
3. Raul Hilberg, *The Politics of Memory: The Journey of a Holocaust Historian* (Chicago, 1996), 133.
4. David Patterson, *Along the Edge of Annihilation: The Collapse and Recovery of Life in the Holocaust Diary* (Seattle, 1999), 7.
5. Ibid.
6. James Young, *Writing and Rewriting the Holocaust: Narrative and the Consequences of Interpretation* (Bloomington, 1990), 25–26.
7. George Steiner, *Language and Silence: Essays 1958–1966* (London, 1967), 235.
8. Inga Clendinnen, *Reading the Holocaust* (Cambridge, 1999), 12.
9. Saul Friedländer, *The Years of Extermination: Nazi Germany and the Jews 1939–1945* (London, 2007), xv.
10. Cf. Zoë Waxman, "Towards an Integrated History of the Holocaust: Masculinity, Femininity, and Genocide," in *Years of Persecution, Years of Extermination: Saul Friedländer and the Future of Holocaust Studies,* ed. Christian Wiese and Paul Betts (London, 2010), 311–21.
11. Martin Gilbert, *The Holocaust: The Jewish Tragedy* (London, 1987), 828.
12. Primo Levi, "Revisiting the Camps," in *The Art of Memory,* ed. James E. Young (Munich, 1994), 185.
13. Wiesel goes so far as to suggest: "Perhaps every Jew ought to pick a dead man, woman, or child, whether known or unknown, and say: from this point on, I shall live for myself and for him or her." See Elie Wiesel, *Evil and Exile,* (Notre Dame, 1990), 37. The United States Holocaust Memorial Museum suggests a similar idea by offering each visitor an "ID card" containing details about a victim of approximately the visitor's age.
14. See Zoë Vania Waxman, *Writing the Holocaust: Identity, Testimony, Representation* (Oxford, 2006).
15. Raul Hilberg, *The Destruction of the European Jews,* 3 vols. (Chicago, 1961).
16. Hilberg, *The Politics of Memory,* 133.

17. Lucy S. Dawidowicz, *The Holocaust and the Historians* (Cambridge, MA, 1981), 177.

18. David G. Roskies, ed., *The Literature of Destruction: Jewish Responses to Catastrophe* (Philadelphia, 1989), 25. He goes even further to argue that testimony needs to be contextualised as a specifically Jewish phenomenon to be understood as part of the continuum of Jewish responses to persecution—as part of "the library of Jewish Catastrophe" (ibid., ch. 2). At the same time, however, we need to remember that even the most assimilated of Jews were not spared.

19. Cf. Sara Horowitz, *Voicing the Void: Muteness and Memory in Holocaust Fiction* (Albany, 1997), ch. 3.

20. See Dawid Sierakowiak, *The Diary of Dawid Sierakowiak: Five Notebooks form the Łódź Ghetto*, ed. Alan Adelson (London, 1997); and Primo Levi, *The Drowned and the Saved* (London, 1988).

21. Sierakowiak, *The Diary of Dawid Sierakowiak*, 20.

22. Primo Levi, *If This is a Man* and *The Truce* (London, 1987), 129.

23. Roskies, ed., *The Literature of Destruction*, 26.

24. It is estimated that only two Łódź ghetto diarists survived the war. As such only a very small sample of the diaries written in the ghetto remain.

25. Roskies, ed., *The Literature of Destruction*, 558. Cf. Zalman Gradowski, "Manuscript of Sonderkommando Member," in *Amidst a Nightmare of Crime: Manuscripts of Members of Sonderkommando*, ed. Jadwiga Bezwinska and Danuta Czech (Cracow, 1973), 75–108. For a history of the manuscript and its discovery, see Ber Mark, *The Scrolls of Auschwitz* (Tel Aviv, 1985). Cf. Nathan Cohen, "Diaries of the Sonderkommando in Auschwitz: Coping with Fate and Reality," *Yad Vashem Studies* 20 (1990): 273–312; and Cohen, "Diaries of the Sonderkommando," in *Anatomy of the Auschwitz Death Camp*, ed. Yisrael Gutman and Michael Berenbaum (Bloomington, 1994), 522–34.

26. Cited in Roskies, ed., *The Literature of Destruction*, 548.

27. Waxman, *Writing the Holocaust*, 81–85.

28. Emmanuel Ringelblum, *Notes from the Warsaw Ghetto: The Journal of Emmanuel Ringelblum* (New York, 1958), 31. Similar archives were set up in Łódź (renamed Litzmannstadt by the Germans); Kovno (Lithuanian: Kaunas); Białystok; Vilna (Lithuanian: Vilnius); Cracow; and Lvov (Polish: Lwów; German: Lemberg).

29. Emmanuel Ringelblum, "O.S.," in Joseph Kermish, ed., *To Live with Honor and Die with Honor!* (Jerusalem, 1986), 18.

30. Chaim A. Kaplan, *The Warsaw Diary of Chaim A. Kaplan* (New York, 1973), 144.

31. Ibid., 340.

32. Cited in Richard Breitman, *The Architect of Genocide: Himmler and the Final Solution* (London, 1991), 243.

33. See Isabel Wollaston, *A War Against Memory? The Future of Holocaust Remembrance* (London, 1983).

34. Shoshana Felman and Dori Laub, *Testimony: Crises of Witnessing in Literature, Psychoanalysis and History* (New York, 1992), 75–92.

35. Cited in Nora Levin, *The Holocaust: The Destruction of European Jewry 1933–1945* (New York, 1973), 324–25.

36. Cited in Patterson, *Along the Edge of Annihilation*, 274.

37. Cf. Alexandra Garbarini, *Numbered Days: Diaries and the Holocaust* (New Haven, 2006), 5–6.

38. This can be seen in the assumptions all too often made about women's Holocaust experiences where testimonies that depart from traditional gendered expectations are often overlooked. See Zoë Waxman, "Unheard Testimony, Untold Stories: The Representation of Women's Holocaust Experiences," *Women's History Review* 12, no. 4 (2003): 661–77, and "Testimony and Silence: Sexual Violence and the Holocaust," in *Feminism, Literature, and Rape Narratives*, ed. Zoe Brigley and Sorcha Gunne (London, 2010), 117–29.

39. Theodor W. Adorno, *Minima Moralia: Reflections from Damaged Life* (London, 1978), 166.

40. Primo Levi, *The Periodic Table* (London, 1984), 139–40.

41. Bert Lewyn and Bev Saltzman, *Holocaust Memoirs: Life on the Run in Nazi Berlin* (Philadelphia, 2001), 437.

42. Felman and Laub, *Testimony,* 59.

43. Ibid., 59–60.

44. Ibid., 60.

45. The furor surrounding the publication of the fraudulent testimony by Benjamin Wilkomirski has had further explosive implications for this debate. See Binjamin Wilkomirski, *Fragments: Memories of a Childhood, 1939–1948* (London, 1996); Daniel Ganzfried, "Die Geliehene Holocaust-Biographie—The Purloined Holocaust Biography," *Die Weltwoche* (27 August 1998); Philip Gourevitch, "The Memory Thief," *New Yorker* (14 June 1999): 48–68; Elena Lappin, "The Man with Two Heads," *Granta* 66 (1999): 7–65; and Stefan Maechler, *The Wilkomirski Affair: A Study in Biographical Truth,* trans. John E. Woods (New York, 2001).

46. Christopher Browning, *Collected Memories: Holocaust History and Postwar Testimony* (Madison, 2003).

47. Kaplan, *The Warsaw Diary of Chaim A. Kaplan,* 30.

48. Ibid.

49. James Young, "Between History and Memory: The Uncanny Voice of the Historian and the Survivor," *History and Memory* 9, nos. 1–2 (1997): 56.

50. Donald Bloxham and Tony Kushner, *The Holocaust: Critical Historical Approaches* (Manchester, 2004), 157. Kushner further argues regarding oral history, that "How a person puts together their life experiences in a coherent way tells us as much about their life *now* as about their past, for all are bound together in creating the individual's identity." See Tony Kushner, "Holocaust Testimony, Ethics, and the Problem of Representation," *Poetics Today* 27, no. 2 (2006): 282.

51. Kushner, "Holocaust Testimony," 283.

52. Ibid., 287.

53. Ibid. See Mark Roseman, *The Past in Hiding* (London, 2000).

54. Kushner, "Holocaust Testimony," 287. See Mark Roseman, "Surviving Memory: Truth and Inaccuracy in Holocaust Testimony," *Journal of Holocaust Education* 8, no. 1 (1999), 1–20.

55. Levi, *The Drowned and the Saved,* 82.

56. Bruno Bettelheim, *Surviving and Other Essays* (New York, 1979), 297–98.

57. Levi, *The Drowned and the Saved,* 23. In the first volume of his memoir, *All Rivers Run to the Sea,* Elie Wiesel has gone so far as to admit: "I must warn you that certain events will be omitted, especially those episodes that might embarrass friends and, of course, those that might damage the Jewish people. Call it prudence or cowardice, whatever you like. No witness is capable of recounting everything from start to finish anyway. God alone knows the whole story." Elie Wiesel, *All Rivers Run to the Sea: Memoirs* (New York, 1995), 17.

58. Levi, *If This is a man and The Truce,* 381.

59. On survivor testimony in the early years after the war, see Henry Greenspan, *The Awakening of Memory: Survivor Testimony in the First Years After the Holocaust, and Today* (Washington, DC, 2004).

60. Cf. Annette Wieviorka, who writes: "Today … the purpose of testimony is no longer to obtain knowledge.... [T]he mission that has devolved to testimony is no longer to bear witness to inadequately known events, but rather to keep them before our eyes." "On Testimony," in *Holocaust Remembrance: The Shapes of Memory,* ed. Geoffrey H. Hartman (Oxford, 1994), 24.

61. On "The Failure of Liberation," see David Patterson, *Sun Turned to Darkness: Memory and Recovery in the Holocaust Memoir* (New York, 1998), 179–96.

62. Bertha Ferderber-Salz, *And the Sun Kept Shining* (New York, 1980), 56.

63. Gisella Perl, *I Was A Doctor in Auschwitz* (New York, 1948), 137.

64. Cf. Annette Wieviorka, *The Era of the Witness* (Ithaca, 2006), xii.

65. Andrea Reiter, *Narrating the Holocaust* (London, 2000), 96.

66. R. G. Collingwood, *The Idea of History* (New York, 1956), 2–3.

67. Geoffrey H. Hartman, "Introduction: Darkness Visible," in *Holocaust Remembrance,* ed. Hartman, 4.

68. See Geoffrey H. Hartman, *Scars of the Spirit: The Struggle Against Inauthenticity* (New York, 2002). Henry Greenspan has argued that "So much have we come to celebrate the act of testimony … that the specific content of the testimony is left as background." *On Listening to Holocaust Survivors: Recounting and Life History* (Westport, CT, 1998), 48.

69. Elie Wiesel, "Jewish Values in a Post-Holocaust Future: A Symposium," *Judaism* 16, no. 3 (1967): 288.

70. Terrence Des Pres, *The Survivor: An Anatomy of Life in the Death Camps* (Oxford, 1976), 177.

71. Saul Friedländer, "Introduction," in *Probing the Limits of Representation: Nazism and the "Final Solution,"* ed. Saul Friedländer (Cambridge, MA, 1992), 19–20.

72. Lawrence L. Langer, *Admitting the Holocaust: Collected Essays* (Oxford, 1995), 93.

73. For a critical account of audiovisual testimonies, see Lawrence L. Langer, *Holocaust Testimonies: The Ruins of Memory* (New Haven, 1991).

74. Cf. Wieviorka, *The Era of the Witness,* 56.

75. Ibid., xii.

76. Cf. Emanuel Tanay, "On Being a Survivor," in *Bearing Witness to the Holocaust, 1939–1989,* ed. Alan Berger (Lewiston, 1992), 17–31.

77. Elie Wiesel, "A Plea for Survivors," in *A Jew Today* (New York, 1978), 237–38.

CHAPTER 8

Studying the Holocaust
Is History Commemoration?

DORIS L. BERGEN

In an interview he gave late in his life, Raul Hilberg insisted that the study of the Holocaust was "not for amateurs." He contrasted the serious scholarship being done in Germany and Austria with what he deemed the dismal state of the field in the United States. The Holocaust, he concluded, "is not for untrained people, it is not for philosophers":

> It is for people who know languages, who know history, who know political science, who know economics, etc. At the root they must be well trained. The Holocaust is not today, as it might have been in the beginning, a subject for the laymen.[1]

In the same interview and on numerous other occasions, Hilberg praised Norman Finkelstein, whose excoriation of the "Holocaust Industry" caused a scandal that Finkelstein's supporters claim cost him tenure at DePaul University.[2] Hilberg's admonition, Finkelstein's work, and the proliferation since the 1990s of Holocaust commemorative and educational projects all over the world raise a question that is rarely voiced aloud: What is the relationship between academic study of the Holocaust and public commemoration?

There are, of course, easy answers, pronounced so frequently that they have become platitudes: study preserves memory of the Holocaust; study counters denial; study of the past can prevent genocide in the present and future. But confronted with Hilberg's warning and mindful of the narrow (Central European) usage of the verb "to study"—that is, study as an academic pursuit, something done within the context of a discipline and often a university, distinct from education of school children and from public outreach—these responses

---

Notes for this section begin on page 172.

seem inadequate. Why should the Holocaust be a subject of academic study, and in particular of ongoing historical inquiry? Is history commemoration?

The answer posited here is "no" or, more accurately, not "yes." History and commemoration are related but distinct. Study sometimes supports commemorative and activist work but it always challenges and complicates and occasionally even undermines those public projects. Precisely that challenge—a function of the degree of scholarly integrity and independence that counters overt instrumentalization—can serve to open up what are often presented as self-evident lessons and to integrate the Holocaust into an understanding of the world, indeed, to reveal it as a part of the world.

This chapter focuses on four familiar lessons, or slogans, in public discourse around the Holocaust and suggests ways these insights (and clichés) are at once unsettled and deepened by historical study. The first to be addressed might be labeled the lesson about bystanders, captured in the often-quoted line: "all it takes for evil to triumph is for good men to stand by and do nothing." The second, summed up in the phrase the "power of one," refers to individuals. Third comes what could be dubbed the claim of a happy ending, the "triumph of the human spirit." The fourth and final section examines what might be characterized as the political lessons of the Holocaust or the activist challenge expressed in the common invocation: "never again."

"All It Takes for Evil to Triumph Is for Good Men to Do Nothing"

It is impossible to avoid these words in materials prepared for events commemorating the Holocaust or for school teachers and students. Although the eighteenth-century political philosopher Edmund Burke is most often cited as the source, there is no record of his having written any version of this sentence.[3] The underlying claim, of course, is that it was the "bystanders," those who remained "silent" and "did nothing" in the face of Nazi evil, who enabled, even caused, the murder of millions of Jews. This version of events is compelling for educators and activists of all kinds because it shifts the focus from the perpetrators and victims—two groups with whom few people can or want to identify—to the "bystanders." Often invoked in arguments that link Holocaust commemoration and education to the prevention of bullying in schools, "all it takes" has become one of the most popular and portable "lessons" of the Holocaust.

Historical scholarship reveals the narrative implied by the bystanders slogan to be misleading. The Holocaust did not happen because "good" men and women did nothing, but because people of all kinds under particular circumstances did "bad" things, which in turn made it harder for them and others to do good things, or even to know what those might be. By drawing attention away from perpetrators to "those who did nothing," the slogan neglects the questions most important to historians of the Holocaust: Who carried out the attacks on Jews and other targets, on their property, their communities, their dignity, and their lives? What were the dynamics that escalated and spread extreme violence from individual acts of cruelty akin to schoolyard bullying to genocide and world war?

In what has become a classic work on Holocaust perpetrators, *Ordinary Men*,[4] Christopher Browning demonstrated the hands-on nature of much of the killing. The men of Order Police Battalion 101 worked on their own and in conjunction with the Einsatzgruppen, mobile murder squads, to murder Jews. It took an enormous effort—physical and emotional—to destroy so many human lives. Some members of the battalion preferred not to participate in killing operations; a few of them requested and received other assignments; some developed their own techniques for rationalizing their involvement. One man reported after the war that he preferred to wait until a co-worker had shot a woman with a child and then he would kill the child in what he deemed an act of mercy: after all, how could a child survive without its mother?[5] Others insisted they always aimed away from their targets or drank themselves into oblivion in order to carry out their grisly task. Most of them got used to it. Members of this and other killing units murdered over 1 million Jews in Poland, Ukraine, and the Baltic States. In most cases they shot them at close range. Likewise, the estimated 1.5 million Jews murdered in Ukraine were not transported to killing centers; Germans and local collaborators massacred them on site.[6]

Browning and his critic Daniel Goldhagen do not agree on what motivated the perpetrators of the Holocaust: Browning emphasizes the ordinariness of the killers and their motives—peer pressure, careerism, the disorientation and brutalization of war—whereas Goldhagen insists on the centrality of a uniquely German form of "eliminationist antisemitism."[7] But both reveal the agency and labor of the killers. As Goldhagen put it elsewhere, committing genocide involves physical effort for the perpetrators; it is "a hard thing to do." It is about "at some point one person deciding to raise his arm and strike the person down—or to shoot him or her at close range."[8]

In contrast to the message of "good people" who did nothing, historical research reveals that people of all kinds did many things during the Holocaust. Omer Bartov's work on Buczacz, a multi-ethnic town in eastern Poland (after the war in Ukraine), shows the complexity of actions and repercussions in the midst of war, occupation, and genocide.[9] Local Ukrainians stole Jewish property and murdered Jews; some also helped Jews by providing food or hiding places. Some of those who took terrible risks to rescue Jews extorted money and other valuables from them and then betrayed them to the Germans. The situation of Poles in the region was fraught in additional ways. Ukrainian nationalists targeted them for expulsion and used the vacuum left by German retreat at the end of the war to carry out "ethnic cleansing." Some Poles helped Jews; most tried to help themselves and their families. Occasionally these goals were linked; more often they were mutually exclusive.

"Doing nothing" was not an option for anyone during the period in which the town of Buczacz endured a year and a half of Soviet rule, three years of Nazi German occupation, and ongoing clashes between local units organized around interests and identities that both hardened and confused categories of ethnicity, religion, politics, and clan. Indeed, one of the problems with the "all it takes" slogan is the way it collapses years of hardship into a split-second decision. By the time the war in Europe ended in May of 1945, there were few bystanders, few left untouched and uncompromised by the chains of complicity.[10]

The morally appealing simplicity of the "all it takes" version of the Holocaust belies the deadly dynamic of extreme violence and its contagious spiral of brutality. Richard S., in 1940 a 12-year-old Jewish boy from Wadowice in southwestern Poland, described how his forced labor squad was taken by German police to do some of the grunt work of throwing Poles out of their homes in preparation for the arrival of *Volksdeutschen* being resettled in the Incorporated Territories of conquered Poland. "They brought us into the houses and made us take out the belongings," Mr. S. recalled, decades later. "One image is imprinted in my brain," he continued:

> The Poles in our town were very religious. They had a lot of pictures of Mary, Jesus, and saints in their houses, crucifixes, things like that. One SS man pointed to a crucifix hanging on the wall and then shouted at us: "*Mach dem Jud runter!*" [Take that Jew down!].[11]

Where in this scenario were the good people doing nothing? Instead the German conquerors manipulated the desperation of enslaved Jews to help expel disempowered Poles, some of whom in the preceding weeks and months had plundered the homes and businesses of Jews who fled the German invasion in September 1939. It was not one-time decisions to "stand aside" that drove the escalating violence of the Holocaust; it was a radicalizing and ongoing process of divide and rule that broke down communal solidarity and set each against all. Richard S. grasped both the horrible irony and the disastrous repercussions of the Germans' methods. "There are probably Poles walking around today who remember that," he observed, "or maybe they have told their children and grandchildren that when the Germans threw us out of our homes, Jews were there too, helping them."[12]

In the force field of genocide, even people who did "good things" could end up enabling and legitimating atrocities. In July 1941, two German military chaplains in Western Ukraine tried to intervene on behalf of some ninety Jewish children, whose parents had already been shot. Locked in a school with nothing to eat or drink, the crying children attracted the attention of soldiers, who turned the case over to their chaplains. The two clergymen—a Roman

Catholic named Ernst Tewes and his Protestant counterpart Wilczek—dared to speak out and even managed to enlist the support of two additional chaplains and at least one officer. They stalled the process by a few days, but in the end, the children were murdered, too, whether by Germans or Ukrainian auxiliaries.[13] Both chaplains remained in military service until the end of the war. The soldiers who appealed to them to do something for the children no doubt felt some relief at having "dealt with" the problem and assuaged their consciences. In the context of a genocidal war, gestures of opposition could be transformed into new forms of legitimation, and evil could triumph even when "good men" did "something."

The slogan "all it takes" is a call for civil courage. It urges us to stand up, to speak out against injustice. At the same time, it assumes a softened version of the Holocaust that is politically safe and even comforting, because it involves no killers, only victims and witnesses. Many commemorative events present the Holocaust this way, a perspective that makes sense when the purpose is to remember those who suffered and died but that can become counterproductive when the goal is to address the central historical questions of agency and causality. The enormous popularity of Elie Wiesel's *Night*, an account of the Holocaust in which the perpetrators are abstract and at key moments altogether absent, coupled with the resonance of his injunctions to protest injustice and fight indifference, embody this phenomenon.[14] It is commendable and indeed urgent to work toward a world where people take responsibility for one another, and references to the Holocaust in service of this cause are powerful and honorable. But study of the Holocaust as history complicates the equation of memory and activism by presenting us with something even more painful than the failure of "good men" to "do something": the combination of the horrific deeds of the killers and their humanity.

"The Power of One"

Many commemorative events and educational programs are organized around the concept of individual responsibility, the conviction that one person can make a difference. The more pithy phrase, "the power of one" appears, among other places, in materials generated by the educational organization, Facing History and Ourselves, notably in the eponymous traveling exhibit that opened in 2003;[15] it originated as the title of a 1989 novel and subsequently movie about apartheid in South Africa,[16] and was used by Nike as the slogan for an advertising and outreach campaign in the 2000s.[17] The appeal of this approach in public discussions of the Holocaust is obvious: it transforms suffering into a source of inspiration, and speaks to the desire, especially among young people, to have an impact on the world. Heroic rescuers—Oskar Schindler, Chiune Sugihara, Tuvia Bielski, Raoul Wallenberg—and articulate, appealing victims—Anne Frank, Etty Hillesum, Hannah Senesch—fit the needs of educators in an individualistic society that seeks role models for its youth.

The problem is that study of the Holocaust indicates in many ways the opposite of this slogan. It is not the power but the powerlessness of many individuals that cries out from the past. Jewish parents were powerless to protect their children, as evident by wrenching decisions to hide children, or to refuse to relinquish them, or to vacillate from one course of action to another. Most paths ended in death. In *Maus,* Art Spiegelman's father Vladek recounts how, in 1942 his sister-in-law Tosha poisoned the three children in her care, including his son Richieu, rather than allow them to fall into the hands of the Germans.[18] A collection published by Yad Vashem includes a letter from Sara and Yehiel Gerlitz of Będzin who entrusted their 6-year-old daughter into the care of a Polish friend. "We are leaving," the mother wrote:

> to an unknown destination. I do not know, my dear child, if I will ever see you again. I take with me … your smile and your tears which my heart, the heart of a mother could not allay…. Remember us and do not blame us! As for me, your mother—forgive me…. Forgive me, my dear child, for having given birth to you. … I implore you[:] … don't blame us.[19]

This crushing admission of powerlessness nevertheless ended on a note of defiance:

> There is one thing more I want you to know: that your mother was a proud person, despite our enemies' scorn and mistreatment, and when she was going to die, she did so without mourning and crying, but with a smile of contempt for the enemy on her lips![20]

Jewish leaders, prominent, intelligent, successful people, also turned out to be powerless to save lives, even their own. Adam Czerniaków, head of the Jewish Council in the Warsaw Ghetto, committed suicide in July 1942, tormented by his inability to save the orphans, the weakest members of his community, from death. According to Raul Hilberg, before his suicide, Czerniaków wrote a note in which he said of the German request that he organize removal of the orphans from the Warsaw Ghetto to be sent to Treblinka: "They want me to kill the children with my own hands."[21] Privilege often bought time, but as the fates of heads of Jewish Councils Chaim Rumkowski, Moshe Merin, and so many others proved, it guaranteed nothing.[22] Resourceful people used their connections, ingenuity, and funds to try to find ways to escape the trap that Europe became during the war, via Shanghai, Cuba, Tashkent, Turkey, and every conceivable destination. Some managed against the odds, but most found the ways blocked, the doors closed.[23]

For those like Victor Klemperer, left behind in Europe, every day was a reminder of impotence. Klemperer bent lower and lower under the measures heaped on him as a Jew in Germany after 1933: no pet, no library privileges, no typewriter.[24] Suicide rates among German Jews from 1933 on skyrocketed.[25] The isolation of individuals was terrible and in many cases total. In the German client state of Slovakia, as of September 1941, even letters mailed by Jews were to be marked with a Star of David, so that they could be opened by police and destroyed.[26] Concealed in cellars and closets, some Jews lost their judgment, or their minds, or their hope.[27] Even God, it was said, hid his face.[28]

Massive forces aligned against the individual: the bureaucracy, military, judicial and educational systems, economic interests. Add to that the antisemitism, self-interest, indifference, and fear on the part of non-Jews brutalized by war and deprivation, and the physical weakness of the human body—the ruthlessness of hunger, the fragility of the old, the vulnerability of the very young—and it is obvious that study of the Holocaust does not support a simplistic notion of the power of the individual. Even time was an enemy.

According to Alexandra Garbarini's study of diaries, already by 1942, many Jews expected Germany to lose the war but feared victory would come too late to save Jewish existence in Europe.[29] By mid-1944, Herman Kruk, a Warsaw librarian in the Vilna Ghetto and later a prisoner in a labor camp in Estonia, understood that every moment counted. Kruk wrote in his diary on 23 July 1944:

> Yesterday was a day of some tension. Today new rumors are spreading: the men will be castrated, the women sent to Königsberg.... Since the latest events on the Eastern Front, since the assassination attempt on H., since Estonia and the entire Baltic has been surrounded, our situation seems to be coming to a head. We are so upset, our nerves choke us, and every day is superfluous. Everything is more and more irritating. We count not just the days, but the hours and minutes: any minute we may get out of hell.[30]

Kruk was shot by the Germans and his body burned, in September 1944, one day before Red Army units reached the area. Liberation came too late to save many victims.

There are two important twists to the concept of power and powerlessness. The first involves the massive power wielded by some individuals, above all, by perpetrators. Hitler, Himmler, and Mengele but also minor tyrants in their own spheres exercised enormous, indeed boundless power over the lives and deaths of other people. People like the physician Friedrich Menecke who consigned thousands of people to death under the program code-named 14f13 while enjoying his dessert, wielded immense and deeply corrupting power.[31] Their situation was akin to what Joseph Conrad described for Europeans in colonial Africa.[32] Camp guards, administrators, kapos, social workers, women and men—all enjoyed a chance to "be someone" in the Nazi system. German racial policy created *Volksdeutschen,* ethnic Germans, in some cases overnight, and vested them with powers to dispossess and kill their neighbors.[33] Backed by the mighty forces of the state and the military, as symbolized and expressed by uniforms, certain individuals vaulted from weakness to vast, destructive power. In occupied Poland, ethnic Germans put on swastika armbands and went in search of everything from socks and bicycles to factories and women's bodies.[34]

People suddenly vested with enormous power over others often used it not only to destroy but to humiliate their victims, perhaps as a way to highlight their power against the powerlessness of those they crushed. This dynamic extended far down the hierarchy of Nazi brutality and privilege. Consider an individual case, taken from the memoir of Liana Millu, an Italian Jewish prisoner in Auschwitz in 1944.[35] Millu depicts a female kapo, a German called Mia.[36] Enraged when her Polish kapo lover showed affection toward a beautiful Hungarian Jewess, Mia beat her rival half to death, then handed her over to Mengele to be sent to the gas: "'This one, *Herr Doctor.*' She pointed to Lili. 'Always *kaputt*. She can't do the work.'"[37] Neither an ideology of racial supremacy nor some kind of antisemitism, eliminationist or otherwise, motivated Mia, herself a prisoner in the camp, to destroy Lili. Instead her ability to inflict death on a Jew was a result, a by-product, of the Nazi war of annihilation. This dynamic that harnessed everyday routines and feelings—insecurity, jealousy—to the cause of mass murder helps explain how genocide magnified the power of those who served as agents of destruction.

Rescuers too wielded power, but research indicates they did so less as extraordinary individuals than when backed by institutions. The sociologist Helen Fein has posited that significant numbers of Jews avoided killing in places where the heads of established religious organizations spoke out publicly against persecution.[38] Sugihara, Schindler, and Wallenberg are all cases of individuals whose power to save depended on access to formal power, even in the case of Sugihara where Japanese authorities objected to his issuing visas to Jews.[39] In Le Chambon-sur-Lignon, where Pastor André Trocmé and his wife Magda Trocmé spearheaded shelter of some 5,000 Jews, they relied on the authority of the pulpit and their network of Protestant congregants and neighbors, not on the force of their individual goodness.[40] Six thousand "righteous among the nations" have been recognized in Poland, more than in any other country. Yet those people—forced by circumstances to operate as individuals—in most cases could save one or a handful of Jews.[41] Compared to the isolation and hopelessness of Europe's Jews, targeted for death and indeed after systematic mass killing began, in the eyes of non-Jews, already in effect dead, rescuers exercised considerable power. Compared to the tyranny of the perpetrators, however, they were weak unless supported by organizations larger than any one person.

The second twist has to do with the issues of choice and agency on the part of victims. Rather than pleading powerlessness or begging for understanding for their failings, a surprising number of Jewish memoirists claim a high degree of individual agency. Indeed many wildly exaggerate the power or room to maneuvre they had, in tormented efforts to expose their own implication in the processes of destruction. Adina Szwajger, a young doctor in the Warsaw ghetto in 1942, agonized throughout her memoir about administering lethal injections to a group of children in the ghetto hospital, to spare them from torment at German hands.[42] In July 1943, she helped her husband Stefan, who was in hiding in a greengrocer's cellar in Mokotow, to get a place in the "Hotel Poland," as part of a group escaping to Hungary. But the scheme was a trap, and Szwajger's husband, like all the others, ended up on a transport to Auschwitz. When she saw prison lorries, Szwajger wrote, she knew: "I knew beyond doubt, that it was all over. And that I had done it to him, with my own hands. Although he had wanted it, if not for me he wouldn't even have known that this could be his escape from life."[43]

Central to the memoir of Olga Lengyel from Transylvania is her insistence that the death of her loved ones at Auschwitz was somehow her fault. "*Mea culpa*," she declared in the first line of her book, "my fault, *mea maxima culpa!* I cannot acquit myself of the charge that I am, in part, responsible for the destruction of my own parents and of my two young sons."[44] Separated from her husband and father upon arrival at the camp, Lengyel stood on the ramp with her mother and two sons. The SS "selector" sent the younger boy with the children and elderly but paused before the older boy, who was almost twelve, Lengyel wrote, and "big for his age." Assuming children and old people would be spared the worst, Lengyel urged her son and mother to go to the left. In her words, "I had condemned Arvad and my mother to death in the gas chambers."[45]

Even those personal accounts that admit powerlessness do so with some sense of shame, not perhaps the shame of someone who has done wrong but the sting of humiliation. An instructive case comes from Robert Melson, who was born in 1937 and survived the war with his parents, young Polish Jews who passed as members of a noble Catholic family.[46] Based on interviews with his parents and his own recollections, Melson's book is a remarkable testament to his mother's charm, his father's courage, and his own childish intuition. In one unforgettable passage, Melson's father recounts a dinner he and his wife "Nina," Melson's mother, hosted in Krakow for their German neighbor Colonel Kruk and his Jew-killing friends:

> Nina had made a Hungarian goulash. They loved her and her cooking. We couldn't get rid of them. They were happy and contented—just the kind of people you'd see in a Munich beer hall.... Nina and I were a big hit and so was Bobi.... When they left, Nina and I avoided looking at each other. That night we went to bed without exchanging a word.[47]

Melson, little "Bobi" at the time, writes that in retrospect he feels, not ashamed, but somehow "degraded and humiliated" at the same time as he takes pleasure in having helped to elude "the hunters one more time."[48]

How do such assertions of responsibility—personal, moral, universal in scale—fit into accounts of the Holocaust? What functions did and do they serve? At one level, expressions of shame and guilt and acts of self-criticism reflect the Shoah's crushing force: a devastation that cut into the very sense of self, with its pernicious methods of divide and conquer and its cunning proclivities at creating "self-service hells" where the worst suffering is what a person does to herself.[49] Whatever the purpose of such claims for those who made them, for readers of their words, these assertions of agency lead back to the unending trauma of the Holocaust, a horror magnified by the degree to which perpetrators managed to shift blame onto their victims.

At another level, we might interpret unrealistic claims of agency on the part of survivors as an expression of what is misleadingly referred to as "survivor guilt"—a sense of the arbitrariness of one's survival and perhaps unworthiness compared to the many who were murdered. Here the claims of agency with regard to wrong decisions and destructive actions intersect with a widespread refusal to take credit for one's own survival. It was just chance, we read in account after account and hear in interview after interview, when survivors are confronted with the common question: how did you manage to survive against all odds? Primo Levi put his finger on the point. In a system of radical and contagious evil, he wrote, it was impossible to survive without compromise.[50] Acts of compromise might be as small and, viewed in retrospect, as insignificant as Levi's decision to share some water he found with his friend Alberto and no one else. What difference would it have made, after all, if he had tried to distribute this meagre treasure more widely? Nevertheless, according to Levi, a sense of having failed contributed to some kind of shame, no doubt related to the loss of self-worth reported by so many victims of violence.

Might the overblown claims of agency in survivors' accounts be understood in part as an effort to insist on their humanity, to demand acknowledgement of moral autonomy, even under the most horrific circumstances? By pointing to her role in the death of her mother and son, Olga Lengyel positioned herself, even on the platform at Auschwitz, in that arbitrary selection between immediate death and a chance at survival, as an agent, a person who knew right from wrong, although she could not discern in the moment the correct course of action. By telling how she ended the lives of a group of children in the Warsaw ghetto in September 1942, Adina Szwajger presented herself then and later as a fully human person, capable of profound love and loyalty, conscious of the difficulty, indeed impossibility of doing the right thing in a situation where there was no right choice, but nevertheless deciding herself how to act and acting, not as a victim or a pawn but as a person, despite everything, still capable of partaking in the universal moral law that gave Immanuel Kant such cause to marvel. In other words, might we understand the paradox of agency, of claims of power on the part of the powerless, as an existential statement, a rejection of retreat into passivity and the release from responsibility such a retreat would entail? Perhaps there is a moral insight here: for victims and targets of assault, an emphasis on agency equals an assertion of humanity and dignity. For the perpetrators, denial of power is an attempt to evade responsibility and avoid the judgment of others and themselves. Both reflect some sense of shame, a reminder that humans are fundamentally moral beings with an awareness of right and wrong. It is not much, but perhaps that shared humanity offers a slim basis for hope.

"The Triumph of the Human Spirit"

Popular representations of the Holocaust often end in triumph, with the happy or at least uplifting endings expected of Hollywood movies. The Academy-Award winning *Schindler's List* and *Life Is Beautiful,* for all their pathos, both fit this pattern, as do the more somber *The Pianist* (where a "good German" saves Władysław Szpilman from starvation in the last days of the war) and *Defiance,* where the Bielski brothers succeed in keeping thousands of Jews alive in their forest otriad.[51] In public statements, the film's director, Edward Zwick, described his decision to make a film about Jewish resistance as motivated by a sense of shame. Ban Ki-moon, the Secretary General of the United Nations, in a speech for Holocaust Commemoration Day in January 2010, referred to the triumph of the human spirit.[52] The notion that suffering purifies or ennobles people offers a silver lining to the horror of genocide and holds out the possibility of meaning in the midst of meaningless misery. These are important messages for commemorative events: people need to build the future on hope not despair.

The problem from the perspective of scholarship is that the Holocaust was not a story of triumph. In the words of Joan Ringelheim, "oppression does not make people better; oppression makes people oppressed."[53] One need not look far to find evidence of this grim fact. Henry Friedman spent most of 1943 hidden in the loft of a barn in eastern Poland with his mother, younger brother and school teacher. A teenager at the time, he remembers voting to have the baby to which his mother was about to give birth killed in order to increase the rest of the group's chances of survival. With the help of the woman who hid them, this was done.[54] Rather than point to the obvious: the complete desperation of the situation, his absolute powerlessness and total dependence on the Ukrainian woman who sheltered them in terribly dangerous conditions (she was having an affair with the local police chief, a notorious hater and hunter of Jews), Friedman claimed responsibility, even casting the decision in terms of a vote. His younger brother Isaac, Friedman maintained, does not remember voting and denies any input in the decision. By mentioning his brother's conflicting memory of the event, Friedman highlighted his own choice, not only to remember but to speak of his role. "I'm no hero," Friedman insisted throughout his memoir—and announced in its title.

Toward the end of *Neighbors,* his searing examination of the murder of the Jews of Jedwabne in July 1941 by gentile Poles, Jan Gross provides an account from Karolcia Sapetowa, a former nanny who sheltered two Jewish children from March 1943 until the end of the war. Her neighbors were uneasy, Sapetowa recalled, because they knew the children were in her home and they understood that if the Germans discovered them, the entire village could be punished. At first she was able to appease the villagers with gifts or promises, but increasingly they pushed her to get rid of the children. "Don't kill us yet today," the little girl and boy would beg her. Desperate, Sapetowa said, she "got a brilliant idea":

> I put the children on a cart, and I told everybody that I was taking them out to drown them. I rode around the entire village, and everybody saw me and they believed, and when the night came I returned with the children.[55]

What does it tell us, Gross adds after quoting Sapetowa's testimony, that residents of a Polish village could sleep in peace only when they were convinced that their neighbor, with her own hands, had just drowned two children?

These and other accounts reveal precious little triumph. Instead they show widespread destruction, failures, and betrayals extended and even exacerbated in the postwar period by the imposition of Communism in large parts of Europe and by resentments that put the erstwhile rescuers of Jews at risk of ostracism and violence.[56] Herman Kruk, the diarist from the Vilna ghetto, understood that genocide has a long afterlife: "There is a legend," he wrote: "On the graves of murdered innocents grow poisonous plants."[57] The Germans who masterminded the mass murder of the Jews were drunk and demoralized, Kruk observed; the Lithuanians were morally destroyed by their role as collaborators; and Jews, collectively and individually, were broken and divided. What, Kruk wondered, would become of children who never knew anything but lies, theft, and death?[58]

Leah K., a survivor of the killing fields of Transnistria, offers one answer. By the age of fourteen, she had lost her entire family: Romanians murdered her father and a brother; her mother and twin sisters died of starvation. Hunted by Ukrainian children and betrayed by Jewish police, Leah managed to escape time and again and to "pass" as a poor Russian orphan. After liberation, she struggled to convince authorities that she was Jewish. She eventually succeeded, only to be consigned to an orphanage back in Romania, where she was beaten and forced to work for the local population. Rather than relief, reunification with her one surviving brother "was the beginning of much pain," and she soon ran away from his cruelty. A family in Canada took her in, but they had no idea what to do with her, and she left after six months to fend for herself, even as she "struggled with feeling ashamed of her pain."[59]

But here, too, there is a twist. This most temptingly facile of the lessons of the Holocaust offers a profound challenge to academic scholarship and the widespread assumption that irony, pessimism, and despair are smart; hope is not. From the cover of his book, the young and dashing Henry Friedman smiles at the world; on the back he shares a belly laugh with Julia Symchuck, the Ukrainian woman who as an 18-year-old girl in 1942 warned Friedman's father that the Gestapo were coming for him.[60] Friedman's resilience appears irrational, like the prayers he offered from his desolate hiding place:

> We had with us a Hebrew prayer book, a *siddur,* which I read to myself. I didn't understand the words, although I could read Hebrew phonetically. I pretended that the words were God's language, that He was listening to my prayers. Most of the time this was the only hope I had, whispering to God in His language.[61]

But perhaps it is precisely that quality of irrationality, of incomprehension and incomprehensibility, that make each desolate flicker of hope so powerful.

In a brief exchange in *Shoah,* Claude Lanzmann asks Mordechai Podchlebnik, one of the very few survivors from Chełmno, why he smiles all the time. In the original interview, the question follows Podchlebnik's description of how he worked unloading corpses from the death vans. On the third day, when he saw his wife and children among the dead, he tried to get killed himself, but the Germans refused. The interpreter has to repeat the question before Podchlebnik understands. "What do you want me to do, cry?" he retorts: "At one time you smile, at one time you cry, and when you live … it's best to smile."[62] Podchlebnik's answer brings to mind the biblical character Job, who does not triumph over suffering but endures, clinging to existence and to some spark of life and even hope.

"Never Again"

The most often invoked of all the lessons of the Holocaust, "never again" is also the most venerable. According to Raul Hilberg, it was the liberated inmates at Buchenwald, the most organized and vociferous of them Communists not Jews, who first displayed these words in April 1945.[63] In the decades since, "never again" has been pledged for many causes: from Israel to Bosnia, Darfur, Iraq, and far beyond. A vow to take action against injustice, oppression, war, and genocide, "never again" presents a political and moral challenge. At the same time, as Peter Novick has pointed out, in another way, it offers an odd comfort, as if the Holocaust were sealed off in some distant past, unconnected to anything before or after.[64] Study, as usual, reveals that reality was more complicated.

On the one hand, "never again" implies that the Holocaust was unique and unprecedented. It draws attention to specific aspects of the Shoah, above all, to antisemitism as the "longest hatred." On the other hand, "never again" implies comparability, both in its genesis in the mixed victim groups of Buchenwald in the spring of 1945 and in its gesture toward the fundamental sameness of all acts of extreme violence. "Never again" hints at patterns and even direct links that connect the Holocaust to other genocides: murderous ideologies, the behaviors of perpetrators, use of propaganda, methods of humiliating victims.[65] Christian Gerlach has identified a tendency of extreme violence to spiral from the original target groups to ever-widening circles of victims.[66] Ben Kiernan has observed that genocide itself is contagious: those who plan and perpetrate extreme violence look to the past for models and rationalizations.[67]

Observers of the Holocaust have not failed to note these connections. With the 1994 genocide of Tutsis in Rwanda, Hilberg noted in the 2003 edition of *Destruction of the European Jews,* "History has repeated itself."[68] Elie Wiesel, at the opening of the United States Holocaust Memorial Museum in 1993, turned to President Bill Clinton and said, "Mr. President, I have been in the former Yugoslavia last fall. I cannot sleep since what I have seen. We must do something to prevent the bloodshed. Something, anything must be done."[69] In his memoir, Henry Friedman described his 1984 experience in India, when Indira Gandhi was assassinated by her Sikh bodyguards. The response was a massive outburst of violence against Sikhs, including destruction of property and killing. Friedman had a flashback to his wartime experience:

> I remembered when we were in hiding and through a hole in the side of the barn I could see Polish farmers being thrown into the fire and burned to death by the Ukrainians. These Sikhs were innocent people being killed indiscriminately by their own countrymen.

He intervened with the chef and manager of his hotel who intended to kill a young Sikh employee, and after numerous drinks and hours of conversation, got an assurance of the man's safety. The next morning, the Sikh sat behind the desk, to Friedman's relief: "I felt that no matter what else had happened in my life, my mission on earth was fulfilled because I had saved a man's life."[70]

Study of the Holocaust shows how understandings of the Holocaust itself have been influenced, indeed transformed, by developments elsewhere. Scholarship in other words is porous. In the 1990s, the nature of genocide in Rwanda, with its obviously arbitrary "racial" categories and direct, hands-on killing,[71] drew historians of the Holocaust to pay more attention to those phenomena in their own research. The prominence of rape in the wars associated with the breakup of Yugoslavia prompted scholars to revisit issues of sexual violence in the Holocaust.[72] Research on genocide in Cambodia drew attention to the spiral effect that linked various victim groups.[73] Work on the Armenian genocide sparked renewed interest in links between the Holocaust and war and nation building. Investigations of genocides in "settler societies" raised awareness of the long afterlife of extreme violence.[74] "Never again" implies the Holocaust was an exception, whereas study of the Holocaust challenges us to confront familiar elements between various pasts and the present and to see how the histories and fates of people are connected.

Is history commemoration? Not exactly: the relationship between them is complex. Study can be an anchor for commemoration and activism but it also poses a challenge from its position of independence. Of course scholarship itself is implicated in the contexts in which it is practiced, but even the claim of independence opens a space for debate and a possibility of integrity. Study of the Holocaust is open to all who are willing to devote their time and energy to the endless process of research, interpretation, and reinterpretation. As Hilberg insisted, there is still so much we do not understand.

At the 2008 Lessons and Legacies Conference in Evanston, Illinois, the renowned historian Henry Friedlander spoke for the first time in public about his experiences in the Holocaust. Born in Berlin in 1930, Friedlander and his parents were sent in 1941 to the Łódź ghetto and from there to Auschwitz, where his mother was murdered. In the fall of 1944, with the help of a kapo from Wedding, the Berlin district where the Friedlanders had also lived, he managed to escape from a selection that targeted teenaged boys for the gas chambers. Friedlander recounted how he had approached the kapo in the death barracks and said to him, in the Berlin dialect they shared, the first words that came into his head: "I don't belong here." The man ordered him to go to his barracks and not make a sound. There the fourteen-year-old Henry lay on the bare cement, afraid even to breathe. He could hear the screams and cries of the boys being loaded onto trucks to be taken to the gas. "Sometimes I still hear them," he told his listeners. "I am a historian," he continued. "I know how to write about the Holocaust. But how do I write about that?"[75]

Notes

1. "Is There a New Anti-Semitism? A Conversation with Raul Hilberg," *Logos* 6, nos. 1–2 (2007), available online at http://www.logosjournal.com/issue_6.1-2/hilberg.htm (accessed 18 May 2010). On Hilberg, see also Nathaniel Popper, "A Conscious Pariah," *The Nation* (19 April 2010); and of course Hilberg, *The Politics of Memory: The Journey of a Holocaust Historian* (Chicago, 1996).

2. Norman G. Finkelstein, *The Holocaust Industry: Reflections on the Exploitation of Jewish Suffering* (London, 2000).

3. On the many variants of the "all it takes" quotation and its absence in the writings of Edmund Burke, see Martin Porter, "'All that is necessary for the triumph of evil is that good men do nothing' (or words to that effect): A Study of a Web Quotation," http://tartarus.org/~martin/essays/burkequote.html (accessed 18 May 2010). Porter calls "all it takes" the "commonest political quote you will find anywhere on the World Wide Web." A Google search for "all it takes for evil to triumph" and "Holocaust" turned up 204,000 results, including use of the quote (with attribute to Edmund Burke) in teaching materials circulated by the United States Holocaust Memorial Museum in Washington, D.C. and the Holocaust Educational Trust of Ireland.

4. Christopher R. Browning, *Ordinary Men: Reserve Police Battalion 101 and the Final Solution in Poland* (New York, 1992). See also James Waller, *Becoming Evil: How Ordinary People Commit Genocide and Mass Killing* (Oxford, 2002); Hilary Earl, *The Nuremberg SS-Einsatzgruppen Trial, 1945-1958* (New York, 2009); Karin Orth, *Das System der nationalsozialistischen Konzentrationslager. Eine politische Organisationsgeschichte* (Hamburg, 1999); Sybille Steinbacher, *"Musterstadt" Auschwitz. Germanisierungspolitik und Judenmord in Ostoberschlesien* (Munich, 2000); and Edward Westermann, *Hitler's Police Battalions: Enforcing Racial War in the East* (Lawrence, 2005).

5. Browning, *Ordinary Men*, 73.

6. On the Holocaust in Ukraine, see Wendy Lower, *Nazi Empire-Building and the Holocaust in Ukraine* (Chapel Hill, 2005); Karel Berkhoff, *Harvest of Despair: Life and Death in Ukraine Under Nazi Rule* (Cambridge, MA, 2004); Patrick Desbois, *The Holocaust by Bullets* (Basingstoke, 2008); also the contributions in Ray Brandon and Wendy Lower, eds., *The Shoah in Ukraine: History, Testimony, Memorialization* (Bloomington, 2008); and contributions in Zvi Gitelman, ed., *Bitter Legacy: Confronting the Holocaust in the USSR* (Bloomington, 1997).

7. Daniel Jonah Goldhagen, *Hitler's Willing Executioners: Ordinary Germans and the Holocaust* (New York, 1996).

8. Goldhagen in conversation with Joanne J. Myers, Carnegie Council, transcript at http://www.cceia.org/resources/transcripts/0225.html (accessed 18 May 2010); see also Daniel Jonah Goldhagen, *Worse Than War: Genocide, Eliminations, and the Ongoing Assault on Humanity* (New York, 2009), esp. ch. 5, "Why the Perpetrators Act"; Goldhagen's exchange with Elie Ngarambe, the Hutu killer whom Goldhagen quotes in the interview and also in the documentary is on 182–83.

9. Omer Bartov, "Interethnic Relations in the Holocaust as Seen Through Postwar Testimonies: Buczacz, East Galicia, 1941–1944," in *Lessons and Legacies VIII*, ed. Doris L. Bergen (Evanston, 2008), 101–24.

10. Useful for understanding networks of involvement and complicity in different ways are Martin Dean, *Collaboration in the Holocaust: Crimes of the Local Police in Belorussia and Ukraine, 1941–44* (New York, 2000); Götz Aly, *Hitler's Beneficiaries: Plunder, Racial War, and the Nazi Welfare State* (New York, 2005); Adam Tooze, *The Wages of Destruction: The Making and Breaking of the Nazi Economy* (New York, 2006); and Jan T. Gross, *Fear: Antisemitism in Poland after Auschwitz* (New York, 2006).

11. Interview with Richard S., May 2010, Toronto, Canada; notes in possession of the author.

12. Interview with Richard S.

13. On the two chaplains and the massacre of Jewish children in Belaya Tserkov, see the reminiscences of Ernst Tewes, "Seelsorger bei den Soldaten 1940–1956. Aufzeichnungen und Erinnerungen," in *Das Erzbistum München und Freising in der Zeit des nationalsozialistischen Herrschaft*, ed. Georg Schwaiger, vol. 2 (Munich, 1984), 244–87; also see the account in Bernd Boll and Hans Safrian, "Auf dem Weg nach Stalingrad: Die 6. Armee 1941/42," in *Vernichtungskrieg. Verbrechen der Wehrmacht, 1941–1944*, ed. Hannes Heer and Klaus Naumann (Hamburg, 1995), 260–96.

14. Elie Wiesel, *Night* (New York, 2006).

15. See http://www.facinghistory.org/news/choosing-participate-exhibition-los-angeles-central-library.

16. Bryce Courtenay, *The Power of One: A Novel* (New York, 1989); the movie is *The Power of One* (1992), dir. John G. Avildsen (starring Stephen Dorff, Armin Mueller-Stahl, and Morgan Freeman).

17. Nike promotional materials for 2008 exhibition and charity auction in Hong Kong at http://www.freshnessmag.com/2008/03/08/nike-hk-the-power-of-one; for the 2005 Nike Foundation campaign on behalf of adolescent girls in developing countries, see http://www.nikebiz.com/responsibility/documents/6_Nike_CRR_Foundations_C.pdf.

18. Art Spiegelman, *Maus: A Survivor's Tale*, vol. 1, *My Father Bleeds History* (New York, 1986), 109.

19. Reuven Dafni and Yehudit Kleiman, eds., *Final Letters: From the Yad Vashem Archive* (London, 1991), 75–76.

20. Ibid., 77.

21. On 22 July 1942, Czerniaków wrote: "The most tragic dilemma is the problem of children in orphanages, etc. I raised this issue—perhaps something can be done." *The Warsaw Diary of Adam Czerniakow*, ed. Raul Hilberg, Stanislaw Staron, and Josef Kermisz (Chicago, 1999), 385; also see remarks by Raul Hilberg in *Shoah*, dir. Claude Lanzmann (Les Films Aleph, 1985); transcript in Lanzmann, *Shoah: An Oral History of the Holocaust* (New York, 1985), 188–90. For

discussion of this scene from *Shoah* and Hilberg's identification with Czerniaków, see Marianne Hirsch and Leo Spitzer, "Gendered Translations: Claude Lanzmann's *Shoah*," in *Claude Lanzmann's Shoah: Key Essays*, ed. Stuart Liebmann (New York, 2007), 183–84.

22. An influential interpretation of the Jewish Councils is Zygmunt Bauman, *Modernity and the Holocaust* (Ithaca, NY, 1989), esp. 129–50. See also Isaiah Trunk, *Judenrat: The Jewish Councils in Eastern Europe under German Occupation* (London, 1972); and Piotr Wróbel, "Hitler's Helpers? The *Judenräte* Controversy," in *Lessons and Legacies IV: Reflections on Religion, Justice, Sexuality, and Genocide*, ed. Larry V. Thompson (Evanston, 2003), 152–62.

23. Among the countless memoirs that show the twists and turns of successful and failed efforts to escape Europe are the following: Barbara Ruth Bluman, *I Have My Mother's Eyes: A Holocaust Memoir Across Generations* (Vancouver, 2009) and Anka Voticky, *Knocking On Every Door* (Toronto, 2010); also notable on this theme is Kelly Iggers, "Through the Trap Door: Czechoslovak-Jewish Immigration to Canada, 1938–1945," (unpublished paper, University of Toronto, 2009).

24. Victor Klemperer, *I Will Bear Witness: A Diary of the Nazi Years*, Vol. 1: *1933–1941* (New York, 1998); typical is the entry for 1 March 1941: "In the morning the milkmaid refused to come up. She is no longer allowed to deliver to Jews' houses.... In the afternoon the news that Bulgaria had joined the Tripartite Pact. So Greece is lost, so Russia looks calmly on, so the route to Egypt through Turkey-in-Asia is open, so Germany appears to be winning the war. In the evening we wanted to eat something at the Pschorrbräu and found nothing edible without meat coupons, went to the Monopol and found only turnips, went to the station and found nothing at all, went back to the Monopol and ate the turnips. ... As soon as we were home there was a police check. One day in my life in the Third Reich" (377).

25. Depression and suicide are recurring topics in Victor Klemperer's diary. See for instance the entry of 20 September 1941: "Frau Kreidl downstairs going round weeping everywhere, does not want to go on living" (435); and the entry of 9 November 1941: "Frau Neumann's uncle, Atchen Fink's older brother, a man late in his sixties committed suicide with his wife in Berlin, when they were to be deported. Neumann said to me he would rather be dead and know his wife dead, than see her 'louse-ridden and rebuilding Minsk'" (443). Suicide of German Jews receives significant attention in Marion A. Kaplan, *Between Dignity and Despair: Jewish Life in Nazi Germany* (New York, 1998); and in Christian Goeschel, *Suicide in Nazi Germany* (Oxford, 2009).

26. See Raul Hilberg, *Die Vernichtung der europäischen Juden* (Frankfurt/M, 1982), vol. 2, 774–75.

27. On the mental and emotional toll of hiding—and of caring for those in hiding—see Adina Blady Szwajger, *I Remember Nothing More* (New York, 1990), esp. chs. 18 and 19, "Children in Hiding" and "Adults in Hiding" (136–50). One of the people in hiding whose despair led him to take a risk that proved to be deadly was Szwajger's husband, Stefan (132–35).

28. E. Levinas, "To Love the Torah More than God," *Judaism: A Quarterly Journal of Jewish Life and Thought* 28, no. 2 (1979): 216–33.

29. According to Garbarini, "This consciousness that the war's end would not bring about the resumption of Jewish communal life reverberated throughout Jews' diaries from the last three years of the war." Alexandra Garbarini, *Numbered Days: Diaries and the Holocaust* (New Haven, 2006), 90.

30. Herman Kruk, *The Last Days of the Jerusalem of Lithuania*, ed. Benjamin Harshav (New Haven, 2002), 697–98.

31. On Mennecke and 14f13, see Henry Friedlander, *The Origins of Nazi Genocide: From Euthanasia to the Final Solution* (Chapel Hill, 1995), 145–50. Excerpts from Mennecke's letters to his wife in Jeremy Noakes and Geoffrey Pridham, eds., *Nazism: A Documentary Reader*, Vol. 3: *Foreign Policy, War and Racial Extermination*, rev. ed. (Exeter, 1997), 436–37. Friedlander drew attention to the lure of power in his analysis of the T4 managers and supervisors. Among the benefits of their jobs, he observed, was "power over others, the right to command, and the ability to make life-and-death decisions." Friedlander, *The Origins of Nazi Genocide*, 196.

32. Joseph Conrad, *Heart of Darkness,* 4th ed. (New York, 2005). For the Nazi context, see Michael Wildt, *Generation des Unbedingten. Das Führungskorps des Reichssicherheitshauptamtes* (Hamburg, 2002); also Elizabeth Harvey, *Women and the Nazi East: Agents and Witnesses of Germanization* (New Haven, 2003).

33. See Doris L. Bergen, "Tenuousness and Tenacity: The 'Volksdeutschen' of Eastern Europe, World War II, and the Holocaust," in *The Heimat Abroad: The Boundaries of Germanness,* ed. Krista O'Donnell, Renate Bridenthal, and Nancy Reagin. (Ann Arbor, 2005), 267–86.

34. See, for instance, the 1940 case of an apprentice gardener from the Kulm (Chełmno) area, who put on his armband from the *Selbstschutz,* the ethnic German militia in Poland, and forced Poles to give him their possessions. In this manner he acquired a bicycle, phonograph, and clothes of various kinds including socks. Records in Sondergericht Bromberg, judgment signed Hennig, Dr. Kruschewski, no date, 2, 4–5, 11–12, Archiwum Państwowe w Bydgoszczy, 80/195, 4, 6–7, 13–14. On the *Selbstschutz* and its campaign early in the war of plunder, rape, and dismemberment, see Christian Jansen and Arno Weckbecker, *Der "Volksdeutsche Selbstschutz" in Polen 1939/40* (Munich, 1992); also the early piece by Eva Seeber, "Der Anteil der Minderheitsorganisation 'Selbstschutz' an den faschistischen Vernichtungsaktionen im Herbst und Winter 1939 in Polen," *Jahrbuch für Geschichte der sozialistischen Länder Europas* 13, no. 2 (1969): 3–34.

35. Liana Millu, *Smoke over Birkenau* (Evanston, 1991).

36. For discussion of Millu's memoir, see Elizabeth R. Baer, "Rereading Women's Holocaust Memoirs: Liana Millu's *Smoke Over Birkenau,*" in *Lessons and Legacies VIII,* ed. Bergen, 157–74.

37. Millu, "Lili Marlene," 47.

38. "The majority of Jews evaded deportation in every state occupied by or allied with Germany in which the head of the dominant church spoke out publicly against deportation before or as soon as it began." Helen Fein, *Accounting for Genocide: National Responses and Jewish Victimization during the Holocaust* (Chicago, 1979), 67; see also ch, 4, "The Keepers of the Keys: Responses of Christian Churches to the Threat against the Jews," 93–120.

39. On Chuine (Sempo) Sugihara, see Hillel Levine, *In Search of Sugihara: The Elusive Japanese Diplomat Who Risked his Life to Rescue 10,000 Jews from the Holocaust* (New York, 1996).

40. On rescuers, see Samuel P. Oliner and Pearl M. Oliner, *The Altruistic Personality* (New York, 1988); Mordechai Paldiel, *The Path of the Righteous: Gentile Rescuers of Jews during the Holocaust* (Hoboken, 1993).

41. On individual rescuers versus institutional failure, see Michael Phayer, *The Catholic Church and the Holocaust, 1930–1965* (Bloomington, 2000); also Phayer and Eva Fleischner, *Cries in the Night: Women Who Challenged the Holocaust* (Kansas City, 1997).

42. Szwajger, *I Remember Nothing More,* 52–58.

43. Ibid., 135.

44. Olga Lengyel, *Five Chimneys: The Story of Auschwitz* (New York, 1983), 1.

45. Ibid., 15–16.

46. Robert Melson, "Choiceless Choices: Surviving on False Papers on the 'Aryan' Side," in *Gray Zones: Ambiguity and Compromise in the Holocaust and Its Aftermath,* ed. Jonathan Petropoulos and John K. Roth (New York, 2005), 91–100. A longer exposition, although without the same development of the topic of shame, is Melson, *False Papers: Deception and Survival in the Holocaust* (Urbana, 2000).

47. Melson, "Choiceless Choices," 97.

48. Ibid., 96–97.

49. Jan Kott refers to Jean-Paul Sartre's postwar play, *No Exit,* in which "the dead in hell are surprised not to see torturers. Hell is organized like a self-service cafeteria.... 'an economy of man-power or devil-power. The customers serve themselves.'" Kott, "Introduction," to Tadeusz Borowski, *This Way for the Gas, Ladies and Gentlemen* (New York, 1976), 22.

50. Primo Levi, *The Drowned and the Saved* (New York, 1989), esp. passage on "Shame," 78–85.

51. Both movies are based on books: Roman Polanski directed *The Pianist*, W. Szpilman, *The Pianist;* Edward Zwick directed *Defiance*, Nechama Tec, *Defiance*.

52. See in particular the remarks of UN Secretary-General Ban Ki-moon on Holocaust Remembrance Day, 27 January 2010: "Countless men, women and children suffered the horrors of the ghettos and Nazi death camps, yet somehow survived. All of them carry a crucial message for all of us. A message about the triumph of the human spirit." 2010 Observance Holocaust Remembrance Day, http://www.un.org/holocaustremembrance/2010/index.shtml (accessed 18 May 2010).

53. Joan Ringelheim, "Women and the Holocaust: A Reconsideration of Research," in *Different Voices: Women and the Holocaust,* ed. Carol Rittner and John K. Roth (St. Paul, 1993), 387.

54. Henry Friedman, *I'm No Hero: Journeys of a Holocaust Survivor* (Seattle, 1999), 25–27.

55. Testimony from the Jewish Historical Institute, Warsaw (ŻIH 301/579) (quoted in Jan T. Gross, *Neighbors: The Destruction of the Jewish Community in Jedwabne, Poland* (Princeton, 2001), 108).

56. Indeed, recognition of the vulnerability of gentile rescuers of Jews in post-World War II Poland is the point of departure for Jan Gross's pathbreaking 2006 book, *Fear.*

57. Kruk, *The Last Days,* 598.

58. Ibid., entry of 2 January 1942, "Lithuania, Lithuanians": "A Lithuanian policeman of the fourth precinct complained that the Lithuanians are worse off than the Jews.... When Lithuania is liberated, the Jews will go free and pure, as martyrs; but the Lithuanians will always remain in history with a bitter testimonial" (151); entry of 24 April 1942, "Something is Rotten among the Germans" (269); and undated narrative, "Underground Ghetto": "When everyone, family and strangers is raped and beaten, when all is hollow and naked, and everything is right before your eyes and cannot be hidden, why should we be amazed?" (598).

59. Account of Leah K., 11 February 1992, in *Shards of Memory: Narratives of Holocaust Survival,* ed. Yehudi Lindeman (Westport, 2007), 123–29. The personal accounts collected in this book come from videotaped interviews in the Living Testimonies collection in Montreal.

60. Friedman, *I'm No Hero,* 15, photos on front and back and between pages 146 and 147.

61. Ibid., 25.

62. Mordechai Podchlebnik, in Claude Lanzmann *Shoah;* for details, see "Transcript of the *Shoah* Interview with Mordechai (Michael) Podchlebnik," (April 2008), 19 on finding his wife and children and 32 on smiling: http://resources.ushmm.org/intermedia/film_video/spielberg_archive/transcript/RG60_5026 (accessed 18 May 2010). Lanzmann's question and Podchlebnik's answer are also discussed by Marcel Ophüls, "Closely Watched Trains," in *Claude Lanzmann's Shoah,* ed. Liebman, 82–83.

63. Hilberg refers to the "never again" slogan's use at the liberation of Buchenwald in the Logos interview.

64. Peter Novick, *The Holocaust in American Life* (Boston, 1999).

65. See Dan Stone, ed., *The Historiography of Genocide* (Basingstoke, 2008), esp. Stone, "Introduction," 1–6; Anton Weiss-Wendt, "Problems in Comparative Genocide Scholarship," 42–70; David Moshman, "Conceptions of Genocide and Perceptions of History," 71–92; and A. Dirk Moses, "Genocide and Modernity," 156–93. Of particular interest here is Stone's contribution, "The Holocaust and Its Historiography," esp. 387–91, "Holocaust and/as Genocide" and "Conclusions." See also Donald Bloxham, *The Final Solution: A Genocide* (Oxford, 2009).

66. Christian Gerlach, "Extremely Violent Societies: An Alternative to the Concept of Genocide," *Journal of Genocide Research* 8, no. 4 (2006): 455–71.

67. Ben Kiernan, *Blood and Soil: A World History of Genocide and Extermination from Sparta to Darfur* (New Haven, 2007). Kiernan identifies "the prominence in genocidal ideology of cults of antiquity" as one of the four major themes of his analysis, along with a "fetish for agriculture," "ethnic enmity," and "imperial and territorial conquests" (2–3): "Hitler considered classical Sparta a model racialist state, and the fate of Carthage served as a metaphor for mass killing and planned destruction in the minds of perpetrators from the conquistadors to the Nazis" (27–28).

68. Christopher R. Browning, "Spanning a Career: Three Editions of Raul Hilberg's *Destruction of the European Jews,*" in *Lessons and Legacies VIII,* ed. Bergen, 191–202.

69. "Elie Wiesel's Remarks at the dedication ceremonies for the United States Holocaust Memorial Museum, April 22, 1993," at http://www.ushmm.org/research/library/faq/languages/en/06/01/ceremony/?content = wiesel (accessed 18 May 2010).

70. Friedman, *I'm No Hero,* 156.

71. Jean Hatzfeld, *Machete Season: The Killers in Rwanda Speak* (New York, 2003); also Philip Gourevitch, *We Wish to Inform You that Tomorrow We Will Be Killed with Our Families* (New York, 1998); and Mahmood Mamdani, *When Victims Become Killers: Colonialism, Nativism, and the Genocide in Rwanda* (Princeton, 2001).

72. See Alexandra Stiglmayr, ed., *Mass Rape: The War Against Women in Bosnia-Herzegovina* (Lincoln, 2004); and Beverly Allen, *Rape Warfare: The Hidden Genocide in Bosnia-Herzegovina and Croatia* (Minneapolis, 1996).

73. See Ben Kiernan, *The Pol Pot Regime: Race, Power and Genocide in Cambodia under the Khmer Rouge, 1975–79* (New Haven, 1996); also Edward Kissi, "Genocide in Cambodia and Ethiopia," in *The Specter of Genocide: Mass Murder in Historical Perspective,* ed. Robert Gellately and Ben Kiernan (Cambridge, UK, 2003); Chanthou Boua, "Genocide of a Religious Group: Pol Pot and Cambodia's Buddhist Monks," in *State-Organized Terror: The Case of Violent Internal Repression,* ed. T. Bushnell, V. Shlapentokh, C. K. Vanderpool, and J. Sundram (Boulder, 1991), 227–40.

74. A fascinating discussion of one case is Chris Mato Nunpa, "Dakota Commemorative March: Thoughts and Reactions," *The American Indian Quarterly* 28, nos. 1–2 (2004): 216–37.

75. Henry Friedlander's remarks at the Lessons and Legacies conference in Evanston, Illinois, November 2008, reproduced from notes taken while he spoke. He subsequently spoke in Germany about his experiences in Auschwitz; see "Zur Wiederherstellung des Rechts. Ausstellungsbericht," an account of the opening of an exhibition about the Auschwitz Trial and the Bergen-Belsen Trial in the Niedersächsischen Landtag, Hannover, in January 2009, in *Nachrichten und Berichte. Information und Kommunikation,* Fritz Bauer Institute. Sandor (Suti) Weisz (who after the war went by the name Yitzhak Livnat), a Hungarian Jew from Nagyszollos, described surviving the same selection, as a 15-year-old, in a similar way. Weisz appealed to a kapo he knew for help, and that man had him pulled out of the group and sent to his own barracks. See recounting by Susan M. Papp in *Outcasts: A Love Story* (Toronto, 2009), 171–73.

Part III

ANOTHER LOOK AT A CLASSIC OF HOLOCAUST HISTORIOGRAPHY

CHAPTER 9

An Integrated History of the Holocaust
Some Methodological Challenges

SAUL FRIEDLÄNDER

"With history," wrote Michel de Certeau, "you begin by putting aside, gathering, thus transforming into 'documents' certain objects that have been distributed differently. This new cultural distribution is the first task. In reality, it consists in *producing* such documents by copying, transcribing or photographing these objects and, in so doing, changing their place and their status."[1] In collecting "documents" for the history of the Holocaust, several very different archives have been constituted and several quasi-autonomous histories written. This chapter will deal with reshuffling or, in other words, reorganizing such previously separate entities in order to produce an integrated history of the extermination of the Jews of Europe.

I shall first define the very concept of an integrated history of the Holocaust, then turn to a few narrative and interpretive choices demanded by such an approach, and, finally, evoke some issues that were previously downplayed or ignored.

The Concept of an Integrated History of the Holocaust

The need for an integrated history of the Holocaust first became clear to me during the debates of the mid- and late 1980s, and particularly as a result of my confrontation with Martin Broszat, at the time director of the Institute of Contemporary History in Munich, regarding his 1985 "plea for the historicization of National Socialism." One of Broszat's arguments was directed against the traditional, simplistic, black-and-white representation of the Third

---

Notes for this section begin on page ?.

Reich; in his view, it had to give way to various shades of gray. Broszat's barely hidden subtext, which emerged during our exchange of letters at the end of 1987, contended that the Jewish survivors' perception of this past, as well as that of their descendants, albeit "worthy of respect," nonetheless represented a "mythical memory" that set a "coarsening obstacle on the path of a rational German historiography."

This view perpetuated the intellectual segregation of the history of the Jews during the Nazi epoch. My own work, *Nazi Germany and the Jews,* was meant to show that no distinction was warranted between historians of various backgrounds in their professional approach to this subject, that *all* historians dealing with this theme had to be aware of their unavoidably subjective approach, and that all could muster enough self-critical insight to restrain this subjectivity. What mattered most to me in my own project was the inclusion of the Jewish dimension, along all others, within an integrated historical narrative. Such a narrative could be identified as follows:

First, the history of these events cannot be limited to German decisions and measures only; it has to include the initiatives and reactions of authorities, institutions, and of the most diverse social groups throughout the occupied and satellite countries of German-controlled Europe. Second, at each stage, Jewish perceptions and reactions, collective or individual, cannot and should not be considered as a secluded domain within the general historical rendition, as they impacted, in various degrees, upon all other elements of this history; finally, a simultaneous representation of the events—at all levels and in all different places—enhances the perception of the magnitude, the complexity, and the interrelatedness of the multiple components of this history. Let me very briefly address each of these points.

We do not need to belabor the fact that the history of the extermination of the Jews of Europe cannot stop at the borders of the Reich, nor be limited to German decisions and measures only. However, one aspect of the German and European scene, marginalized at times, demands to be stressed: the awareness among European elites and populations of what these anti-Jewish measures and policies were leading to. Nowadays we know that a considerable amount of information about the extermination was available throughout Europe from a rather early stage on. The Polish underground was openly referring to the mass murder as soon as it started; the Swiss Federal authorities explicitly evoked the consequences of the hermetic closing of borders for Jews, in mid-summer 1942. In Germany itself, the fate of the Jews was quite openly alluded to at various levels of the population.

"In Bereza-Kartuska where I stopped for lunch," Wehrmacht Private H. K. wrote home on 18 June 1942, "1,300 Jews had just been shot on the previous day.... Men, women, children had to undress completely and were then liquidated with a shot in the back of their neck. The clothes were disinfected and used again. I am convinced that if the war goes on much longer, the Jews will be turned into sausage and served to Russian war prisoners and to Jewish specialized workers." A few months later, Private S. M., on his way to the front, wrote from the town of Auschwitz: "The Jews arrive here, that is to Auschwitz, at a weekly rate of 7 to 8,000; shortly thereafter, they die a heroes' death." He added: "It is really good to see the world." In Minden (Westphalia), the inhabitants had been discussing the fate of deportees from their own town as early as December 1941 and publicly mentioned that Jews who were unable to work were shot.

German elites showed precise information. As early as February 1942, Bishop Berning of Osnabrück noted that "admittedly there is a plan to exterminate all the Jews." In recent studies, Peter Longerich, Frank Bajohr and Dieter Pohl, Bernward Doerner and, previously, Jörg Echternkamp confirmed an awareness strenuously denied for decades. Echternkamp, in his massive volume on German wartime society, although still minimizing the extent of open allusions to the extermination, nonetheless offered an eloquent summary of that awareness: "The lie of Auschwitz became the lie of German society, whereby secret knowledge of secret evil was passed off as ignorance.... Living a lie was normality in German war society.... Only a few beacons of truth ... rose above the sea of liars."[2]

Let us now turn to the Jewish dimension of this history. Works dealing with German and related policies generally pay little attention to the properly Jewish dimension of the events: The Jews, it is usually assumed, were passive victims, an amorphous mass, whose history could be reduced to mere statistical data: A given percentage of the Jewish population exterminated in such and such a country, a different number in another one, and so on throughout occupied Europe. Yet, important historical work had been developing since the late 1940s, so to speak behind closed doors, including the gathering of vast collections of documents, the publication of diaries and the writing of monographs devoted to the everyday lives of the Jews and to their path to death, by country, city, community, ghetto, and camp.

This internal history of the Jewish people during the years of persecution and extermination has most often remained a domain apart whose traces in the general history of these times were mainly limited to Jewish armed resistance or to the issue of Jewish leadership. In fact, the contribution of this history to our grasp of the Shoah (and thus the need for its integration into the overall narration of the events) applies to a fundamental point. In contradistinction to vast segments of surrounding society, the victims did not understand what was ultimately in store for them. In Germany and in the West, the information available to the Jews had somehow not been pieced together; in the East, the Jewish populations in their immense majority refused to believe that what they heard about other areas would also apply to them. This lack of comprehension decisively contributed to the smoothness of the extermination process and to the so-called passivity of the victims. In terms of reactions and initiatives, expecting terrible hardship and even widespread death is one thing, expecting immediate murder, quite another.

The history of the destruction of European Jewry at the level of individuals can be reconstructed from the perspective of the victims on the basis of postwar depositions, interviews and memoirs, but mainly owing to the unusually large number of diaries (and letters) written during the events and recovered over the following decades. These diaries and letters were written by Jews of all countries, all walks of life, all age groups, either living under direct German domination or within the wider sphere of persecution. Of course, the diaries have to be used with the same critical attention as any other document. Yet, as a source for the history of Jewish life during the years of persecution and extermination, they remain crucial and irreplaceable.

I have given priority to the individual voice for yet another reason, beyond its testimonial value. The victim's voice, suddenly arising in the course of the narration of these events, can, by its eloquence or its clumsiness, by the immediacy of the cry of terror, or by the naivety of unfounded hope, tear through the fabric of the "detached" and "objective" historical rendition. Such a disruptive function would hardly be necessary in a history of the price of wheat on the eve of the French Revolution, but it is essential to the representation of extreme historical events such as the Holocaust, which ordinary historiography necessarily domesticates. The individual cries and whispers of the victims introduce into the most precise historical narrative a primary and essential sense of disbelief.

It has often been stated that witnessing the Shoah is impossible in essence as, in Primo Levi's words, "those who touched bottom, those who saw the Gorgon have not returned to tell about it or have returned mute."[3] In the abstract this is undeniable. However, no less evident remains the fact that the victims' notations inscribed in the descent towards extermination come ever closer to what the diaries of members of the *Sonderkommandos* almost touched: The moment of murder.

Let us now consider the third aspect of an integrated history of the Holocaust: simultaneous representation. Only the succession of phases, each presenting the synchronicity of events both throughout occupied Europe and within each country can indicate the interrelatedness and the very dimension of this history. An example of usually separately described yet related events taking place in the Reich at the end of 1941 may help in clarifying this point.

In late December 1941, the decision to exterminate all the Jews of Europe had been made. At the same time, the main representative institution of the German Evangelical Church, the Church Chancellery, responding to the violently antisemitic stance taken by a number of local churches adhering to the German-Christian line, issued a statement of its own denying any solidarity with converted Jews. This was made brutally clear in a circular letter published on 23 December by the Chancellery's deputy director, Günther Fürle: "The breakthrough of racial consciousness in our people, intensified by the experience of the war and the corresponding measures taken by the political leadership, has brought about the elimination of the Jews from the community of us Germans. This is an incontestable fact which the German Evangelical Churches … cannot heedlessly ignore. Therefore, in agreement with the Spiritual Council of the German Evangelical Church, we request the highest authorities to take suitable measures so that baptized non-Aryans remain separate from the ecclesiastical life of the German congregations. The baptized non-Aryans will have to find the ways and means to create their own facilities to serve their particular worship and pastoral needs." The Confessing Church protested but its protest was that of a minority and did not call for any countermeasures.

A few weeks earlier, several Catholic bishops, led by Bishop Preysing of Berlin, circulated a text meant to express support for converted German Jews sent to the "East." The majority of the Bishops' Conference rejected any such motion, even in its most timid phrasing. Of course, neither Protestants nor Catholics addressed the fate of the immense majority of the deportees, the non-converted Jews. In other words, as the deportations from the Reich and the Protectorate were sending tens of thousands of Jews to the East, as the huge massacre of Jews in occupied Soviet territory became common knowledge, and as Chełmno, the first extermination site, had just been activated, Hitler and his acolytes could rely on the passivity of the Christian Churches, the only counter-force that had once challenged the regime about its criminal policies: the killing of the mentally ill.

The simultaneity of the decision to murder all the Jews of Europe and the declared non-intervention of the Christian Churches even regarding converted Jews sets the early phase of the "Final Solution" in its wider German context. The same context takes on an additional tragically-ironic meaning as, at the very same time, in the last days of 1941, in the Reich and all over occupied Europe, Jews were celebrating their oncoming liberation in view of the Soviet successes in front of Moscow. Only in Vilna and somewhat later in Warsaw did a tiny group become aware that the overall extermination was just starting.

Narration and Interpretation

A discussion of the narrative form adapted to an integrated history of the Holocaust is primarily meant here at a quasi-technical level and not in any way as a follow up to the debate with Hayden White about the representation of the Holocaust.[4] We are dealing with events occurring in Germany, in every single country of occupied and satellite Europe, and well beyond. We are dealing with institutions and individual voices, with ideologies, religious traditions, etc. As just mentioned, no general history of the Holocaust can do justice to the significance of this diversity of elements by presenting them as independently juxtaposed. Thus, analytic categories like those used by Raul Hilberg in *The Destruction of the European Jews,* for example, have to be replaced by a succession of time units. For this reason and, furthermore, in order to follow the fate of individual Jews, mainly that of the diarists, a chronological representation of the entire process becomes unavoidable. In other words, an integrated history, as presented here imposes a return to a chronicle-like narration. But, as historian Dan Diner pointed out, not to a form of chronicle that predated conceptualization; in this case, chronicle remains the only recourse after major interpretive concepts have been tried and found lacking.

Such form of chronicling does not exclude partial interpretations nor does it exclude assumptions about the general historical context of the Holocaust, the collapse of liberalism in continental Europe and the related surge of extreme antisemitism, for example, nor, more specifically, does it exclude assumptions about the historical place of the extermination of the Jews within the vast array of Nazi goals and policies. This last issue brings us back to a point that was implicitly present in Broszat's argument: his objection to the centrality of the Holocaust within the general history of the Third Reich.

The promoters of the historicization agenda stressed quite correctly that Nazi crimes had been, out of necessity, set at center stage in the history of the Third Reich for the needs of the postwar trials. Later, according to the same argument, the centrality of the criminal dimension and the black-and-white representation became imperative at least for a German historiography aimed at educating the nation (*eine volkspädagogische Geschichtsschreibung*). Thus, according to the same view, the time had come (in 1985) to perceive the policies of the regime within a much wider and differentiated context.

And indeed, in some recent works the persecution and extermination of the Jews of Europe became but a secondary result of policies pursued towards entirely different goals. These goals included, for example, the creation of a new economic and demographic equilibrium in occupied Europe by way of murdering surplus populations; ethnic reshuffling and decimation of Eastern populations to facilitate German colonization or, in the immediate, to ensure sufficient food supply for the *Wehrmacht;* systematic plunder of the Jews of Europe in order to allow the waging of a total war without putting too heavy a material burden on German society or, more precisely, in order to protect the economic and social foundations of Hitler's *Volksstaat.*

These interpretations were often based on new documentary material, but they projected the limited or local significance of this material unto an overall explanation of the Holocaust as such. As a result, all such interpretations imply the primacy of instrumental rationality to explain the policies of expropriation, slave labor, and extermination. Instrumental rationality means modernity and, implicitly, in this case, the pitilessness of modern capitalism. This brings us back, on a more sophisticated level, to some of the early Marxist attempts to explain Nazism. To analyze these approaches here would be impossible. Suffice it to mention some marginal but telling events that become significant "anomalies" and put in question the validity of such a paradigm. What, for example, would be the rationale behind the Reichsführer SS's personal demand, in the summer of 1942, to Finland's Prime Minister to have his country deliver its thirty to forty foreign Jews into Germans hands? Why would the Germans take the trouble to deport the small and impoverished Sephardic communities from the Aegean islands in July 1944 while the Reich was crumbling? Or, why would they round up and deport hundreds of Jewish children from France to Auschwitz, a few days before the liberation of Paris?

The only approach that seems plausible in writing an integrated history of the Holocaust—and I am aware that this goes against oft used universalizing perceptions of this history—is to consider the Jewish issue as one of the most central tenets of the regime's worldview and thus of its policies. "All in all," Goebbels noted after a long conversation with Hitler at the end of April 1944, "a long-term policy in this war is only possible if one considers it from the standpoint of the Jewish Question." This crazed obsession was enthusiastically supported and implemented by Hitler's closest acolytes, by party and state agencies, by officials and technocrats at all levels of the system, and, as we saw, by important segments of the population. The "logic" behind this anti-Jewish passion was constantly spewed by the regime's propaganda. In fact, as Jeffrey Herf has shown, propaganda molded an increasingly ominous image of "the Jew" as the lethal and relentlessly active enemy of the Reich, intent on its destruction. Thus, within the same hallucinatory logic, once the Reich had to fight on both fronts, East and West, without the hope of a rapid victory and with some early intimations of defeat, Hitler opted for immediate extermination. Otherwise, as he saw it, the Jews, like in 1917–1918, would destroy Germany and the new Europe from within. And, after the military situation became ominous, the extermination was accelerated to its utter limits.

In Conclusion: Questions, Answerable and Unanswerable

An integrated history leads in and of itself to comparative queries and, more generally, to connections that are otherwise but dimly perceived. Let me present one telling example: the glaring lack of an overall Jewish solidarity in the face of catastrophe.

The German Jewish leadership attempted to bar endangered Polish Jews from emigrating from the Reich to Palestine, in late 1939 and early 1940, in order to keep all emigration openings for German Jews only; native French Jewish leadership (the *Consistoire*) ceaselessly demanded from the Vichy government a clear-cut distinction between the status and treatment of native Jews and that of foreign ones. The Councils in Poland—particularly in Warsaw—were allowing a whole array of privileges to members of the local middle class who could afford paying bribes, while the poor, the refugees from the provinces, and the mass of those devoid of any influence were increasingly pushed into slave labor, or driven to starvation and death. Once the deportations started, Polish Jews in Łódź, for example, turned against the deportees from the West. In Westerbork, German Jews, the elite of the camp, closely working with the German commandants, protected their own and put Dutch Jews on the departure lists, while, previously, the Dutch Jewish elite had felt secure and was convinced that only refugees (mainly German Jews) would be sent to the local camps, then deported. The hatred of Christian Jews by their Jewish brethren, and vice versa, particularly in the Warsaw Ghetto, is notorious.

Yet, a strengthening of bonds appeared within small groups sharing a specific political or religious background. Such was typically the case in political youth groups in the ghettos, among Jewish scouts in France, and, of course, among this or that group of Orthodox Jews. In looking at the big picture, we may reach the conclusion that in a majority of cases, specific ethnic-cultural, political or religious bonds shared by any number of sub-groups took precedence over any feeling of shared "Jewishness."

★

On 27 June 1945, the world-renowned Jewish-Austrian chemist Lise Meitner, who in 1939 had emigrated from Germany to Sweden, wrote to her former colleague and friend, Otto Hahn, who had continued to work in the Reich. After mentioning that he and the scientific community in Germany knew much about the worsening persecution of the Jews, Meitner went on: "All of you have worked for Nazi Germany and never tried even passive resistance. Certainly, to assuage your conscience, here and there you helped some person in need of assistance but you allowed the murder of millions of innocent people, and no protest was ever heard." Meitner's *cri de coeur* addressed through Hahn to Germany's most prominent scientists, none of them active party members, none of them involved in criminal activities, could have applied as well to the entire intellectual and spiritual elite of the Reich (with some exceptions, of course) and to wide segments of the elites in occupied or satellite Europe.

An even more unsettling aspect of the same question arises in regard to the attitude of the Christian churches. In Germany—again with the exception of a few individuals, none of whom belonged to the higher reaches of the Evangelical or Catholic Church—no Protestant bishop or Catholic prelate protested publicly against the extermination of the Jews. When men of good will, such as Bishop Preysing of Berlin or the voice of the Confessing Church, the Württemberg Bishop Theophil Wurm, were ordered to stop their attempts at confidential protests, they submitted.

That an important number of personalities belonging to Germany's intellectual or spiritual elites did not take a public stand against the murder of the Jews is easily understood. That not even a few prominent voices were publicly heard is puzzling; that not a single personality of major stature was ready to speak out remains, as some other aspects of this history, a continuous source of disbelief.

Notes

1. Quoted in Georges Didi-Huberman, *Images in Spite of All* (Chicago, 2008), 97–98.

2. Excerpted in Max Hastings' review of Echternkamp's volume, "Germans Confront the Nazi Past," *The New York Review of Books* (26 February 2009), 17. Regarding the other studies, see mainly Hans Mommsen, "Der Holocaust und die Deutschen: Aktuelle Beiträge zu einer umstrittenen Frage," *Zeitschrift für Geschichtswissenschaft* 56, no. 10 (2008): 844–53.

3. Primo Levi, *The Drowned and the Saved* (New York, 1988), 83–84.

4. For this debate, see in particular Saul Friedländer, ed., *Probing the Limits of Representation: Nazism and the "Final Solution"* (Cambridge, MA, 1992).

CHAPTER 10

Truth and Circumstance
What (If Anything) Can Be Properly Said about the Holocaust?

HAYDEN WHITE

Under what circumstances would it be impertinent, tactless, or simply irrelevant to ask of a discourse which manifestly refers to the real world, past, present, or future, the question: "Is it true?" And if there are certain utterances (expressions, allusions, suggestions, statements, propositions, or assertions) about the real world for which the question "Is it true?" is beside the point, what kinds of responses, if any, would be appropriate for utterances of this kind?

I pose these questions in the context of an ongoing discussion of what would constitute a "proper" representation of the Holocaust, an event so traumatic for so many individuals and groups that, when irrefutable evidence of its occurrence became public, incredulity was the first and most dominant response to it. Even after incredulity gave way to outrage over the fact that a "modern," "enlightened," "Christian," and "humanistic" nation like Germany could betray the values of the European civilization of which it had been an esteemed representative, the question of what "the Final Solution" amounted to, what it signified about European values themselves, what it told one about modernity, Germany, "the Jews" and Judaism, and "Europe" in general remained pressing and seemingly intractable. For historians—professional custodians of Western historical consciousness and cultivators of a putative science of history—the principal question raised by the Holocaust was its identity as a specifically "historical" event and the best way to inscribe it within, insert it into, assimilate it to the normative narrative account of Europe's history. At the same time, the sense that the Holocaust was an "unusual," "novel," and possibly even a "unique" event in Europe's history raised the possibility of having to

---

Notes for this section begin on page 201.

revise this history radically in order to do justice to the insights into the *real* nature of European civilization which the event had seemingly provided. In fact, the "extremity" if not the uniqueness of the Holocaust event raised crucial questions about the theoretical presuppositions underlying and informing modern Western ideas about "history," the methodologies utilized by modern professional historians in their efforts to know the historical past, and the protocols and techniques used for the presentation of historical reality in their discourses.

These questions were rendered more difficult to answer due to the fact that modern media had made possible the recording and circulation of so many personal accounts of survivors' experiences of the event and, moreover, the demand on the part of many of these "witnesses" to the event that their remembered experiences be factored into the "official" or "doxological" record being built up by the historians on the basis of their examination of the documentary and monumentary evidence available to them. Beyond that, while the historians' reconstruction of what had really happened in the Final Solution and/or the Holocaust was proceeding at a customarily glacial pace, the field of Holocaust Studies was being flooded by a plethora of memoirs, autobiographies, novels, plays, movies, poems, and documentaries, which, from the standpoint of many historians, threatened to aestheticize, fictionalize, kitschify, relativize, and otherwise mythify what was an undeniable fact (or congeries of facts) and as such "properly" studied only by means and methods more or less scientific. This meant that, from the standpoint of many historians, when presented with any representation of the Final Solution or the Holocaust, the first and most basic question had to be: "Is it true?" And if the answer to that question was either no or contained some equivocation, then the representation in question had to be rejected as being not only a misrepresentation of reality but, given the nature of the hurt visited upon the victims, a violation of victims' moral right to a true and accurate account of what they had experienced.

But what about that vast mass of testimony of survivors? Should it be submitted to the same criterion of truthfulness as that demanded of a historian's account of some event in the past? We must undoubtedly demand that the person bearing witness to some experience at least wishes to tell the truth, but is a correspondence model of truth our principal interest in the testimony of survivors? Obviously, it must be our primary concern if the testimony is offered in a court of law where the determination of what happened and who was responsible for it are our principal interests. But when it is a matter of giving voice to what it felt like to be subjected to the kind of treatment that the victims of the Holocaust experienced, a correspondence ideal of truthfulness would seem to be an improper demand. Even the coherence model of truthfulness would seem to have little relevance in the assessment of the authority of the testimony of a victim. Here the question "Is it true?" should only be posed as a rhetorical one.

I will return to the status of victims' testimony later on. For the moment, I want to extend the investigation of the pertinence of the question "Is it true?" to the consideration of artistic and specifically literary treatments of the Holocaust. Of course, artistic and literary treatments of the Holocaust must be a problem for historians of the Holocaust who regard this event as having something like a sacral status. And this is especially the case when "artistic" is identified with "aesthetic," and "literature" is identified with "fiction." It is the necessity of these two sets of identifications that I wish to question.

If the Holocaust is conceded an ontological status that would prohibit its representation in images or as an occasion for anything other than reverence or celebration, then obviously any artistic or literary treatment of the Holocaust would have to be viewed as approaching near to the status of blasphemy. This attitude would rule out in advance any historiographical treatment of the Holocaust insofar as it might use aestheticizing or fictionalizing strategies in the composition of the presentation. And yet, in my view at least, this is exactly what a narratological treatment of the Holocaust or any part of it would do. This is why, for example, the philosopher (and my dear friend) Berel Lang counsels the abandonment of any attempt to narrativize the Holocaust and suggests instead that accounts remain at the level of a chronicle, a simple listing of the facts in the order of their occurrence as established by a literalist reading of the documentary record.

Berel Lang is quite right to view narrative or narrativization or more simply storytelling as less a veridical mimesis of a course of real events than a "dangerous supplement" to a rigorously truthful account of them.[1] For Berel Lang, the making of a story out of the events of the Holocaust is another instance of figuration which sacrifices any possibility of a literal account of it to the exigencies of aesthetic fancy or play. An aesthetic treatment of the Holocaust, in his view, subordinates the truth of fact to the egoistic display of the artist's technique or the ambiguating effects of rhetorical or poetic figuration. In this view, Berel Lang joins forces with Carlo Ginzburg's efforts to defend the historian's truth from the corroding effects of skepticism and relativism. Ginzburg objects to relativism because it eschews the possibility of a single correct view of the world and to skepticism because—in his view—it forecloses the very possibility of truth itself. Pluralism and skepticism together license an "anything goes" attitude toward truth and an "any given view is as valid as any other" attitude towards values.[2] Lang provides arguments against aestheticism and fictionalism in the treatment of any event with the moral weight and ontological substance of the Holocaust.

Now, in my contribution to the conference "The Final Solution and the Limits of Representation," organized by Saul Friedländer and Wulf Kansteiner at UCLA in 1990, I took the position that the problem of representing the Holocaust should not be conceptualized in terms of traditional (late nineteenth-century) notions of realism, history, representation, aesthetics, fiction, ideology, discourse, storytelling, and mimeticist notions of description. The idea was that, as the occurrence of the Holocaust itself had made obvious, the combination of the new reality manifested in World War II and the consolidation of modernist notions of the nature of discourse, representation, history, and art itself had rendered questionable if not nugatory the pre-World War II notions of these issues.

I do not wish to rehearse once more my attempts to formulate these issues as I did then. What I want to do, rather, is try to confront the issue of how to present the Holocaust as a historical phenomenon, the "novelty" not to say the "anomalous" nature of which in modern European history I willingly concede, by a consideration of the stakes that are involved in the posing of the question "Is it true?" when confronted with any and every instance of Holocaust representation, in historiography, in literature, in film, in photography, in philosophy, in social science, and so on.

And this assessment extends to the manifestly artistic versions of victims' testimony, to memoirs such as Primo Levi's *Se questo è un uomo* (*If This Is a Man*) to comix like Art Spiegelman's *Maus*, films like Cavani's *Il portiere di notte* (*The Night Porter*) movies like Spielberg's *Schindler's List*, and Benigni's *La vita è bella* (*Life Is Beautiful*). Although all of these artistic works are manifestly *about* the real historical event, the Holocaust, they are viewed by many historians as not only "unhistorical" but as "fictionalizing" or "aestheticizing" of an event which, by its nature, has a moral right to a strictly truthful account of its reality.[3]

And it is here that I wish to question the pertinence, aptness, tactfulness, and adequacy of the question "Is it true?" to *all* discourses making reference to real historical events in the course of their elaboration. My answer to this question will be something like, yes, it is always pertinent to raise the question "Is it true?" of any account of the past presenting itself as a *historical* account thereof. But, I will suggest, this question "Is it true?" is of secondary importance to discourses making reference to the real world (past or present) cast in a mode other than that of simple declaration. This is especially the case with artistic (verbal, aural, or visual) representations of reality (past or present) which, in modernity, are typically cast in modes other than that of simple declaration—for example, the interrogative, imperative, and subjunctive modes.[4]

The question I have posed, "When is the question, 'Is it true?' irrelevant," etc., is often discussed in terms of the morality of truth-telling: for example, when is it proper or desirable to tell a lie or, put another way, do circumstances make it "better" to tell a lie rather than the truth? This question does not interest me. I am interested in the question, is it proper to forego asking the question "Is it true or false?" in the presence of a specific kind of discourse of which witness literature would be a paradigm and a modernist literary treatment of the Holocaust would be an instance.[5] This question interests me because of a belief amongst some historians that a history and all of the statements made about history or the past must "tell the truth." Moreover, it is a principle of historiographical statements that they must not "lie," "distort," "misrepresent," or deny, leave out, negate or disavow those "facts" which have been established with regard to some aspect of past "reality." All of this is bad enough, according to the moral epistemology that informs much of current thought about historical writing, but it is much, much worse to "fictionalize" history either in the sense of presenting "fictional" things as "facts," the sense of turning "facts" into fictions, or mixing facts with fiction as in the nefarious historical novel or historical movie or the so-called "docudrama" (which is supposed to be a "dramatization" of some historical reality). This crime, sin, or misdemeanor is deemed to be akin to the feared "mythification" of reality or "metahistorical" treatment of historical reality after the manner of Hegel, Marx, Nietzsche, Spengler, Toynbee, and so on.

Now, in my opinion Holocaust "discourse" is not only about the kinds of questions I have listed above; it also includes the actual histories or historical treatments of the Holocaust insofar as they present or perform certain answers to theoretical questions in the course of their attempts to provide answers to a set of purely "factual" questions. And this is so from the moment when the question "What is it?" is posed all the way over to the time when, in the book or article actually published, one can see manifested the statement "This is what happened." The *theoretical* question "What is it I see before me?" belongs to the same discourse as the answer cast in the mode of a set of facts which add up to the statement: "What you see before you is a Holocaust, genocide, extermination, etc." And because the theoretical question "What is it?" belongs to the same discourse as the answer "It is an X," we cannot legitimately (i.e., with a logic that is not tautological) point to any given history of the Holocaust written by any given historian as an *example* of a "proper" treatment of it.

What is proper to anything is both a question of fact (What does it look like or what are its attributes? What did it do?) and a question of morality (what is its "nature," its "essence," its "substance" in reference to which alone one might determine the "propriety" which is to say, the "self-sameness" of a thing's motion, movement, desire, judgment, action, etc.). *Authenticity* (the circumstance in which a thing *appears to be* exactly what it is or always *is* what it appears to be) might also be defined as doing the proper thing, at the proper time, and in the proper place, with the proper aim, object, and goal in mind and the proper means for doing just that thing and not something else. The difficulty of living up to this ideal of authenticity is manifest in situations in which it is the "nature" of the thing that is being assessed as to its authenticity or self-sameness that is at issue.

Thus, if in support of a particular notion of what the Holocaust is or might be or must be taken to have been, etc., I bring out a specific representation of it as an example of what an authentic or proper presentation of it is to be taken to be, my judgment of it has to be taken to be either assertoric, categorical, or problematical, which is to say, either in the mode of a hypothesis, in the mode of an imperative, or in the mode of a question. If *assertoric,* then the example can be considered for use as a model generating hypotheses to be tested out in the manner of an interrogation. If *categorical,* then the example is to be taken as a paradigm or original instance that will not only suggest to us what kinds of questions are properly posed to the thing being interrogated, but also the moral stance proper to the inquiry. Whereas a *problematical* example features aporia, or the difficulty of deciding whether the proper is to be considered an assertoric or a categorical instance. Here I follow the Kant of *Groundwork of the Metaphysics of Morals.*[6]

Kant thought that in any inquiry into an ethical matter, we could not legitimately use an example to suggest the principle being sought by which to guide inquiry "properly," because the principle in question had to be sought in the operations of a reason purged of both moral and aesthetic "interests." But if the issue in question is the proper, which is a moral question, pure (or scientific) reason cannot provide what we are looking for in seeking the rule of "propriety" in the first place. If in making a statement of what one *ought* to do in trying to compose a representation of an event like the Holocaust with proper concern for its real "nature," I advance an argument giving my reasons for recommending one mode of approaching the phenomenon over another, my statement has to be taken as a kind of recommendation or an imperative. Here is an example: Consider this way of treating the history of the Holocaust (that of, for example, Christopher Browning rather than that of Daniel Goldhagen) or, alternatively, Write the history of the Holocaust in this way and no other!

Now, in neither case is "Is it true?" a proper response to utterances of the kind: "Consider this" or "Do this!" Is it true that I ought to consider writing my history of the Holocaust on the model of X? Or alternatively: Is it true that I must write the history of the Holocaust, not only in a given manner but that I must also cast my history in a particular mode (by which I mean a specific attitude of submission, reverence, or care vis-à-vis the object of study)? For the question "Is it true that I *ought* to do P?" is a deontological question, which is to say, a matter of obligation, and one proper response to it is to ask either: "Says who?" or "To what or whom am I obligated to do P?" And if the answer to this question is something like, you are obligated by the very nature of the event of which you are writing a history, you can see that we are back to the original question: What is the nature of this event called the Holocaust?

The difficulty in which much of Holocaust discourse has become mired is that the telling of the truth about anything can come modalized in ways other than an answer to the simple declarative sentence which is usually taken by philosophers to be the model of statements claiming to be true. To be sure, statements of the kind "It is the case that (or it is true that) snow is white or the cat is on the mat" are properly responded to by the question "Is it true that … ?" But statements cast in the form of questions ("Where is the cat?"), desires ("Would that I had a cat"), even imperatives ("Find the cat!") are hardly answerable by the question: "Is it true?"

All this is elementary, to be sure. But if we extend the idea of modality from sentences to whole discourses, we can even entertain the idea that whole novels, dramas, histories, and (who knows?) even philosophical discourses might be cast in a variety of modes that deprives even their factual statements of the force of declaratives. Limiting my remarks now to my own area of interest and the hypothesis that there is more than one way to "tell the truth about the past," I wish to suggest that both the historical novel and the novelesque history are instances of non-declarative discourses, that their truth may consist less in what they *assert* in the mode of factual truth-telling than in what they *connote* in the other moods and voices identified in the study of grammar: which is to say, the *modes* of interrogation, conation or coaction, and subjunction and the *voices* of action, passion, and transumption. Thus, for example, it might make less sense to respond to a poem or a novel or a history cast in the mode of a question or a wish with the query: "Is it true?" than it does to respond to one cast in the mode of a command. The "proper" response to a command might be "Yes, Sir" or "No, Sir" but it is not necessarily (in the case in which a command is uttered outside a military or a master-slave relation) improper to respond, as in the case with Melville's "Bartleby the Scrivener," with the subjunctive statement "I would prefer not."

Considerations such as these move us over into the domain of Speech Act theory, in which propriety of response to an utterance is "context specific" and "conditions of felicity" (which is to say, propriety) may apply. In the case of research into the past, there are a number of different ways of addressing, observing, hailing or otherwise investing the past. Thus, for example, one might approach the past as a place from which one or one's group has descended. Or (quite a different matter) one might regard the past as a place of one's origin. Again, one might take up a position vis-à-vis the past as what has already happened or what has been done or what has been made before one had appeared on the scene. This sense of the past as that which has already been done might in turn be taken up as either a heritage or as a burden to be cast off and, in either case, a presence *which seems to present itself* (apodictically) either as an enigma (a puzzle waiting to be solved—as in Pynchon's *Crying of Lot 49*) or an anomaly (a real problem for which there may be no solution)—as in Toni Morrison's *Beloved*).

I would like to recall that Speech Act theory was intended, according to J. L. Austin, its founder, to undermine ("play old Harry with") two fetishisms: the "true/false fetish" and the "value/fact fetish."[7] According to Austin, the crucial instance of Speech Act theory is to be found in the class of speech-acts he calls "Behabitives," which is to say, such behaviors as "apologizing," "congratulating," "commanding," "consoling," "cursing," and "challenging."[8]

Behabitives belong, according to Austin, to one of five classes of speech acts which also include: Verdictives (giving a verdict, appraising), Exercitives (appointing, voting, ordering), Commissives (promising, announcing, espousing), and Expositives (arguing, conversing, illustrating, exemplifying). Austin goes on to say that he finds the last two classes of Speech Acts, that is, Expositives and Behabitives, "most troublesome: behabitives ... because they seem too miscellaneous altogether; and expositives because they are enormously numerous and important, and seem both to be included in the other classes and at the same time to be unique in a way that I have not succeeded in making clear even to myself. It could well be said that all aspects are present in all my classes. ..." In other words, by Austin's own account, his effort to define or identify the essence of Speech Acts is problematic: his discourse is expositive but leaves open the ethical (or behabitive) question: given this exposition of the phenomenon called Speech Acts, what should I do?

So, supposing I am a historian, interested as I am in the history of modern Germany, the history of Jewish communities in modern Europe, the "places" of the Final Solution, the Holocaust, the genocide, the extermination, and so forth, in these histories, the meaning of this event for the understanding of what was really happening in the times and places of these histories. And because I am aware of the "special" or "extreme" or "exceptional" nature of this event—its embarrassment not only to Europeans but to many other groups to their own *amour propre* and the *threat* that this event poses to their sense of their own individual and group identity—supposing that I know that this event has a significance that is not only factualistic (in the sense that it happened where and when and how it did) but also ethical, insofar as it manifests the violation of a fundamental principle of our humanity, namely, thou shalt not treat another human being as less than human, which is also the rule of modern humanistic historiological inquiry, namely, that thou shalt treat every human being in history as partaking in the *humanitas* which all humans share in. Given these suppositions, the question arises: does the evidence that comes to us from this event which we are studying in order to find out not only *that* it happened and *how* it happened, but also and more importantly, does it tell us what were the conditions of possibility of its happening? Which, if we are to take Aristotle seriously (and how could we not?), puts the ball out of the court of both philosophy and history and into that of *poiesis*: "poetry" or literary art understood as a mode of cognition focused on the possible, rather than on the actual (history, as Aristotle understood it) and the universal (philosophy as he understood it). Indeed, I would suggest at this point in my own discourse that the Speech Act theory of J. L. Austin (who was practical enough to have participated in the planning of the Normandy invasion) is or can legitimately be considered to be a theory of the poetic function of language (as against its referential, expressive, conative, phatic, and metalinguistic functions), for what else is poetic utterance but a doing or making of something by a particular mode, manner or style of saying something?[9]

Recall now that for Austin a speech act is "illocutionary," that is, an action in which, in saying something, one not only says *something* but also *does* something, that is to say, changes a relationship either of the speaker to the world, of one part of the world to another, or of the world to the speaker. And if this is right—as many of Austin's commentators seem to think that it is—then we might begin to think about discourses, of which "historiography" would be one, as speech-acts which, in saying something about the world, seek to change the world, the way one might relate to it, or the way things relate to one another in the world. In other words, Austin's theory of speech-acts might be used to contrive a discourse or a congeries of discourses such as "historiography" as a praxis, which is to say, an action intended to change or have an impact on the world by the *way* it says something about it. (I take it that such a principle underlies the belief in the right of courts to deem Holocaust denial a crime to be punished by a fine or incarceration or some other sanction. The Holocaust denier has not only said something, he has also *done* something in the saying, that is, he has changed or tried to change relationships in the real world in the way that a curse or magical spell is supposed to do. Which is why those historians who objected to the designation of Holocaust denial as a crime perceived aright what the courts had overlooked, namely, that if denial of a fact established by historians constitutes a crime, then the distinction between honest error and malicious error must go by the board. The proper response to someone who denies the Holocaust is not "Is it true?" but, rather, the question, what motivates the desire driving the denial?)

An example of a text which, although manifestly *about* the real world and specifically the world of Auschwitz, to which a response cast in the form "Is it (historically) true?" would be tactless, is Primo Levi's memoir of his time in Auschwitz in the late months of World War II. Obviously, Levi's *Se questo è un uomo*[10] contains a multitude of declarative utterances which ask to be taken as true in the literal sense of that term (that is, as referentially true and semantically meaningful). But the title of Levi's memoir is taken from the poem that serves as the epigraph of the work and as the paratextual paradigm of the work's intended meaning-effect. It begins with a title: "Shema," the Jewish declaration of faith in Israel, and an address, not to the prospective reader, but to an anonymous "you":

You who live secure	Voi che vivete sicuri
In your warm houses,	Nelle vostre tiepide case,
You who return at evening	Voi che trovate tornando a sera
To find warm food and friendly faces	Il cibo caldo e visi amici:
Consider if this is a man	Considerate se questo è un uomo
Who works in mud	Che lavora nel fango
Who knows no peace	Che non conosce pace
Who fights for a piece of bread	Che lotta per mezzo pane

Who dies by a yes or a no	Che muore per un si o no.
Consider if this is a woman,	Considerate se questo è una donna
Without hair or a name	Senza capelli e senza nome
Without strength to remember	Senza più forza di ricordare
With vacant eyes and a cold womb	Vuoti gli occhi e freddo il grembo
Like a frog in winter	Come un rana d'inverno
Meditate on these things	Meditate che questo è stato:
I charge you with these words.	Vi commando queste parole.
Engrave them on your hearts	Scolpitele nel vostro cuore
When at home or on the way	Stando in casa andando per via.
When you retire and when you rise.	Coricandovi alzandovi;
Repeat them to your children	Ripetele ai vostri figli.
Or may your house crumble	O vi sfaccia la casa,
Disease afflict you,	La malattia vi impedisca,
Your children turn their faces from you.[11]	I vostri nati torcano il visi da voi.

While the use of a poem or a prayer as an epigraph of a memoir is not unusual, this poem instructs the reader to meditate upon the significance of life in Auschwitz for what it tells us about the capacity of human beings to humiliate their own kind. "Consider," the second stanza of the poem suggests, whether the humiliation endured by the *Häftlinge* of the camps made them less than "men" or "women." This suggestion to "consider" is not itself glossed in the poem, but the reader is told, in the first two lines of the next stanza: "Meditate (*meditate*) on these things: / I charge you (*commando*) with these words."[12] Then follows the curse upon those who might fail to "inscribe them in [their] hearts" while waking and sleeping, at home or abroad, or fail to "repeat them to [their] children."

> Or may your house crumble,
> Disease afflict you,
> Your children turn their faces from you.[13]

It has to be said that this is not the kind of epigraph that one would normally expect to find at the beginning of a "historical" account of a life or a memoir of an episode in a life. The threat of a curse is a kind of speech act quite different from the kind conventionally used as an epigraph; it indicates that the discourse to follow will be anything but a coolly objective account of the facts or a contribution to the documentary record.

Nonetheless, as I have tried to demonstrate in my reading of *Se questo è un uomo* in the journal *Parallax*, the specific *literariness* of Levi's text, that is, its poetic rather than documentary nature, excuses it from the kinds of questions we might ask of it in a court of law.[14] This is not to suggest that it is "fictional" and it certainly does not mean that it is "aesthetic." It is simply to say that it uses literary devices (for example, traditional literary or mythological plot structures—Dante's descent into Hell is the model), figures and principles of linguistic connection and psychological association more tropological than logical in kind.

Levi uses tropes (such as catachresis, metonymy, irony, synecdoche, etc.), and figures (especially for transforming persons into the kind of "characters" or "types" that one finds in myths, legends, and novels) to depict a real situation in which choice and decision involved the life and death of self and others on a daily basis. In many respects, Levi's text conforms to the principles of the genre of confession, since it is his own exculpation for having survived that he seeks, as well as that of others.

But of course it is not only his own redemption that is at issue. Levi's is or purports to be an account of what life and death were like in the concentration camp Auschwitz. It is not an imaginary world, and yet it can scarcely be described except poetically. I have often pointed out that Levi adds nothing in the way of factual information that could not be had in any reference book. Instead of telling us "what happened," he tells us "what it felt like" and what it took in self-humiliation to "survive in Auschwitz."

Are we in the domain of fiction then?

Hardly.

In the preface to the Italian edition of *Se questo è un uomo,* Levi addresses the problem of the genre to which his book belongs: "I recognize," he writes, "and beg forgiveness for the structural defects of the book." But, he adds, "If not actually, in both intention and conception it was born already in the last days of the Lager." The need, he says, *"di raccontare agli 'altri,' di fare gli 'altri' partecipi,"* had assumed among the survivors the "character of a spontaneous (immediate) and violent impulse" (*tanto da rivaleggiare con gli altri bisogni elementari: il libro è stato scritto per soddisfare a questo bisogno; in primo luogo quindi a scopo di liberazione interiore*).[15] "Whence," he adds, "its fragmentary character; the chapters were written, not in the order of logical succession, but in the order of urgency." The secondary revision, the putting in order and fusion, came later. Thus, Levi with a kind of *captatio bene volentiae* sends his book forth, warts and all, as we say. But not before adding a sly warning to the historians: *"Mi pare superfluo aggiungere che nessumo dei fatti e inventato."*[16]

Thus, the work was conceived as if in a dream and then worked out or worked up on reflection and consideration. What does this mean for the factual content of the work? Levi's answer is laconic and ambiguous: "It seems superfluous to add that none of the facts was invented." I cannot resist pointing out that this last sentence can be read in two ways: either "none of the *facts* was invented" (which leaves it open for other things than the facts to have been invented) or "none of the facts was *invented*" (which simply says what we all expect, namely, that the facts were found or given, rather than "made up"). In any event, by this sentence, Levi alerts us to the idea that his discourse is somewhat more or other than either fact or fiction. And why not? By his own account of life in the Lager, the very distinction between fact and fiction had become as nebulous as the distinction between good and evil. Everything existed in that "Gray Zone" which Levi would limn in his late work, *The Drowned and the Saved*. His point was or seems to me to have been that in the world of the Lager, things were as difficult to make sense of as any life in "history."

To sum up: did the experience of the victims, survivors, or casualties of the Holocaust constitute a new kind of experience hitherto unknown to "history"? And if so, what could possibly be said about this experience that would not violate or otherwise diminish the sense of its exceptionality? My suggestion has been that we cannot establish on the basis of any strictly factual account, whether the Holocaust was a new event, a new kind of event, or simply an old kind of event with a different face. If it is a new kind of event, an event peculiar to our modernity, then this would account for our unease in the face of conventional historiographical treatments of this event. I have suggested that the straightforward declarative mode favored by traditional historians cannot do justice to the vast mass of witness literature insofar as the historian must ask of it, "Is it true?" I have suggested further that one might want to consider the possibility that the witnesses of the kind of extreme events in which the last (and our own) century abounds might very well be writing or speaking in a different mode of expression, such as the interrogative, the imperative, and the subjunctive. I go further: I suggest that, when it comes to an *artistic* version of witness testimony, such as Levi's *Se questo è un uomo*, the question of the factual truth of the account is of a lesser importance. It is, rather, a question of mode rather than of mimesis.

Notes

1. Berel Lang is the foremost proponent of the idea that the Holocaust is a "literal event," by which he means an event about which anything other than the plain truth ought not to be said about it. In Lang's view, the Holocaust is an event which by its nature precludes any ornament, poetic or rhetorical, and any "imaginative" treatment other than that of a reverence all but silent. He has developed, qualified, and refined this idea with philosophical tact and ethical acumen in a number of texts: from his "The Representation of Limits," in Saul Friedländer, ed., *Probing the Limits of Representation: Nazism and the "Final Solution"* (Cambridge, MA, 1992), 300–17; through *Holocaust Representation* (Baltimore, 2000); down to *Philosophical Witnessing: The Holocaust as Presence* (Lebann, NH, 2009). See also Isabel Wollaston, "'What Can—and Cannot—Be Said': Religious Language after the Holocaust," *Journal of Literature and Theology* 6, no. 1 (1992): 47–57; and Zachary Braiterman, "Against Holocaust-Sublime," *History and Memory* 2, no. 2 (2000): 7–28.

2. Carlo Ginzburg, "Just One Witness," in Friedländer, ed., *Probing the Limits of Representation*, 82–96.

3. I recently met a young historian who had been teaching Levi's *Se questo è un uomo* in a course on the Holocaust. He told me that he was constantly worried about how much of the text had been "made up" as against what there was in it of factual significance.

4. Todd Presner, "Subjunctive History: The Use of Counterfactuals in the Writing of the Disaster," *Storiografia: Rivista annuale di storia* 4 (2000): 23–38.

5. Of course, there is a great deal of work on the ways in which an artistic or poetic treatment of the Holocaust inevitably "aestheticizes" it, as if "aestheticize" translates to beautifying or making it desirable in some way. By the same token, some theorists seem to think that a "literary" treatment of the Holocaust will inevitably "fictionalize" it, as if literary writing equated with

fictional writing only. The trouble here is with the ideas of "aesthetics" and "literary" that are being used. I take aesthetics to have to do with the effect of the perception of an object, scene, or event on the bodily senses and the cognitive weight of such an effect. By "literary" I would mean the use of certain identifiable devices, techniques, and symbolizations by which to endow things, real or imaginary, with meaning. See Ernst van Alphen, "Caught by Images: On the Role of the Visual Imprints in Holocaust Testimonies," *Journal of Visual Culture* 1 (2000): 205–22; and Georges Didi-Huberman, *Images in Spite of All: Four Photographs from Auschwitz* (Chicago, 2008), for another take on the "what is properly shown about Auschwitz" debate.

    6. Immanuel Kant, *Groundwork of the Metaphysics of Morals*, ed. Mary McGregor (Cambridge, UK, 1997), 24–28.

    7. J. L. Austin, *How To Do Things with Words* (Oxford, 1973), 150.

    8. Ibid., 151.

    9. Roman Jakobson, "Closing Statement: Linguistics and Poetics," in Thomas Sebeok, ed., *Style in Language* (New York, 1960), 353–57.

    10. Primo Levi, *Se questo è un uomo*, in *Opere*, vol. 1, ed. Marco Belpoliti (Rome, 2009), 3.

    11. Based on the translation of Ruth Feldman and Brian Swann, available online at http://www.poemhunter.com/poem/shema/.

    12. The translators of this poem, Ruth Feldman and Brian Swann, put English "Consider" for Italian "Meditate." I keep "meditate" because it suggests the idea of "reflect upon." "Consideration" is a particular way of putting images and thoughts together, as in a montage or collage. A meditation might follow upon a consideration. Thus, I can account for the fact that the line telling the reader to "meditate that this has been," ends with a colon, and is followed by the words: "I commend these words to you." The imperative translated as "consider" by Feldman and Swann is actually *"commando"* which has the sense of "obey" rather than English "commend." The anaphoric repetition of *"Considerate se ... "* with its telling "if" is now "that"—the "might be" now has happened.

    13. Feldman and Swann have: "Disease render you powerless" for *"La malattia vi impedisca."*

    14. Hayden White, "Figural Realism in Witness Literature," *Parallax* 10 (2004): 113–24.

    15. Levi, *Se questo*, 5–6.

    16. Ibid., 6.

CHAPTER 11

Modernist Holocaust Historiography
*A Dialogue between
Saul Friedländer and Hayden White*

WULF KANSTEINER

Many years before Saul Friedländer started to write his own comprehensive history of the Holocaust he described the difficult balancing act that a successful synthetic history of Nazi genocide would have to accomplish. In his view, such a comprehensive account should reflect state-of-the-art historical scholarship, including an exhaustive study of available primary documents and testimonies. Only full command of the facts can "establish as reliable a narrative as possible," convey the true extent of the Nazi crimes, and thus counter lingering revisionist or otherwise apologetic renditions of Nazi history.[1] However, while Friedländer invoked and embraced the rigors of academic historical research as a benchmark for epistemological success, he also stressed the need to transcend the parameters of conventional historical writing. Standard historical prose tends to normalize the past, offering its authors and readers an illusion of control and closure especially vis-à-vis the many disturbing aspects of contemporary history. Therefore, a comprehensive history of the Holocaust could only succeed as an ethical intervention if it featured an innovative aesthetic design capable of communicating the horror of Nazi genocide and resisting the temptations of intellectual domestication.[2]

Friedländer recommended three literary strategies to avoid the pitfalls of "simplistic and self-assured historical narrations."[3] He suggested that Holocaust historians include a running commentary into their writing intended to "disrupt the facile linear progression of the narrative, introduce alternative interpretations, question any partial conclusion, withstand the need for closure."[4] For the same reason, they should tell the history of the Final Solution from

Notes for this section begin on page 224.

a number of different vantage points and recover the voices of the victims in order to avoid the domestication of death and despair. Friedländer recognized full well that his allegiance to standard rules of evidence, on the one hand, and his call for new formats for the writing of Holocaust history, on the other hand, formed a contradictory, even explosive mixture and that this blueprint for future Holocaust historiography might be difficult to carry out.

Given Friedländer's concerns about the sedative, normalizing effects of conventional historical writing it is not surprising that he developed a great interest in the theoretical insights of the linguistic turn in the humanities. In fact, while contemplating the theoretical, ethical foundations of successful Holocaust syntheses, Friedländer was particularly intrigued by the work of Hayden White and, in 1990, organized a conference in Los Angeles titled "Probing the Limits of Representation" which was specifically designed to test the viability of White's ideas in the field of Holocaust studies.[5] Therefore, it makes a lot of sense to analyze the narrative design of Friedländer's two-volume *Nazi Germany and the Jews* from the perspective of White's narratological critique of historical writing. In my assessment, the methodological dialogue between White and Friedländer reveals that Friedländer has indeed succeeded in transcending the aesthetic and ethical limits of historical writing. Especially the second volume represents a truly unusual combination of scholarly erudition, innovative narrative design, and ethical integrity. But Friedländer's achievements also inadvertently highlight and render vulnerable some essential, axiomatic illusions that have sustained professional academic historiography since its inception. *Nazi Germany and the Jews* constitutes a wake-up call for historians—and an elegant verification of White's philosophy of history.

Narratology of History: An Unfinished Project

Hayden White launched his provocative analysis of historical writing and historiographical ideology in two steps in the early 1970s and early 1980s respectively. In *Metahistory* he proposed a systematic, structuralist methodology for the study of the poetics of history that set the models of causality, the ideological orientation, and rhetorical styles of a given work of history in relation to its overall narrative structure. White emphasized that historical texts are first and foremost narrative constructs the aesthetic complexities of which can be fully appreciated only if the texts are subjected to the type of narratological critique that has been conventionally reserved for the analysis of narrative fiction. To this end, White probed the writings of nineteenth-century historians and philosophers, for instance Michelet and Marx, with narratological methods derived from Northrop Frye and others. Readers of *Metahistory* were treated to a powerful and insightful critique of the historians' craft, but they walked away from the book with a complicated, partly redundant, and generally unwieldy tool kit for the analysis of historical writing. Reading *Metahistory* sometimes raises more questions than it answers: How precisely did White conceptualize the relationship between modes of emplotment and the four basic tropes? Are there really only sixteen registers for the analysis of historical prose as White suggests in the introduction of *Metahistory*?[6]

In the years after the publication of *Metahistory* White continued his critique of historical practice by revisiting nineteenth-century classics, exploring the relationship between literature and historiography, and publishing reflections on historical theorists like Michel Foucault and Paul Ricoeur.[7] Unfortunately, White never developed his structuralist methodology further, for instance, by analyzing contemporary works of history.[8] But White's essays nevertheless presented important additional insights into the concrete mechanics of historical narrative, which became particularly apparent when White published a collection of his essays in 1987.[9] Already in the first chapter of *The Content of the Form,* White presented a seemingly pedestrian yet radical argument. By exploring the relationship between historical chronicles and historical narratives White demonstrated in a particularly compelling fashion that works of history cannot be reduced to the sum of their factual components. According to White, the writings of professional historians contain many factual statements that can be verified by generally agreed-upon rules of evidence, but the narrative frameworks that integrate facts into coherent stories are imposed on the data and are not found in the historical record. In essence, White saw facts in a state of narrative innocence; he recognized no epistemological relation between specific factual statements or specific types of historical data and the different story lines that historians employ to make sense of these facts and to convey their insights about the past to their readers.[10]

White also developed new terminology to grasp the complex relationship between historiography and its discursive and non-discursive contexts. For White, works of history relate to at least two different referents. The primary referent encompasses past events and actants whose factuality has been confirmed by established rules of evidence. By adhering to these rules of evidence, historians differentiate themselves from novelists and mark their writing as works of nonfiction. But on the level of the secondary referent, fact and fiction can no longer be clearly distinguished from each other, because the secondary referent of a work of history includes the narrative conventions and associated political and aesthetic preferences that historiography shares with other genres and media of narrative communication.[11] Historiography might be appreciated for its apparently authentic representation of past events, but this reality-effect is a carefully crafted illusion produced by the systematic conflation of primary and secondary referents. Historians and their audiences (primarily other historians) pretend that the secondary referents of their writings have the same factual integrity as their primary referents, although this is manifestly not the case. The past never occurred in the form of stories and most certainly not in the form of the kind of stories one finds in history books. Facts become history and can help fulfill the social and communicative function of history only when they are integrated into narrative frameworks that might have all kinds of qualities, but factual accuracy is not one of them.

White focused on the macro level of historical writing. He dealt with the broad strokes, the overarching narrative schemes that historians employ to make sense of the world. White's penchant for the philosophical side of historiography has never brought him face to face with the less glamorous, more pedestrian aspect of historical writing. He has never scrutinized a set of standard historical monographs to figure out how average historians set up their main concepts or try to back up their particular historical emplotments in their notes. As a result, White has little to say about the linguistic contexts in which primary and secondary referents meet, that is, about the long and often tedious passages of detailing prose in which historians arrange their facts in ways that, presumably, support their specific narrative choices. In this respect, the narratological-semiological analysis of historiography is an unfulfilled promise of the 1970s and 1980s.

White and Holocaust Historiography

In 1982, White famously argued that Holocaust deniers violate fundamental rules of evidence of the historical profession by rejecting the fact that the Nazi government and its collaborators murdered six million Jews. But he added immediately that many other Holocaust emplotments that one might consider unacceptable do not suffer from the same epistemological shortcoming. White gave two examples for such morally flawed but factually accurate interpretations of the Holocaust. He imagined a (neo-)Nazi emplotment of the "Final Solution" that acknowledges all the details of the genocide of European Jewry but celebrates it as a brave and admirable act of necessary racial cleansing. White also invoked the Zionist interpretation of the Holocaust that sublates the horrors of the "Final Solution" within an overarching narrative of Jewish martyrdom and heroism. He found neither of these stories politically acceptable, but emphasized that both could be written in such a way that they live up to the standards of evidence developed in the historical profession.[12]

White provided excellent examples to illustrate that factual accuracy, moral integrity, and political effectiveness are independent variables in Holocaust culture (and historical culture in general) that might coexist in a given representation of the "Final Solution" but that are not linked conceptually. One can easily find other suitable examples of comic and romantic emplotments of the Holocaust that support White's argument, especially in the realm of popular culture. By celebrating Holocaust survivors, rescuers, and liberators, the vast genre of popular films and documentaries about the "Final Solution" thrive on the challenge of casting the seemingly gloomy topic of Nazi genocide into optimistic, uplifting, and factually accurate narratives of great entertainment and monetary value.[13] Both sides of the narrative equation, the gloom as well as its cheerful deconstruction, are carefully constructed aesthetic effects. In 1990, however, White equally famously seemed to reverse himself when challenged by Saul Friedländer to develop further his provocative remarks on the politics of Holocaust historiography. In a paper delivered at UCLA, White then conceded that "in the case of an emplotment of the events of the Third Reich in a comic or pastoral mode, we would be eminently justified in appealing to the facts in order to dismiss it from the list of competing narratives of the Third Reich."[14] Unfortunately, in 1990 White did not explain this passage or his position on the matter in any detail.[15] Consequently, the ambiguity and possible reversal can be read as White's acknowledgment of and adaptation to the perceived limits of academic culture.[16]

White has dealt with Holocaust representations on a number of occasions since 1990. He has demonstrated, for example, that Holocaust testimony succeeds in conveying the horrors of the camps only through the extensive use of figurative language. Primo Levi's writing is a case in point. Levi took pride in his plain, scientific language while modeling the plot structure of *Survival in Auschwitz* after Dante's *Divine Comedy*. In addition, Levi's exceptionally compelling characterization of the people and situation he encountered in Auschwitz relies on a wide range of rhetorical devices, including prolepses, ellipses, similes, and anthropomorphisms. Levi's testimony is factual in the sense that he did not invent events and people; but White argues that *Survival in Auschwitz* "derives its power as testimony, less from the scientific and positivistic registration of the 'facts' of Auschwitz, than from its enactment as poetic utterance of *what it felt like* to have had to endure such 'facts.'"[17] Thus for White, there is "no conflict between the referential function of Levi's discourse and the expressive, affective, and poetic functions."[18] Quite the contrary, Levi's realism, his ability to capture the feelings induced by an experience of extraordinary violence, could be accomplished only through extensive narrative and non-narrative figuration.

With White's analysis of *Survival in Auschwitz* we have already started a close reading of *The Years of Extermination*. Levi and Friedländer write in different contexts, and their books belong to different genres, but they deploy similar stylistic means for similar ends. They use seemingly simple and understated, at times terse, at times slightly ironic, language and avoid explicit moralizing and extensive explanation. In this way they try to capture the many nuances of the experiences of the victims. At the same time, Friedländer and Levi pursue different scales of analysis and address different audiences. Levi writes a memoir about Auschwitz designed to express his subjective experience as faithfully as possible. Friedländer deals with the totality of the Holocaust in a book of professional scholarship. His readers expect information about the causes and consequences of the "Final Solution" as well as insights into the experiences of the victims, with the first expectation conventionally taking precedence over the second. As a result of these differences, *Survival in Auschwitz* is an artful but ultimately consistent book, whereas *The Years of Extermination* is a deeply ambivalent text.

Friedländer's mastery consists of using the potentially debilitating conflict between explanation and emotion as an additional, powerful channel of communication. While apparently keeping the conflict undecided, he actually tips the balance ever so slightly toward emotion, using the historian's focus on explanation as a way to make his readers look at the events of the Holocaust from the vantage points of the victims. This effect is accomplished through the book's dispersive structure which stages (and hides) a pervasive yet subtle deconstructive dialogue between our attempts to explain the Holocaust and our recognition that some facets of its history seem to defy explanation. In essence, in the last resort *The Years of Extermination* sacrifices explanation for moral insight and thus shatters the limits of conventional historical writing.

Put into White's terms, *The Years of Extermination* is a modernist text that captures the reality of the modern event "Holocaust" through a figurative performance. As a result of the innovative design of his book, Friedländer addresses the lingering and debilitating effects of Holocaust violence much more successfully than conventional historical prose ever could. *The Years of Extermination* and White's thoughts on Levi thus mark an interesting convergence. While White and Friedländer took very different intellectual paths that only crossed occasionally, for instance in Los Angeles in 1990, they have ultimately drawn similar radical conclusions about historical writing after Auschwitz.[19]

Historical Empathy and the Origins of the "Final Solution"

Friedländer writes a transnational European history of the "Final Solution" that pays particular attention and tribute to the victims of Nazi genocide. This focus is one of the reasons for the unfamiliar structure of the book. Each chapter and most subchapters deal with seemingly clearly defined chronological segments of the history of the Holocaust. But each of these segments incorporates a multitude of historical locations and features an impressive array of Jewish and non-Jewish eyewitness testimony culled mostly from diaries found after the war. Let's consider, for example, subchapter VI in chapter 7.[20] The chapter covers events from July 1942 to March 1943 and deals with deportations and the situation in the Eastern European ghettos. The subchapter begins with two and a half pages on the Łódź ghetto featuring no fewer than eleven quotes from three different diaries. Some quotes are quite extensive, and they are carefully interwoven to provide multiple perspectives on the same events or topics. The next page refers to Lwów and focuses on the diarist Bruno Schulz. The last two pages of the subchapter describe the situation in Vilna, citing ten passages from four different diaries. All of this happens within seven pages. Subchapter VII, dealing with the confusion among European Jews as a result of the Nazi onslaught, presents an even more rapid change of locations causing the reader to experience a faint echo of that state of confusion: Amsterdam, Vilna, Theresienstadt, Paris, Dresden, Łódź, Warsaw, London, The Hague, Brussels—almost all of these locations are represented through quotes and all of this is achieved in the course of five and a half pages.[21]

Friedländer never ends a chapter, not even the final chapter, with an explicit analytical message. He never spells out what specific insights the events offer that he has just described, and he does not finish the book by expounding lessons of history regarding the origins of the "Final Solution" and the need to prevent its reoccurrence. Instead, the chapters end as they began: *in medias res* and often with an eyewitness having the last word. Friedländer keeps the reader historically up to date, that is, he tells the audience the location and time of the specific events under description, but he refuses to keep the reader analytically up to date, that is, he refuses to tell the audience what the preceding text means for Holocaust historiography in particular and Holocaust history in general. Friedländer thus entices the reader to consider the events from the perspective of the victims of the "Final Solution" who had historical insight (meaning they can tell us a lot about their specific experience if one bothers to ask them) while frequently lacking analytical insight into the reasons for their suffering. At the end of each of the chapters, as a result of their circular structure, the reader is again with the victims and therefore also more likely to consider the next chapter and the next Nazi attack from the vantage point of the victims. Through the precise thematic and visual foci, the rapid changes of location, and the relative dearth of analytical exegesis, *The Years of Extermination* engages the audience emotionally; the readers are invited to feel their way into the past and get a sense of how the events were experienced by people directly involved in them.

Friedländer faces an interesting dilemma. He set out to write a synthetic history of the Holocaust that pays close attention to the perspective and experiences of the victims of the "Final Solution." Yet the victims, as Friedländer emphasizes repeatedly, did not cause their own destruction and had little knowledge of the factors that set the Nazi genocide into motion. They speculated frequently and widely about the motives of their opponents and possible strategies of survival, but had only limited insight into the political, social, and ideological dynamics of the different levels of the Nazi bureaucracy.[22] Friedländer's most unusual and most extensively used sources, the diaries of the victims, provide intriguing answers to his primary research question, that is, what did the Holocaust mean to its victims, but they are largely silent on the problem of causation, which has to play a decisive role in any comprehensive history of Nazi genocide.

Friedländer begins his study with a series of prolepses; the most powerful of these is featured in the epigraph at the very beginning of the book. Citing the diarist Stefan Ernest, Friedländer tells his readers, "[T]his is not the truth, this is only a small part, a tiny fraction of the truth."[23] This gesture of humility is followed by other disarmingly frank admissions of gaps and problems. Friedländer explains that for lack of sources some questions will probably never be answered satisfactorily, for instance, concerning the attitudes of some of the bystanders.[24] He also emphasizes that "no single conceptual framework can encompass the diverse and converging strands" of the history of the Holocaust.[25] Thus Friedländer's conceptual focus, "the centrality of ideological-cultural factors as the prime movers of Nazi policies," represents for him the most important fraction of the truth but hardly the whole truth.[26]

In Friedländer's description, Hitler was the spider in the middle of an antisemitic web that spanned all of Germany and ultimately almost all of Europe. Hitler adapted his public display of antisemitism to his tactical priorities since he had to accommodate many powerful social, economic, and political constituencies. As a result, "the imperatives of anti-Jewish ideology had ... to be attuned to a multiplicity of structural hurdles."[27] But Friedländer stresses time and again that Hitler never wavered in his extreme, redemptive antisemitic views.[28] Moreover and more important, Hitler also pulled the political strings by closely monitoring the anti-Jewish policies of the regime: "No matter of any importance in the ongoing anti-Jewish harassment could be settled without Hitler's consent."[29] For Friedländer, the Holocaust would not have happened without Hitler.[30]

Yet Friedländer does not simply analyze Hitler's antisemitic convictions; rather, at key junctures in the story, he puts Hitler on stage and makes him perform his antisemitism. For instance, over ten pages of the book, Friedländer quotes extensively from anti-Jewish statements that Hitler made on over twenty-five different occasions in the weeks between 2 October and 17 December 1941.[31] Friedländer chooses this rhetorical strategy to demonstrate the causal connection between Hitler's intense anti-Jewish hatred and the final decision to exterminate the Jews of Europe that was made in the fall of 1941 and, according to Friedländer, probably after 11 December as a result of the American entry into the war.[32] The ten-page-long chronicle of condensed, repetitive invectives counts among the most unusual and powerful passages of the book. In a sense, these ten pages are the performative equivalent of a Hitler order that probably never existed on paper. But on closer examination one can still raise a lot of questions about the following sentence that captures Friedländer's strategy in a nutshell: "As the deadly threats spewed by 'the highest authority' became one continuous rant, the ever more murderous campaign developed apace."[33] How are the first and the second part of the sentence related? The phrase "developed apace," which appears frequently in the book as a result of its many parallel narrative strands, begs the question of who precisely does the developing and for what reasons while Hitler is ranting.[34]

Friedländer provides a series of multi-layered answers to these questions that are not developed in as much detail as his analysis of Hitler's antisemitism, but that nicely correspond to and corroborate that analysis. In a sense, the answers take on the shape of a set of Russian dolls that tightly fit into each other. Friedländer first points toward the Nazi leadership. He emphasizes that the ideologically reliable party old-timers often developed idiosyncratic antisemitic styles and occasionally butted heads, but generally collaborated frightfully effectively.[35] According to Friedländer, the same is true for the second and third tier of Nazi officials. In this context, however, Friedländer's language assumes an almost circular structure:

> In order to be effective, however, the ideological impetus had to emanate not only from the top but also be fanatically adopted and enforced at intermediate levels of the system by the technocrats, organizers, and direct implementers of the extermination—by those in short who made the system work, several levels below the main political leadership. Key figures in the agencies involved—particularly some of the best organizers and technocrats—were motivated by anti-Jewish fanaticism.[36]

It seems here as if Friedländer invokes the terrible effectiveness of the system as proof of the ideological cohesion of the Nazi bureaucracy. What if antisemitic fanaticism was only one of many factors that made the system so effective? Maybe the ideological impetus assumed its destructive force not primarily by being replicated on the lower levels of Nazi bureaucracy and society, but by absorbing and integrating a wide range of motives and emotions into the crime of genocide.

Goebbels is the next Russian doll that Friedländer carefully unwraps for us. For Friedländer, Nazi propaganda in general and Goebbels's efforts in particular provided the communicative conduit between the Führer and his people. Time and again Friedländer emphasizes how effectively Nazi propaganda, especially Nazi cinema, indoctrinated the German soldiers and "penetrated the minds of the Volksgenossen."[37] In his discussion of Goebbels's "total war" speech, Friedländer once more casts his argument into a particular compelling image: "Tens of millions of Germans, glued to their radios, were engulfed in a rhetoric of rage and vengeance."[38] Obviously, in Friedländer's assessment, these Germans were not just glued to the radio but also glued to one another by their shared antisemitic convictions.

Friedländer puts particular blame on the traditional elites and especially the churches. Due to the traditional religious antisemitism inherent in Christianity, the vast majority of Catholic and Protestant officials remained publicly silent about deportations and exterminations, and only occasionally extended a helping hand in private, and then primarily to converted Jews. These "basic facts," as Friedländer calls them, set a powerful example for the ninety-five percent of the German population who regularly attended religious services.[39] Unfortunately, church officials were hardly the only members of the elite who failed their people. Military leaders also quickly adapted their antisemitic ways to radical Nazi anti-Judaism.[40] Even members of the military opposition to Hitler, who were willing to risk their lives in the fight against the Führer, saw no need to abandon long-held antisemitic views.[41]

At this stage, we have amassed a depressingly vast collection of antisemitic dolls: Hitler, his immediate entourage, old Nazi fighters, Nazi technocrats, ordinary soldiers, regular Germans, church officials, military leaders, and resistance fighters. But the collection is still not complete. Friedländer writes a transnational history of the Holocaust and thus adds more layers of analysis that appear to fit perfectly around their German core. Friedländer sees a combination of "modern anti-Jewish hostility" and "national anti-Semitic rantings" sweeping half of Europe, including Portugal, Spain, Poland, Hungary, Slovakia, Romania, Croatia, and France.[42] In the course of his analysis Friedländer adds Lithuania and Belgium to the list[43] and highlights the antisemitic leanings of key officials in the British and U.S. governments.[44] On several occasions Friedländer explicitly mentions additional motives like greed, fear, and political opportunism.[45] But it is clear that, for Friedländer, antisemitism was the single most important cause of the anti-Jewish policies of the German government and the submissiveness, passivity, assistance, and occasional all-out support with which these policies were greeted across Europe.

Friedländer develops a powerful metaphor that brings all the layers together and that conveys his explanatory model in a particularly vivid way:

> This anti-Jewish frenzy at the top of the Nazi regime was not hurled into a void. ... [T]he flames that the Nazi leader set alight and fanned burned as widely and intensely as they did only because, throughout Europe and beyond ... a dense underbrush of ideological and cultural elements was ready to catch fire. Without the arsonist the fire would not have started; without the underbrush it would not have spread as far as it did and destroyed an entire world.[46]

Causation and Analytical Unease

In my summary of the book I have in a sense committed an error that many Holocaust historians are guilty of and that Friedländer identified in his introduction: I have domesticated the disturbing history of the "Final Solution" by casting it into standard, consistently structured historical prose. I have accomplished this act of discursive normalization in three steps: (1) by eliminating the voices of the victims since they do not speak to the question of causality; (2) by rearranging Friedländer's fragmented story into neat little packages that are part of a clear, hierarchical structure reaching from Hitler to the European periphery; (3) by deploying the metaphors of the spider web and the Russian doll that convey the structure of my argument to the reader and that thereby enhance the summary's appeal and legitimacy.[47]

One might assume that providing such a consistently structured summary is an appropriate way to explain and test Friedländer's analytical model. After all, the synopsis is based on a close reading of the text and identifies Friedländer's most important *explicit* statements about the origins of the Holocaust. Nevertheless, in some respects the summary is already a serious misrepresentation of Friedländer's work because it completely ignores the text's many *implicit* and ultimately negative statements about historical causality that are expressed through the book's unusual structure. We have already seen that *The Years of Extermination* can induce a subtle feeling of spatial confusion. On closer examination, every single passage and statement can be clearly linked to a specific location. But the rapid sequence of sometimes seemingly haphazardly arranged sites of action conveys a faint echo of the sense of displacement that the victims of Nazi policies experienced as they were cut off from society and rushed through Europe toward their death.

A similar effect is triggered by the way that Friedländer deals with time. On first inspection, his narrated time follows a clear chronological sequence. Each chapter covers an explicitly identified period, and the book takes the reader in an orderly fashion from "September 1," 1939 on page 3 to "May 1 or 2," 1945 on page 661. But Friedländer juggles so many different people, locations, and narrative strands that the seemingly strict chronological chapter sequence gives way to a multidirectional chronological web once the reader enters the narrative. The text displaces linear concepts of time and space by rapidly oscillating between different locations and points in time. Consider, for example, chapter 5. During the first thirteen pages, and then again during the last forty pages of the chapter, Friedländer's timeline jumps violently back and forth between September and December 1941 as he covers many different aspects of that crucial period. In subchapter II, Friedländer slows down narrated time, as he is often forced to do, by going over the same days again and again, each time from a different perspective. He covers Hitler's state of mind, the mood among pessimistic, somewhat less pessimistic and starkly divided Jews, before turning towards the German high command, Goebbels, the U.S. president, and Charles Lindbergh.[48] Matters are further complicated by the fact that some voices are clearly identified while other quotes are only attributed to the last names of diarists who have not made an appearance in over fifty pages. The precise yet redundant time coordinates and the vague personal and geographical information have a similar effect; they ever so slightly destabilize the historical referents of Friedländer's text. The ten successive pages in the middle of the chapter that do unfold in a strict chronological fashion are a massive exception both in the chapter and in the book as a whole. These ten pages cover the already mentioned performance of Hitler's antisemitism.[49] Thus the book is certainly not a strictly chronologically structured account, as a number of reviewers have suggested.[50] Quite the contrary, linear chronology is such an unusual occurrence in the book that Friedländer can use it as an extraordinarily effective tool of rhetorical emphasis.

The constant chronological vacillation can have some rather disturbing effects, as the example of Reinhard Heydrich illustrates. Heydrich, who died on 4 June 1942 after having been wounded by Czech commandos a few days earlier, is featured prominently in *The Years of Extermination*. He appears on seventy-three pages of the book. On some of these pages, however, Heydrich literally returns from the dead. Heydrich dies for the first time on pages 349 and 350; he is alive again on page 352, dead on page 357, alive on pages 362, 367, and 368, dead on page 374, alive on page 377, and then never mentioned again. In every single instance that Heydrich appears, the context explains the situation completely adequately. But the readers have no way of knowing if the zombie-like Heydrich will be dead or alive during his next appearance. They cannot with any precision position themselves vis-à-vis the trajectory of Heydrich's life because they can't aggregate the available information about the book's structure into a reliable narrative road map that allows them to predict the circumstances of Heydrich's next visit. The same applies to the book as a whole. The outcome of the Holocaust (and Heydrich's life) is well known to all readers. They are familiar with the stages of historical progression reflected in the terse, yet sensible chapter headings. But that information gives them no chance to predict the historical locations, scenes, and actors they will encounter on the very next page. They don't even know if time will move forward or backwards. Friedländer combines brutal certainty on the macro-level of narrative events with relentless unpredictability on the micro-level of historical action. Thus, over large passages of the book, readers remain chronologically and geographically uprooted and alienated from any sense of narrative progression, let alone narrative resolution, for instance, in the form of a survivor story. They are unlikely to experience the degree of historical control that history products convey on a routine basis. Instead, they are subjected to a skillfully arranged abundance of subplots and multidirectional timelines that simultaneously confirm and deconstruct comforting illusions of linear time to which historians conventionally subscribe.

But the challenge of *Years of Extermination* extends beyond its confusing surface structure. The committed reader could reassemble the disparate pieces of a specific subplot for instance by extracting Friedländer's description of the events in France from multiple segments of the book. That exercise should go a long way in reestablishing narrative cohesion in the same way that Heydrich's life and death can be fairly easily rearranged in proper chronological sequence. But this type of "repair work" raises pressing and ultimately debilitating questions about the precise conceptual relation between the many different stories lines of *The Years of Extermination*. Upon closer analysis, Friedländer's cultural-ideological framework, which seems to hold the book together so efficiently, comes tumbling down and standard concepts of causality become questionable. While Friedländer explicitly identifies antisemitism as the common causal denominator of the transnational history of the Holocaust, a close reading of his collage of countless, small-scale and large-scale events provides plenty of evidence that calls into question the primacy of anti-Jewish ideology. There is simply no easy exit from the book's semantic labyrinth as the following "repaired" story lines indicate:

- Friedländer reports that the Dutch, especially those living in the cities, were very tolerant of Jews. Nevertheless, the docile Dutch police and the highly efficient Dutch bureaucracy proved terrible weapons in the quest to rid the country of Jews, most of whom had lived in the Netherlands for many generations.[51] Belgium, in comparison, featured rabidly antisemitic, pro-German organizations whose members staged their own pogroms.[52] Yet many foreign-born Jews who had found refuge in the country without being integrated into Belgian society were ultimately rescued by ordinary citizens.[53] Timing, administrative structures, and other factors appear to have played a much more important role in these cases than seemingly malleable anti-Jewish dispositions.
- The situation seems to have been similarly confusing in France. The French elite with their picture-perfect, antisemitic credentials collaborated quite enthusiastically in the deportation of Jewish immigrants. But the very same leaders were far more hesitant to hand over their Jewish compatriots.[54] Real and imagined xenophobic divisions appeared to have played a more important role than antisemitic convictions.
- Friedländer recounts on several occasions that the Jewish community in Palestine, especially its leadership, displayed a disturbing indifference about events in Europe. The political elite worried primarily about the dearth of future immigrants once European Jewry had been exterminated.[55] Since antisemitism does not appear to be a likely motive in this case, reactions in Palestine raise interesting questions about contemporary European societies. Maybe the social-psychological dynamics at play in Palestine also explain the widespread indifference with which most Europeans and Americans responded to Nazi anti-Jewish policies.
- In his extensive coverage of German perpetrators and bystanders, Friedländer systematically focuses on their antisemitism. On several occasions, however, he discusses Nazis and soldiers who did not appear to hate Jews but nevertheless (as far as we know,) contributed their share to the success of the genocidal mission. The most famous person in this category is Kurt Gerstein,[56] but Friedländer mentions many others including a soldier who "does not read like a born murderer or dyed-in-the-wool antisemite, but rather like someone who just went along and enjoyed his

newly acquired power." Friedländer adds that "this was probably the case of most soldiers of the Ostheer."[57]

- Friedländer puts a lot of blame on the shoulders of church officials for failing to provide moral guidance and occasionally even egging on the killers of Jews. He links that behavior to pervasive Christian antisemitism. Friedländer is particularly interested in explaining the passivity of the pope. In the end, he attributes it to political motives and concludes "there is no specific indication that the pope was anti-Semitic or that his decisions during the war stemmed, in part, from some particular hostility toward Jews."[58] Moreover and more important, on many occasions, often in passing, Friedländer reports that church officials played an important role in rescue operations and in bringing about a reversal of anti-Jewish policies. The change of heart came toward the end of the war, but it occurred all across Europe, including in countries whose leaders had been particularly eager collaborators.[59]
- Friedländer mentions that some Eastern Europeans took German occupation as an opportunity to stage spontaneous anti-Jewish riots, but he also reports that on many occasions the *Einsatzgruppen* initially failed to convince Poles, Russians, Ukrainians, and Lithuanians to launch pogroms against their Jewish compatriots despite significant propaganda efforts.[60]
- Ironically, the Italian government and Italian troops quickly emerged as the most efficient protectors of Jews in Croatia, France, and Greece.[61] Yet after German troops occupied Italy, Italian police officers occasionally rounded up Jews on their own volition without German prodding.[62] What role if any did antisemitism play in these contradictory events in Catholic Italy?
- Similarly, we learn very little about the motives of large collectives of helpers in Denmark, Bulgaria, and Belgium. What kind of people acting under what circumstances escaped the grasp of antisemitism or intervened despite their anti-Jewish prejudices in the age of ideology?
- According to Friedländer, the deportation of the Jews of Salonika resulted from a range of factors including the presence of collaborators and "periodic tensions" between Greeks and post-World War I Jewish refugees. Friedländer stops short of calling the Greeks antisemitic; nevertheless the deportations proceeded depressingly swiftly.[63]

The more one studies the multiple facets of Holocaust history presented in *The Years of Extermination,* the more the key concepts that Friedländer has so carefully erected begin to fray at the edges and appear questionable. As a result of Friedländer's evenhandedness and scrupulous fairness in the handling of evidence, readers are left with a lot of different antisemitisms that had different consequences in different settings. Plus, we get a sense of other factors at work, but only a few of them are identified for us, and Friedländer never integrates these factors into an overarching analytical model. The explicit framework "antisemitism" is implicitly overwhelmed by empirical excess if one starts to straighten out Friedländer's "twisted road to Auschwitz." Friedländer's dispersive structure can apparently handle a lot more contradictory evidence than conventional historical prose. Only on a few rare occasions does Friedländer even explicitly question the soundness of his own analytical model. For instance, on the one hand, Friedländer puts a lot of emphasis on the extent and success of Nazi antisemitic propaganda and stresses the fact that the Nazi leadership paid close attention to public opinion. On the other hand, Friedländer concedes in passing that the success of the Nazi propaganda efforts was ultimately unimportant because "German policies regarding the Jews did not depend on the level of anti-Semitism in German and European opinion."[64]

The list above provides the basis for an illuminating counterfactual scenario. If Friedländer had first and foremost aimed at providing a comprehensive, analytically fully satisfactory explanation of the Holocaust, he could have easily developed a more complex causal model that systematically integrates a variety of factors. If we consider, for a moment, the tensions and contradictions in *The Years of Extermination* as an analytical problem, social-psychological models could indeed provide an analytical solution so long as they included an important role for ideology.[65] The German scholar Harald Welzer, for instance, has developed social-psychological methods for perpetrator research that stress the importance of ideological factors, especially in providing mass murderers with an interpretive framework that renders their task meaningful.[66] His methods offer the opportunity to conceptualize the many crimes and crime scenes that make up the vast event of the Holocaust as the outcome of complex constellations of factors whose precise composition could have differed from case to case despite the fact that all contributed to the same outcome. By way of Welzer's insights, Friedländer's relatively static, explicitly causal model could easily be transformed into a more dynamic and flexible conceptual framework that accounts for the existence of different types of antisemitism and their different effects in different settings.[67] In addition, a more dynamic framework could more effectively explain, following the lead of Christopher Browning, how groups of German men and non-German collaborators who did not feel passionately about Jews in one way or another nevertheless quickly turned into efficient killers.[68]

The point is, however, that Friedländer does not want to present a comprehensive, analytically pleasing explanation of the Holocaust. There are a number of hints to that effect throughout the book, in addition to the very explicit statement in the introduction where Friedländer announces that he wishes "to offer a thorough historical study of the extermination of the Jews of Europe, without eliminating or domesticating that initial sense of disbelief" caused by the recognition that the Nazis indeed intended to murder all Jews without exception.[69] To maintain that sense of disbelief, Friedländer has to protect it from knowledge that "rushes in and smothers it," as he puts it on the same page. The task of producing and protecting disbelief entails, among other things, that Friedländer implicitly trips up his own analytical framework, thus rendering antisemitism both omnipresent and opaque.

Friedländer maintains a sense of analytical unease by refusing to explicitly address and resolve the tensions between his forcefully presented analytical framework (that is, antisemitism), and the many truthful historical vignettes that demand additions to and revisions of that framework.[70] On a few occasions, Friedländer explicitly addresses analytical problems inherent in the historical record, but rather than resolving them he simply highlights them. Thus, when acknowledging the puzzling willingness of so many Belgians to rescue Jews, he simply calls the issue "unresolved" and "probably unresolvable."[71] In addition, on a few more occasions, he endorses the sense of confusion among eyewitnesses not as a reasonable but as an accurate interpretation of events. In this vein he cites Ruth Klüger, who calls the behavior of helpers, like the Belgians, "incomparable and inexplicable."[72] For the same reason, Friedländer highlights the inconclusiveness of the testimony of his star witness Viktor Klemperer: "To Klemperer the attitudes of the population appeared as contradictory as ever," meaning that Germans refused to act consistently antisemitically despite all the evidence that attests to their anti-Jewish dispositions and that Friedländer has carefully assembled for us.[73]

The eyewitness testimonies and Friedländer's refusal to adopt the role of omniscient historian are linked in other ways as well. By leaving the reader alone with the analytical dissonances triggered by his text, Friedländer administers small homeopathic doses of analytical unease and yet again simulates the perspective of the victims who did not fully understand the reasons for the persecution they endured but could not afford to ignore the riddle that the behavior of the perpetrators presented to them. *The Years of Extermination* is a narrative balancing act designed to protect Friedländer's key concept from implosion while raising just enough doubt about the tools of the trade, including his own concepts, to impress on the reader the very fragility and fundamental insufficiency of historiographical semantics.[74]

So is *The Years of Extermination* a truly modernist or postmodern text? Sometimes the surface of the text certainly looks that way. The book does not have a proper end with scenes of liberation and closure as we see in the movies. Instead, the reader learns that Germans were still antisemitic, that most of the diarists whom they have met in the previous 660 pages were murdered though a few had stayed alive, and that the suffering continued because the survivors were trapped in the past: "Recurrently it pulled them back into overwhelming terror and, throughout, notwithstanding the passage of time, it carried along with it the indelible memory of the dead."[75] The book also lacks a conventional narrative focus. Hitler, who comes closest to filling that role, performs very often but acts very rarely; he floats above the events as they are unfolding.

At other times the text looks like a chronicle or a realist novel in the tradition of Tolstoy's *War and Peace*.[76] These similarities to pre-modern and realist forms of historical writing highlight the genre-busting, hybrid qualities of *The Years of Extermination*. In the last analysis, however, the book is indeed a thoroughly (post)modernist work of history. On a structural level, Friedländer performs a radically self-conscious deconstruction of notions of causality that have informed professional historiography since its beginnings in the nineteenth century and that did not exist at the time when Tolstoy finished his study of the Napoleonic wars.

White generally prefers the term modernism and praises modernist aesthetics when urging historians to broaden their narrative horizons. But he might as well have recommended the study of postmodern philosophy. In White's assessment, the concerns of literary modernism align very nicely with postmodern philosophical pursuits.[77] In his view, familiarity with either intellectual movement, especially concerning the critique and redeployment of narrative techniques, would have gone a long way in bringing historians into the twentieth century. However, in the special case of *The Years of Extermination*, which finally puts into practice some of White's recommendations, the label modernist, even if applied primarily in a metaphorical sense, seems indeed more plausible than the designation postmodern.

Perhaps the metaphor is best explored through some examples. *The Years of Extermination* does not seem to revel in playful intertextuality or contribute to the parodic deconstruction of the historical referent. Such objectives are generally attributed to postmodern historiographic metafictions ranging from E. L. Doctorow's *Ragtime* to, most recently, Jonathan Littell's *The Kindly Ones*.[78] These texts more or less elegantly conflate fact and fiction even if they feature fairly conventional narrative and chronological structures. Instead, Friedländer's magnum opus shares a number a traits with *Ulysses*, the modernist novel par excellence. The characters in *Ulysses* are firmly grounded in time and space, for instance by way of the 1904 street map of Dublin which Joyce regularly consulted during the writing process. But Joyce's strictly chronological and realistic geographical coordinates are overwhelmed by flashbacks and paratactical excess, deployed, among other purposes, for exploring the disjunction between internal and external time which was a major concern of many modernist writers.[79] *The Years of Extermination* stages a less radical but similarly enlightening clash between objective historical time and victim/survivor/trauma time through a relentless repetition of antisemitic acts presented in a subtly disorienting rhythm of chronological and geographical oscillation. Modernists like Joyce, Proust, and Woolf had not given up on the pursuit of truth in representation; they chose unusual aesthetics to capture the truths of human consciousness.[80] Friedländer had similar objectives in mind when he applied unusual historiographical strategies of representation in order to convey the psychological truths of human suffering during Nazi persecution. In a sense, all these intellectuals developed new ways of thinking about loss and mourning while avoiding conventional religious, philosophical, and cultural rituals of consolation.[81] The modernist enterprise—and by extension White's philosophy of history as well as Friedländer's innovative volume—seek to give "a shape and a significance to the immense panorama of futility and anarchy which is contemporary history," as T. S. Eliot put it in his 1923 review of *Ulysses*.[82]

History, Identity, and Truth beyond Epistemology

So what is the primary, and what is the secondary referent of *The Years of Extermination*? What messages is Friedländer sending his readers by way of the unusual structure of his book? What is the point in trying to induce a sense of analytical unease? Let me first try to summarize the primary referent of the book, that is, the basic, historical plot structure of *The Years of Extermination*:

> A small group of extreme racial antisemites managed to organize an unprecedented genocide because they had political power and found many collaborators in Germany and abroad who held less radical, yet compatible views. Together, with the small group always in control, they invented a bureaucratic, technological process for mass murder that combined conventional mass shootings with new technologies for mass murder, ultimately succeeding in killing six million Jews. Several hundred thousand perpetrators committed the crime and a very large number of people knew about it. Yet the people in occupied Europe and beyond did not intervene to stop the genocide because they failed or did not want to understand the full extent of the crime, and because many profited from the policies of the National Socialist regime. First and foremost, however, people did not intervene because they shared a traditional, Christian, antisemitic worldview and thus failed to identify with the victims. The victims themselves were increasingly desperate and isolated from society. Some communities managed to maintain a sense of cultural identity for a surprisingly long time. Others disintegrated more quickly as Jews were forced to participate in their own destruction. In the end, the behavior of the victims, including isolated attempts at armed resistance, did not have any effect on the outcome of the murder campaign.

This basic plot summary applies to a number of books that have been written about the Holocaust, for instance Leni Yahil's *The Holocaust*.[83] But Friedländer adds an important twist to the story that radically changes the form of the book and constitutes its secondary referent. I would call this secondary referent the historiographical plot structure of *The Years of Extermination*. On this level, the book is without precedent in Holocaust historiography:

> Understanding the perpetrators and the origins of the "Final Solution" is important, but it is time to shift focus and pay close attention to the victims: first, because the victims deserve our empathy, and that empathy has not been forthcoming to a sufficient degree from mainstream Holocaust historians; and second, and much more crucial, because in important respects we are still in the same epistemological boat as the victims were. Our boat is not tossing and turning constantly and throw-

ing us into the abyss, but it is rolling to such an extent that we cannot always be one hundred percent sure about our bearings. I know the history of the Holocaust as well as any scholar and I am convinced that antisemitism was the most important factor. But as our boat keeps moving, mainly as a result of the upheaval that was the Holocaust, I see aspects of the history of the "Final Solution" that complicate and cloud the picture. Occasionally, I even wonder about the soundness of my conceptual convictions. These complicating aspects need to be included in the story. It is a question of honesty and truthfulness about history, historiography, and the relationship between the two. Moreover, in acknowledging the complicating aspects of the story and keeping alive that sense of disbelief that the victims experienced in a much more radical way, historians are making a small contribution to building a morally sensitive cultural universe, consumers of which are hopefully more willing to transform disbelief into resistance than their twentieth-century relatives were.

The historiographical plot structure of the book, its secondary referent, is an ethical axiom that informs every single page of the book. It is also the book's most important message, and it cannot be verified or falsified according to any established rules of evidence.

Friedländer's radical and honest balancing act exposes the contradictory raison d'être of historical writing with exceptional clarity. Historians certainly seek to establish facts and explore origins and causal links, but they also address the really important moral and political questions that other social scientists working within empirically more rigorous and intellectually less imaginative contexts often cannot tackle directly. Friedländer provides models and evidence of causality, but he accomplishes a lot more. The book invents for the reader a complete narrative universe, a simulation of the 1940s, that contains all the main players and factual events as well as countless minor players and factual occurrences, and, on the basis of that total, yet contradictory, vision, captures the atmosphere in Europe during World War II, creates empathy with the victims of Nazi persecution, renders a verdict of moral justice about the behavior of victims, bystanders, and perpetrators, and, last but not least, by nurturing a sense of disbelief, insists on the hope that, despite all the evidence to the contrary, the Nazi genocide will remain a unique event, perhaps not in the world but at least in the West. One might disagree with every single aspect of Friedländer's vision, with the way he captures the atmosphere, his standards of moral judgment, his utopian hope, or, least likely, even the way in which he creates empathy for the victims. But these assessments are not subject to the rules of historical evidence. Friedländer's opinions regarding these big topics can be questioned on the basis of diverging emotions, tastes, intuitions, reasons, philosophies, and identities. They cannot be proven untruthful in the way that specific factual statements in his account might turn out to be false, for instance, regarding the number of victims that the Finnish government handed over to Nazi authorities.[84]

Reviewers have enthusiastically welcomed the publication of *The Years of Extermination*, especially Friedländer's inclusion of the voices of the victims, into his integrated history of the Holocaust.[85] They have often mentioned

Friedländer's intention to maintain a sense of disbelief in the face of the "Final Solution" and have occasionally voiced polite reservations about his model of causality.[86] But they have refused to fully engage with Friedländer's conceptual preferences, narrative design, and empirical claims. Instead, they quickly have elevated *The Years of Extermination* to the status of a historical monument that is unworthy of historiographical squabble.[87]

Many factors have influenced the critics' reaction. First and foremost, *The Years of Extermination* is indeed a stunning achievement. None of the other synthetic studies of the subject presents a truly transnational history of the "Final Solution" *and* systematically integrates into that history the perspectives and voices of the victims. But the critics' humility is also the result of other factors, including the fact that the field of Holocaust studies has recently moved in Friedländer's direction. After a string of publications in the 1990s that emphasized non-ideological factors and the importance of decision-making processes on the ground in occupied Eastern Europe, the pendulum has again swung the other way. New research stresses that local perpetrators were closely attuned to Berlin's ideological priorities as a result of direct interventions and frequent visits by Himmler and other Nazi leaders.[88]

In addition, there is a question of historiographical etiquette linked to Friedländer's status as Holocaust survivor/scholar. As we have seen, it would make some analytical sense to criticize Friedländer for not discussing the motives of the perpetrators in terms of a multi-dimensional, social-psychologically informed research design that some of the methodologically more innovative Holocaust scholars have adopted during the last fifteen years. But it does not make much political or moral sense to tell the survivor Friedländer, who has written the first truly victim-centered comprehensive history of the Holocaust, that he has failed to understand the perpetrators—that, in essence, he lacks historical empathy for the thousands of German and non-German murderers who perhaps held no antisemitic views before they embarked on their careers as mass murderers.

Finally, the critics might have preferred praise over detailed critical engagement because Friedländer's resistance to the domestication of disbelief raises uncomfortable questions about Nazi perpetrator research, Holocaust historiography, and historical writing in general. *The Years of Extermination* excels in moral and epistemological terms because, unlike so many colleagues before him, Friedländer recognized that a history of an event like the Holocaust can succeed as an ethical and intellectual intervention only if the text acknowledges the limits of historical explanation, and features honest reflections on these limits as an integral part of its narrative design. Friedländer subjects his own text to a healthy dose of skepticism. Consequently, if the critics were to take their praise of the book as seriously as they should, they would never write history in the same way again.

It would be foolish to suggest that Friedländer's emphasis on eyewitness testimony and his insistence on a certain measure of inexplicability in Holocaust history are unrelated to his personal experience as a victim of Nazi persecution.[89] Friedländer is certainly also reflecting on his own subject position and responsibility as scholar and survivor when he cites Walter Laqueur in his introduction: "There are certain situations which are so extreme that an extraordinary effort is needed to grasp their enormity, unless one happened to be present."[90] Perhaps Friedländer's intuitions are more immediately applicable to some research questions rather than others. His intuitions might be a particular asset for the study of victims' testimony and less useful for the research on Nazi decision-making dynamics, or vice versa. But then there is hardly an independent vantage point from which to measure the intellectual potential and truthfulness of scholarly passion. Perpetrator researchers in Germany, for instance, have followed their own intuitions when they have analyzed the mindset and institutional culture of Nazi and Wehrmacht murderers. Their research has yielded impressive results, but it is hardly surprising that German scholars have either assumed or concluded that the organizers and implementers of the "Final Solution" were perfectly normal individuals whose behavior can be fully explained on the basis of the available data and research tools. After all, it might be comforting to know that people living in other times and other cultures can learn the business of genocide just as easily as the murderers to whom one is linked by name, culture, and family ties. In this sense Martin Broszat's bizarre claim, in his exchange with Friedländer, that German academics can study the Holocaust more objectively than their Jewish colleagues retains a troublesome relevance today.[91]

Emplotment and Modernism

White faces an interesting strategic and also ethical dilemma when he encourages historians to embrace the creative potential of their craft and write attractive and compelling histories in support of all kinds of progressive causes. It is unclear how historians should assume this kind of political agency if they are no longer able to speak in the name of historical truth, which is the one quality, however illusory it may be, that the public still appreciates about academic historiography. White always had conceptually and intellectually compelling answers for this kind of criticism, but he did not show the way toward narrative formats of historical writing that combined popular and political success with epistemological relativism.[92] Friedländer is the first historian who has found a practical solution for the problem by casting seemingly conventional historical prose into a decidedly dispersive narrative structure with the result of crafting an ethical intervention of exceptional lucidity.

Translated into the terminological world of *Metahistory*, Friedländer's achievements could be described in the following way.[93] On a meta-tropological level, Friedländer's book is an ironic treatment of the history of the Holocaust that negates on the figurative level what is positively affirmed on the literal level, for instance the causal force of antisemitism.[94] On the one hand, Friedländer's irony highlights the fallibility of language and calls into question the belief of his colleagues who assume that they can capture the truth of the Holocaust in conventional, large-scale historical narratives. On the other hand, meta-tropological irony claims a special space for successful, non-figurative representation of the "Final Solution." Friedländer reserves this space for eyewitnesses and especially victims, to whom he ascribes the ability to provide truthful insights into the emotional experience of persecution on a lesser scale of narrative complexity.

On a tropological level, the ironic effect of *The Years of Extermination* is achieved through a vigorous fight between the two master tropes of metonymy and synecdoche. In a classic gesture of synecdoche, Friedländer rigorously integrates his book under the ideological-cultural sign of antisemitism. At the same time, the book teems with metonymic detail that cannot be reduced to any overarching causal principle. This figurative clash is not a weakness—quite the contrary. White has argued that routine works of history are often consistently structured according to one dominant trope, whereas historical masterpieces thrive on the tension between conflicting tropological centers of gravity.[95] By this standard, the epic struggle among irony, synecdoche, and metonymy that takes places in the pages of *The Years of Extermination* will endure for many generations.[96]

Stuck between a profession that is refusing to leave behind nineteenth-century realism and a hyperactive and interactive twenty-first-century postmodern culture, White and Friedländer have decided to split the difference and have developed a fondness for early twentieth-century high modernism. It is hard to tell from the reactions of their colleagues in history, however, if the subtle and responsible play with time, space, and causality, which was a provocative literary statement ninety years ago, will finally find a home in history departments across the West, or if all the accolades and prizes that Friedländer has garnered also attest to a profound sense of helplessness with which professional historians react to the fact that one of their own has gone all-out modern.

Notes

1. Saul Friedländer, *Memory, History, and the Extermination of the Jews of Europe* (Bloomington, 1993), x.
2. Ibid. See also Saul Friedländer, *Nazi Germany and the Jews: The Years of Persecution, 1933-1939* (New York, 1997), 5.
3. Friedländer, *Memory, History*, 131.
4. Ibid., 132.

5. Saul Friedländer, ed., *Probing the Limits of Representation: Nazism and the "Final Solution"* (Cambridge, MA, 1992).

6. Hayden White, *Metahistory: The Historical Imagination in Nineteenth-Century Europe* (Baltimore, 1973), 29.

7. Hayden White, *Tropics of Discourse: Essays in Cultural Criticism* (Baltimore, 1978); Hayden White, *The Content of the Form: Narrative Discourse and Historical Representation* (Baltimore, 1987).

8. This reluctance is also noticeable in White's contribution to the present volume. He focuses for instance on the literary qualities of Primo Levi's memoirs, arguing that they share many aesthetic qualities with conventional historical writing. But White apparently prefers not to engage directly in a close reading and narratological analysis of standard historical prose.

9. White, *The Content of the Form*; see also Nancy Partner, "Hayden White: The Form of the Content," *History and Theory* 37, no. 2 (1998): 162–72.

10. White, *The Content of the Form*, 24–25. In his text in the present volume White uses the terms "declarative utterance" or "declarative mode" for simple linguistic statements that primarily serve a referential function and that consequently can be considered true or false depending on how successfully they fulfill this function.

11. Ibid., 43.

12. Ibid., 76–80.

13. Judith Doneson, *The Holocaust in American Film*, 2nd ed. (Syracuse, 2002); and Lawrence Baron, *Projecting the Holocaust into the Present: The Changing Focus of Contemporary Holocaust Cinema* (Lanham, MD, 2005).

14. Hayden White, "Historical Emplotment and the Problem of Truth," in *Probing the Limits of Representation,* ed. Friedländer, 37–53, 40; reprinted in Hayden White, *Figural Realism* (Baltimore, 1999), 27–42.

15. Wulf Kansteiner, "Hayden White's Critique of the Writing of History," *History and Theory* 32, no. 3 (1993): 273–95. In 2000, White explicitly commented on the apparent reversal of his 1990 opinion, claiming that such a reversal never took place; see Hayden White, "An Old Question Raised Again: Is Historiography Art or Science? (Response to Iggers)," *Rethinking History* 4, no. 3 (2000): 402.

16. In 1990, many historians, especially those of White's and Friedländer's generation, were still intellectually engaged in the Historians' Debate that had erupted in West Germany in the mid-1980s. In the course of that debate a number of highly respected conservative historians of modern German history had been massively attacked for emplotments of Nazi history that constituted small, incremental deviations from mainstream postwar German historiography but that had considerably fewer radical implications than White's counterfactual Nazi emplotment of the "Final Solution." In seeking to distance himself from this conservative crowd (and avoid their fate) White illustrated the importance of political factors in the writing of history while unfortunately discouraging others from engaging in radical, narratological critiques of Holocaust historiography. On the generational dimension of the historians' debate, see Norbert Frei, "Farewell to the Era of Contemporaries: National Socialism and Its Historical Examination en Route into History," *History and Memory* 9, nos. 1–2 (1997): 59–79.

17. Hayden White, "Figural Realism in Witness Testimony," *Parallax* 10, no. 1 (2004): 123 (emphasis in original); see also White, "Historical Discourse and Literary Writing," in *Tropes for the Past: Hayden White and the History/Literature Debate,* ed. Kuisma Korhonen (Amsterdam, 2006), 25–33.

18. Hayden White, "Introduction: Historical Fiction, Fictional History, and Historical Reality," *Rethinking History* 9, nos. 2–3 (2005): 149. See also White's remarks about Levi's work in the present volume.

19. See in this context Robert Eaglestone's interesting dialectical reading of the relationship between Friedländer's work and Derridean deconstruction in *The Holocaust and the Postmodern* (Oxford, 2004), 191–93.

20. Saul Friedländer, *The Years of Extermination: Nazi Germany and the Jews, 1939–1945* (New York, 2007), 433–38.

21. Ibid., 438–44.
22. Ibid., xxiv–xxv, 43, 440–41.
23. Ibid., vii.
24. Ibid., xii.
25. Ibid., xvi.
26. Ibid., xvii.
27. Ibid., xxi.
28. Ibid., 645.
29. Ibid., 142; see also 471.
30. Ibid., xvii.
31. Ibid., 272–81. Friedländer uses the same rhetorical strategy on other occasions albeit on a smaller scale, or, more precisely, he very effectively reminds the reader of the chronicle of outbursts documented on pages 272–81 by deploying phrases like "crescendo," "diatribes," "deluge of anti-Jewish tirades," or "full-scale raving"; see 335, 402, 541, and 660.
32. Friedländer follows the assessment of Christian Gerlach, who argued forcefully for a December decision. Gerlach, *Krieg, Ernährung, Völkermord: Forschungen zur deutschen Vernichtungspolitik im Zweiten Weltkrieg* (Hamburg, 1998). In this respect, Friedländer disagrees with most Holocaust historians, who assume that Hitler had already settled on genocide earlier in the fall; see, for example, Christopher Browning, *The Origins of the Final Solution: The Evolution of Nazi Jewish Policy, September 1939–March 1942* (Lincoln, 2004); see also Christopher Browning, "Evocation, Analysis, and the Crisis of Liberalism," *History and Theory* 48 (2009): 238–47. It is interesting to note, however, that after having made a strong case for a December decision, Friedländer backs off and concludes that "the decision was taken sometime during the last three months of 1941" (286). For Friedländer, it is ultimately not that important to settle the factual question about the timing of the decision, which other Holocaust historians have debated with much vigor. Acknowledging a certain measure of indecidability seems to be the most appropriate position to take in light of the existing gaps in the archival record. Plus, that measure of indecidability serves Friedländer's aesthetic, moral, and historiographical objectives very well.
33. Friedländer, *The Years of Extermination*, 282.
34. For similar phrasing see ibid., 144, 160, 170, 237, 282, 356, 495, and 544.
35. Ibid., 23, 75.
36. Ibid., 479; see also 502.
37. Ibid., 513. On the successful indoctrination of soldiers, see also 28, 134, 189, and 211–12, and on Nazi film, see 19–22, 99–102, and 160.
38. Ibid., 473.
39. Ibid., 574, 55. The failure of the churches is extensively covered in *The Years of Extermination*; see, for instance, 72–75, 94, 184–87, 229, 298–303, 465–66, and 561–77, and here especially 574.
40. Ibid., 210.
41. Ibid., 55, 635; see also 513.
42. Ibid., 71.
43. Ibid., 221, 259.
44. Ibid., 85, 89; see also 270.
45. Ibid., 53, 180, 479, 500, 535.
46. Ibid., xix.
47. Incidentally, some reviewers have chosen to offer such a "translation" of *The Years of Extermination*; see, for instance, Jeffrey Herf, "The Whole Horror," *New Republic* (10 September 2007).
48. Friedländer, *The Years of Extermination*, 267–70.
49. Ibid., 272–82.
50. See, for example, Stephan Speicher, "Von Mördern und Mitläufern," *Literaturen* 2 (2007): 55–59, 59.

51. Friedländer, *The Years of Extermination*, 122, 375, 406, 609.
52. Ibid., 259.
53. Ibid., 423.
54. Ibid., 175, 378, 551.
55. Ibid., 153, 305–06, 457, 597.
56. Ibid., 459.
57. Ibid., 209–10.
58. Ibid., 571.
59. For example: Slovakia, 373, 485; Netherlands, 410; France, 421, 553–54; Belgium, 423; Romania, 450; Bulgaria 485; Italy, 561; Hungary 620. With regard to the actions of church officials, Friedländer constructs an interesting contradiction. In his discussion of the German clergy he points out that church officials had considerable influence on public opinion and could therefore, for instance, force the Nazi government to conduct euthanasia killings in much less visible ways. Consequently, Friedländer finds their silence about the Holocaust particularly blameworthy (*The Years of Extermination*, 202, 303). At the same time, he seems to suggest that the public statements of bishops in other Catholic countries had no influence on the population: "A few Catholic bishops courageously spoke out in their diocese but these were lone voices that could not have a major impact on the attitude of the Hungarian population" (ibid., 620).
60. Ibid., 223–24.
61. Ibid., 230, 453, 489, 553.
62. Ibid., 612.
63. Ibid., 487–88.
64. Ibid., 189.
65. Friedländer dismisses the explanatory power of "common social-psychological reinforcements, constraints, and group dynamical processes" if they are considered "independent of ideological motivations." He does not try to integrate the two factors within one overarching causal model (*The Years of Extermination*, xx).
66. Harald Welzer, *Täter: Wie aus ganz normalen Menschen Massenmörder werden* (Frankfurt/M, 2005). Welzer refers extensively to Friedländer's *The Years of Persecution* and his concept of redemptive antisemitism and has only one point of criticism. For Welzer there is nothing unusual or inexplicable about the process that turns normal people into murderers: see *Täter*, 74–75.
67. Jörg von Bilavsky, "Die Chronik des Unfassbaren," *Das Parlament* (29 January 2007).
68. Christopher Browning, *Ordinary Men: Reserve Police Battalion 101 and the Final Solution in Poland* (Cambridge, MA, 1992).
69. Friedländer, *The Years of Extermination*, xxvi.
70. The term "analytical unease" is derived from Friedländer's theoretical writings about Holocaust historiography; see Friedländer, *Memory, History*; see also Friedländer, *Den Holocaust beschreiben: Auf dem Weg zu einer integrierten Geschichte* (Göttingen, 2007), 102–16; and his contribution to this volume.
71. Friedländer, *The Years of Extermination*, 423.
72. Ibid., 578.
73. Ibid., 518. Even a brief look at *The Years of Extermination* illustrates that Friedländer departed from his original plans for his Holocaust synthesis as he laid them out in *Memory, History and the Extermination of the Jews of Europe*. As intended, he adopted poly-perspectival writing strategies and successfully recovered the voices of the victims. But he had also anticipated addressing the reader through a continuous commentary in order to unsettle the story and prevent narrative closure (132). Instead of following that route, Friedländer opted for the more elegant solution of having the narrative unsettle itself. His text narratively performs historical unease through a manipulation of the basic historiographical vectors of time, space, and causality. It is now easy to see why he made that decision. It would have been difficult to resist the temptation of having the comments explain to the reader the complex narrative world of the book and thus undermine its artfully constructed reading experience. For the same reason, Friedländer ends each subchapter

with particularly vivid and disturbing stories and testimonies, which thus take the place historians conventionally use for providing summary and context. In short, he chose narrative complexity and emotional focus over explanation.

74. Alon Confino has described this balancing act very well; see Confino, "Narrative Form and Historical Sensation: On Saul Friedländer's The Years of Extermination," *History and Theory* 48, no. 3 (2009): 199–219; and Confino's chapter in this volume.

75. Friedländer, *The Years of Extermination*, 663.

76. Incidentally, in an analysis of Tolstoy's *War and Peace* White argued in 2007 that one of the archetypical texts of literary realism consists of "a series of vignettes, anecdotes, [and] small histories" that braid together three different genres—political history, everyday history, and philosophical treatise—and render the past "unreasonable and incomprehensible," all for the purpose of conveying "what it felt like to fight in a battle, to be wounded, march beyond exhaustion, suffer imprisonment or risk death." Thus White makes *War and Peace* look very much like *The Years of Extermination* (minus Friedländer's radical self-reflexive edge) in an essay appropriately titled "Against Historical Realism," *New Left Review* 46 (2007): 89–110 (quotes from 90, 91, and 109).

77. White, *Figural Realism,* 40.

78. On the genre of historiographic metafiction in general and *Ragtime* in particular, see the interesting exchange between Linda Hutcheon and Frederic Jameson in Hutcheon, *A Poetics of Postmodernism* (New York, 1988), 89; and Jameson, *The Cultural Logic of Late Capitalism* (Durham, 1991), 22–23.

79. See, for example, Pericles Lewis, *The Cambridge Introduction to Modernism* (Cambridge, 2007), 161; see also Peter Nicholls, *Modernisms: A Literary Guide,* 2nd ed. (London, 2009), 7.

80. Or, as White put it, the style of Woolf for example reveals her to be "both a modernist and a historicist at the same time" (White, *Figural Realism*, 98).

81. Tammy Clewell, *Mourning, Modernism, Postmodernism* (London, 2009), 2.

82. T. S. Eliot, *Selected Prose* (London, 1975), 177. Having outed Friedländer as a modernist both in terms of form and ethics raises interesting questions about the limits of his innovation. Postmodern critics like Lyotard have maintained that modernism fell victim to its own success as the aestheticization of loss through compelling formal consistency became itself a source of solace and pleasure (Jean-François Lyotard, *The Postmodern Condition: A Report on Knowledge* (Manchester, 1984), 81). Like his modernist predecessors, Friedländer indeed delivers an elegantly written, self-sufficient text conveying subdued hope of historical emancipation. In this context, one might even invoke the book's success as proof for its lack of transgressive potential, as Amos Goldberg has done ("The Victim's Voice and Melodramatic Aesthetics in History," *History and Theory* 48, no. 3 (2009): 220–37). In the end, however, following Dominick LaCapra's assessment in *Writing History, Writing Trauma* (Baltimore, 2002), I still prefer modernist cultural forms of mourning to postmodern fetishizations of trauma, and that preference applies most specifically to the fetishization of perpetrator trauma manifest in Jonathan Littell's transgressive novel *The Kindly Ones*.

83. Leni Yahil, *The Holocaust: The Fate of European Jewry, 1932–1945* (New York, 1990).

84. Compare Friedländer, *The Years of Extermination*, 449 with Dieter Pohl, "Der Chronist der Apokalypse," *Der Spiegel* (9 October 2006).

85. For representative reviews, see Ulrich Herbert, "Die Stimmen der Opfer," *Süddeutsche Zeitung* (29 September 2006); and Norbert Frei, "Gesichter des Schreckens," *Neue Züricher Zeitung* (2 October 2006).

86. Hans Mommsen, for instance, not known for critical reticence, mentions that the role of the German bureaucracy and the key turning points in the Nazi persecution of Jews are not described with as much precision as he would have liked to see, and then concludes that "we owe a debt of gratitude to Friedländer for his impressive humanitarian lifetime achievement;" see "Fassungslosigkeit, die sich mitteilt," *Frankfurter Rundschau* (4 October 2006). Dieter Pohl, in "Der Chronist der Apokalypse," offers a few factual corrections, for instance regarding the collaborative measures of the Finnish government, and points out that Friedländer might have exaggerated the extent of antisemitism in Eastern Europe in general and in Poland in particular, and then insists

in closing, citing Ranke, that "anybody who wants to know what really happened has to read this book." See also Richard Evans's "Whose Orders," *New York Times* (24 June 2007).

87. Klaus-Dietmar Henke calls *The Years of Extermination* "the historiographical monument for the murdered Jews of Europe" (*Frankfurter Allgemeine Zeitung* (4 October 2006)).

88. Dan Stone, *Histories of the Holocaust* (Oxford, 2010), ch. 2.

89. Saul Friedländer, *When Memory Comes* (Madison, 2003); see also Karolin Machtans, *Zwischen Wissenschaft und autobiographischem Projekt: Saul Friedländer und Ruth Klüger* (Tübingen, 2009).

90. Friedländer, *The Years of Extermination*, xxv.

91. Martin Broszat/Saul Friedländer, "Um die 'Historisierung des Nationalsozialismus:' Ein Briefwechsel," *Vierteljahrshefte für Zeitgeschichte* 36 (1988): 343; see also Friedländer's chapter in this volume; and Nicolas Berg, *Der Holocaust und die westdeutschen Historiker* (Göttingen, 2003). Dan Stone has wisely concluded that debates like the Broszat/Friedländer exchange should be revisited in light of "the continued stress on a more or less positivist methodology in the history-writing of the Holocaust—especially in perpetrator research;" see Stone, "*Nazi Germany and the Jews* and the Future of Holocaust Historiography," in *Years of Persecution, Years of Extermination: Saul Friedländer and the Future of Holocaust Studies*, ed. Christian Wiese and Paul Betts (New York, 2010), 344.

92. For a passionate critical exploration of White's relativism, see A. Dirk Moses, "Hayden White, Traumatic Nationalism, and the Public Role of History," *History and Theory* 44, no. 3 (2005): 311–32; see also White's compelling response, "The Public Relevance of Historical Studies: A Reply to Dirk Moses," *History and Theory* 44, no. 3 (2005): 333–38, and Moses's rejoinder to White, "The Public Relevance of Historical Studies: A Rejoinder to Hayden White," *History and Theory* 44, no. 3 (2005): 339–47.

93. This slightly unorthodox application of White's methods is inspired by Richard Vann, "Hayden White, Historian," in *Re-Figuring Hayden White*, ed. Frank Ankersmit, Ewa Domańska, and Hans Kellner (Stanford, 2009), 304–31.

94. The precise place of irony in White's work has been subject to substantial discussion; see Herman Paul, "An Ironic Battle against Irony: Epistemological and Ideological Irony in Hayden White's Philosophy of History, 1955–1973," in *Tropes of the Past*, ed. Korhonen, 35–44.

95. White, *Tropics of Discourse*, 70.

96. One can also describe Friedländer's achievement in different theoretical terms and call his refusal of historicization and closure a narrative performance of the sublime; see F. R. Ankersmit, *Sublime Historical Experience* (Stanford, 2005). *The Years of Extermination* thus also constitutes a powerful negative and practical answer to Martin Broszat's "Plea for the Historicization of National Socialism," in *Reworking the Past: Hitler, the Holocaust, and the Historians' Debate*, ed. Peter Baldwin (Boston, 1990), 77–87.

Part IV
THE HOLOCAUST IN THE WORLD

CHAPTER 12

The Holocaust and European History[1]

Donald Bloxham

My title alludes to a particular contextualization of the Holocaust. It is obviously not the only possible contexualization, and cannot claim to be an especially appropriate one, because what qualifies as appropriate depends upon the particular questions asked of the thing contextualized. Dirk Moses' fascinating chapter discusses the subject in the context of world history; I seek to narrow the focus in a complementary way. My goal is to examine the Holocaust in a spatiotemporal *Raum* of great violence against population groups, but in a way that retains the historian's sensitivity to specificity: I portray the Holocaust as an only partly discrete episode within a wider process. Mine is an attempt to marry the study of *ethnopolitics* with the study of *geopolitics* and straightforward *politics*, within an overall framework that encapsulates something about Europe's experience of late modernity.

This modernity was not manifested for most Europeans in a series of abstract Enlightenment ideas, but in rough realities developing in a particularly pronounced manner from the later nineteenth century through the first half of the twentieth. New political boundaries were formed within states in the form of class politics, and between states as borders changed. Rural depression and urban industrialization loomed, accompanied by mass migration and followed by urban depression. Hereditary dynasties were replaced by dictatorships purporting to rule in the interests of the titular people, which used the rhetoric of that people as a legitimation for the increasingly radical exclusion of "others." War was both a product of these forces and the forum in which ethnic, racial, religious, and other forms of exclusion could be pushed to their most violent conclusions. The murderousness that Europe had projected into its colonies in

---

Notes for this section begin on page 252.

the nineteenth century was brought back into the continent from the end of that century as the continent imploded under its own competitive pressures.

Within this longer term set of socio-economic developments, the *geopolitical* parameters of my space are provided firstly by the crises and dissolution of the older European multinational empires—the Ottoman, Romanov, and Habsburg states—from the later nineteenth century onwards, though the Ottoman retreat and its associated ethnic violence can be dated further back. Secondly, we have the establishment in the wake of these empires of a string of insecure and often aggressive and heterophobic new nation-states. Thirdly, we have the intrusion of three new imperial influences into the contested spaces vacated by that process of imperial dissolution, from the Baltic to the Black Sea and the eastern and southern Mediterranean, and from the changing eastern and western borders of Germany and Russia respectively: Italy, the Soviet Union, and, particularly for our purposes, the "Third Reich." The contested areas were the places where, for the most part, the most violent population politics were enacted during the World War II era, but they were also the site of much other violence in the quest for land and ethnic supremacy, particularly from the time of the substantial end of the Ottoman Empire in mainland Europe in the eastern crisis of 1875–1878.

The *politics* of the matter are, naturally, manifold, but two aspects are particularly salient. The first is that the new imperial forms were shaped by new ideological norms—fascism, Nazism and Stalinism—which gave a particular coloring and radicalism to the expansion and consolidation of their empires, and gave an inflection to their conduct as great powers. The concept of great powers brings us to the second, somewhat countervailing point. However different these empires were from others before them, they were still confronted with some of the established problems of existing at or near the heart of the world economic system and its associated power structures. They were born into a world of other great powers with which they were necessarily in upclose competition or collaboration, and of lesser powers which they sought to incorporate within spheres of influence, and which in turn decided their alliance or neutrality policies according to established tenets of survival in a Europe whose stock in trade had been military and commercial alliance systems. And, of course, the new great powers were confronted with internal ethnic, religious, economic, and social problems that could not always be simply resolved by force.

As to *ethnopolitics,* they too were multifarious, and barely an ethnic group in Europe escaped some sort of violence leveled against it "as such," in the language of the genocide convention, whether that violence was in the form of forced assimilation, forced movement, or outright murder. But the geopolitical context also houses the interface of the three great monotheistic religions, and it is a widely overlooked aspect of the period (except insofar as the question is reduced to Christian antisemitism) that many of the most vicious intergroup dynamics at this time of geopolitical flux were superimposed on religious cleavages. That was true for the different Christian sects in the Polish-Ukrainian and Croat-Serb conflicts, just as for the Muslim-Christian and Christian-Jewish dynamics.

It is not at all paradoxical that an intrinsic part of the force-paced *modern* continental re-ordering was the murder or systematic eviction of some of Europe's very *oldest* "others." Understanding why requires comprehending how that overused and under-defined concept "modernity" actually interacted with pre-existing traits of the civilizations of our greater Europe. That, in turn, requires a more anthropologized understanding of Europeans' fears and perceptions than is generally allowed in a historical literature that is itself in thrall to the Eurocentric self-conception of rational action.

The status of minorities shifted in the context of the same systemic developments that produced new social classes and socio-economic strife. The combined impact of the European Enlightenment, the French political revolution and the British industrial revolution reshaped the sociological contours of the continent as elites had to broaden and rationalize political participation to some degree in the interests of social cohesion and productivity, and, therefore, overall state power. That such shifts necessitated radical changes in patterns of life meant they invariably created new resentments—not least nationalisms—and poured oil on the smouldering fires of old ones—not least religious antagonisms. The "rise" of this or that nation, or ethnos, or political philosophy, or social group, was held by protagonists to be the cause, rather than the consequence, of the longer term modernizing process and its associated traumas, and was so held because of the cultural preconceptions of superiority-inferiority and morality-immorality that were part of Christian (and Muslim) civilization. The concept of life or death struggle to rectify the situation fed on social Darwinism, which seemed so apt a doctrine as the great power system of diplomatic accord broke down under the strains of the later nineteenth century.

The greatest ethnoreligious violence of the second half of the nineteenth century had Muslims as it victims, as Tsarist Russia expanded its borders at the expense of the Ottomans, and the new Balkan states established themselves in violence. Then it was the turn of the Ottoman Christians to suffer the most extreme anti-civilian violence in the World War I era. The Armenians and Assyrians suffered waves of massacre culminating in genocide in 1915–1916; Greek Orthodox Ottomans from sensitive coastal regions were expelled (around 200,000) and internally deported (around 300,000) respectively at the end of the Balkan wars and during World War I, prior to their near complete eructation from Anatolia by murder and expulsion during and after the Greco-Turkish war of 1921–1922. At the end of the World War I era, the internationally-sponsored ethnic cleansing of "Turks" and "Greeks" (meaning Greek Muslims and most of the remaining Ottoman Orthodox Christians) was the last major burst of such violence—until the murder of tens of thousands of

Bosnian Muslims by Serbian Četniks and others in World War II, the further Bulgarian expulsion of "Turkic" Muslims in the early 1950s, and then the violence against Yugoslav Muslims after the Cold War. In World War II, Jews were the preeminent victims, having already suffered greatly at the hands of the Tsarist regime in 1915 and again during the Russian civil war.

Whatever its intriguing macro level patterns and interconnections, this violence was manifestly not all of the same intensity or direction. Very schematically, we may say that: (a) the fate of many Muslims in Christian Russia and the Balkans was one of eviction or "ethnic cleansing," that is, removal from a particular politico-geographical space; (b) the fate of many Christians in the Ottoman Empire was one of mass murder or genocide but largely confined to a particular politico-geographical space, namely the interior of the perpetrator state; and (c) the fate of the Jews during World War II was one of genocide that exceeded the interior of the perpetrator state and the lands ruled directly by it. What do we make of the differences?

Comparative genocide studies has been preoccupied with legislating harshly on similarities and differences between cases, especially insofar as the questions concern the relationships (1) between the Holocaust and other genocides and (2) between genocide and "non-genocidal" mass killing or eviction. Such approaches are rather sterile from the historian's perspective, which is concerned with balances of the general and the particular. The historian may be left simply with Wittgenstein's "family resemblances": with things that look similar to some others in certain respects, and to yet others in different respects, but with none looking absolutely identical to any other in all facets, and none the definitive family member against whom others can be measured according to their distance. The legal or social-scientific boundary separating genocide from not-genocide is not centrally significant here: family resemblances are more respectful of the "ragged edges" of historical actuality than regimented typologies of genocidal violence such as that of Kurt Jonassohn.[2] Ideal types by their very name have the virtue that their creators know they are reductive abstractions, as with my (a)(b)(c) schema above. As we shall see on a closer examination of the events outlined in that schema, when the cases are understood historically, that is as temporally evolving processes rather than unitary events viewed from the perspective of the finished act, each shares elements with the others: at the risk of sounding overly-schematic myself, (a: "Muslims")→(b: "Christians")→(c: "Jews") represents a progression of destructive ambition but, regressively, (c) has elements of (b) and both have elements of (a). What follows is an analytical approach that is both contextual in the sense of exposing the broad shared framework of (a), (b), and (c), and comparative in the sense of accounting for the "progression" by identifying key variables within that context. It also illustrates just how blurred the lines can be between one and another stage/type of destruction.

Muslims

The ethnic cleansing of Muslims into "Asian" Anatolia is perhaps simplest to explain in general terms, because its basic condition was change in the overlordship of the territories from which it was conducted. Flight and expulsions from the Crimea and the north Caucasus were a function of the consolidation of Russian security and the rule of territory conquered from the Ottoman Empire, colored by a Russian Christian chauvinism. The expulsions from the Balkan nation-states varied slightly in motivation over time, combining similar chauvinisms with resentment against a people historically associated with dominance, and increasingly a desire to reshape the demographic map in perpetuity with the aim of creating ethnically homogeneous nation-states.[3] Nevertheless, given the transnational, regional nature of anti-Muslim violence and the involvement in it of a major power from beyond the Balkans—Russia—we can conclude that the perpetration of such violence was in some way civilizational. The combined total of refugees created in both these long drawn sequences was in the millions, and perhaps as high as five million between the 1850s and the mid 1920s.[4] If neither sequence quite reached the proportions of unequivocal genocide, then we also need to remember that murder was nevertheless a key part of the process of eviction, partly *pour encourager les autres,* and partly because of the potential for escalation that was intrinsic to such actions—the deliberate opening of a window for the settling of scores, for rape, plunder, and sadism that were intrinsic to the ongoing process of inter-communal polarization. Thus in the very short period of the Balkan wars of 1912–1913, the death toll of Balkan Muslim civilians reached at least 40,000, and at least 400,000 more were expelled southeastwards out of mainland Europe; the corresponding figures were in the same general scale, and probably greater, in 1877–1878 alone.[5]

Moreover, there *was* at least one borderline case in these sequences, a possible genocide: Tsarist "pacification" and then eviction policy against the "Circassians" of the north Caucasus from the early 1860s, in which the death toll associated with the expulsion policy is at least in the range of the lower hundreds of thousands of people. One context for the most radical measures was war, the earlier Crimean conflict, and one of the tributary rationales was that the Circassians (like the Crimean Tatars also forced out from the time of the Crimean War) had sympathies with the Ottomans and indeed Britain. A Muslim death toll of perhaps 100,000 was also established in central Asia during World War I in relation to the European conflict: the "Urkun" was the net result of the Tsarist regime's policy of reprisal against the Kyrgyz in light of their refusal to conscript.[6] These two episodes encapsulate some of the dynamics which contributed to a definite instance of genocide during World War I, when the embattled Ottoman Empire was the perpetrator.

Christians

The deportation of the Armenians was justified by the Committee of Union and Progress (CUP) regime as a state security measure enacted in light of Armenian wartime subversion, as allegedly manifest in alliance with the empire's wartime opponents, Britain and, especially, adjacent Russia. As with earlier Russian policy towards the Caucasian Muslims, though to a greater degree given prior relations, the *Feindbild* was of an inner enemy in league with an outer enemy, the internal minority gaining strength as the fifth column of a larger force. For the first time in war, in the 1914–1918 conflict the Ottoman Empire was ranged against the powers who had traditionally posed as friends of the Armenians and had correspondingly interfered in the empire's internal affairs.

The longer-term context for this inner-outer enemy association, and of the violence of the measures enacted to address it, was the diminution of the empire, such that securing sovereign control of its remaining rump lands in Anatolia was a matter of absolute priority, and potentially separatist populations were viewed with increasing suspicion. Like the Jews in Europe, Christians in the Ottoman state had long been culturally stereotyped, based particularly on ideas of economic exploitation and trans-national affiliation, and subjected to abuses based on their alleged religious inferiority. Those abuses provided the locus for great power intervention on behalf of the minorities, while the stereotypes provided the template into which new ethno-nationalist conceptions of their dangerous otherness could fit as the great powers intervened. A vicious circularity was manifest. The notion that Armenian Christians had broken the compact with the Muslim state, and the inherently superior Muslim population, by appealing to the great powers for the "protection" enshrined at the end of the "eastern crisis" in the 1878 Berlin Treaty, was a key moment in the deterioration of relations that led to the massacres of around 80,000 Armenians in 1894–1896.[7]

With the loss of territory and Christian populations, and the influx of Muslim refugees, the empire was becoming unprecedentedly Islamicized, and the growing suspicion of nationalizing non-Muslim populations boded ill for Christians even without war, as the 1894–1896 massacres had shown. Many Armenians consequently emigrated to Russian territory, and successive late Ottoman elites had deliberately settled Muslim immigrants and refugees and sedentarizing Kurds in places of remaining Armenian concentration in order to dilute their presence and, thereby, their claim to territorially-specific protection. In the years leading up to 1914, some western Anatolian Greeks had been terrorized into leaving for the Greek state, just as "Turks" and Bulgarian Christians fled in either direction from Bulgaria and the Ottoman Empire during the Balkan wars. World War I greatly increased the sense of Ottoman existential crisis and, as everywhere, reduced moral constraints, but it also complicated the issue of how to remove the Armenians from their eastern Anatolian homelands.

As late as the beginning of May 1915, an Ottoman general proposed evicting Armenians from the border provinces into Russia as one option among others. The idea was taken no further because the logic perceiving extant Russian-Armenian collaboration predicted that Armenian refugees driven into the Caucasus would openly join Russian forces in greater numbers.[8]

Within a week, the direction of eviction was finally decided: it would be southwards, to the internal exile of the deserts of present-day Syria and Iraq. The CUP measures quickly became more extensive, as from late May through the summer, deportations spread from the border regions throughout the whole of eastern Anatolia and westwards even into Thrace, though there were not always deportations of entire communities in the western extremities.[9] Many of the deportees were massacred and abused on a colossal scale by local Muslim populations, paramilitaries, and gendarmes, and a huge number also died of attrition en route, but the ultimate destinations of the deportations nevertheless remain significant in themselves. The destinations were significant partly because prior to the war Circassian refugees had been settled in these arid areas, where infrastructure was absent and settlers were liable to be attacked by nomadic Bedouins: the mortality had been great even in peacetime and with some governmental effort at assisting the Muslim refugees.[10] So even if there had been no massacres, and a "territorial solution" only (to use Uwe Adam's term for the Nazi "Jewish reservation" designs[11]), the CUP knew that deporting Armenians to these inhospitable areas was akin to a death sentence for many in the medium term at most, and given general wartime shortage even that term was liable to be sharply reduced. This specific sort of removal was the most straightforward way of rendering Armenians "harmless" in the immediate term and preventing them from returning in the medium and longer terms. But these barren deportation destinations were also important in their particular spatial relationship to the deportees' homeland, as the human geographer Kerem Öktem has pointed out.[12] They were largely outside Anatolia, south of the Berlin-Baghdad railway line, which was one of the lines tacitly associated with great power spheres of influence and was also an area of predominantly Arabic populations. The CUP might well have expected to lose the areas to the south of the railway were the Central Powers to be defeated in the war, but in any case the area to the north of the railway was seen as the Turkic-Muslim heartland that had to be purified and (thus) demographically secured for the future.

It is difficult, and probably illusory, to separate cleanly the eviction aspects of the Armenian genocide from the directly murderous aspects. Many of the Armenian deportations from western Anatolia and Cilicia, for instance, were not accompanied by massacre en route since they were conducted away from the east where wartime "security" issues were most pronounced, and where the paramilitary forces operated, and where future land loss was especially feared—nevertheless they still ended up perishing in huge numbers at their desert destinations. On the other hand, when the Ottoman armies later regrouped and pressed into the Caucasus later in the aftermath of the Russian revolution and consequent military retreat, the massacres they conducted of Armenians in formerly Russian territory showed that killing could extend to anywhere the state wished to incorporate within its future territory. These divergent examples simply illustrate the practical elision, under particular circumstances, of the distinction between the ideal types of eviction and outright murder. The ethnocentric desire for Turkic-Muslim homogeneity within a designated territory was served either way. The episode also suggests that other instances of ethnic cleansing might well have developed into genocide had they not been immediately successful in virtue of having somewhere viable on this earth to dispatch their victims to.

There was radicalization within radicalization. It is still not clear exactly how pre-planned all the massacres were, though we can be certain that the initial killings of Armenian soldiers, community leaders, and menfolk more generally were directly ordered to remove the community's ability to mobilize itself, while the involvement of CUP central committee members in authority over the paramilitary forces that attacked deportation convoys reveals absolute approval of the thrust of the measures. However they began, the measures swiftly snowballed. Widespread popular participation in the massacres was the result of some local Muslims' desire to express their heightened sense of community at an extreme moment, but as important was the sense that the Armenians had been declared fair game for robbery, abuse, and sexual enslavement by the state's decision to deport and effectively outlaw them.

Radicalization also issued in the more intensive pursuit of Armenians within areas already targeted. For instance, the Interior Ministry became concerned about the issue of forced Armenian converts to Islam, and ordered deportations from within that group. While conversion was at points allowed for women and children who could be forcibly assimilated into the Turkic-Muslim body politic, the Interior Ministry's views on that matter changed from ambiguity to outright suspicion that some converts (presumably particularly males) would remain "inner Armenians" and thus a threat by dint of their very identity. Finally, while some men (and parts of their families) working in trades deemed vital for the war effort or for local economies were sometimes left alone, many others were sought out and deported, including many that the empire's allies saw as economically essential. It is probable that, had not the back-and-forth of the Russian-Ottoman front in 1915–1917 increasingly destroyed state authority over eastern Anatolia, this process of evermore fine combing of the Armenian population would have continued. As a testament to that probability, around a year after the decisions that set the genocide in motion in spring 1915, the desert concentration centers were host to extensive massacres of the survivors of the deportations, whichever part of the empire the deportees originated from. Mass murder, once embarked upon, seems to have developed something of its own momentum, even at the cost of some—though not all—immediate practical rationales.

Jews

The policies that culminated in the "final solution" of the Jewish question also began with a spatial goal, the emigration of Jews from Germany, rather than a goal of physical eradication. If this gives the impression that we are instantly inveigled in a functionalist interpretation of the development of the genocide, then that impression must be tempered by recognition that it is often impossible to delineate clearly between spatial and "existential" "solutions" as such. The various Jewish "reservation" plans—Lublin, Madagascar, beyond the Urals[13]—provide the progressively expansive and radical links between the two ideal types. Like the deserts of Iraq and Syria, the conditions in each of these human dumping grounds were obviously highly attritional if not genocidal, which suggests that while we cannot talk of outright decisions for genocide prior to the invasion of the USSR, an unfolding *logic* of escalating destruction is again evident.

The spatial location of the reservations was also vital to understanding the perpetrators' imaginary. Lublin was on the then-eastern periphery of the German empire as it then stood; and the others were definitively outside *Europe* as far as the Nazis were concerned—Madagascar obviously so, but the Urals too, when we recall that many Europeans saw them as a natural border with Asia, and the SS planned correspondingly to build a great *Ostwall* along the range. The same went for Palestine, the (post-Ottoman) "near *eastern*" place, increasing Jewish emigration to which had broad German institutional support in the mid-1930s.

As with CUP Armenian policy in 1915, getting Jews out of the salient geopolitical-cultural space and having them die cannot really be conceptually or temporally separated in the consideration of the deportation designs. Even when mass murder of Jews began, with the first *Einsatzgruppen* killings in the USSR in late June 1941, these co-existed easily for a while with the idea of a spatial solution. Those killings should be taken on the terms on which they were first conducted. Murder of many adult male Soviet Jews began immediately upon the invasion, but it was not initially intended as a way of wiping out all Jews, and the subsequent escalation of measures was not planned from the outset. It was a paranoid, racist security policy, the aim of which was decapitating the Jewish community and the "Judeo-Bolshevik" state and preempting potential resistance.[14] Over the first six to eight weeks ever more men between the ages of 15 and 60 were shot on the basis that this was the surest way to destroy the Jewish-Bolshevik "intelligentsia" and its potential manpower. (At approximately the same time, the German military authorities in occupied Serbia also used Jewish and Roma men as hostages alongside ethnic Serbs, and in much greater numbers relative to the respective populations, and murdered them in "reprisal" for partisan action.) Such suppositions explain why at first over the coming weeks and months the developing German murder policy was less extreme in Jewish communities that had been part of Poland rather than the USSR before 1939: Polish Jews were at that point considered to be less immediately dangerous, and were to be dealt with as part of a more comprehensive but as yet unknown overall "solution."[15]

Clearly none of the reservation plans reached fruition, because of varying combinations of their intrinsic impracticability and frustrations relating to the course of the war. The spatial aspects of Nazi Jewish policy that were more or less successful in their own terms were either effectively rendered irrelevant by developments—as with forced emigration from Germany and Austria, because of the incorporation of millions more Jews in the occupied territories conquered from 1939—or were only ever supposed to be transitional measures in the direction of full eructation—as with ghettoization *within* the occupied East. Given that literal removal of some sort from German-ruled territory was the priority, if that was to happen it had to be achieved by different means than the removal of Muslims from Europe, which was the rough equivalent of forcing Jews out of Germany in 1933–1939, and also by different means than the dumping of Anatolian Christians into the deserts, which was the rough equivalent of the reservation plans.

If we need analogues to corroborate the idea of genocidal escalation based on frustrated removal efforts, we need look no further than Germany's ally Romania, the second largest state murderer of Jews in World War II, as it killed increasingly large numbers of Jews in Bessarabia and Bukovina from late June, and in Transnistria from later summer 1941. Before falling under Romanian authority, Transnistria, on the eastern side of the Dniester River, was the area into which Romania sought to evict Jews from Bessarabia and Bukovina, which had just been "recovered" for Romania from the USSR in the wartime expansionist drive. Ion Antonescu assumed that a rapid German victory would allow the Jews to be driven yet further eastwards, even beyond the Urals.[16] That did not come to pass. As the German forces in the USSR refused to allow the Jews to accumulate in their rear prior to the Romanian assumption of power in Transnistria, escalated massacres became the Romanian measure of choice against this population of refugees. Further massacres of scores of people ensued upon the Romanian accession in Transnistria, and vast numbers also died of privation and disease in hastily constructed camps.[17]

Where the growing German murder of the Soviet Jews differed from that of Romania's killings is that in the Romanian case the murder did not spread westwards to incorporate the Jews of "old Romania" indiscriminately (though Romanian Roma were often deported to Transnistria irrespective of their place of dwelling), whereas Nazi policy did expand back westwards and became increasingly inclusive of Jews wherever they lived and whatever their citizenship status. More generally, on the Romanian side, there was a desire to "cleanse" Romania of Jews as a whole, but in stages, and as only the ideologically most important part of a more general campaign of "Romanianization." As with any state policy, the realization of this vision, and the form by which it was achieved, was contingent on events.

The escalation and de-escalation of Romanian Jewish policy tells us less about levels of antisemitism than about the relationship of antisemitism to developing state strategy. The Antonescu regime believed that lenient treatment of Jews would improve Romania's prospects at an Allied-orchestrated postwar settlement, and from the second half of 1942 it was becoming increasingly clear who the likely victors would be. Important too in that connection was a sense of national *amour propre* regarding subordinate relations to Germany and equality with other allied states, especially at a time when other Axis partners were becoming increasingly reluctant to acquiesce to German pressure to deport their Jews. Then in 1944 Romania switched sides in the war. A lesser European power had to play the triangulation game to survive, as Hungary belatedly tried to before being invaded by Germany in 1944.[18]

As for Germany itself, the deportations of German Jews themselves developed from a more straightforward eviction agenda. The German regional leaders drove to remove Jews from their areas, out of a combination of the ideological desire to become "Jew-free," and the competitive desire to do so at least as quickly as anyone else. The Gauleiter had been lobbying Hitler for these deportations from well before they began in autumn 1941. The SS facilitated their deportation initially without, it seems, a precise medium-term plan about what would happen to them. The question of whether German Jews should be murdered outright was not settled by the decision to deport them eastwards. What these deportations did do was add to the logistical problems on the ground in Poland and the USSR, where the initiatives of regional civilian and military administrations and SS leaders—especially the regional Higher SS and Police leaders, or HSSPFs—were vital in developing the most radical "solutions" to these problems in order, again, to get their own areas "free of Jews." (One thinks here of Hans Frank's reluctance to accept Jews into the *Generalgouvernement,* and then his embrace of Berlin's empowerment to "liquidate them yourselves" in situ given the very *absence* of an overall destination.[19]) Thus, in the broader context of radicalization created by the German-Soviet war and the escalation of murder in the Soviet territories, autumn 1941 saw the beginning of a series of local initiatives in annexed western Poland and the *Generalgouvernement* to establish murder facilities using gas to dispose of indigenous ghettoised Jews who were too ill, young, or old to work, both for its own sake but also to make space for incoming German and other Central European Jews. The dynamic was established of a constant sifting of the Jewish population for murder, in which overcrowding and disease in the captive group served as an important proximate motivation for murder.[20]

The foregoing paragraph is a highly simplified description of the process of escalating murder in the German empire. By depicting it I am firstly seeking to reinforce the point that the developing Jewish policy was possessed of a certain logic of radicalization given the imperatives of wartime rule, the closing down of options during war, and the self-created dilemmas of a broad functional elite for whom removing Jews by some means was a political bottom line. By the same token, in the Armenian case, different proximate rationales served an overall logic of destruction: Armenian men could be murdered on deportation marches to "pre-empt" resistance, while women and children could be murdered in the deserts as spreaders of disease. In the USSR the circle of victims vastly expanded over the late summer and autumn of 1941, less because of discrete central orders than the radical ethos of the SS police forces, their open-ended pacification remit, and competition between different German agencies[21]; in Poland, ghetto overcrowding and disease meant that the same end of increasingly total murder was approximated only a number of months later. This process of policy convergence across a very large terrain was the result of an accumulation of ad hoc measures, in which different proximate rationales for killing served in different contexts,[22] though it is important to stress that ad hoc certainly does not mean purely fortuitous.

Yet—and here I come to my second point—if these dynamics of radicalization are accepted they account "only" for the murder of Jews within Germany's expanded borders, which I take to include Germany's eastern empire plus "greater Germany" itself, and the lands annexed to it from 1938 to 1941, as well as the Netherlands which was scheduled to be incorporated. By extension, as total mass murder became standard practice wherever Germany had sufficient control and could implement its agenda of rendering huge areas "free of Jews," the dynamics also explain the extension of genocide to areas like Greece and Serbia. The dynamics do not account for that aspect of the "final solution" that has so contributed to its particular notoriety, the aspect that begs the question not just *why eviction from a particular space,* or *why mass murder within that space,* but *why mass murder beyond that space*? Certainly a very important seed of the expansion of genocide lay in Hitler's longstanding view of the Jews, and the views of many of his chief collaborators. Taken in the abstract from well before 1933, these views justified the removal of any moral or spatial limitation on the measures taken to combat the Jewish peril, pointing to the "need" for a reckoning that transcended issues of territory. Each of the ethno-religious dynamics considered heretofore devolved significantly on issues of the power of one group over another, but the antisemitic tradition that Hitler took to new extremes differed from the Christian-Muslim dynamic in ascribing a ubiquitous, conspiratorial agenda to the objects of its suspicion. However, this cultural-cum-ideological stereotype simply cannot do all the necessary work in explaining the breadth of the "final solution" because there is no rule of history stating that the inherent possibilities of ideas must reach any of their inherent conclusions.

It is teleological to ask how the logic of Hitler's ideas was realized; instead, the question must be how a complex political, bureaucratic, military, and (to some extent) social process evolved temporally against the horizon of antisemitic meaning and possibility established jointly by Hitler, the other true believers, a number of opportunists, and a range of cultural preconceptions that predated Nazism. Given the institutional character of the Nazi regime there was at once considerable possibility for competitive radicalization within and beyond the boundaries of the state administration as traditionally defined, and a lack of precise blueprints and concrete visions, which is why metaphor, and its relation euphemism, played enduring roles in Jewish policy. The violence of the language emanating from the top of the regime, and the cumulative weight of policy pronouncements against Jews in the 1930s, gave clear signs about basic direction, though not about precise destination, and the atmosphere of permissiveness inculcated over years of Nazi rule liberated all manner of fantasies about how this interpretative gap might be filled. But the context in which these fantasies expanded to their most ambitious was provided not just—as is now well-known—by war in the east, but also by the formal and informal alliances created by Germany's agenda as a great power acting within a set of continental ethnopolitical and geopolitical parameters.

Here we move from the solely comparative study of genocide towards a more contextualized account of the Holocaust within a wider and longer process of violent European restructuring. To the extent that the Holocaust was a European process in European contexts, the answer to the question about the extent of the "final solution" must also be European in its scope. Like the eviction of the Muslims, the destruction of the European Jews was an international crime perpetrated by lesser and greater state and substate actors pushing basically in the same direction and thereby reinforcing each other.

Europe

As with the Muslims, transnational violence against Jews (and Romanies) was facilitated by the fact that they were targets on whom very many European nationalists could agree without fear of contradiction by domestic and international co-participants. Jews were the victims of a particularly channeled international persecution at a time when alliance politics and German preferences inhibited violence against certain other minorities—say Ukrainians or Hungarians in Romanian territory, or "ethnic Germans" anywhere outside of territory still ruled by the Soviet Union—even where that dynamic had greater local political immediacy than the Jewish/non-Jewish dynamic—as with the

Ukrainian nationalists who were primarily anti-Russian/Soviet and anti-Polish, yet spent much of 1941–1942 slaughtering Volhynian Jews under German command. The constellation of alliance factors could also moderate violence via the established precedent of "population exchange," which was deployed between ethnic Romanians and Bulgarians, and would likely have provided the solution of the Transylvanian question in the strained Romanian-Hungarian alliance, given an Axis victory in the war. But it bears emphasizing that of the ethnic conflicts not involving Jews in the period, some of the most vicious and unrestrained were either enacted as Germany was losing control (mutual Polish-Ukrainian massacres) or in the face of sometime German opposition given Berlin's concern for stability (Croat-on-Serb massacres).[23]

There were significant European dimensions to the relationships with protagonists as well as with allies of convenience. As with the murder of the Ottoman Christians, the state of war also meant that the great power "protectors" of the minority in question—the "Judaeo-Bolshevik" state and the "Jewish-manipulated" capitalist states during World War II, Britain and Russia during World War I—were now not only less able to interfere but were directly opposed militarily. The "inner" and "outer enemies" could be targeted simultaneously and as extensions of each other, just as the USSR deported its Volga German population in the face of the Third Reich's military advance. What had been a hindrance in peacetime had become a window of opportunity in wartime, just as the German retreat in turn opened a different window of opportunity—for the expulsion of the ethnic German "clients" of the Reich by Germany's former allies and dominions alike. In both sequences of eviction, the perpetrating states also had somewhere to expel the ethnic Germans to, respectively the USSR's own interior and Germany itself. It bears repeating that on practical as well as ideological grounds these options of simple eviction were not available in most of Europe during World War II.

The extent to which each set of state and proto-state actors within the German orbit participated in genocide on their own account varied considerably, and that can partly be attributed to the patterns of intergroup action and stereotype that preceded the war. Muslim-Jewish relations were at that point the least violent of the interfaith interactions in the former Ottoman dominions. This was perhaps because Jews and Christians had together been subject to Muslim domination and the particularities of the Ottoman social order there. Whatever the reason, with the exception for very specific reasons of Romania, the Balkan states emerging from the Ottoman Empire also lacked the intensity of antisemitism of those states to the north, and provided less of an indigenous impetus to the World War II genocide of the Jews.

In the former Habsburg domains, Jews were often depicted by antisemites as arch beneficiaries of the former anti-nationalist imperial order. By this view, they were parasitical on Austro-Hungarian power and exploitative of the "suppressed peoples" in virtue of the economic functions the Habsburgs had seen fit to deploy some of them in. Hungarian, Slovak, and even Croat policy towards the Jews had a particular economic coloring as well as a function of removing a people historically associated with domination and now suspected of yearning for the days before the nation-state.

In many parts of the former Romanov domains, economic stereotypes also existed, there as elsewhere dovetailing with religious stereotypes; nevertheless strong indigenous antisemitic agendas tended to develop only when the "Jewish question" fitted into overlapping nationalist dynamics. This may explain why Belarus, with no strong nationalist movement or history of independence, produced many collaborators in the "final solution" but no pogroms outside of the more predominantly Polish western areas, and probably fewer perpetrators motivated by overtly ideological factors.[24] Latvia, Lithuania, and Ukraine had differing histories of toleration of Jews, but they were each characterized by relatively strong nationalist sentiment. Further, all had lost their independence at various points to the Soviet Union, as had the eastern territories of Poland in 1939, and they had experienced the privations, persecutions, deportations, and summary economic re-ordering associated with Soviet rule. Together, these factors suggest why in June–July 1941 Latvia, Lithuania, "western Ukraine," and parts of the northeast of Poland experienced a wave of massacres with extensive local participation on the arrival of German forces.[25]

In each instance, prior Soviet rule and its hardships were equated with the political ascendancy of Jews. The proportional overrepresentation of Jews in the local communist parties and in the ranks of the NKVD cannot be denied, nor that many Jews welcomed the arrival of Soviet forces; but nor can the fact that Jews suffered more than most groups from Soviet economic restructuring and the deportation of "bourgeois elements." Present, perhaps, in this ostentatious antisemitism was a desire to create the false impression that Jews had been the only collaborators with Soviet rule, to be contrasted with the majority non-Jewish "victims." As in the case of the militias of the Organisation of Ukrainian nationalists, heightened antisemitism also served as an appeal to German sympathies. In the absence of state authority, and then its arrival in the form of licentious Nazi rule, any number of imaginary scores could be settled in a way that recalls pogroms in 1905 and 1918. Ultimately, what was at issue was not the actual number of Jews involved in Communist rule, but the association of Jews with Bolshevism on the grounds of Bolshevik atheism, modernity, and commitment in principle to the equality of Jews and non-Jews—and, relatedly, the simple fact that any Jews at all should find themselves in unprecedented positions of political authority over Christians.[26]

Right across the continent, and indeed the occident, the Russian revolution had stimulated particularly virulent expressions of antisemitism. Many contemporary French newspapers, for instance, attributed the Bolshevik revolution to Jewish influence.[27] Romania's June 1941 Iași pogrom was triggered by an empirically unsubstantiated claim that Jews were signaling Soviet bombers in that border area.[28] The Bolshevik revolution itself fitted into a pre-existing set of perceptions that Jews were beneficiaries of industrial-commercial modernity and of ruptures in Europe's social order that began with the egalitarian, secularizing rhetoric of the French revolution, and found contemporary political expression through the rise of liberalism and the European left, and the minorities treaties imposed on the lesser European powers in 1878 and 1918–1923 as they emerged from the shell of the dynastic empires.

The far-reaching impact of the Nazi agenda transcended *some* of the cultural particularities of the successor peoples of the former dynastic empires as far as influence on their anti-Jewish actions was concerned. Germany's strategy as a great power in the run-up to war had involved playing on ethnic fears and antagonisms as a way of fracturing the 1918 peace settlement. As it divided up Eastern and Southeastern Europe in sometime partnership with the USSR in 1938–1941, Germany was in a position to reverse a number of the post-World War I boundary awards, with Hungary and Bulgaria gaining territory at the expense of Romania, Greece, Yugoslavia, and Czechoslovakia. As territory changed hands, any so-called "foreign" populations dwelling on it were in danger from their new masters. They were in danger because they were seen as potential grounds for future irredentist claims by the recently dispossessed state; because as non-conationals they were simply distrusted; and because in freshly acquired territory, there were often fewer issues of citizenship and fewer ties of residual compassion to concern oneself with. Thus as well as following up its acquisition of Dobruja from Romania with the Bulgarian-Romanian population exchange, Bulgaria was prepared to allow Germany to deport to their deaths Jews from the Macedonian and Thracian territories acquired from Greece and Yugoslavia. From June 1941 Hungary evicted into Ukraine and eastern Galicia foreign and allegedly stateless Jews from the areas it acquired from Slovakia, including Jewish refugees who had fled Poland. Romania swiftly learned the Dobruja lesson of creating demographic faits accomplis against distrusted minorities, as we saw in the cases of Bessarabia and Bukovina.

It was not, however, just a matter of the German agenda influencing other states and peoples and presenting new opportunities and "threats"; the process worked in reverse too. Perhaps it would be better to think in terms of a series of unequal dialectics. Let us briefly consider four modalities of German/non-German interaction, of which the first concerns nationalist groups and collaborators within the Nazi eastern empire. It is no coincidence that the first SS *Einsatzgruppe* (A) to progress to the murder of Soviet Jews of all ages and both sexes did so in the context of much local collaboration in killing in the Baltic. Without the newly-stoked indigenous nationalistic antagonisms that, along with material factors, prompted tens of thousands of Latvians, Lithuanians, and Ukrainians to collaborate with German forces in the Soviet territories and beyond, the "final solution" simply could not have achieved the dimensions it did there.

Secondly, independent states could also take the lead. On 18 August 1941 Hitler not only suggested that Europe was presenting a "united front" against the Jews; he also implied that Antonescu was actually showing the way by being more radical than Germany had been *so far*, by which he was obviously referring to the sheer extent of Romania's killing in Bessarabia and Bukovina, which was greater at that point than the SS-Police murder in neighboring German-occupied Ukraine. Hitler's invocation of "Europe" here was particularly pointed. Goebbels recounted that in the same conversation the Führer recalled his own 30 January 1939 "prophecy" that should the Jews bring about another world war the result would be the destruction of the Jewish race in *Europe*.[29]

Barely a week after Hitler's reflections on the Romanian situation, a third tributary of murderous radicalization manifested itself. If groups of indigenous activists added impetus in the Baltic, and Romania had shown what other states could do on their own account, there were also inadvertent but important interactions between the demographic policies of different Axis states. At the end of August, what Klaus-Michael Mallmann calls a "qualitative leap" occurred in the murder of Ukrainian Jewry, when a massacre of about 23,600 people at Kamenets Podolsky by forces under the regional HSSPF Friedrich Jeckeln more than doubled the entire death toll inflicted by all SS-Police agencies in the region to that point. The "problem" of overcrowding and people-management that they sought to solve by massacre had been partly created by Hungary: most of the Jews had been expelled by Hungary.[30] The Jews who had been forced into eastern Galicia by Hungary also compounded "overcrowding" in that district and so contributed to the proximate reasons by which the local SS and Police Leader Friedrich Katzmann ordered the killing of the "superfluous" at Stanislavow on 12 October. This was the first massacre on anything like its scale in the *Generalgouvernement*, to which eastern Galicia had been annexed after the invasion of the USSR. Eastern Galicia acted as a sort of policy "bridge" between the USSR and Poland, with (H)SSPFs liaising not just with Berlin but with each other, and at the end of October the radicalization of Jewish policy in Poland was entrenched by the initial preparations for the Bełżec extermination camp in the Lublin district.[31]

As to the expanding program of eastward deportations into the killing zones of Germany's empire, that was shaped through the fourth modality, inter-state interaction of a more deliberate sort. From the end of October 1941 the German Foreign Office approached Romania, Slovakia, and Croatia about the possibility of deporting Jews of their citizenship who happened to be living in Germany. This would help fill deportation quotas of German Jews bound for Poland, and in retrospect it set a precedent for later, more extensive deportations from those states themselves. The three agreed in principle (subject to Slovakia's concerns about securing the wealth of the deportees), not caring less about the people involved. Unsurprisingly, the "European" idiom was deployed once again. In the following month, on 28 November 1941, Hitler revealed to the

Grand Mufti of Jerusalem that "Germany has resolved, step by step, to ask one European nation after the other to solve its Jewish problem, and at the proper time, direct a similar appeal to non-European nations as well."[32] The language is instructive, alluding to a more global "solution" to the Jewish question as the aggregate of a number of individual "national solutions." Around the same time, the minister for the occupied Soviet territories Alfred Rosenberg made a similar distinction when he proclaimed that "the Jewish question is solved *for Germany* only when the last Jew has left German territory, and *for Europe* when not a single Jew lives on the European continent up to the Urals."[33]

If in Hitler's and Rosenberg's terms of late autumn 1941 the solution of Europe's and Germany's Jewish questions were not yet fully merged as a German project, the merger had certainly occurred by the time of the Wannsee conference, when every country in Europe was listed as a target for deportations. So why did Germany ultimately seek not just to facilitate the destruction of other countries' Jewish populations but also to drive that process? The answer lies, I would argue, with those German organizations that had something to gain by capitalizing on the opportunities Europe had just presented for "Europeanization."[34]

The initial diplomatic convergence with Romania, Slovakia, and Croatia explains the certainty of Reich Security Head Office (RSHA) chief Reinhard Heydrich and the Foreign Office representative Martin Luther at the Wannsee conference of January 1942, as Luther proclaimed to foresee no great difficulties in getting the Western and Southeastern European states to surrender their Jews.[35] The significance of Heydrich's and Luther's offices is that these were the two organizations whose influence in Jewish policy was, unlike most other organizations, heavily invested in its extension beyond Germany's imperium. Such is obviously true by definition of the Foreign Office's remit, but it is also true to a significant degree of the RSHA, despite the earlier leadership Heydrich had shown and been granted in emigration policy and then murder policy in the first weeks of the invasion of the USSR.

Since the early weeks, in Poland and the USSR, other much larger SS and police agencies (notably the HSSPFs with the Waffen-SS and Order Police forces at their disposal) had driven Jewish policy at least as murderously. Meanwhile, various civil authorities and military had incorporated many surviving Jews into work projects. Heydrich's leadership on Jewish policy had been compromised. If there could be competition to "solve" the "problem" of Jews under German rule in ever more radical and immediate fashions, one way of reframing the problem was expanding the scope of the whole policy according to quite ordinary imperatives of organizational life: growth, innovation, seizing the moment. Battling the Jewish "threat" also presented opportunities, and the RSHA, vanguard of the SS vanguard that it was, capitalized on those opportunities. It cannot be stressed enough that this combination of amoral ambition and expansive aggression only made rational sense within the framework of the antisemitism that gave it direction—there was a confluence of ideological and institutional logics within German power structures and, for a while from around 1938 through to around mid-1942, a conducive continental atmosphere too.

Perhaps one could say that Hitler's January 1939 "prophecy" came true. Stripped of its messianic pretensions, a "prophecy" is a prediction. Such utterances are not uncommon in the history of genocide, and some have been blunter.[36] But observers do not need political leaders to spell things out in such explicit terms, which is where *logics* of unfolding developments have their own manifest force without requiring the aid of precise visions, let alone "blueprints." The predictions of mass murder in Rwanda shortly prior to the 1994 genocide are well known. Austrian and British observers alike recognized months before the Armenian genocide that Istanbul's entry into the war against the Entente put Ottoman Christians in mortal peril.[37]

Self-evidently Hitler was better placed than most to comprehend the forces Germany could unleash in war. The SS, and more specifically the men of the RSHA, were straining at the leash to prove themselves in Germany's existential battles. At the beginning of 1939 Hitler could not have known what precise form the "destruction of the Jewish race in Europe" would take, but he knew his men. He also knew Europe in a way that can only be comprehended by appreciating the cultural-political phobias preoccupying so many of the continent's nationalists at that point. He was a keen student of history, and his very selectiveness made him focus on the most violent parts of it. He saw himself as the solution to the continent's problems, and was gratified though, one suspects, not that surprised when Europe warmed to his theme.

There were limits to Hitler's and Heydrich's predictive powers, however—limits imposed by different existential calculi across the German sphere of influence. Heydrich's superficial certainty about expanding the genocide to a fully continental level did not meet with anything like complete realization. From shortly after the time of his death, with Axis setbacks from late summer 1942, and especially the loss at Stalingrad at the turn of the year, the earlier "multiplier effect" was cancelled out. A burgeoning continental consensus on Jewish policy was fractured as Germany's allies triangulated and rejected the surrender of Jews from areas beyond their contested borderlands or—often the same thing—of Jews with full citizenship. More extensive deportations thereafter tended only to happen where, as in Hungary, deportation policy was foisted onto the states in question, and even in Hungary the deportation programme was not completed because of the combination of increasing Magyar resistance to the deportation of Jews from the central Hungarian lands, especially under the concerned eyes of the Allies, and the changes wrought in intra-Axis politics by Romania's defection.[38]

As a great power fighting for outright hegemony, Germany was less interested in and equipped for triangulation than its allies. Nevertheless it would be wrong to think that Germany was determined to impose its Jewish policies on other states at any cost to the war effort. Germany's calculus by the second half of the war entailed fighting ever harder, a few feeble westward peace overtures notwithstanding. The occupation of Hungary was precisely to keep a wavering Budapest within the Axis, and the deportation of the Hungarian Jews was, I would argue, a way of binding Budapest to Berlin in a community of guilt that was also a community of fate, as well as an expression of the expanding but manifestly not inexorable systemic logic of mass murder. Conversely, where states like France, or Bulgaria, or Romania looked like they were committed to military and/or economic collaboration, their reservations about handing over Jews for murder (whether Jews from particular areas or particular categories of citizen) were tolerated to varying degrees. The destruction of the Jews was part of the existential calculus, and for a while it dovetailed with the war against the Allies, but for a Nazi regime whose raison d'être was war-fighting ability there was no sense practically *or* ideologically in pursuing the former to the detriment of the latter. "Europe" could be a decelerator of genocide as well as an accelerator.[39]

Notes

1. I thank Mark Levene, Jürgen Matthäus, and Dan Stone for comments and advice on drafts of this chapter, and Ahmet Efiloğlu for statistics on the deportations of Ottoman Greeks.
2. Frank Chalk and Kurt Jonassohn, eds., *The History and Sociology of Genocide* (New Haven, 1990).
3. On these shifts in rationale, Mark Biondich, *The Balkans: Revolution, War, and Political Violence since 1878* (Oxford, 2011).
4. Generally on these issues see Justin McCarthy, *Death and Exile: The Ethnic Cleansing of Ottoman Muslims, 1821–1922* (Princeton, 1995).
5. Biondich, *The Balkans*, 29–30.
6. McCarthy, *Death and Exile;* Stephen D. Shenfield, "The Circassians: A Forgotten Genocide?" in *The Massacre in History*, ed. Mark Levene and Penny Roberts (Oxford, 1999), 149–62; John Anderson, *Kyrgyzstan: Central Asia's Island of Democracy?* (London, 1999).
7. For the deep geopolitical context of the genocide, see Donald Bloxham, *The Great Game of Genocide: Imperialism, Nationalism, and the Destruction of the Ottoman Armenians* (Oxford, 2005), chs. 1–2.
8. Taner Timur, *Türkler ve Ermeniler* (Ankara, 2000), 33. Fuat Dündar, "Pouring a People into the Desert: The 'Definitive Solution' of the Unionists to the Armenian Question," in *A Question of Genocide: Armenians and Turks at the End of the Ottoman Empire*, ed. Ronald Grigor Suny, Fatma Müge Göçek, and Norman N. Naimark (New York, 2011), 281–82.
9. On the pattern of deportations and exemptions: Hilmar Kaiser, "Genocide at the Twilight of the Ottoman Empire," in *The Oxford Handbook of Genocide Studies*, ed. Donald Bloxham and A. Dirk Moses (Oxford, 2010), 365–85; Taner Akçam, *A Shameful Act: The Armenian Genocide and the Question of Turkish Responsibility* (London, 2007); Raymond Kévorkian, *Le Génocide des Arméniens* (Paris, 2006); Dündar, "Pouring a People into the Desert," 283–84.
10. Dündar, "Pouring a People into the Desert," 278–80.
11. Uwe Dietrich Adam, *Judenpolitik im dritten Reich* (Düsseldorf, 1972), 303–13.

12. Kerem Öktem, "Reconstructing Geographies of Nationalism: Nation, Space and Discourse in Twentieth Century Turkey," PhD thesis, Oxford University, 2006.

13. Götz Aly, "'Jewish Resettlement': Reflections on the Political Prehistory of the Holocaust," in *National Socialist Extermination Policies: Contemporary German Perspectives and Controversies,* ed. Ulrich Herbert (New York, 2000), 53–82.

14. Christoph Dieckmann, "The War and the Killing of the Lithuanian Jews," in *National Socialist Extermination Policies,* ed. Herbert, 240–75; Ralf Oggoreck, *Die Einsatzgruppen und die "Genesis der Endlösung"* (Berlin, 1996).

15. See previous note and Peter Klein, ed., *Die Einsatzgruppen in der besetzten Sowjetunion 1941/42* (Berlin, 1997).

16. Radu Ioanid, *The Sword of the Archangel: Fascist Ideology in Romania* (New York, 1990), 215; Jean Ancel, *Transnistria, 1941–1942. The Romanian Mass Murder Campaigns* (Tel Aviv, 2003), vol. 1, 89; Radu Ioanid, *The Holocaust in Romania: The Destruction of Jews and Gypsies Under the Antonescu Regime, 1940–1944* (New York, 2000), 142.

17. For Romanian policy, see previous note, plus Mark Levene, "The Experience of Genocide: Armenia 1915–16 and Romania 1941–42," in *Der Völkermord an den Armeniern und die Shoah,* ed. Hans-Lukas Kieser and Dominik Schaller (Zurich, 2002), 423–62.

18. See notes 16 and 17, plus Martin Broszat, "Das dritte Reich und die rumänische Judenpolitik," *Gutachten des Instituts für Zeitgeschichte* 1 (1958): 102–83, and Holly Case, *Between States: The Transylvanian Question and the European Idea during World War II* (Stanford, 2009).

19. Kurt Pätzold and Erika Schwarz, eds., *Tagesordnung Judenmord: Die Wannsee-Konferenz am 20. Januar 1942: Eine Dokumentation zur Organisation der "Endlösung"* (Berlin, 1992), doc. 15.

20. Peter Longerich, *Politik der Vernichtung: Eine Gesamtdarstellung der nationalsozialistischen Judenverfolgung* (Munich, 1998); Bogdan Musial, *Deutsche Zivilverwaltung und Judenverfolgung im Generalgouvernement: Eine Fallstudie zum Distrikt Lublin 1939–1944* (Wiesbaden, 1999).

21. Michael Wildt, *Generation des Unbedingten: Das Führungskorps des Reichssicherheitshauptamtes* (Hamburg, 2003); Jürgen Matthäus, "Controlled Escalation: Himmler's Men in the Summer of 1941 and the Holocaust in the Occupied Soviet Territories," *Holocaust and Genocide Studies* 21, no. 2 (2007): 218–42.

22. On the local quality of decision-making, Longerich, *Politik der Vernichtung,* 440.

23. On Ustasha policies, see Alexander Korb, "Understanding Ustasha Violence," *Journal of Genocide Research* 12, nos. 1–2 (2010): 1–18.

24. Roger Petersen, *Understanding Ethnic Violence: Fear, Hatred, and Resentment in Twentieth Century Eastern Europe* (Cambridge, UK, 2002).

25. Ibid.; Dieter Pohl, "Schauplatz Ukraine," in *Ausbeutung, Vernichtung, Öffentlichkeit,* ed. Norbert Frei, Sybille Steinbacher, and Bernd Wagner (Munich, 2000), 135–73; Pohl, *Nationalsozialistische Judenverfolgung in Ostgalizien: Organisation und Durchführung eines staatlichen Massenverbrechens* (Munich, 1997), 43–67; Hans-Heinrich Wilhelm, "Antisemitismus im Baltikum," in *Die Normalität des Verbrechens: Bilanz und Perspektiven der Forschung zu den nationalsozialistischen Gewaltverbrechen,* ed. Helge Grabitz, Klaus Bästlein, and Johannes Tuchel (Berlin, 1994), 85–102.

26. See previous note. On Ukrainian nationalist antisemitism, see John-Paul Himka, "Ukrainian Collaboration in the Extermination of Jews during the Second World War," in *The Fate of the European Jews, 1939–1945: Continuity or Contingency,* ed. Jonathan Frankel (New York, 1997), 170–89.

27. Léon Poliakov, *The History of Anti-Semitism, Vol. IV* (Philadelphia, 2003), 274–78.

28. Ioanid, *The Holocaust in Romania,* 66–67.

29. Joseph Goebbels, *Die Tagebücher von Joseph Goebbels* ed. Elke Fröhlich (Munich, 1998), part II, vol. 1, 269. On the comparative scale of massacres, see Alexander V. Prusin, *The Lands Between: Conflict in the East European Borderlands, 1870–1992* (Oxford, 2010), 152–53.

30. Klaus-Michael Mallmann, "Der qualitative Sprung im Vernichtungsprozeß. Das Massaker von Kamenez-Podolsk Ende August 1941," *Jahrbuch für Antisemitismusforschung* 10 (2001): 239–64; Christopher R. Browning with Jürgen Matthäus, *The Origins of the Final Solution: The Evolution of Nazi Jewish Policy, 1939–1942* (Lincoln, 2004), 291.

31. Pohl, *Nationalsozialistische Judenverfolgung.*
32. Browning and Matthäus, *Origins,* 379, 406.
33. Browning and Matthäus, *Origins,* 404. This pronouncement had a number of precursors.
34. The arguments in the following paragraphs stem substantially from chapter 6 of Donald Bloxham, *The Final Solution: A Genocide* (Oxford, 2009).
35. Pätzold and Schwarz, eds., *Tagesordnung Judenmord,* doc. 24.
36. On the eve of the East Pakistan genocide of 1971, General Yahya Khan is reputed to have stated that the Bengalis would start eating out of Pakistan's hands were three million of them killed. Robert Payne, *Massacre: The Tragedy of Bangladesh and the Phenomenon of Mass Slaughter throughout History* (New York, 1973), 50.
37. On the Armenian case, see footnote 36 in Donald Bloxham, "Three Imperialisms and a Turkish Nationalism," *Patterns of Prejudice* 36, no. 4 (2002): 48.
38. For the horrific Hungarian anti-Jewish violence after Himmler's stop order, and the murderous forced-march deportations of around 76,000 Hungarian Jews for forced labor in the Reich from October 1944, see Bloxham, *The Final Solution,* 250–51, 253.
39. Bloxham, *The Final Solution,* ch. 6.

CHAPTER 13

Fascism and the Holocaust[1]

FEDERICO FINCHELSTEIN

In this chapter I want to explore the relations between intellectual history and political history vis-à-vis transnational approaches in historiography. My comments are rooted in my own research and theoretical experiences as an historian of transnational fascism and genocide.

I will first engage in a historiographical reading of fascism as a critical subject of global history. I will then deal with fascism's ultimate and more extreme realization, the Holocaust. Understood as the product of ideological global encounters, the Shoah poses significant challenges to the global history of ideology and politics.

It is somewhat puzzling that two historical formations that are contextually connected are generally not connected by historians.[2] This chapter aims to reconnect them. It attempts to establish a dialogue between two historical fields that often avoid talking to each other. Most historians of the Holocaust have overwhelmingly rejected the notion of fascism as a causal explanation for its intellectual genealogies. At the same time, many historians of fascism present the Holocaust as a particular event that is not central enough to fascist historiography.

My aim is not to domesticate Holocaust historiography under yet another grand narrative, as many historians of generic fascism tend to do, but rather to explore the intellectual and experiential links between the Holocaust and fascism. These links have been often downplayed by most historians of fascism and the Holocaust. In contrast, these links were highlighted by both victims and perpetrators. The Holocaust signals a central methodological dimension of the difficulties that fascist studies often encounter when they attempt to participate in global discussions about transnational history. I would argue that the transnational study of fascism and the Holocaust highlights the interplay between

Notes for this section begin on page 266.

the global and the national in history and historiography. In this context, establishing dialogical connections between the historiographies of fascism and the Holocaust can illuminate larger methodological trends in the field of history and the current attempts of historians to think the global and the political.[3]

As an ideology that found followers throughout the world, that is a globalized form of political ideology such as Marxism or liberalism, fascism has always been considered a global object of study. However, it has been traditionally presented as the target of a somewhat mutually exclusive methodological binary. Sometimes this binary of mutual exclusion appears to work in tandem with a classic division of labor among historians. According to this approach, many "working historians" test the hypothesis developed by a group of historical theorists, the generic historians of fascism. As a result, generic notions shape national understandings of fascism. At the same time, a transnational phenomenon like the Holocaust is displaced.

Such an understanding of fascism as a generic phenomenon is not new. Since its inception, fascism was theorized in many ways, quite often as a global puppet of capitalism or communism. However, in the 1960s and 1970s comparative studies of fascism stressed fascism's peculiarities, especially in terms of its many national particularities as well as its structural international similarities. Until the 1990s, this was the prevailing tendency among historians who were mainly working on national cases. Fascism was part of different national histories.[4] However, in the 1990s and early 2000s the study of fascism has consolidated as a distinctly global field of knowledge. This is a field that regards consensus as a structural foundation. In this view, historical progress is ascribed a sense of totality. Closure becomes a latent historiographical desire.[5]

Unlike their more focused predecessors, generic historians turn fascism into an ossified theory, ready to be used for cataloguing fascism according to its different national expressions. These historians present definitions of fascism which are often closed to further historical inquiry. They tend to consider specific cases of fascism as mere illustrations of their consensual definitions. This is not a truly global historiography. To be sure, it deals with fascism as a universal entity. However, most historians of Italian fascism in Italy, or of Latin American, Japanese, or German fascism in Germany, for example, do not participate in the generic consensus or even ignore its success among English readers interested in fascism. Generic fascism relies on a closed body of intra-textual references. As far as theory is concerned, self-referentiality is a defining mark of the generic scholarship. This does not seem to be a problem for generic historians insofar as they see studies of fascism as mere illustrations of their theories. Thus, global expressions of fascism are often presented as case studies that "qualify" as fascist within the framework of a variety of historical definitions. These are forms of "high theory" that defy global contextualization, especially with respect to the Holocaust and other genocides outside Europe.

In fact, such generic notions of fascism have a specific origin, a *Sonderweg* of sorts. The founding father of the generic school was the German historian Ernst Nolte in the 1960s. Nolte started his inquiry with a prefabricated definition that was highly influential for later generic historians who regarded him as "pioneer."[6] Nolte presents fascism as being primarily a dialectical reaction to liberalism, and more importantly to Marxism. The latter is for Nolte the consequential culmination of the former.[7] Nolte argues that Nazism is the synthetic form of fascism, something close to its ultimate realization. He defines Nazism as a platonic form of fascism: "National Socialism was the death throes of the sovereign, martial, inwardly antagonistic group; it was the practical and violent resistance to transcendence."[8]

Nolte continues by noting that transcendence is a metahistorical phenomenon that Nolte defines as "looking back on what has been and forward to what is coming, reaches out towards the whole."[9] It may be possible to note the Heideggerian undertones of Nolte's understanding of transcendence, notably as an integration of the possibility of "authenticity" with a functional "being" in the world.[10] In more specific terms, however, transcendence is a term that for Nolte relates to the historical in probing the "hidden structures of fascism." But is "resistance to transcendence" a more existential metamorphosis of anti-Marxism or of "the death throes of the sovereign, martial, inwardly antagonistic group"? For Nolte the three elements constitute the hierarchical levels of his generic understanding of fascism. Fascism as anti-Marxism is the historical phenomenological definition *per se*. In sharp contrast "the death throes of the sovereign, martial, inwardly antagonistic group" and "resistance to transcendence" are progressively ontological questions. Nolte affirms that the former is not within history but at its foundations and the latter is well beyond history. This distinction exemplifies Nolte's understanding of the relation between history and theory. In self-ascribed Hegelian fashion, Nolte understands theory as philosophy and history as an empirical science subjugated to theory. As an illustrative science, history provides theory with a phenomenological apparatus. And with its help Nolte theoretically defines fascism as a political phenomenon and more importantly as a metapolitical one. Nolte's "gift" to generic historians is not only in the field of the hypothesis (especially in terms of his understanding of fascism as a resistance to transcendence) but also in terms of the methodological. Nolte's view of history as an illustration is a rare methodological import for historians. Endowed with it, generic studies represent notorious attempts to bring closure to the question of the relationship between history and theory in historiography. History is all about illustrating abstract theoretical questions that surpass in importance and complexity the simple historical ones. Thus, for generic historians, fascism in its historical sense is less interesting than fascism in the metapolitical sense. In this context, historical cases of fascism and fascist theory are part of the history of fascism but they do not represent significant dimensions of the fascist phenomenon. They are perceived as manifestations of generic fascism's realizations.

Therefore, fascism as a generic object of study becomes a subject only when it is "ideal typed."[11] Examples of this paradigmatic displacement of agency (from fascist theory to historical theorists) are, to be sure, quite diverse and sometimes even opposed.[12] But most generic historians of fascism see their task as that of finding the "fascist minimum," a sort of Holy Grail of fascist historiography.[13] Ironically, this view coincides with Mussolini's own view about an essential kernel of fascism that transcended its more national and political connotations.[14] But generic scholars are not very interested in fascist self-understanding and its transnational notions of the abject in politics. They tend to reify important aspects of fascism such as notions of national rebirth, modernism and/or biopolitics. Thus, fascism is often unidimensionally presented as either exclusively focused on a form of radical nationalism that aims to renew the nation as well an example of political modernism and/or symbolic and corporal forms of political representation and repression.[15] Other generic historians, actually a minority of them, radically oppose action to theory.[16] For generic historians fascism can either be empty rhetoric or rhetoric as ideology.[17] In their varied generic narratives, these dichotomist understandings of praxis and theory tend to displace the peculiar intertwining of fascist theory and practice in the past. This radical connection between action and theory is what I would call experiential ideology. Although this connection was not specific to fascism, it was with fascism that it became radicalized in an extremely novel political formation. I understand experiential ideology as one of the most significant aspects of transnational fascism, in other words, how and why fascists acted out ideological constructs through extreme forms of violence. Violence became the ultimate form of theory. This fascist connection between ideology and practice defies generic notions which are not sufficiently anchored in the past insofar as the fascist ideological experience was embedded in a historical agency. It is precisely this agency that these historians tend to displace. Interpretative experiences complicate the linearity of hindsight-based definitions.

Let me turn to the question of fascism and victimization in the context of the Holocaust. The Holocaust might be the first transnational experience of genocide and for this reason still poses, and it is symptomatic of, the problems and perspectives opened by a critical global history of fascism. By the end of the Holocaust, Argentine writer Jorge Luis Borges thought of Nazi ideology as a theory of violence. In 1945 Borges considered violence, literally, as fascist ideology. Borges also realized that the victims of this radical form of political violence—the Jewish otherness in the Holocaust case—were turned into sacrificial objects. For the Borgesean Nazi character, Camp commander Zur Linde, for example, the fascist body and the national organism are sacrificial objects as well. Moreover, for Zur Linde the sacrifice of the fascist self is, in a sense, even a more significant source of ideological self-determination through violence.

Before being executed by the Allies, Zur Linde argues that: "An inexorable epoch is spreading over the world. We forged it, we who are already its victim. What matters if England is the hammer and we the anvil, so long as violence reigns and not servile Christian timidity? If victory and injustice and happiness are not for Germany, let them be for other nations. Let heaven exist, even though our dwelling place is Hell. I look at myself in the mirror to discover who I am, to discern how I will act in a few hours, when I am face to face with death. My flesh may be afraid; I am not."[18]

In Borges's view, the Nazi idea of the sacrifice of the Jews implied for Hitler's followers an end in itself, namely bare physical violence.[19] For a fascism that transcended national borders and cultures, the Jew represented absolute darkness. This violence is presented as a naked innate form of authenticity but, according to Borges's interpretation, it leads to an ideological maelstrom.

Fascism ends when it achieves its ideological sacred imperative of violence. It ends with the sacrifice, the destruction of the fascist self. Fascism is fully entropic. Entropy leads to the destruction of reason as exemplified in the split between the flesh and the ego in the body and memory of Zur Linde. The killing of the ego is the result of the over-determination of the forces of desire in politics, the equation of authenticity with victimization, sacrifice, and violence. For Borges this is a wrong kind of universalism, the fascist international that aims to establish violence through victimization as the only politics.

Some years before, Sigmund Freud considered Nazi victimization as a central element of global fascist ideology, especially in terms of its mythical ideological formations and its reification of desire over reason.[20] Both the Argentine Borges and the Austrian Freud considered the Nazi victimization of Jews as an essential element of fascist ideology. To be sure, their view was more sophisticated than the more simplistic view shared by the majority of their fellow antifascists. For the latter, fascism was simply an evil, a brute yet silly aberration from normative politics. Fascism had no ideology.[21] Borges and Freud postulated the opposite view. Fascism was above all a radical ideological event that threatened enlightened civilization. The reasons for this distinctive perspective in the context of antifascism were especially related to the Borgesean and Freudian emphasis on antisemitism as a central source of ideological fulfillment in Nazi ideology, as well as their inclusion of the latter within a broader fascist notion of desire and the unconscious.

It was in the camps that the ideological implications of fascist ideology were first experienced and later interpreted. Jean Améry, an anti-fascist and a member of the resistance against Nazism, would talk of "real fascism and singular Nazism."[22] Améry was concerned about the spread of under-contextualized theories of fascism that reduced fascist ideologies to common generalities or worse. They used fascism to conflate political movements and regimes of various kinds with the radical victimizing dimensions of Nazism.[23] For Améry, "Hitler-fascism was not an idea at all, but depravity."[24]

The tendency to identify fascism with Nazism was widespread during the time of the Holocaust, especially among the victims. In the Warsaw Ghetto, for example, Chaim Kaplan used it to aptly explain the Nazi-fascist attempt to create a new world order.[25] For Kaplan, this world order clearly posed victimization as an ideology of conquest and persecution. In contrast, for historians of the Holocaust, the limits of historiographical notions of fascism and Nazism explained the need to exclude fascism altogether as an analytical tool for understanding the Holocaust. As a result many historians often overlooked the actual ideological connections between the global intellectual history of fascism and the historical conditions for the Holocaust.

Primo Levi, who became a member of a fascist youth group in 1924 when he was only 5, came to realize the victimizing implications of the Italian variant of fascism. He saw and experienced the grip of fascism from the perspectives of substantially different "gray zoned" subject positions, namely semi-mandatory fascist youth, onlooker, anti-fascist and Jewish victim. For Levi, the "exaltation of violence" opened the way to the fascist ideological attack against reason. Levi, who conceived Nazism as the "German version of fascism," saw the former as a radical version of fascist ideology. The camps were the model for the fascist "New Order."[26]

Levi reflected on the sacrificial aspects of fascist violence. Fascist violence had the ultimate aim of destroying the humanity of the self. Levi traced the continuum of fascist violence from the Italian fascist squads of 1922 to Auschwitz: "The Blackshirts had not just killed Turin's trade unionists, Communists and Socialists. First they made them drink half a kilo of castor oil. In this way a man is reduced to tatters, is no longer human.... There's a direct connection between the Turin massacres [of 1922] and the entry ceremony in the Nazi camps, where they stripped, destroyed your personal photographs, shaved your head, tattooed you on the arm." He concluded: "This was the demolition of man; this is Fascism."[27]

Fascists across the globe shared this view albeit not its ethico-political implications. For the fascists the victimization of the enemy was another example of the centrality, and desirability, of violence in fascist ideology. Mussolini, the Argentine and Brazilian fascists, or the Romanian fascists considered the enemy to be a defining character of their own notion of the self.[28] In short, Jews and other enemies defined what the fascists were not, and by opposition, what they actually were.

Not all fascist ideologies were as radical as Nazism in terms of their negative and nonetheless projective self-identification with the enemy. Similarly, other forms of fascism were not as extreme in terms of their desire, their "will," to put their fantasies about violence and victimization in practice. For most "sources" living during the time of fascism (1919–1945), Nazism was a peculiarly radical version of fascism. In other words, Nazism was "German fascism." This appreciation was shared by most fascists and anti-fascists. After the war and the Holocaust, this experiential conceptualization of fascist ideology was displaced by newer forms of historical meaning making and selective post-war memory processes. Whereas before 1945, global fascism served the purpose of illuminating the global ideological implications of Nazi processes of victimization, after 1945 fascism as an explanatory device often obscured central dimensions of the Shoah experience, especially those of its victims.

After the war and until recently, fascism and Nazism were generally conflated. This conflation buttressed a form of collective silence about the identities of the victims of the Holocaust and hence the ideological peculiarities of Nazi persecution. This was the case when these notions of generic fascism were embraced either in Western or in Eastern Europe.[29] In the East and the West the inclusion of Nazism within global fascism, and/or global totalitarianism, served the purpose of downplaying the main features of Nazi victimization.

Generic fascism obliterated the history and memory of victims. It also obscured the particularities of transnational fascism as it was understood at the time of the Shoah. Most historians of fascism and the Holocaust presented an uncritical take on this transnational peculiarity of fascism. In fact, they often ended up mutually excluding their respective fields of knowledge. They replaced a mutually inclusive living field of ideological experiences and genocidal practices in the past with definitions, glossaries, and "high theory" from the present.

In light of this exclusion and due to the absence of any meaningful approach to the Holocaust by generic historians, historians of the Holocaust have concluded that fascism has no connection whatsoever with Nazism.[30] For example, Saul Friedländer stresses the singularity of what he aptly calls Nazi redemptive antisemitism. Friedländer emphasizes the pseudo-religious dimension of the Holocaust, saying the extermination was a "sacred end and not a means to other ends."[31] Friedländer concludes that no similar trait can be found in other countries.[32] In Friedländer's *Nazi Germany and the Jews* and *The Years of Extermination*, the global history of Nazi endeavors is explained through the enactment and reception of Nazi policies, both nationally and internationally. To be sure, Friedländer states that the Holocaust "is an integral part of 'the age of ideology.'" But he also clearly differentiates between global fascism "in Italy and elsewhere" and Nazism in Germany. In other words, for him fascism can be a transnational ideology but not in Germany. The canonic status of Friedländer's work is especially related to its emphasis on the experience of the victims. In this context, the lack of references to fascism as experienced and interpreted by the victims is surprising. This is a result of what Amos Goldberg has presented as the book's overwhelmingly cogent "melodramatic" narrative and the sense that victims could not do anything about their genocidal destiny.[33] I would argue that as a result of this melodramatic stress the victims' political interpretations of global ideology are not significant enough in Friedländer's approach. The intellectual history of global interpretations of fascism could provide another angle for thinking the Nazi transnational project of conquest and destruction, especially in terms of how it was interpreted by its victims.

Developing transnational approaches outside the framework of the Nazi empire seems to be anathema in Holocaust historiography. However, the adoption of a global historical approach to Nazism may not necessarily mean a general downplaying of the Holocaust as a unique event in history.[34] Eurocentrism, which is also a trademark of many generic studies, plays an important role in current pleas for uniqueness in Holocaust historiography, and Friedländer is not an exception. Whereas Africans and also Arabs experienced an equally unique brand of Italian racism in the forms of mustard gases and other chemical weapons, summary executions, and killings of civilians, the Nazis executed one of the most extreme events in history. In short, it was a radical departure, a turning point in history. But empire, fascism, and racism link the Holocaust with the world outside Europe. More recently many historians of Nazism have focused on German, and European, imperialism as a central precursor of the Nazi genocide in the East.[35] All in all, as Arendt suggested many years ago in her *The Origins of Totalitarianism*, global ideologies and imperialism are central elements of the history and pre-history of fascism and the Holocaust.[36]

To be sure, historians of the Holocaust are not alone in dismissing global fascism as an actor in the Holocaust. In fact, historians of fascism like Renzo De Felice,[37] Gilbert Allardyce,[38] and Zeev Sternhell[39] have stressed the peculiarities of Nazism vis-à-vis fascism. In turn, Friedländer and Yehuda Bauer bluntly suggested the inadequacy of global fascism as a conceptual tool for understanding the Holocaust.[40] These arguments are especially powerful when confronting generic theories of fascism. But their explanatory power lapses when they are contrasted with the ideological experiences of victims and perpetrators. The result of this mutual exclusion of Holocaust and fascist studies is that the Holocaust and fascism are not studied as partaking of a single global context of radical ideological politics.

Whereas Holocaust historiography often sees the study of fascism as a threat to its claims on historical uniqueness, fascist historiography generally sees the study of the Holocaust as a menace to its methodological imperative to enforce definitions. This mutually excluding dual perspective downplays contextual notions of ideology during the period of global fascism. At the same time, and paradoxically, this historical perspective avoids the study of the empirical connections between fascist sources across Europe and beyond. On one hand most historians of the Holocaust did not study the ideological links between Nazism and other fascisms.[41] On the other hand, most historians of fascism studied these connections without taking into account Nazism's most fateful and distinctive feature: the extermination of the Jews in Europe. I would argue that it would be important to engage these historiographies and unmake their politics of mutual exclusion.

By establishing a critical dialogical exchange between these two converging and yet mutually exclusive historical fields, I attempt to highlight the problems of "high theory" and closure in historiographical formations. The premise here is to put in question this mutual exclusivity while at the same time, paradoxically, enforcing some important boundaries between the two historical phenomena of fascism and the Holocaust. Thus, it is important to stress the connections between the theory and ideological experience of fascism vis-à-vis the history and historiography of the Holocaust. While it is also important to state significant distinctions, I emphasize the relational nature of these two historical experiences but also explore the conceptual limitations that theories of fascism face when confronted with limit events such as the Holocaust.

The Holocaust poses a challenge to generic theories of fascism. It also provides an opportunity for thinking the ideological and aesthetic dimensions of fascism and its conceptual representations, especially with respect to fascist genocidal notions of the abject, sacrifice, and the sacred. In this regard, Dominick LaCapra has called our attention to the global role played by ideological processes of victimization in fascism, Nazism, and the Holocaust. LaCapra questions the denial of the relevance of ideology that misleadingly confines ideology to its traditional understanding as an articulated system of beliefs.[42] Fascist ideology, which rejected reason, simply did not work in this way. As Emilio Gentile argues, "[T]he connection between experience and ideology is particularly important in fascism, which maintained from its birth the characteristic of anti-ideological-ideology, an ideology, in other words, which asserted the predominance of action and experience over the theoretical systems of rational ideologies."[43]

For Gentile, the "sacred" aspects of fascism speak to this fascist rejection of theory.[44] Similarly, LaCapra argues that it is essential to rethink the sacralizing dimensions of fascism as centrally connected with its ideological formations: "I would note … that to the extent fascism and especially Nazism arguably have a significant relation to the religious and the sacred, it is, I think, more to a specific form of the immanent sacred, especially when the latter is absolutized and bound up with a quest for total purity that may generate anxiety about contamination and prompt a turn to rituals, including purifying and sacrificial rituals that get rid of phobic, anxiety-producing, typically scapegoated others."[45]

By putting this question at the front of his work, LaCapra displaces the focus of current historiographical approaches.[46] Works on the question of fascism and the sacred by George Mosse, Emilio Gentile, Michael Burleigh, Roger Griffin, Stanley Payne or Roger Eatwell, for example, present the connections between fascism and religion as a mutually excluding binary of sorts. Fascism's connection with the sacred is either about (1) the relations between fascism and formal institutional religions such as Catholicism or Protestantism or (2) the notion of fascism as a form of political religion.[47] Fascism is part of a process of secularization where religious spaces are occupied by modern political parties. Religion is not abandoned, but the actors change. The party replaces the church. For Gentile, "Fascism was a political religion, with its own set of beliefs and dogmas" which "intended to define the meaning and the goal of existence, creating a new political cult centered on the sacralization of the fascist state and on the myth of the Duce, with a tight sequence of collective rites to celebrate the big events of its 'sacred history.'"[48]

For Mosse and Gentile, fascism was characterized by religious forms (language and rituals) that fascism borrowed from institutional religion. In this sense, they see fascism as a radical moment in the history of secularization.[49] For most historians, fascism is a political religion, which simply means that fascists thought of their movement as a displaced form of religion, namely a fanatic political faith. For these authors, fascism as a political religion is just a radical form of politics.[50] Thus, whereas liberal politics presents mild sacralizing aspects, fascism pushes them to the extreme. In contrast, LaCapra shows how the fascist notion of the sacred is intrinsically related to processes of victimization. These processes are complex in both theoretical and contextual terms. The Holocaust is their ultimate outcome.

The radical sacred violence of the Holocaust, as it was understood by its perpetrators, transformed genocidal ideological motivation into a form of elation.[51] This ideological status of violence as a sublime object of fascist desire presents, as LaCapra argues, one of the most extreme dimensions of fascist ideology. It went beyond notions of civic religion. This violence is not reactionary, but it signals the complexity of the fascist bridging of politics and the sacred. For LaCapra, Nazi "post-secular dimensions do not represent some regression to barbarism, much less 'brutishness,' but instead make up what might be termed a constitutive outside of 'modernity'—what is inside modernity as its uncanny repressed or disavowed other."[52] In LaCapra's view fascism represents a further displacement of the secular into the sacred. Against standard theories of secularization, for LaCapra these reoccupations present the possibility of a post-secular fascist ideology.[53]

Elsewhere I have argued that structural violence was a mark of fascism and found its best expression in the war ideal and the concentration camps. I have intimated that fascism brandished power and violence as ideological aims rather than means. In fascist ideology violence exceeds the instrumental and becomes a form of creative intuition, of creation. Fascism renders politics an almost sacred field of action, and in this context violence is perceived as an ethical force that helps fascism achieve a radical break from ordinary concerns.[54]

Violence played a central role in fascism. In their radical display of raw, unmediated physical violence, Nazis pushed the fascist experience to the extreme. In a sense, they became fully different from other forms of fascism. However, fascism exercised its genocidal potential by engaging in genocidal practices in Italian fascist Africa or in Civil War Spain. Global fascism (from France to the

Ukraine) also collaborated in the Nazi Final Solution by providing logistic support and killers. However, Nazism presents a radical departure from other fascist formations. Nazism is not a generic "ideal type" of fascism but its most radical possibility.

The focus on the victims of fascism, and their reception and interpretation of global fascist ideologies, could help historians of fascism and the Holocaust. This focus could move historiography beyond the ongoing focus on generic notions that neglect anti-fascist readings of fascism and at the same time downplay the experiential notion of fascist perpetrators, including the Nazis.

After Borges, Freud, and Levi and many other theorists who were contemporaries of fascism, a distinctive group of critical theories examined the Holocaust as an event that posed central questions to ongoing conceptualizations of history and ideology. The Holocaust epitomizes the radical possibility of a politics of evil. As seen by commentators ranging from Hannah Arendt to the Frankfurt School and Alain Badiou to Slavoj Žižek and Jürgen Habermas and Axel Honneth, fascist ideology constituted part of the explanation.[55] Thus, a variety of critical theorists have used history to illustrate critical notions of modernity that were intrinsically related to fascism and the Holocaust. For them, these events were mutually engaged both in terms of their phenomenological dimensions and in terms of their manifold conceptual layers of historical meaning. The near absence of historians from these engagements is quite remarkable. Even historians who emphasized the centrality of ideology—that as we have seen was often noted by the sources during the period—tend to neglect the ideological processes that genetically connected fascist ideological configurations to the Holocaust.

Dwelling on the similarities and differences in terms of racism and victimization makes historical comparison not useless but necessary, even if one aims to stress differences across the globe. Thus, one limitation underlying many works of Holocaust historiography is that they tend to suggest the futility of any transnational comparison of fascist-like movements and regimes at all. In this view, Nazism was not part of a global ideological formation but rather a German form of extreme antisemitism. Generic theories of fascism provide the dialectical antithesis, and fascism as a global ideology is more significant than national singularities or events, the Holocaust included. This is manifested with forms of historical "high theory." Uncanny, or self-interrogating concepts or events are downplayed or literally put aside. In this context, critical questions relating the Holocaust to fascism are left behind. It would be useful to take a genealogical view of this process of canon formation among historians. As it happened after the war, but now further away from this context of emergence, abstract notions of fascism serve the function of downplaying historical experience, especially the experiences of the victims of fascism. This detachment domesticates the history of fascism, depriving it of its transnational dimensions as a global ideology.

Notes

1. I would like to thank Dominick LaCapra, Ben Brower, Amos Goldberg, Andrew Sartori, Sam Moyn, Manu Bhagavan, Gary Wilder, and Janaki Bakhle for their comments on previous versions of this text.

2. There are significant exceptions among historians of fascism who have explored the connections between fascism and Nazism, as well as those related to the Holocaust. I see this chapter as an elaborative complement to these works. See, for example, Tim Mason, *Nazism, Fascism and the Working Class* (Cambridge, UK, 1995); Geoff Eley, "What Produces Fascism: Preindustrial Traditions or a Crisis of a Capitalist State?" *Politics and Society* 12, no. 1 (1983): 53–82; Enzo Traverso, *Understanding the Nazi Genocide: Marxism after Auschwitz* (London, 1999); Enzo Collotti, *Fascismo, fascismi* (Florence, 1997); George Mosse, *The Fascist Revolution: Toward a General Theory of Fascism* (New York, 1998).

3. On transnational and comparative history see Deborah Cohen and Maura O'Connor, eds., *Comparison and History: Europe in Cross-National Perspective* (New York, 2004). For other approaches to transnational history and comparative issues, see Ann Laura Stoler and Frederick Cooper, "Between Metropole and Colony: Rethinking a Research Agenda," and Samuel Truett and Elliott Young, "Making Transnational History: Nations, Regions, and Borderlands," in *Continental Crossroads: Remapping U.S.-Mexico Borderlands History,* ed. Samuel Truett and Elliott Young (Durham, 2004), 1–32; Carmen de la Guardia and Juan Pan-Montojo, "Reflexiones sobre una Historia Transnacional," *Studia histórica (Historia contemporánea)* 16 (1998); Carlotta Sorba et al., "Sguardi transnazionali" *Contemporanea* 1 (2004): 97–12; Daniel Rodgers, Frederick Cooper, Pierre-Yves Saunier, Michael Werner, and Bénédicte Zimmerman, "Penser l'histoire croisée: entre empirie et réflexivité," *Annales. Histoire, sciences sociales* 58 (2003): 7–36; Gunilla Budde, Sebastian Conrad, and Oliver Janz, eds., *Transnationale Geschichte: Themen, Theorien, Tendenzen* (Göttingen, 2006). On the conceptualization of political history, see Pierre Rosanvallon, "Para una historia conceptual de lo político (nota de trabajo)," *Prismas. Revista de historia intelectual* 6 (2002): 123–33; Pierre Rosanvallon, *Democracy Past and Future* (New York, 2006). For a study of Rosanvallon's place in historiography, see Samuel Moyn's introduction to the book. See also Elias J. Palti, "Temporalidad y refutabilidad de los conceptos políticos," *Prismas. Revista de historia intelectual* 9 (2005).

4. See, for example, Eugen Weber, *Varieties of Fascism: Doctrines of Revolution in the Twentieth Century* (New York, 1964); Walter Laqueur and George Mosse, eds., *International Fascism, 1920–1945* (New York, 1966); S. J. Woolf, ed., *European Fascism* (New York, 1969); Walter Laqueur, ed., *Fascism: A Reader's Guide* (Berkeley, 1976). For an overview of the historiography see Wolfgang Wippermann, *Faschismustheorien. Die Entwicklung der Diskussion von den Anfängen bis heute* (Darmstadt, 1997); Renzo De Felice, *Interpretations of Fascism* (Cambridge, MA, 1977); Emilio Gentile, *Fascismo. Storia e interpretazione* (Rome-Bari, 2002).

5. See, for example, Roger Griffin, "The Primacy of Culture. The Current Growth (or Manufacture) of Consensus within Fascist Studies," *Journal of Contemporary History* 37, no. 1 (2002): 21–43; Stanley G. Payne, "Historical Fascism and the Radical Right," *Journal of Contemporary History* 35, no. 1 (2000): 111; Roger Griffin, ed., *International Fascism: Theories, Causes and the New Consensus* (London, 1998); Roger Eatwell, "Towards a New Model of Generic Fascism," *Journal of Theoretical Politics* 4, no. 2 (1992): 161–94; Aristotle Kallis, "Studying Inter-War Fascism in Epochal and Diachronic Terms: Ideological Production, Political Experience and the Quest for 'Consensus,'" *European History Quarterly* 34, no. 1 (2004): 9–42.

6. Ernst Nolte is famous, and often infamous, among Holocaust historians for having generated the *Historiskerstreit,* that is, the debate among West German historians and critical theorists regarding the German character of the Holocaust. For a variety of reasons, including time and space, I will not deal here with Nolte's most recent position vis-à-vis the subject. Nonetheless my analysis will insist on the somewhat diachronic recognition of the continuities in Nolte's polemical stance with respect to the genetic nature of fascism and Marxism. This is a position that first led him to the minimization of fascism as an event not born out of right-wing traditions but from Marxism and then to the minimization of Nazi extermination policies against the European

Jewish population. See Ernst Nolte, *La guerra civil europea, 1917–1945. Nacionalsocialismo y bolchevismo* (México, 1994), original edition: *Der europäische Bürgerkrieg 1917–1945: Nationalsozialismus und Bolschewismus* (Berlin, 1987). See François Furet and Ernst Nolte, *Fascism and Communism* (Lincoln, 2001.) For Nolte and the *Historikerstreit*, see the texts translated by James Knowlton and Truett Cates, eds., *Forever in the Shadow of Hitler? Original Documents of the Historikerstreit, the Controversy Concerning the Singularity of the Holocaust* (Atlantic Highlands, NJ, 1993). For an analysis for this debate, see Dominick LaCapra, *Representing the Holocaust: History, Theory, Trauma* (Ithaca, 1994), 49–50, 53, 106, and 190 and *History and Memory after Auschwitz* (Ithaca, 1998), 55–59 and 64–65; María Pía Lara, *Narrating Evil: A Postmetaphysical Theory of Reflective Judgment* (New York, 2007); Matthew G. Specter, *Habermas: An Intellectual Biography* (Cambridge, UK, 2010). On Nolte as a pioneer for generic historians, see, for example, Aristotle Kallis, "Fascism—A 'Generic' Concept?" in *The Fascism Reader*, ed. Aristotle Kallis (London, 2003), 46.

7. Nolte argues that if fascism as anti-Marxism aims to "exterminate its opponent, it cannot be satisfied with the mere political defeat of a recognizable party: it must expose the 'spiritual roots' and include them in its condemnation." In Nolte's view even the exterminatory drive of the Nazis was taken after the Soviets. Fascism as a reaction against Marxism is a revolutionary reaction for it aims to change the world that surrounds it. Ernst Nolte, *Three Faces of Fascism: Action Française, Italian Fascism, National Socialism* (New York, 1969), 51, 81.

8. Nolte, *Three Faces of Fascism*, 529.

9. Ibid., 540.

10. In this sense Nolte's approach may be inscribed within the framework of Heidegger's complex relation with post-humanism. LaCapra suggests that Heidegger among others might be seen as an anthropocentric posthumanist who remains within a traditional framework of assumptions about the human. Thus, for LaCapra, Heidegger's critique of humanism and the very term "human" still has an anthropocentric set of assumptions that are related to his view of other animals as well. For this reading of Heidegger, see LaCapra, *Representing the Holocaust*, 158, and LaCapra, *History and Its Limits: Human, Animal, Violence* (Ithaca, 2009). There is another sense in which transcendence and, even the Noltean sense of authenticity, could be as well equated with the progressive Kantian notion of history and its relation to man's release from self-incurred tutelage. This seems to be the interpretation put forward by George Mosse in his perceptive criticism of Nolte; see Mosse's review of Nolte's *Three Faces of Fascism* in *Journal of the History of Ideas* 27, no. 4 (1966): 621–63. See also Immanuel Kant, "What is Enlightenment?" in *On History* (Indianapolis, 1979), 3–10.

11. Griffin presents his own view of fascism as a "consciously constructed ideal type of fascism which sets up to be more heuristically useful to academic research than existing ones." Griffin, *The Nature of Fascism* (New York, 1991), 12; Stanley Payne, *A History of Fascism 1914–1945* (Madison, 1995), 4. For a criticism of Griffin in this regard, see Daniel Woodley, *Fascism and Political Theory: Critical Perspectives on Fascist Ideology* (London, 2010), 8–13.

12. As we have seen for Nolte, fascism is in itself a form of political and metaphysical resistance to transcendence. This resistance is itself imbued with an apparent authenticity that for Nolte is equally transcendental in the metapolitical sense. For Payne, fascism is a radically antagonistic form of revolutionary ultra-nationalism with a vitalist philosophy, vertical conceptions of leadership, war, violence, and mass mobilization. For Roger Griffin, generic fascism is essentially focused on national rebirth, what he calls the palingenetic myth, as a form of historical modernist resistance to liberalism. For Griffin, fascism is both political and metapolitical. For Paxton, fascism is "a form of political behavior marked by obsessive preoccupation with community, decline, humiliation, or victimhood and by compensatory cults of unity, energy and purity, in which a mass-based party of committed nationalist militants, working in uneasy but effective collaboration with traditional elites, abandons democratic liberties and pursues with redemptive violence and without ethical or legal restraints goals of internal cleansing and external expansion." Payne, *A History of Fascism 1914–1945*, 14; Roger Griffin, *Modernism and Fascism: The Sense of a Beginning under Mussolini and Hitler* (London, 2007), xv, 332; Griffin, *The Nature of Fascism*; Robert O. Paxton, *The Anatomy of Fascism* (New York, 2004), 219.

13. See Griffin, *The Nature of Fascism,* and his *A Fascist Century* (London, 2008). See also Payne, *A History of Fascism 1914–1945* and his previous *Fascism. Comparison and Definition* (Madison, 1980), 167–76; Paxton, *The Anatomy of Fascism;* Roger Eatwell, "On Defining the 'Fascist Minimum': the Centrality of Ideology," *Journal of Political Ideologies* 1 (1996), 303–19; Aristotle Kallis, *Fascist Ideology: Territory and Expansion in Italy and Germany (1919–1945)* (London, 2000).

14. Federico Finchelstein, "On Fascist Ideology," *Constellations: An International Journal of Critical and Democratic Theory* 15, no. 3 (2008): 320–31.

15. For some sophisticated recent examples, see Griffin, *Modernism and Fascism,* and Aristotle Kallis, *Genocide and Fascism: the Eliminationist Drive in Fascist Europe* (London, 2008).

16. See, for example, Paxton, *The Anatomy of Fascism,* 16, 19, 53. In his excellent study, Paxton often establishes a dichotomy between practice and theory (ideas). By the end, of the book, however, he states that fascist ideas are better explained by focusing on fascist practice: "I believe that the ideas that underlie fascist actions are best deduced from those actions." To be sure, as Paxton argues, fascist actions were often conceived as forms of ideological actualization. Practice in his view can be an implicit idea. But Paxton does not consider explicit fascist ideas (and there were many of them) as highly significant. For a criticism of Paxton in this regard, see Zeev Sternhell, "How to Think about Fascism and its Ideology," *Constellations: An International Journal of Critical and Democratic Theory* 15, no. 3 (2008): 280–90.

17. Generic historian Aristotle Kallis tries to combine theory and practice without sufficiently emphasizing the fluidity of both constructs in the fascist context. He sees fascism as a combination of mutually excluding variables from theory to praxis. The result is an ideal type of fascism that constructs fascism as the sum of rhetoric as ideology and empirical data related to its institutional traits. See his thought-provoking *Fascist Ideology.*

18. See Jorge Luis Borges, "Deutsches Requiem," in Borges, *Obras Completas* (Buenos Aires, 1996), vol.1, 581; Jorge Luis Borges, *Labyrinths* (New York, 1964), 147. On Borges and Zur Linde, see my *El Canon del Holocausto* (Buenos Aires, 2010) ch. 4.

19. For historical reflections on the role of bare violence in history, see Benjamin Brower, "Force of Empire," working paper. See also Etienne Balibar, "Outlines of a Topography of Cruelty: Citizenship and Civility in the Era of Global Violence," *Constellations: An International Journal of Critical and Democratic Theory* 8, no. 1 (2001): 15–29; Martin Jay, *Refractions of Violence* (New York, 2003); LaCapra, *History and Its Limits.* For an excellent analysis of Nazism's genealogy of violence, see Enzo Traverso, *The Origins of Nazi Violence* (New York, 2003). See also Angelo Ventrone, *La seduzione totalitaria. Guerra, modernità, violenza politica (1914–1918)* (Rome, 2003), and Francisco Sevillano Calero, *Exterminar. El terror con Franco* (Madrid, 2004); Philippe Burrin, *Nazi Antisemitism* (New York, 2005).

20. See Federico Finchelstein, "Fascism Becomes Desire: On Freud, Mussolini and Transnational Politics," in *The Transnational Unconscious,* ed. Mariano Plotkin and Joy Damousi (London, 2009), 97–125.

21. On antifascism and its view of fascism see Benedetto Croce, *Scritti e discorsi politici, 1943–1947* (Bari, 1963), vol. 1, 7; vol. 2, 46, 357. See also Renzo De Felice, *Interpretations of Fascism* (Cambridge, MA, 1977), 14–23; Pier Giorgio Zunino, *Interpretazione e memoria del fascismo: gli anni del regime* (Rome, 1991), 11–142; Zunino, *La Repubblica e il suo passato: il fascismo dopo il fascismo, il comunismo, la democrazia: le origini dell'Italia contemporanea* (Bologna, 2003); Enzo Collotti, ed., *Fascismo e antifascismo: Rimozioni, revisioni, negazioni* (Rome-Bari, 2000); Filippo Focardi, *La guerra della memoria. La Resistenza nel dibattito politico italiano dal 1945 a oggi* (Rome-Bari, 2005); Leonardo Paggi, "Antifascism and the Reshaping of the Democratic Consensus in Post-1945 Italy," *New German Critique* 67 (1996): 101–10; Claudio Pavone, *Alle origini della Repubblica. Scritti su fascismo, antifascismo, e la continuità dello stato* (Turin, 1995); "La Resistenza in Italia: alcuni nodi interpretativi," *Ricerche di Storia Politica* 5, no. 1 (2002): 31–38.

22. Jean Améry, *At the Mind's Limits* (Bloomington, 1980), x.

23. Ibid., ix–x.

24. Ibid., 31.

25. Chaim Kaplan, *Scroll of Agony: The Warsaw Diary of Chaim A. Kaplan* (New York, 1973), 280–81.

26. Primo Levi, *The Black Hole of Auschwitz* (London, 2005), 8, 33, 72.

27. Ian Thomson, *Primo Levi* (London, 2002), 26–27.

28. On notions of the enemy, see Enzo Traverso, *À feu et à sang. De la guerre civile européenne (1914–1915)* (Paris, 2007); Federico Finchelstein, *Transatlantic Fascism: Ideology, Violence and the Sacred in Argentina and Italy, 1919–1945* (Durham, 2010), and Angelo Ventrone, *Il Nemico Interno. Immagini, parole e simboli della lotta politica nell'Italia del Novecento* (Rome, 2005).

29. See Enzo Traverso, *Le Passé, modes d'emploi: Histoire, memoire, politique* (Paris, 2005).

30. In this sense, it is interesting to note generic historians' tendency to disengage from recent, and not so recent, debates in Holocaust historiography. For many of them, the approach of Daniel Goldhagen seems to be a fruitful approach to the Holocaust. This is a symptomatic aspect of an elective affinity between approaches that reduce their topic to their formulaic explanations. See for example Kallis, *Genocide and Fascism*, 6–7, 27.

31. Saul Friedländer, "Nazism: Fascism or Totalitarianism," in *The Rise of the Nazi Regime: Historical Reassessments*, ed. Charles S. Maier, Stanley Hoffmann, and Andrew Gould (Boulder, 1986), 30. See also Friedländer, *Memory, History, and the Extermination of the Jews of Europe* (Bloomington, 1993), 26; Friedländer, "Mosse's Influence on the Historiography of the Holocaust," in *What History Tells: George L. Mosse and the Culture of Modern Europe*, ed. Stanley G. Payne, David J. Sorkin, and John S. Tortorice (Madison, 2004), 142.

32. Friedländer pushes his point radically enough so as to limit any kind of comparison. In his critique of the work of the German historian Wolfgang Schieder, Friedlander argues: "and a point, on which it seems useless to dwell, Nazi anti-Semitism has been compared to the 'racism' of Italian fascists toward Africans, slaves, and the Germans of southern Tyrol." Friedländer, "Nazism: Fascism or Totalitarianism," 27. For a more nuanced approach, see Ian Kershaw, *Hitler, the Germans and the Final Solution* (New Haven, 2008), 345.

33. See Saul Friedländer, *Nazi Germany and the Jews: The Years of Persecution, 1933–1939* (New York, 1998), and *The Years of Extermination* (New York, 2007), xvii, 69–70. Before the appearance of Amos Golberg's pathbreaking essay, most historians did not criticize Friedländer's book rendering his book an almost "ideal typical" canonic artifact. See Amos Goldberg, "The Victim's Voice and Melodramatic Esthetics in History," *History and Theory* 48, no. 3 (2009): 220–37.

34. For important works on these connections, see A. Dirk Moses, ed., *Empire, Colony, Genocide: Conquest, Occupation, and Subaltern Resistance in World History* (New York, 2008); Dan Michman, *Holocaust Historiography: A Jewish Perspective. Conceptualizations, Terminology, Approaches and Fundamental Issues* (London, 2003); Jean-Michel Chaumont, *La concurrence des victimes. Génocides, identité, reconnaissance* (Paris, 2002); Omer Bartov, *Mirrors of Destruction. War, Genocide and Modern Identity* (New York, 2000); Marcello Flores, *Tutta la violenza di un secolo* (Milan, 2005); Dan Stone, *History, Memory and Mass Atrocity: Essays on the Holocaust and Genocide* (London, 2006); Richard H. King and Dan Stone, eds., *Hannah Arendt and the Uses of History: Imperialism, Nation, Race and Genocide* (New York, 2007); A. Dirk Moses and Dan Stone, eds., *Colonialism and Genocide* (London, 2007).

35. Matthew P. Fitzpatrick, "The Pre-History of the Holocaust? The *Sonderweg* and *Historikerstreit* Debates and the Abject Colonial Past," *Central European History* 41, no. 3 (2008): 477–503; Edward Ross Dickinson, "The German Empire: an Empire?," *History Workshop Journal* 66 (2008): 129–62; Olivier Le Cour Grandmaison, *Coloniser, exterminer: sur la guerre et l'état colonial* (Paris, 2005); Isabel Hull, *Absolute Destruction: Military Culture and the Practices of War in Imperial Germany* (Ithaca, 2005); George Steinmetz, *The Devil's Handwriting: Precoloniality and the German Colonial State in Qingdao, Samoa, and Southwest Africa* (Chicago, 2007); Joël Kotek, "*Sonderweg*: Le génocide des Herero, symptôme d'un Sonderweg allemand?" *La Revue d'histoire de la Shoah* 189 (2008): 177–97; Donald Bloxham, *The Final Solution: A Genocide* (Oxford, 2009).

36. On this topic see Angelo Del Boca, *I gas di Mussolini: Il fascismo e la guerra d'Etiopa* (Rome, 1996); "La leggi razziali nell'impero di Mussolini," in *Il regime fascista*, ed. Angelo Del

Boca, Massimo Legnani, and Mario G. Rossi (Rome-Bari, 1995), 329–51; R. J. B. Bosworth, *Mussolini's Italy: Life, Under the Fascist Dictatorship, 1915–1945* (New York, 2006), 4.

37. In De Felice's view the differences are not marginal but substantial. He states: "The different tempers of these two peoples; the fact that in National-socialism, the idea of Volk played a radical role and had a radical ground and tradition that by no means can be compared to any factor of fascist ideologies; and, lastly, the different degree of totalitarianization of national life carried out by both regimes." See De Felice, *Interpretations of Fascism*; Renzo De Felice, *El Fascismo. Sus interpretaciones* (Buenos Aires, 1976), 341. On De Felice and the Holocaust, see my "Rileggendo il canone: Renzo de Felice fra storia e teoria," *I Viaggi di Erodoto. Trimestrale di Cultura Storica* 43–44 (2001): 52–67, and Traverso, *Understanding the Nazi Genocide*, 77. On de Felice in general, see Giovanni Aliberti and Giuseppe Parlato, eds., *Renzo De Felice: il lavoro dello storico tra ricerca e didattica* (Milan, 1999); *Incontro di studio sull'opera di Renzo De Felice: Roma, Palazzo Giustiniani, 4 giugno 1997* (Rome, 2000); Emilio Gentile, *Renzo De Felice. Lo storico e il personaggio* (Rome, 2003), and Giovanni Mario Ceci, *Renzo De Felice storico della politica* (Soveria Mannelli, Catanzaro, 2008).

38. See Gilbert Allardyce, "What Fascism Is Not: Thoughts on the Deflation of a Concept," *American Historical Review* 84, no. 2 (1979): 367–88.

39. In his important work on the origins of fascism, Sternhell argues that fascism cannot be identified with Nazism because of Nazi antisemitism and the Holocaust. These two related features of Nazism show that the differences between Nazi Germany and fascism "are no less significant than similarities." Zeev Sternhell, with Mario Sznajder and Maia Asheri, *The Birth of Fascist Ideology*, 4–5.

40. Yehuda Bauer, *Rethinking the Holocaust* (New Haven, 2001), 83, 113–15, and Friedländer, "Nazism: Fascism or Totalitarianism."

41. Fascism does not have a significant role in the most important histories of the Holocaust; in addition to Saul Friedländer's master work, see also Raul Hilberg, *The Destruction of the European Jews* (New Haven, 2003), and, more recently, Christopher R. Browning with Jürgen Matthäus, *The Origins of the Final Solution: The Evolution of Nazi Jewish Policy, September 1939–March 1942* (Lincoln, 2004). For a critique of Hilberg's canonic status, which in many ways resembles the way Saul Friedländer's is currently appraised, see Federico Finchelstein, "The Holocaust Canon: Rereading Raul Hilberg," *New German Critique* 96 (2005): 3–48. For analysis of the problem of canonization in historiography, see Dominick LaCapra, "Canons, Texts, and Contexts" in *Representing the Holocaust*, 19–41.

42. To be sure, the understanding of the systemic, integralist nature of fascist thinking is a central dimension, but especially in the case of the history of political theory, the history of ideas needs to be connected with what Roger Chartier has called the logic of practice. An excellent example of the understanding of fascism as a system of concepts is Zeev Sternhell, *The Anti-Enlightenment Tradition* (New Haven, 2010). See also Roger Chartier, *Escribir las prácticas. Foucault, De Certeau, Marin* (Buenos Aires, 1996).

43. Emilio Gentile, "Fascism and the Italian Road to Totalitarianism," *Constellations: An International Journal of Critical and Democratic Theory* 15, no. 3 (2008): 291–302.

44. Gentile, "Fascism and the Italian Road to Totalitarianism."

45. Dominick LaCapra, "Fascism and the Sacred: Sites of Inquiry after (or along with) Trauma," 10–11. This text belongs to Chapter 5 of his new book *History, Literature, Critical Theory* (forthcoming, 2013).

46. LaCapra has presented insights and elaborated on these connections between fascism, ideology, and sacrifice in his books *Representing the Holocaust*; *History and Memory after Auschwitz*; *Writing History, Writing Trauma* (Baltimore, 2001); *History in Transit: Experience, Identity, Critical Theory* (Ithaca, 2004); and *History and Its Limits*.

47. See Michael Burleigh, "National Socialism as a Political Religion," *Totalitarian Movements and Political Religions* 1, no. 2 (2000): 1–26; Payne, *A History of Fascism 1914–1945*, 9, and his review essay of Emilio Gentile's *Le religioni politiche* in *Totalitarian Movements and Political Religions* 3, no. 1 (2002): 122–30; Roger Griffin, "God's Counterfeiters? Investigating the Triad of Fascism, Totalitarianism, and (Political) Religion," in *Fascism, Totalitarianism, and Political Religion*,

ed. Roger Griffin (London, 2005), 1–31; Emilio Gentile, "New Idols: Catholicism in the Face of Fascist Totalitarianism," *Journal of Modern Italian Studies* 11, no. 2 (2006): 143–70, and his essay, "Fascism, Totalitarianism and Political Religion: Definitions and Critical Reflections on Criticism of an Interpretation," *Totalitarian Movements and Political Religions* 5, no. 3 (2004): 327–75.

48. Gentile, "Fascism and the Italian Road to Totalitarianism," 298.

49. See George Mosse, *The Nationalization of the Masses: Political Symbolism and Mass Movements in Germany from the Napoleonic Wars Through the Third Reich* (Ithaca, 1991), and Emilio Gentile, *Le religioni della politica. Fra democrazie e totalitarismi* (Rome-Bari, 2001); Gentile, *Il culto del littorio: la sacralizzazione della politica nell'Italia fascista* (Rome-Bari, 1993). For a critical interpretation of Mosse and Gentile, see Enzo Traverso, "Interpreting Fascism: Mosse, Sternhell and Gentile in Comparative Perspective," *Constellations: An International Journal of Critical and Democratic Theory* 15, no. 3 (2008): 303–19. On Mosse, see also Emilio Gentile, *Il fascino del persecutore: George L. Mosse e la catastrofe dell'uomo moderno* (Rome, 2007), and the collective volume: Payne, Sorkin, and Tortorice, eds., *What History Tells*.

50. See for example, Michael Burleigh, *Sacred Causes: Religion and Politics from the European Dictators to Al Qaeda* (New York, 2006); Roger Griffin, Robert Mallett, and John Tortorice, eds., *The Sacred in Twentieth-Century Politics: Essays in Honour of Professor Stanley G. Payne* (New York, 2008); and Griffin, *A Fascist Century*.

51. On the Posen Speech, see Friedländer, *Memory, History, and the Extermination of the Jews of Europe,* 110–11.

52. LaCapra, "Fascism and the Sacred: Sites of Inquiry after (or along with) Trauma," 27.

53. For the notion of reoccupation, see Hans Blumenberg, *The Legitimacy of the Modern Age* (Cambridge, MA, 1983). On processes of secularization vis-à-vis the sacred, see also Jose Casanova, *Public Religions in the Modern World* (Chicago, 1994).

54. See Finchelstein, "On Fascist Ideology."

55. See, for example, Max Horkheimer and Theodor Adorno, *Dialectic of Enlightenment* (Stanford, 2002); Jürgen Habermas, *The Philosophical Discourse of Modernity* (Cambridge, MA, 1987); Axel Honneth, *Pathologies of Reason: On the Legacy of Critical Theory* (New York, 2009); Slavoj Žižek, *Did Somebody Say Totalitarianism?: Five Interventions in the (Mis)use of a Notion* (New York, 2002); Alain Badiou, *The Century* (Cambridge, UK, 2007); Hannah Arendt, "The Seeds of a Fascist International," in *Essays in Understanding 1930–1954,* ed. Jerome Kohn (New York, 1994), 140–50.

CHAPTER 14

The Holocaust and World History
Raphael Lemkin and Comparative Methodology[1]

A. Dirk Moses

Introduction

"The Holocaust and world history" is not a theme usually posited by philosophers of history or world historians. It is implied most often by scholars in Jewish studies, Holocaust historiography and genocide studies when they declare that the Nazi attempt to exterminate European Jewry is unique, unprecedented, unparalleled, or singular—compared to other genocides in world history. Such claims have roots that long precede the genocide of the 1940s. Already in 1846, the prominent German-Jewish historian Heinrich Graetz lamented, "This is the eighteenth hundred-year era of the Diaspora, of unprecedented suffering, of uninterrupted martyrdom without parallel in world history," indeed adding that this exile "was a history of suffering to a degree and over a length of time such that no other people has experienced."[2] If, by the middle of the nineteenth century, this "lachrymose history" (Salo Baron) of Jewish life since the destruction of the second temple constituted unparalleled suffering, the Holocaust that occurred a hundred years later required an updating of the world-historical claim. It has four not entirely compatible versions.

In the first, the Holocaust's irrational, purely-ideological character is stressed. Only the Jews were targeted for ideological reasons alone.[3] Whereas in other genocides, an actual civil or military conflict subtended the targeting of civilians, the Holocaust was driven by hallucinatory ideology devoid of a social or political reality.[4] The second version of the claim maintains that the Nazis aimed to destroy all Jews everywhere whereas other genocides were only local and partial.[5] The third version invokes the significance of the Enlightenment

---

Notes for this section begin on page 286.

and technology. In this vein, Frank Chalk, in his pioneering co-edited book on genocide through the ages, figured the Holocaust's meaning in terms of its German perpetrators as representatives of western civilization:

> The Holocaust has a special meaning for Western civilization: unlike the dead of ancient genocides, unlike the Cathars, the Japanese Christians, the Pequots and the Hereros, unlike the Armenians and the victims of Stalin's terror, the Jews and Gypsies were murdered in post-Enlightenment Europe by a people steeped in Western culture and rich in scientific knowledge.... We agree that in the challenge it poses to Western values from within our society, the Holocaust stands alone in the history of the West and in the history of genocide.[6]

Again, the judgment is made against the horizon of world history.

Still another version of the claim for the world-historical nature of the Holocaust is entailed by the special status of the victims: Jews as representatives of western civilization. Their intended destruction was therefore not a regular case of genocide, but rather a nihilistic attack on that civilization, that is, on the monotheistic values that the Nazis denied and violated: "God, redemption, sin and revelation."[7] For this reason, Dan Diner refers to the Holocaust as a "profound civilizational break."[8] This last point derives from an associated claim within Jewish theology and later, in a secularized form in Jewish politics, about the unique role of the Jews in human history. Graetz linked the question of unique suffering to the uniqueness of the victims' message when he wrote:

> The proscribed, outlawed Jew, pursued over the entire earth, felt an exalted, noble pride in bearing, and in suffering for a doctrine which reflected eternity and by which the nations would eventually be educated to the knowledge of God and to morality, a doctrine from which the salvation and redemption of the world would go forth.[9]

The "exalted, noble pride in bearing, and in suffering for a" redemptive doctrine for humanity as a whole persists in the present day. Jewish religious and Israeli political leaders commonly refer to a special Jewish moral mission for humanity—and therefore a mission in world history. David Ben Gurion, for example, regarded Jews as a "unique people" whose destiny was to be a "light unto the nations," not by converting others as in Christianity or Islam, but by "redeeming" their ancestral land and establishing a just society.[10] The Israeli president, Shimon Peres, underlined this point when he said in 2009, "The State of Israel is not merely the Jews' protective shield, but an ideal of historic import: to be a nation with a moral message."[11] Since 1945, the light of monotheism—"God, redemption, sin and revelation"—has been replaced by the secular ideals of human rights and minority protection via memory of the Holocaust as a unique genocide. This position is now the official Zionist and even United Nations (UN) position, exemplified by the successful Israeli attempt at the UN to institute a Holocaust Memorial Day.[12]

In all four assertions, human history becomes a backdrop for the uniqueness claim, a means of interrogating the Holocaust's world-historical import and of endowing it with meaning; while, in turn, the Holocaust becomes an episode in the unique Jewish mission to "sanctify life and prevent murder and discrimination," that is, to impart the universal yet characteristically Jewish values of human rights and minority protection. In the fourth version, in particular, history becomes a kind of theodicy, the evil committed against the Jews eliciting the revelation of human rights and the genocide prevention. In this mode, Holocaust historiography is as much an ethical discourse, indeed a political theology, as a secular investigation.

For all their claims to universality, the uniqueness claims betray the generally ethno- and western-centric matrix from which they stem, much like Graetz's much earlier reasoning about why diasporic Jews did not become "a vagabond horde of gypsies"—it is because they had the civilizing Law.[13] Their particularity is revealed by those who directly experience its effects. Any listener would naturally wonder what a Palestinian would think when Peres brandishes Israel's ethical mission and behavior:

> We never set out to conquer. We did not rush towards domination. We rejected lordship, we fought discrimination, we protested slavery, we forbade violence. We believe in the preeminence of man, and we pray for *Tikkun Olam* [repairing the world] and world peace.

Indeed, non-European critics regard the humanism proclaimed in uniqueness positions as the very source of their own oppression, because it distinguishes so starkly between civilization and barbarism (or savagery). The view from outside the North-Atlantic consensus looks very different. W. E. B. Du Bois, for instance, wrote in *The World and Africa* in 1947 that

> [t]here was no Nazi atrocity—concentration camps, wholesale maiming and murder, defilement of women or ghastly blasphemy of children—which the Christian civilization of Europe had not long been practicing against colored folks in all parts of the world in the name of and for the defense of a Superior Race born to rule the world.[14]

For this reason, the Nigerian writer Wole Soyinka, explicitly challenges the uniqueness thesis by arguing that the Atlantic slave trade, not the Holocaust, places "the first question mark on all claims of European humanism—from the Renaissance through the Enlightenment to the present-day multicultural orientation."[15] Similarly, Frantz Fanon argued that the enduring problem was racism against and, exploitation of, non-whites. The Holocaust was an intra-European affair: "They are hunted down, exterminated, cremated. But these are little family quarrels." Whereas Jews are "slaves of an 'idea'" (antisemitism), he was enslaved "by his own appearance." Although he recognized certain commonalities in the Jewish and Black experiences, Fanon observed that the latter embodied the lowest cultural values, indeed evil itself, in Europe's collective unconscious.[16] Finally, there is the criticism that the very ambition to write world history can evince a Euro-American hegemonic global imaginary, in fact that their "world conquest and ideological structures ... produced the notion of 'world history' in the first place."[17]

Like the Holocaust uniqueness claims, these positions are indentured to a particular stance and similarly questionable ethical discourse: equating antisemitism with anti-Black prejudice in the name of a generic anti-racism, flattening out the differences between all genocides, and attributing all evil in world history to European imperialism.

There are, then, two rival narratives about the meaning of the Holocaust and the course of modern global history: one that insists on its uniqueness, even if coded by other terms like "unprecedented" and so forth, and links Holocaust memory both to the universal values of human rights and the particular geopolitical agenda of Israel; and the other that regards the Holocaust less as a racially-driven genocide against a helpless minority than the logical outcome of imperial-racial conquest that it holds Zionism to embody. In both cases, blindness to their subject positions leads the protagonists of each narrative to a Schmittian friend/enemy stance and therefore to express empathy selectively in scholarly as well as political analyses. They impute malevolent (greed) or purely irrational motives (fanaticism/racial hatred) to the enemy-other, while their favored object's behavior is explicable by the laws of cause and effect: if their own "side" commits an act of violence, they were "forced" to do so *defensively* by the unbridled and unprovoked *aggression* of the enemy-other.

How does one avoid this competitive discourse of uniqueness and counter-uniqueness with their overshadowing geopolitical stakes and unsatisfactory methodological implications? Demonstrating that the underlying bone of contention is metahistorical claim-making about the Holocaust is the first task—as I hope I have shown here. The second task is to conceive of a viable methodology for historians writing about the Holocaust in world history. I do so by reconstructing the first serious attempt to address this question: that of Raphael Lemkin (1900–1959), the Polish-Jewish jurist who coined the term "genocide" in 1943 and wrote an unpublished world history of genocide after World War II. How did this complex figure, proud Jew and non-Zionist Polish patriot, conceive of world history and the Holocaust's place in it? We will see that he extricated himself from these metahistorical discourses in two ways: first, by proposing an immanent and cosmopolitan discourse that, by extending empathy to *all* victims of genocide and persecution, applied social scientific explanations to *both* victims and perpetrators; and second, by proposing a comparative approach that did not take any particular genocide as the prototype, model, or paradigm against which all the other are judged. He linked his moral purpose—to prevent and criminalize genocide—by seeking to explain its occurrence throughout history with the latest scholarly tools, deployed in an even-handed manner.[18] Consequently, this chapter does not contextualize the Holocaust in world history, an impossible undertaking in a short contribution. Instead, it explicates Lemkin's methodology as a guide for current and future research, which is thematized in the last section.

Raphael Lemkin, World History, and the Holocaust

It is no accident that Lemkin, a Jew from Eastern Europe, where consciousness and experience of nationality was so intense and where Jews had been persecuted for centuries, invented a concept to name the destruction of nationalities and pressed for its criminalization. Raised in an observant Jewish environment in which children studied the Bible and Jewish literature, his imagination was accordingly animated by the fate of nations and peoples. Like many Jews, he was drawn to the ancient Hebrew prophets. Suffering for their struggle, their "words lived long for they were deeds dressed as words." These sentiments would have been compelling to a youth who as a boy heard about pogroms, like that in Białystok, 50 miles away, in 1906. From Isaiah's call to "Cease to do evil; learn to do well; relieve the oppressed; judge the fatherless, plead for the widow" (Isaiah 1:17), he drew a cosmopolitan conclusion: it "sounded to me so urgent, as if the oppressed stood now outside our door. The appeals for peace by converting swords into ploughshares seemed to recreate his presence."[19] The hints he left in his unpublished autobiography indicate that, as a boy, he had also read widely about the persecution of human cultural groups since antiquity, beginning with the Roman Emperor Nero's attempted extermination of Christians. By learning about the travails of many ethnic groups over the centuries—the Huguenots of France, Catholics in Japan, Muslims in Spain— he concluded that ethnic destruction was a universal and enduring problem. While the persecution of Jews was part of this sorry tale—indeed, he called them "that classical victim of genocide"[20]—his sympathies were for people everywhere; their suffering was part of the same human story: "A line of blood led from the Roman arena through the gallows of France to the pogrom of Białystok."[21] His was a cosmopolitan rather than sectarian moral imagination that carefully negotiated the differences and similarities between cases, avoiding the temptation either to flatten out or to hypostasize distinctions.[22]

> I identified myself more and more with the sufferings of the victims, whose numbers grew, and I continued my study of history. I understood that the function of memory is not only to register past events, but to stimulate human conscience. Soon contemporary examples of genocide followed, such as the slaughter of the Armenians. It became clear to me that the diversity of nations, religious groups and races is essential to civilization because every one of these groups has a mission to fulfil and a contribution to make in terms of culture. To destroy these groups is opposed to the will of the Creator and to disturb the spiritual harmony of mankind. I have decided to become a lawyer and work for the outlawing of Genocide and for its prevention through the cooperation of nations. These nations must be made to understand that an attack on one of them is an attack on them all.[23]

This quotation also makes clear that Lemkin couched his appeal to end genocide not in terms of abstract human rights and individual suffering, but in relation to an ideal of world civilization whose constituent parts were national, religious, and racial groups. However Jewish his roots and sympathies—he wrote for Jewish and Zionist newspapers in the 1920s while working as a lawyer in Poland—he seemingly did not became a Zionist or devote exclusive attention to the Jewish experience in World War II.

Misunderstanding his cosmopolitanism, Lemkin's commentators have accused him of illegitimately conflating the experiences of Jews and other groups, and of succumbing to a false (Christian) universalism, even implying that he did so for careerist reasons. The implicit charge that he neglected the metahistorical significance of the Holocaust is also based on the proposition that he did not fully understand the ambition of the Nazi genocide of Jews when he coined the term genocide.[24] Indeed, Lemkin thought the Nazis' policies unprecedented towards a number of victim groups, not just Jews. And even then he said they recalled other cases of genocide.

> The above-described techniques of genocide represent an elaborate, almost scientific, system developed to an extent never before achieved by any nation. Hence the significance of genocide and the need to review international law in the light of the German practices of the present war. These practices have surpassed in their unscrupulous character any procedures or methods imagined a few decades ago by the framers of the Hague Regulations. Nobody at that time could conceive that an occupant would resort to the destruction of nations by barbarous practices *reminiscent of the darkest pages of history.*[25]

For all that, Lemkin was acutely conscious of the Jewish experience. Although he fled his native Poland in 1939, he was well informed about subsequent Nazi rule. He devoted a separate chapter in his book *Axis Rule in Occupied Europe* (1944) to the Nazi treatment of Jews, outlining the "special status" for them in every conquered country, as well as noting that they were "one of the main objects of German genocide policy." Indeed, they were "to be destroyed completely." He knew about the extermination camps.[26] His analysis of Nazi policy towards the Jews exemplifies his deft touch, shuttling back and forth between the similarities and specificities of the Jewish case.

In Sweden until 1941, he collected Nazi occupation documents and published them with extended commentary in *Axis Rule*, the book in which he introduced the genocide concept. In terms of Lemkin's view of historical progress, the Nazi occupation marked a dramatic regression to "the wars of extermination, which occurred in ancient times and in the Middle Ages," when the distinction between civilians and combatants was not well observed. This was how he described premodern genocide in *Axis Rule*:

> As classical examples of wars of extermination in which nations and groups of the population were completely or almost completely destroyed, the following may be cited: the destruction of Carthage in 146 B.C.; the destruction of Jerusalem by

Titus in 72 A.D.; the religion wars of Islam and the Crusades; the massacres of the Albigenses and the Waldenses; and the siege of Magdeburg in the Thirty Years War [May, 1631]. Special wholesale massacres occurred in the wars waged by Genghis Khan and by Tamerlane.[27]

The difference between barbarism and civilization was the distinction between civilians and combatants, and he saw international law as advancing this marker of civilization. From its inception, then, the genocide concept, like the Jewish genocide (Lemkin did not use the term Holocaust, which was not common currency in the 1940s), was embedded in a world historical frame.

Rather than study the Jewish case alone, Lemkin wanted to study genocide, which he said was a "generic notion" that applied to any human situation in the present and the past.[28] One could only understand the significance of the Jewish experience by relating it to the experience of others. His basic point was that genocide named a single evil—the destruction of peoples: "Genocide is a new word, but the evil it describes is old. It is as old like [sic] the history of mankind. It was necessary, however, to coin this new word because the accumulation of this evil and its devastating effects became extremely strong in our own days."[29] For that reason, he explained, "All cases of genocide, although their background and conditions vary, follow, for the most part, the same pattern. The object of destruction is a specific human group."[30]

Already while he was lobbying for the UN Convention on the Punishment and Prevention of Genocide (1948), Lemkin turned to popularizing and legitimating his new concept by writing a major academic study of genocide. His correspondence with funding organizations and publishers shows that he was soliciting interest in a book on the subject as early as 1947 and that he had produced substantial draft chapters by the next year.[31] Wanting to encourage the ratification of the UN genocide convention, he noted, "The historical analysis is designed to prove that genocide is not an exceptional phenomenon, but that it occurs in intergroup relations with a certain regularity like homicide takes place in relations between individuals."[32] Lemkin's point was that genocide was not sacred but profane, to use Durkheim's distinction; far from the irruption of the inexplicable and irrational into normal life, it was the outcome of normal—and explicable—social interaction.

This agenda naturally told against making the Holocaust, let alone genocide, a metahistorical-singular event; after all, why devote a lifetime to criminalizing something so rare and specific that it is unlikely to recur? Moreover, how could countries be convinced to ratify the Genocide Convention if they thought it really pertained only to the Jewish Holocaust and therefore did not immediately concern them? Regarding his lobbying of UN delegates, he said that his *Axis Rule* book and "the Nazi experience was not a sufficient basis for a definition of genocide for international purposes. One cannot describe a crime by one criminal experience alone; one must (rather) draw on all available experiences of the past."[33] Accordingly, Lemkin routinely referred to the world history of genocide in his public advocacy of ratification.[34]

Alas, Lemkin's book never eventuated. Publishing houses and funding agencies did not think it a viable or marketable proposition.[35] His book proposals and chapters are scattered in three North American archives; while some are seemingly lost, it is still possible to reconstruct his project in considerable detail.[36] In his "Description of the Project" for his book, *Introduction to the Study of Genocide* (the first of a projected two-volume work), Lemkin detailed how he would combine legal and historical analyses for consciousness-raising purposes:

> This book will deal with the international and comparative law aspects of this crime. Moreover, the particular acts of genocide will be illustrated by historical examples from Antiquity, the Middle Ages and Modern Times. These examples are necessary not only to prove that genocide has always existed in history, but also to explain the practicality of the Genocide Convention which up to now has been ratified by the parliaments of 58 nations.[37]

The project was to be interdisciplinary because genocide, like the nationhood it attacked, was multidimensional.

> The etiology and the reasons motivating the crime of genocide in different periods of history and in different cultures will be examined. The research will deal also with matters of psychology, economics, political science and cultural anthropology, the latter playing a great part in cases where genocide can be explained as resulting from a cultural conflict.[38]

Why did genocide occur? Lemkin listed a number of hypotheses:

> One of the basic reasons for genocide is a conflict of culture as it appeared for example in the migrating nomadic societies and sedentary ones. Also this conflict was particularly violent when the ideas of the absolute appeared in the course of the encounter of various religions. The economic and political expectations which were attached to the annihilation of a group worked always as a generating force of genocide. Also colonialism cannot be left without blame. The basic difficulty consists in the fact that the standards of conduct between individuals disappear in relations between one group and another.[39]

It is immediately evident that Lemkin did not set store on inter-group enmity as the starting point for explaining genocide. Such enmity arose from dramatic transformations in the interaction between migratory and sedentary and societies. Material factors were consequently important.[40]

At the same time, emotional factors were paramount to mobilizing a population for genocidal violence. As he made clear in a draft chapter called "The Concept of Genocide in Social and Individual Psychology," situational factors were as important as individual and cultural dispositions in leading to genocidal violence.[41] Above all, he appealed to sociology—the discipline that studies societies with generic concepts—for methodological inspiration. Genocide is "primarily sociological, since it means the destruction of certain social groups by other social groups or their individual representatives."[42] Accordingly, he was interested in tracing various processes that recurred in genocide, combined differently in each case. Murder was the last resort: "Actual physical destruction is the last and most effective phase of genocide." More commonly, genocide was effected by "political disenfranchisement, economic displacement, cultural undermining and control, the destruction of leadership, the break-up of families and the prevention of propagation."[43]

Even so, because Lemkin was acutely conscious of cultural difference and contingency in historical events and social processes like genocide, he opposed the application of a single model for each genocide.[44] Instead, he devised a set of questions for the comparative analysis of historical case studies that would balance careful contextualization with systematic rigor. His template for each case study, reproduced in an abbreviated form below, highlights not only the multi-dimensional nature of genocide but also his eschewal of the Holocaust as a paradigm of genocide.

1. Background-historical
2. Conditions leading to the genocide
3. Methods and techniques of genocide
4. The genocidists
5. Propaganda
6. Responses of victims
7. Responses of outsider groups
8. Aftermath.[45]

He wrote draft chapters on most of the following extensive list. This is how he named and organized the cases:

Antiquity: Canaanites/Biblical genocide, Assyrian invasions, Egypt, Greece, Celts, Carthage, Early Christians, Pagans, Gauls, Genocide in Ancient Greece.
Middle Ages: Goths, Huns, Vandals, Vikings, Charlemagne, Albigeneses, Valdenses, England, Jews, Mongols, Moors, the French in Sicily. By the Vikings, Spanish Inquisitions, Genocide against the Moors and the Moriscos, by the Huns, against the Jews. By the Goths. Crusades.
Modern Times: 1. Genocide by the Germans against the Native Africans, 2. Assyrians in Iraq, 3. Belgian Congo, 4. Bulgaria under the Turk, 5. Genocide against the Greeks, 6. Chios, 7. Greeks and Franks, 8. Greeks in Exile from Turkish occupation, 9. Genocide by Greeks against the Turks, 10. Genocide against the Gypsies, 11. Hereros, 12. Haiti, 13. Hottentots, 14. Huguenots, 15. Hungary under the Turks, 16. Genocide against the American Indians, 17. Ireland, 18. Genocide by Jannisaries, 19. Genocide by the Japanese against the Catholics, 20. Genocide

against Polish Jews, 21. Genocide against Russian Jews, 22. Genocide against Jews in South Africa, 23. Genocide against Rumanian Jews, 24. Korea, 25. Latin America, 26. Genocide against Aztecs, 27. Yucatan, 28. Genocide against the Incas, 29. Genocide against the Maoris of New Zealand, 30. Genocide against Mennonites, 31. Nuremberg Trials, 32. Parsis, 33. Serbs, 34. Slavs, 35. Smyrna, 36. South Africa, 37. Genocide against the Stedinger 38. Tasmanians, 39. Armenians, 40. SW Africa, 41. Natives of Australia.[46]

We do no have the space to examine each chapter but it is worth noting that Lemkin wrote a substantial manuscript on the Nazi policies for the purposes of indicting German leaders for genocide.[47] As in *Axis Rule,* he treated the persecution and murder of European Jewry as a case of genocide among others perpetrated by the Nazis, noting its distinct features while highlighting its similarities. Ever the sober lawyer, he made the case for their guilt in terms explicable to an international readership with secular premises. Lemkin's was the first account of the "Holocaust and world history," then, but it never saw the light of day. His work was promptly forgotten as the uniqueness thesis began to structure the conceptual approach to the study the Holocaust.

The Holocaust and World History: Following Lemkin's Program

How can one revive Lemkin's method today, more than half a century after he wrote his proposals and draft chapters? How can the Holocaust be made interesting or relevant to world historians who are more interested in themes like climate change, demography, migration, and state-formation? To be of genuine global interest, the Holocaust needs to be deprovincialized from its signification within an exclusively Jewish and western narrative about the triumphant achievement of human rights and genocide prevention. That narrative is simply implausible for large sections of the global population and shows no genuine interest in world history. A world history gaze can illuminate some generic features of genocide that recur in the Holocaust. It does not "diminish" the Holocaust—to name the anxiety of those who insist on its uniqueness—to point out such features. Far more, such an exercise is intrinsic to the program set forth by Lemkin, namely to advance immanent rather than transcendental explanations for its occurrence. Of particular interest is the notion that a people could be a hereditary or blood enemy, which meant that all its members were *ipso facto* guilty, to be exterminated with impunity, indeed with divine warrant. In the following brief exposition, I focus mainly on the concept of "enemy people" since Biblical antiquity as an example for this approach.

It has been often pointed out that the Bible contains numerous examples of genocide by the ancient Israelites of their enemies, although they were no exception to Near Eastern norms at the time. Significant for genocide studies is that the Bible deals with the fate of peoples. The Amalek, an enemy people of the Israelites, embodied the concept of hereditary enemy. Just as the Bible teaches that their name was to be "blotted out" (Deuteronomy 25:19), their putative genocidal intentions towards the Israelites serve as ready historical analogy for Israeli leaders today.[48] The Bible was also the source for "the Judeo-Christian history of salvation" in which "the obliteration and replacement of peoples was a principal motor of advance and historical change." Genocide could be thereby imbued with metahistorical significance, as it was for medieval Europeans for whom the Bible provided "ancient prototypes" "for recounting acts of inter-ethnic slaughter."[49]

Other cases in antiquity indicate alternative modalities of enemy people construction. Rome's armies occasionally exterminated entire cities that resisted its rule or rose up in rebellion. To be sure, they did not always destroy the enemy, but nor did they pardon those who could not be trusted. Security considerations dictated their fate.[50] Punishing and avenging treachery and betrayal, experienced as an insult and expression of contempt, was another motivation for destroying a people or city. Rome's attack on Carthage, which it accused of basic breaches of trust, is a classic example of this modality. Carthage's behavior meant that Rome withdrew the right of pity and limited warfare. Vengeance and indignation drove it to impose mass, collective capital punishment rather than ethnic or racial hatred.[51] Betrayal was also a common theme in Asian and Central Asian empires. The Mongols were acutely conscious of treachery by peoples they had absorbed into the multi-ethnic empires. Peoples who broke alliances—and therefore an oath—by joining the enemy were sometimes exterminated years later by Mongol leaders who did not forget such betrayals.[52]

Genocidal intentions could also be generated by the other side of the imperial relationship in a phenomenon called "subaltern genocide."[53] The total extermination of an enemy people was also a common refrain by Chinese nationalists against the Manchu Dynasty in the late nineteenth century, for example. They were to be pulled "out by the roots" for betraying their oath to protect China from foreign penetration. The Manchus were racialized as a "barbarous lineage"; revenge was to be taken on them for their centuries-long humiliating tutelage over the Chinese.[54] Also anti-colonial in nature were the peasant insurgencies in nineteenth-century India. Their targets were not only the British occupiers but Indian tribal groups seen as agents or beneficiaries of colonial rule. Such targeting was often collective, directed "against all members of a given class of enemies without pausing to sort out the 'good' individuals among them from the 'bad,' and secondly ... [hitting] ... out against all classes and sections of the population hostile to the peasantry, irrespective of whichever of these might have been the rebels' initial object of attack."[55] The local people shared consanguinity and territory, rigidly distinguishing between locals and alien newcomers. Theirs was a struggle for the homeland against foreign

Indians, members of other tribes who exploited the peasantry and who were held responsible for moral and material decline, especially if they were money lenders and traders, bearers of the incipient commercial economy. Alien influence was coded as the beginning of general decline. The rebels sought to expel or destroy the commercial interloper to recover a harmonious past as future.[56]

At the same time in North America, European settlers were racializing Apache Indians as enemies who were congenitally dangerous to their presence and should therefore be exterminated. This disposition was, by all accounts, the consensus on the frontier.[57] The tendency to collective thinking of dangerous people was also evident in Imperial Russian elites in their conquest of the Caucasus between the 1830s and 1860s. Noting the French tactics in their pacification of Algeria, the Russians engaged in wholesale population expulsions with virtually genocidal consequences for groups like the Circassians. Decades later, during the Russian Civil war, both Red and White forces routinely "sifted" and "filtered" captured troops and populations for members of suspect groups they regarded as corporate enemy groups. White forces, for instance, executed tens of thousands of Jews, Balts, Chinese, and Communists because they were seen as "incorrigible."[58]

The concept of enemy people (*vrag narodo*) and classes became a central element of the Soviet security paranoia. Stalin thought the so-called Kulaks an irredeemable enemy. Because of their large number and geographical dispersion, he found that expulsion was not an option. Starvation was a substitute policy, with genocidal consequences for Ukrainian and Caucasian peasants.[59] Less well known but equally devastating was the genocidal deportation in 1943–1944 of the Caucasian peoples, who were accused of collaborating with the Nazi invaders. For their alleged betrayal of the Soviet Fatherland, the Chechens became a "bandit nation"; according to Beria, they were a nation of "active and almost universal participation in the terrorist movement directed against the Soviets and the Red Army."[60]

Since the 1920s, the Soviet leadership had felt encircled by enemies abroad and their agents within Soviet borders: peoples thought to be in league with these foreign enemies were necessarily "unreliable elements," "suspect nations," "nationalities of foreign governments." In this context, leaders could make genocidal statements like this one:

> We will annihilate every such enemy, even if he is an old Bolshevik, we will annihilate his entire clan, his family. We will mercilessly annihilate anyone who in actions or thoughts—yes, even in thoughts—who attempts [to undermine] the unity of the socialist state.[61]

Security rather that racial imperatives governed the logic of this rhetoric and policy.

Other aspects of genocide can be briefly noted. In all these empires, terror played an important role in conquest and governance. Massacring entire towns hastened the surrender of others when they heard the news.[62] The relentless pursuit of enemy peoples is also a recurring feature of genocide through the ages. Sometimes the destruction was total, sometimes it was not. Enemies were pursued to the extent that they no longer represented a threat or that sufficient vengeance had been exacted. Equally important is the question of preemption. We know from Richard Tuck's study of western thought on war and peace that one tradition—expressed by Tacitus and Cicero, for instance—justified preemptive strikes against enemies on the basis of fear, glory, and generally *raison d'etat*.[63] We also know that this justification found application in practice, such as the habit of European settlers to preemptively exterminate indigenous peoples collectively because they might pose a threat. Out of fear or by projecting their own genocidal designs onto the other, settlers murdered entire groups on the basis of the proposition that the Native Americans were apparently bent on destroying them.[64]

Now all these aspects of genocide can be detected in the Nazi genocide of European Jewry: the identification of an enemy people that was incorrigible and mortally dangerous, that was responsible for moral and material decline by its commercial activity, that collaborated with and represented foreign enemies, whose fundamental disloyalty was proven by the betrayal of an army in 1917, that was therefore a permanent security risk to attack preemptively and collectively, to be pursued relentlessly, to be terrorized and exterminated. In fact, Hitler referred explicitly to some of these cases—particularly the Romans and the Mongols—in justifying his stance and policies.[65] The Nazis concocted their own genocidal amalgam of these historical examples. To point to their presence in the Holocaust is not to suggest that it is "just like any other genocide in world history"—the dreaded "relativization" of the Holocaust. It is to note, as Lemkin did, that genocides, for all their variation, share recurring features that congeal in different constellations in different conjunctures. It goes without saying that branding "the Jews" an enemy people was based on fantastical notions of global conspiracy—just as paranoia and accusations of "ethnic guilt" that pronounce civilians to be potential security risks is present, in varying degrees, in genocides generally.[66]

Conclusion

What then of "the Holocaust and world history"? Lemkin studied both scientifically as he would any history and any genocide; he seems not to have invested the Holocaust with any metahistorical significance. Taking the perspective of the *longue durée* naturally told against such investment. He observed patterns of immanence rather than transcendence, the quotidian rise and fall of nations and empires, rather than moments of world-historical significance. His own assumption was that the norm of diversity resisted the imposition of homogeneity. Note how he includes the Nazi regime in this list of homogenizing empires:

> At different stages of history some cultures have been stronger, some have been weaker, but the diversity of cultures in the world has been aspired to from earliest times. And once a tendency was felt to impose one culture upon the rest of the world, like in the case of Greece, Rome, Assyria, France (under Louis XVI), Nazi Germany under Hitler, this tendency was always broken up by counter-forces which ultimately secure the principle of diversity.[67]

Despite his valorization of cultural difference, he was no cultural relativist, believing that the West, as the origin of humanitarian international law, was the motor of civilizational development. It drove the transition from the barbarism of total warfare and wars of extermination of antiquity and the Middle Ages to the modern laws of war and occupation with their distinction between civilians and combatants. If this view, shared by other liberal Jews of his generation like Norbert Elias, has been powerfully challenged by critics who associate genocide and the Holocaust with modernity, his nascent theory of cultural learning processes is worth recalling. Memory of genocide spurs the effort to prevent it, perhaps a secular manifestation of the Jewish notion that "the secret of redemption is memory:"[68]

> The history of genocide displays the presence of a vicious circle. The preservation of nations contributes to the creation and development of original cultures. However, the presence of original cultures in certain, especially limitrophe [border zones, ADM], areas of the world caused cultural conflicts and genocide. It also created the concern to prevent genocide by permitting the natural development and co-existence of cultures without excluding one another by violent means.[69]

The terrible events of World War II "created the concern to prevent genocide," he noted, because they "shocked the conscience of mankind," as the UN General Assembly put it in 1946. Contrary to the common view that the Holocaust was the impetus for the drafting of the UN Declaration on Human Rights and the Genocide Convention, the Nazi genocide *and* persecution of many other groups—that is, genocide—was the international community's point of reference: the Holocaust was not a term used at the time, after all.[70]

What of his legacy today? World histories of genocide are being written, alas with no regard for Lemkin's work.[71] The best recent scholarship on the Holocaust to embody the Lemkinian spirit is Donald Bloxham's tellingly-titled study of the Holocaust, *The Final Solution: A Genocide*.[72] A genuine comparativist with expertise in war crimes trials, the Armenian genocide, and geopolitics since the Eastern crisis of the 1870s,[73] Bloxham reasons inductively, showing how the Nazi policies grew out of but also exceeded the ethnic warfare in Europe in the first half of the twentieth century. Along the way, he disposes of the uniqueness myth that the Nazis intended the total destruction of the Jews, while also referencing Lemkin's observation that "crippling" a group was genocidal because it destroyed its agency and prevented its reproduction.

Deftly negotiating the complex historiography of the field, he shows that any one paradigm, whether industrial killing, modernity, antisemitism or imperialism cannot do justice to the Holocaust's complexity, which was, ultimately, a multi-causal event. In the manner of Lemkin, then, Bloxham has successfully deprovincialized Holocaust scholarship.

A world history approach to the Holocaust must also do more than engage in the usual comparative calculus. It must ask after its location in the world system of empire- and nation-states. Mark Levene is the historian to have most systematically pursued this question. Abjuring the distinction between ancient and modern genocide, he thinks the twentieth century *context* is distinctive. Unique is the development of competitive nation-states in a system dominated by old core powers accompanied by newcomers like the United States. Those that wish to catch up, like Imperial Germany whose challenge to the established order had been defeated in World War I, scapegoat domestic minorities held responsible for hindering resource mobilization or betraying previous efforts to break into or dominate the system. This pattern of revisionist challenges to the core powers and the system they govern, exemplified by the Nazi, Soviet, Japanese, and Italian empires of the 1930s and 1940s, are the global context for the genocides of that period.[74] To ask about the Holocaust and world history, then, takes us far from the uniqueness claim, where we began, to a global frame and a genuine interest in all civilizations and cultures facing the challenge of imposing and resisting hegemony in a competitive system of nation- and empire-states. Explicit or implicit ascriptions of transcendent meaning in world history, in particular about the evils of antisemitism or imperialism, can be replaced by middle-range inquiry amenable to empirical testing.

Notes

1. Thanks to Avril Alba, Donald Bloxham, Nick Doumanis, Yotam Hotam, Geoffrey Brahm Levey, Dan Stone, and Natasha Wheatley for critical feedback on drafts of this chapter. An elaborated version of the argument will appear in my *Genocide and the Terror of History*, forthcoming.

2. Heinrich Graetz, "The Diaspora: Suffering and Spirit," in *Modern Jewish Thought: A Source Reader*, ed. Nahum H. Glatzer (New York, 1977), 20.

3. Saul Friedländer, "The Historical Significance of the Holocaust," in *The Holocaust as Historical Experience*, ed. Yehuda Bauer and Nathan Rotenstreich (New York, 1981), 2–4, 15.

4. Daniel Jonah Goldhagen, *Hitler's Willing Executioners: Ordinary Germans and the Holocaust* (New York, 1996), 412 For my critique of this proposition, see A. Dirk Moses, "Paranoia and Partisanship: Genocide Studies, Holocaust Historiography and the 'Apocalyptic Conjuncture,'" *The Historical Journal* 15, no. 2 (2011): 615–45.

5. Steven T. Katz made this thesis the center of his book, *The Holocaust and Historical Context* (Oxford, 1994), an exhaustive examination of other genocides in world history that, he contends, do not evince the intention for total destruction that characterizes the Holocaust.

6. Frank Chalk, "The Ultimate Ideological Genocide," in *The History and Sociology of Genocide: Analysis and Case Studies*, ed. Frank Chalk and Kurt Jonassohn (New Haven, 1990), 325.

7. Uriel Tal, "Forms of Pseudo-Religion in the German *Kulturbereich* Prior to the Holocaust," *Immanuel* 3 (1973–1974): 68–73.

8. Dan Diner, *Beyond the Conceivable: Studies on Germany, Nazism, and the Holocaust* (Berkeley, 2000), 3. Diner also invokes the first version of the uniqueness claim.

9. Graetz, "Diaspora," 22.

10. Ze'ev Tsahor, "Ben-Gurion's Mythopoetics," *Israel Affairs* 1, no. 3 (1995): 65.

11. Shimon Peres address at opening ceremony of Holocaust Martyrs and Heroes Remembrance Day, 20 April 2009, www.mfa.gov.il/MFA/AntiSemitism+and+the+Holocaust/Documents+and+communiques/President_Peres_opening_ceremony_Holocaust_Remembrance_Day_20-Apr-2009.htm.

12. The Israeli representative at the UN noted, "The Holocaust constituted a systematic and barbarous attempt to annihilate an entire people, in a manner and magnitude that have no parallel in human history" and observed its consequences: "By so shocking the conscience of humankind, the Holocaust served as a critical impetus for the development of human rights, the drafting of landmark international conventions, such as the Genocide Convention, and for the very establishment of this organization." See Dan Gillerman, Israeli Permanent Representative to the United Nations, statement at the 60th meeting of the General Assembly, 31 October 2005, http://israel-un.mfa.gov.il/statements-at-the-united-nations/holocaust-remebrance/agenda-item-72-holocaust-remembrance-31-october-2005. Cf. Daniel Levy and Natan Sznaider, *The Holocaust and Memory in the Global Age* (Philadelphia, 2006).

13. Graetz, "Diaspora," 21.

14. W. E. B. Du Bois, *The World and Africa* (Millwood, NY, 1967), 23.

15. Wole Soyinka, *The Burden of Memory, the Muse of Forgiveness* (New York, 1999), 38–39.

16. Frantz Fanon, *Black Skin/White Masks,* trans. Charles Lam Markmann (London, 1986), 115–16, 180–92.

17. Arif Dirlik, "Performing the World: Reality and Representation in the Making of World Hist(ories)," *Journal of World History* 16, no. 4 (2005): 391–92.

18. Cf. Dan Stone, "The Historiography of Genocide: Beyond 'Uniqueness' and Ethnic Competition," *Rethinking History* 8, no. 1 (2004): 127–42. Stone, *Histories of the Holocaust* (Oxford, 2010), ch. 5.

19. Raphael Lemkin, "Autobiography," "First Love and Early Education" chapter, New York Public Library, Lemkin Collection, Box 1, Reel 2, Folder 37. I have corrected Lemkin's spelling in the quotations from his unpublished writings.

20. Raphael Lemkin, "Genocide in Economics," New York Public Library, Lemkin Collection, Box 2, Reel 2, Folder 2.

21. Raphael Lemkin, "Totally Unofficial Man," in *Pioneers of Genocide Studies,* ed. Samuel Totten and Stephen L. Jacobs (New Brunswick, 2002), 370–72.

22. A. Dirk Moses, "Raphael Lemkin, Culture, and the Concept of Genocide," in *The Oxford Handbook of Genocide Studies,* ed. Donald Bloxham and A. Dirk Moses (Oxford, 2010), 19–41.

23. Lemkin, 'Autobiography', New York Public Library, Lemkin Collection, Box 1, Reel 2, Folder 36, 2.

24. John Cooper, *Raphael Lemkin and the Genocide Convention* (Houndmills, 2008), 10, 23, 58–59; Yehuda Bauer, "The Place of the Holocaust in History," *Holocaust and Genocide Studies* 2 (1987): 211–12, 215; Katz, *Holocaust in Historical Context,* 129–30 n. 15.

25. Lemkin, *Axis Rule in Occupied Europe* (Washington, DC, 1944), 90 (emphasis added).

26. Lemkin, *Axis Rule,* 89, 81; cf. 249–50, 77, 21–22.

27. Raphael Lemkin, *Axis Rule,* 80 n. 3. The book was finished in 1943 but negotiations with the publishers delayed its appearance by a year. See Cooper, *Raphael Lemkin and the Genocide Convention,* 54.

28. Lemkin, *Axis Rule,* 80.

29. Raphael Lemkin, "Introduction into Part 1: The New Word and the New Idea," New York Public Library, Lemkin Collection, Box 2, Reel 2, Folder 2, 1.

30. Raphael Lemkin, "Memorandum on the Genocide Convention," American Jewish Historical Association, Lemkin Collection, P-154, Box 6, Folder 5.

31. His research was financed by a special "Genocide Research Fund" at Yale Law School, to which donors contributed. See Harry Starr, Lucius N. Littauer Foundation to Lemkin, 13 February 1951, American Jewish Historical Association, Lemkin Collection, P-154, Box 8, Folder 10.

32. Lemkin to Paul Fejos, Viking Fund, 22 July 1948, American Jewish Historical Association, Lemkin Collection, P-154, Box 8, Folder 10.

33. Lemkin, "Totally Unofficial Man," 390.

34. College Roundtable: United Nations: Genocide Convention (undated), American Jewish Archives, Cincinnati, Collection 60, Box 4, Folder 2, 2.

35. A typical rejection letter from Roger F. Evans, Rockefeller Foundation, to Lemkin, 6 November 1947, New York Jewish Historical Association, Lemkin Collection, P-154, Box 8, Folder 10.

36. Studies of these manuscripts can be found in Dominik Schaller and Jürgen Zimmerer, eds., *The Origins of Genocide: Raphael Lemkin as a Historian of Mass Violence* (Abingdon, 2009), and Cooper, *Raphael Lemkin and the Genocide Convention,* chs. 15 and 16.

37. Raphael Lemkin, "Description of the Project" (undated), New York Public Library, Lemkin Collection, Box 2, Reel 3, Folder 1, 2.

38. Ibid.

39. Ibid., 4.

40. Ibid.

41. Raphael Lemkin, "The Concept of Genocide in Social and Individual Psychology," New York Public Library, Lemkin Collection, Roll 2, Folder 2.

42. Raphael Lemkin, "The Concept of Sociology in Sociology," New York Public Library, Lemkin Collection, Box 2, Roll 2, Folder 2. Cf. Martin Shaw, "Sociology and Genocide," in Bloxham and Moses, *The Oxford Handbook of Genocide Studies,* 142–62.

43. Lemkin, "The Concept of Sociology in Sociology."

44. Raphael Lemkin, "Reflections on Cure and Treatment," New York Public Library, Lemkin Collection, Box 2, Reel 2, Folder 2. "It is therefore useless to apply to it [genocide] the same standards and methods used by chemists or biologists."

45. Raphael Lemkin, "Revised Outline for Genocide Cases," American Jewish Historical Association, Lemkin Collection, P-154, Box 8, Folder 11. This is the bare list: each subheading was supplemented by considerable detail.

46. Lemkin, "Description of the Project," 5. Unfortunately, case "41. Natives of Australia" has not been located. It would be a great service to genocide scholars for these chapters to be published. So far, only his chapter on the Aboriginal Tasmanians has been reprinted, along with an extended commentary by Ann Curthoys: "Raphael Lemkin's 'Tasmania': An Introduction," *Patterns of Prejudice* 39, no. 2 (2005): 162–69; Raphael Lemkin, "Tasmania," in Curthoys, "Raphael Lemkin's 'Tasmania,'" 170–96 (both are reprinted in Moses and Stone, *Genocide and Colonialism,* 66–73, 74–100).

47. Raphael Lemkin, *Raphael Lemkin's Thoughts on Nazi Genocide: Not Guilty?,* ed. Steven L. Jacobs (Lewiston, 1992). Cf. Dan Stone, "Raphael Lemkin on the Holocaust," *Journal of Genocide Research* 7, no. 4 (2005): 539–50.

48. Louis H. Feldman, *"Remember Amalek!": Vengeance, Zealotry, and Group Destruction in the Bible According to Philo, Pseudo-Philo, and Josephus* (Cincinnati, 2004), chs. 7 and 8; Jeffrey Goldberg, "Israel's Fears, Amalek's Arsenal," *New York Times,* 17 May 2009.

49. Len Scales, "Bread, Cheese and Genocide: Imagining the Destruction of Peoples in Medieval Western Europe," *History* 92 (2007): 294–95, 287.

50. Benjamin Isaac, *The Invention of Racism in Classical Antiquity* (Princeton, 2004), 216.

51. David Konstan, "Anger, Hatred, and Genocide in Ancient Greece," *Common Knowledge* 13, no. 1 (2007): 170–87.

52. John Joseph Saunders, *The History of the Mongol Conquests* (Philadelphia, 2001), ch. 4.

53. Nicholas A. Robins and Adam Jones, eds., *Genocides by the Oppressed Subaltern Genocide in Theory and Practice* (Bloomington, 2009); A. Dirk Moses, ed., *Empire, Colony, Genocide: Conquest, Occupation and Subaltern Resistance in World History* (New York, 2008).

54. Peter Perdue, "Erasing the Empire, Re-racing the Nation: Racialism and Culturalism in Imperial China," in *Imperial Formations*, ed. Ann Laura Stoler, Carole McGranaham and Peter Perdue (Santa Fe, 2007), 141–72.

55. Ranajit Guha, *Elementary Aspects of Peasant Insurgency in Colonial India* (Durham, 1999), 24.

56. Ibid., 279–95.

57. Karl Jacoby, "'The Broad Platform of Extermination': Nature and Violence in the Nineteenth Century North American Borderlands," *Journal of Genocide Research* 10, no. 2 (2008): 249–67.

58. Peter Holquist, "Violent Russia, Deadly Marxism? Russia in the Epoch of Violence, 1905–1921," *Kritika: Explorations in Russian and Eurasian History* 4, no. 3 (2003): 627–52.

59. Michael Ellman, "The Role of Leadership Perceptions and of Intent in the Soviet Famine of 1931–1934," *Europe-Asia Studies* 57, no. 6 (2005): 823–41.

60. Jeffrey Burds, "The Soviet War against 'Fifth Columnists': The Case of Chechnya, 1942–4," *Journal of Contemporary History* 42, no. 2 (2007): 270.

61. Ibid., 283.

62. Saunders, *The History of the Mongol Conquests*, 56; Isaac, *The Invention of Racism in Classical Antiquity*, 216.

63. Richard Tuck, *The Rights of War and Peace* (Oxford, 1999), 11–13, 18–23.

64. Jacoby, "'The Broad Platform of Extermination,'" 252.

65. A. Dirk Moses, "Redemptive Anti-Semitism and the Imperialist Imaginary," in *Years of Persecution, Years of Extermination: Saul Friedländer and the Future of Holocaust Studies*, ed. Christian Wiese and Paul Betts (London, 2010), 233–54.

66. Cf. Moses, "Paranoia and Partisanship."

67. Raphael Lemkin, "Part I, Ch. II, Sec. II: The Nature of the Group Concerned," American Jewish Archives, Cincinnati, Collection 6, Box 7, Folder 7/2, 3.

68. Andreas Huyssen, *Present Pasts: Urban Palimpsests and the Politics of Memory* (Stanford, 2003), 32; Stone, "Genocide and Memory," in Bloxham and Moses, *Oxford Handbook of Genocide Studies*, 102–19.

69. Lemkin, "Description of the Project," 5.

70. Symptomatic in conflating the war experience with the Holocaust is Johannes Morsink, *The Universal Declaration of Human Rights: Origins, Drafting, and Intent* (Philadelphia, 1999). For an alternative reading, see Donald Bloxham, *Genocide on Trial: War Crimes Trials and the Formation of Holocaust History* (Oxford, 2001).

71. For example, Ben Kiernan, *Blood and Soil: A World History of Genocide and Extermination from Sparta to Darfur* (New Haven, 2007).

72. Donald Bloxham, *The Final Solution: A Genocide* (Oxford, 2009).

73. Donald Bloxham, *The Great Game of Genocide: Imperialism, Nationalism and the Destruction of the Ottoman Armenians* (Oxford, 2005); Bloxham, *Genocide, the World Wars, and the Unweaving of Europe* (London, 2008).

74. Mark Levene, *Genocide in the Age of the Nation-State*, vol. 1, *The Meaning of Genocide* (London, 2005).

Select Bibliography

Adam, Uwe Dietrich. *Judenpolitik im dritten Reich*. Düsseldorf: Droste, 1972.
Adorno, Theodor W. *Minima Moralia: Reflections from Damaged Life*. London: Verso, 1978.
Agamben, Giorgio. *Remnants of Auschwitz: The Witness and the Archive*. New York: Zone Books, 2001.
Akçam, Taner. *A Shameful Act: The Armenian Genocide and the Question of Turkish Responsibility*. London: Constable, 2007.
Allardyce, Gilbert. "What Fascism Is Not: Thoughts on the Deflation of a Concept." *American Historical Review* 84, no. 2 (1979): 367–88.
Allen, Beverly. *Rape Warfare: The Hidden Genocide in Bosnia-Herzegovina and Croatia*. Minneapolis: University of Minnesota Press, 1996.
Aly, Götz. *Hitler's Beneficiaries: Plunder, Racial War, and the Nazi Welfare State*. New York: Metropolitan Books, 2005.
———. *Into the Tunnel: The Brief Life of Marion Samuel 1931–1943*. New York: Metropolitan Books, 2007.
Ancel, Jean. *Transnistria, 1941–1942. The Romanian Mass Murder Campaigns*, 3 vols. Tel Aviv: Goldstein-Goren Diaspora Research Center, 2003.
Anderson, John. *Kyrgyzstan: Central Asia's Island of Democracy?* London: Harwood Academic Publishers, 1999.
Ankersmit, F. R. "Historical Representation." *History and Theory* 27, no. 3 (1988): 205–28.
———. "Reply to Professor Zagorin." *History and Theory* 29, no. 3 (1990): 275–96.
———. *Historical Representation*. Stanford: Stanford University Press, 2001.
Ankersmit, Frank, and Hans Kellner, eds. *A New Philosophy of History*. London: Reaktion, 1995.
Ankersmit, Frank, Ewa Doma ska, and Hans Kellner, eds. *Re-figuring Hayden White*. Stanford: Stanford University Press, 2009.
Arendt, Hannah. *Eichmann in Jerusalem: A Report on the Banality of Evil*. New York: Viking Penguin, 1963.
———. *The Origins of Totalitarianism*. New York: Harcourt Brace, 1979.
———. *Essays in Understanding 1930–1954: Uncollected and Unpublished Works by Hannah Arendt*, ed. Jerome Kohn. New York: Harcourt Brace, 1994.
Assmann, Aleida. *Erinnerungsräume. Formen und Wandlungen des kulturellen Gedächtnisses*. Munich: C. H. Beck, 1999.
Auschwitz in den Augen der SS: Rudolf Höß, Pery Broad, Johann Paul Kremer. Oświęcim: Auschwitz-Birkenau State Museum, 1997.
Austin, J. L. *How To Do Things with Words*. Oxford: Clarendon Press, 1973.
Badiou, Alain. *The Century*. Cambridge, UK: Polity Press, 2007.
Ball, Karyn. *Disciplining the Holocaust*. Albany: SUNY Press, 2008.

Bankier, David, and Dan Michman, eds. *Holocaust Historiography in Context.* Jerusalem: Yad Vashem, 2008.
Bartov, Omer. *The Eastern Front 1941–45: German Troops and the Barbarization of Warfare.* London: Macmillan, 1985.
———. *Mirrors of Destruction: War, Genocide and Modern Identity.* New York: Oxford University Press, 2000.
———. *Erased: Vanishing Traces of Jewish Galicia in Present Day Ukraine.* Princeton: Princeton University Press, 2007.
———. "Interethnic Relations in the Holocaust as Seen Through Postwar Testimonies: Buczacz, East Galicia, 1941–1944." In *Lessons and Legacies VIII: From Generation to Generation,* ed. Doris L. Bergen. Evanston: Northwestern University Press, 2008, 101–24.
Bauer, Yehuda, "On the Place of the Holocaust in History." *Holocaust and Genocide Studies* 2, no. 2 (1987): 209–20.
———. *Rethinking the Holocaust.* New Haven: Yale University Press, 2001.
Bauman, Zygmunt. *Modernity and the Holocaust.* Cambridge, UK: Polity Press, 1989.
Belke, Ingrid, ed. *Moritz Lazarus und Heymann Steinhal: Die Begründer der Völkerpsychologie in ihren Briefen.* Tübingen: J. C. B. Mohr, 1971.
Beradt, Charlotte. *The Third Reich of Dreams: The Nightmares of a Nation, 1933–1939.* Wellingborough, UK: Aquarian, 1985.
Bergen, Doris L. *War and Genocide: A Concise History of the Holocaust.* Lanham: Rowman & Littlefield, 2003.
———. "Tenuousness and Tenacity: The 'Volksdeutschen' of Eastern Europe, World War II, and the Holocaust." In *The Heimat Abroad: The Boundaries of Germanness,* ed. Krista O'Donnell, Renate Bridenthal, and Nancy Reagin. Ann Arbor: University of Michigan Press, 2005, 267–86.
Berkhofer, Robert F. Jr. *Beyond the Great Story: History as Text and Discourse.* Cambridge, MA: Harvard University Press, 1995.
Berkhoff, Karel. *Harvest of Despair: Life and Death in Ukraine under Nazi Rule.* Cambridge, MA: Harvard University Press, 2004.
Bettelheim, Bruno. *The Informed Heart: Autonomy in a Mass Age.* Glencoe, IL: Free Press, 1960.
———. *Surviving and Other Essays.* New York: Alfred A. Knopf, 1979.
Bezwińska, Jadwiga, and Danuta Czech, eds. *Amidst a Nightmare of Crime: Manuscripts of Members of Sonderkommando.* Cracow: State Museum of Auschwitz-Birkenau, 1973.
Blackbourn, David. *The Conquest of Nature: Water, Landscape, and the Making of Modern Germany.* London: Jonathan Cape, 2006.
Blatman, Daniel. *The Death Marches: The Final Phase of Nazi Genocide.* Cambridge, MA: Harvard University Press, 2010.
Bloch, Marc. *The Historian's Craft.* Manchester: Manchester University Press, 1967.
Bloxham, Donald. *Genocide on Trial: War Crimes Trials and the Formation of Holocaust History.* Oxford: Oxford University Press, 2001.
———. "Three Imperialisms and a Turkish Nationalism." *Patterns of Prejudice* 36, no. 4 (2002): 37–58.
———. *The Great Game of Genocide: Imperialism, Nationalism, and the Destruction of the Ottoman Armenians.* Oxford: Oxford University Press, 2005.
———. "Modernity and Genocide." *European History Quarterly* 38, no. 2 (2008): 294–311.
———. *The Final Solution: A Genocide.* Oxford: Oxford University Press, 2009.
Bloxham Donald, and Tony Kushner. *The Holocaust: Critical Historical Approaches.* Manchester: Manchester University Press, 2004.
Bloxham, Donald, and A. Dirk Moses, eds. *The Oxford Handbook of Genocide Studies.* Oxford: Oxford University Press, 2010.
Blumenberg, Hans. *The Legitimacy of the Modern Age.* Cambridge, MA: MIT Press, 1983.
Blumenthal, Nahman. "Magical Thinking in the Era of Nazi Occupation." *Yad Vashem Studies* 5 (1963): 175–86 (in Hebrew).

Boll, Bernd, and Hans Safrian. "Auf dem Weg nach Stalingrad: Die 6. Armee 1941/42." In *Vernichtungskrieg: Verbrechen der Wehrmacht, 1941–1944*, ed. Hannes Heer and Klaus Naumann. Hamburg: Hamburger Edition, 1995, 260–96.

Borges, Jorge Luis. *Labyrinths.* Harmondsworth: Penguin, 1970.

Bosworth, R. J. B. *Mussolini's Italy: Life under the Fascist Dictatorship, 1915–1945.* London: Arnold, 2006.

Boua, Chanthou. "Genocide of a Religious Group: Pol Pot and Cambodia's Buddhist Monks." In *State-Organized Terror: The Case of Violent Internal Repression,* ed. T. Bushnell, V. Shlapentokh, C. K. Vanderpool, and J. Sundram. Boulder: Westview Press, 1991, 227–40.

Bracher, Nathan. *Through the Past Darkly: History and Memory in François Mauriac's "Bloc-Notes."* Washington, DC: Catholic University of America Press, 2004.

Braiterman, Zachary. "Against Holocaust-Sublime." *History and Memory* 12, no. 2 (2000): 7–28.

Bramwell, Anna. *Blood and Soil: Richard Walther Darré and Hitler's "Green Party."* Bourne End, UK: The Kensal Press, 1985.

Brandon, Ray, and Wendy Lower, eds. *The Shoah in Ukraine: History, Testimony, Memorialization.* Bloomington: Indiana University Press, 2008.

Brather, Hans-Stephan. "Aktenvernichtung durch deutsche Dienststellen beim Zusammenbruch des Faschismus." *Archivmitteilungen* 8, no. 4 (1958): 115–17.

Breisach, Ernst. *On the Future of History: The Postmodernist Challenge and its Aftermath.* Chicago: University of Chicago Press, 2003.

Breitman, Richard. *The Architect of Genocide: Himmler and the Final Solution.* London: The Bodley Head, 1991.

Brink, Cornelia. *Ikonen der Vernichtung. Öffentlicher Gebrauch von Fotografien aus nationalsozialistischen Konzentrationslagern nach 1945.* Berlin: Akademie Verlag, 1998.

Broszat, Martin, "Das dritte Reich und die rumänische Judenpolitik." *Gutachten des Instituts für Zeitgeschichte* 1 (1958): 102–83.

Browning, Christopher R. *Ordinary Men: Reserve Police Battalion 101 and the Final Solution in Poland.* New York: HarperCollins, 1992.

———. *Collected Memories: Holocaust History and Postwar Testimony.* Madison: University of Wisconsin Press, 2003.

———. "Evocation, Analysis, and the 'Crisis of Liberalism.'" *History and Theory* 48 (2009): 238–47.

———. *Remembering Survival: Inside a Nazi Slave-Labor Camp.* New York: W. W. Norton, 2010.

Browning, Christopher R., with Jürgen Matthäus. *The Origins of the Final Solution: The Evolution of Nazi Jewish Policy, September 1939–March 1942.* London: William Heinemann, 2004.

Brüggemeier, Franz-Josef, Mark Cioc, and Thomas Zeller, eds. *How Green Were the Nazis? Nature, Environment, and Nation in the Third Reich.* Athens: Ohio University Press, 2005.

Bunzl, Matti. "*Völkerpsychologie* and German-Jewish Emancipation." In *Worldly Provincialism: German Anthropology in the Age of Empire,* ed. H. Glenn Penny and Matti Bunzl. Ann Arbor: University of Michigan Press, 2003, 47–85.

Burdick, Charles B. "Vom Schwert zur Feder. Deutsche Kriegsgefangene im Dienst der Vorbereitung der amerikanischen Kriegsgeschichtsschreibung über den Zweiten Weltkrieg. Die organisatorische Entwicklung der Operational History (German) Section." *Militärgeschichtliche Mitteilungen* 10, no. 2 (1971): 69–80.

Burds, Jeffrey. "The Soviet War against 'Fifth Columnists': The Case of Chechnya, 1942–4." *Journal of Contemporary History* 42, no. 2 (2007): 267–314.

Burke, Peter. *What is Cultural History?* Cambridge, UK: Polity Press, 2008.

Burleigh, Michael. "National Socialism as a Political Religion." *Politics, Religion and Ideology* 1, no. 2 (2000): 1–26.

———. *Sacred Causes: Religion and Politics from the European Dictators to Al Qaeda.* London: HarperPress, 2006.

Burleigh, Michael, and Wolfgang Wippermann. *The Racial State: Germany 1933–1945.* Cambridge, UK: Cambridge University Press, 1991.

Burrin, Philippe. *Nazi Anti-Semitism: From Prejudice to the Holocaust*. New York: The New Press, 2005.

Casanova, Pascale. *The World Republic of Letters*. Cambridge, MA: Harvard University Press, 2005.

Cesarani, David. "'Integrative and Integrated History": A Sweeping History of the Shoah Rooted in Everyday Life—and Death." *Yad Vashem Studies* 36, no. 1 (2008): 271–77.

Chalk, Frank, and Kurt Jonassohn, eds. *The History and Sociology of Genocide*. New Haven: Yale University Press, 1990.

Chaney, David. *The Cultural Turn*. London: Routledge, 1994.

Chartier, Roger. *Cultural History: Between Practices and Representations*. Cambridge, UK: Polity, 1988.

———. *The Cultural Origins of the French Revolution*. Durham: Duke University Press, 1991.

Chaumont, Jean-Michel. *La concurrence des victimes. Génocides, identité, reconnaissance*. Paris: La Découverte, 2002.

Chéroux, Clément, ed. *Mémoire des camps. Photographies des camps de concentration et d'extermination nazis (1933–1999)*. Paris: Marval, 2001.

Chin, Rita, Heide Fehrenbach, Geoff Eley, and Atina Grossmann. *After the Nazi Racial State: Difference and Democracy in Europe*. Ann Arbor: University of Michigan Press, 2009.

Clendinnen, Inga. *Reading the Holocaust*. Cambridge, UK: Cambridge University Press, 1999.

Cohen, Arthur A. *The Myth of the Judeo-Christian Tradition*. New York: Harper & Row, 1969.

Cohen, Boaz. "The Birth Pangs of Holocaust Research in Israel." *Yad Vashem Studies* 33 (2005): 203–43.

Cohen, Deborah, and Maura O'Connor, eds. *Comparison and History: Europe in Cross-National Perspective*. New York: Routledge, 2004.

Cohen, Jeremy. *The Living Letters of the Law: Ideas of the Jew in Medieval Christianity*. Berkeley: University of California Press, 1999.

Cohen, Nathan. "Diaries of the Sonderkommando in Auschwitz: Coping with Fate and Reality." *Yad Vashem Studies* 20 (1990): 273–312.

———. "Diaries of the Sonderkommando." In *Anatomy of the Auschwitz Death Camp*, ed. Yisrael Gutman and Michael Berenbaum. Bloomington: Indiana University Press, 1994, 522–34.

Collingwood, R. G. *The Idea of History*. New York: Oxford University Press, 1956.

Collotti, Enzo. *Fascismo, fascismi*. Florence: Sansoni, 1997.

Confino, Alon. "Fantasies abouth the Jews. Cultural Reflections on the Holocaust." *History and Memory* 17, nos. 1–2 (2005): 296–322.

———. *Germany as a Culture of Remembrance: Promises and Limits of Writing History*. Chapel Hill: University of North Carolina Press, 2006.

———. "Narrative Form and Historical Sensation: On Saul Friedländer's *The Years of Extermination*." *History and Theory* 48, no. 3 (2009): 199–219.

———. "A World Without Jews: Interpreting the Holocaust." *German History* 27, no. 4 (2009): 531–59.

Cooper, Gregory J. *The Science of the Struggle for Existence: On the Foundations of Ecology*. Cambridge, UK: Cambridge University Press, 2003.

Cooper, John. *Raphael Lemkin and the Genocide Convention*. Basingstoke: Palgrave Macmillan, 2008.

Courtenay, Bryce. *The Power of One: A Novel*. London: Heinemann, 1989.

Croce, Benedetto. *Scritti e discorsi politici, 1943–1947*. Bari: Laterza, 1963.

Cru, Jean Norton. *Témoins: essai d'analyse et de critique des souvenirs de combattants édités en français de 1915 à 1928*. Paris: n.p., 1929.

———. *Du témoignage*. Paris: n.p., 1931.

Curthoys, Ann. "Raphael Lemkin's 'Tasmania': An Introduction." *Patterns of Prejudice* 39, no. 2 (2005): 162–69.

Czerniakow, Adam. *The Warsaw Diary of Adam Czerniakow*, ed. Raul Hilberg, Stanislaw Staron, and Josef Kermisz. Chicago: Ivan R. Dee, 1999.

Dafni, Reuven, and Yehudit Kleiman, eds. *Final Letters: From the Yad Vashem Archive.* New York: Paragon House, 1991.
Darnton, Robert. *The Kiss of Lamourette: Reflections in Cultural History.* New York: Norton, 1989.
Dawes, James. *That the World May Know: Bearing Witness to Atrocity.* Cambridge, MA: Harvard University Press, 2007.
Dawidowicz, Lucy S. *The Holocaust and the Historians.* Cambridge, MA: Harvard University Press, 1981.
Dawidowicz, Lucy S., ed. *A Holocaust Reader.* West Orange, NJ: Behrman House, 1976.
Day, Mark. *The Philosophy of History: An Introduction.* London: Continuum, 2008.
Dean, Carolyn J. "History and Holocaust Representation." *History and Theory* 41, no. 2 (2002): 239–49.
———. *The Fragility of Empathy after the Holocaust.* Ithaca: Cornell University Press, 2004.
———. "Minimalism and Victim Testimony." *History and Theory* 49 (2010): 85–99.
Dean, Martin. *Collaboration in the Holocaust: Crimes of the Local Police in Belorussia and Ukraine, 1941–44.* New York: Macmillan, 2000.
De Felice, Renzo. *Interpretations of Fascism.* Cambridge, MA: Harvard University Press, 1977.
Del Boca, Angelo. *I gas di Mussolini: Il fascismo e la guerra d'Etiopa.* Rome: Editori Reuniti, 1996.
Desbois, Patrick. *The Holocaust by Bullets.* Basingstoke: Palgrave Macmillan, 2008.
Des Pres, Terrence. *The Survivor: An Anatomy of Life in the Death Camps.* New York: Oxford University Press, 1976.
Dickinson, Edward Ross. "The German Empire: An Empire?" *History Workshop Journal* 66 (2008): 129–62.
Didi-Huberman, Georges. *Images in Spite of All: Four Photographs from Auschwitz.* Chicago: University of Chicago Press, 2008.
Dieckmann, Christoph, and Saulius Sužiedelis. *The Persecution and Mass Murder of Lithuanian Jews during Summer and Fall of 1944.* Vilnius: Margi Raštai, 2006.
Diner, Dan. "Zwischen Aporie und Apologie. Über Grenzen der Historisierbarkeit des Nationalsozialismus." In *Ist der Nationalsozialismus Geschichte? Zu Historisierung und Historikerstreit,* ed. Dan Diner. Frankfurt/M: Fischer Taschenbuch Verlag, 1987, 62–73.
———. *Beyond the Conceivable: Studies on Germany, Nazism, and the Holocaust.* Berkeley: University of California Press, 2000.
Dintenfass, Michael. "Truth's Other: Ethics, the History of the Holocaust, and Historiographical Theory after the Linguistic Turn." *History and Theory* 39, no. 1 (2000): 1–20.
Dirlik, Arif. "Performing the World: Reality and Representation in the Making of World Hist(ories)." *Journal of World History* 16, no. 4 (2005): 391–410.
Dorland, Michael. *Cadaverland: Inventing a Pathology of Catastrophe for Holocaust Survival.* Waltham, MA: Brandeis University Press, 2009.
Douglas, Mary. *Purity and Danger: An Analysis of the Concept of Pollution and Taboo.* London: Routledge, 2002.
DuBois, W. E. B. *The World and Africa.* Millwood, NY: International Publishers, 1967.
Eaglestone, Robert. *Postmodernism and Holocaust Denial.* Cambridge: Icon Books, 2001.
———. *The Holocaust and the Postmodern.* Oxford: Oxford University Press, 2004.
Earl, Hilary. *The Nuremberg SS-Einsatzgruppen Trial, 1945-1958: Atrocity, Law, and History.* New York: Cambridge University Press, 2009.
Eatwell, Roger. "On Defining the 'Fascist Minimum': the Centrality of Ideology." *Journal of Political Ideologies* 1 (1996): 303–19.
Ehrenreich, Eric. "Otmar von Verschuer and the 'Scientific' Legitimization of Nazi Anti-Jewish Policy." *Holocaust and Genocide Studies* 21, no. 1 (2007): 55–72.
Eley, Geoff. "What Produces Fascism: Preindustrial Traditions or a Crisis of a Capitalist State?" *Politics and Society* 12, no. 1 (1983): 53–82.
Eley, Geoff, ed. *The "Goldhagen Effect": History, Memory, Nazism—Facing the German Past.* Ann Arbor: University of Michigan Press, 2000.

Elkins, Caroline. *Imperial Reckoning: The Untold Story of Britain's Gulag in Kenya*. New York: Henry Holt & Company, 2005.
Ellman, Michael. "The Role of Leadership Perceptions and of Intent in the Soviet Famine of 1931–1934." *Europe-Asia Studies* 57, no. 6 (2005): 823–41.
Engel, David. *Historians of the Jews and the Holocaust*. Stanford: Stanford University Press, 2010.
Engelking, Barbara, and Jacek Leociak. *The Warsaw Ghetto: A Guide to the Perished City*. New Haven: Yale University Press, 2009.
Fanon, Frantz. *Black Skin/White Masks*. New York: Grove Press, 1967.
Farbstein, Esther. *Hidden In Thunder: Perspectives on Faith, Halachah and Leadership during the Holocaust*. Jerusalem: Mossad Harav Kook, 2007.
Fasolt, Constantin. *The Limits of History*. Chicago: University of Chicago Press, 2004.
Fassin, Didier, and Richard Rechtman. *The Empire of Trauma: An Inquiry into the Condition of Victimhood*. Princeton: Princeton University Press, 2009.
Fein, Helen. *Accounting for Genocide: National Responses and Jewish Victimization during the Holocaust*. Chicago: University of Chicago Press, 1979.
Feldman, Louis H. *"Remember Amalek!" Vengeance, Zealotry, and Group Destruction in the Bible According to Philo, Pseudo-Philo, and Josephus*. Cincinnati: Hebrew Union College Press, 2004.
Felman, Shoshana, and Dori Laub. *Testimony: Crises of Witnessing in Literature, Psychoanalysis and History*. New York: Routledge, 1992.
Ferderber-Salz, Bertha. *And the Sun Kept Shining*. New York: Holocaust Library, 1980.
Finchelstein, Federico. "Rileggendo il canone: Renzo de Felice fra storia e teoria." *I Viaggi di Erodoto. Trimestrale di Cultura Storica* 43–44 (2001): 52–67.
———. "The Holocaust Canon: Rereading Raul Hilberg." *New German Critique* 96 (2005): 1–47.
———. "On Fascist Ideology." *Constellations* 15, no. 3 (2008): 320–31.
———. "Fascism Becomes Desire: On Freud, Mussolini and Transnational Politics." In *The Transnational Unconscious*, ed. Mariano Plotkin and Joy Damousi. Basingstoke: Palgrave Macmillan, 2009.
———. *El Canon del Holocausto*. Buenos Aires: Prometeo Libros, 2010.
———. *Transatlantic Fascism: Ideology, Violence and the Sacred in Argentina and Italy, 1919–1945*. Durham: Duke University Press, 2010.
Finkelstein, Norman G. *The Holocaust Industry: Reflections on the Exploitation of Jewish Suffering*. London: Verso, 2000.
Fitzpatrick, Matthew P. "The Pre-History of the Holocaust? The *Sonderweg* and *Historikerstreit* Debates and the Abject Colonial Past." *Central European History* 41, no. 3 (2008): 477–503.
Flores, Marcello. *Tutta la violenza di un secolo*. Milan: Feltrinelli, 2005.
Flusser, Vilém. *Für eine Philosophie der Fotografie*, 6th ed. Göttingen: Vice Versa, 1992.
Foucault, Michel. *Discipline and Punish: The Birth of the Prison*. London: Allen Lane, 1977.
Frank, Hans. *Deutsche Politik in Polen, 1939-1945. Aus dem Diensttagebuch von Hans Frank, Generalgouverneur in Polen*, ed. Imanuel Geiss and Wolfgang Jacobmeyer. Opladen: Leske + Budrich, 1980.
Fredriksen, Paula. *Augustine and the Jews: A Christian Defense of Jews and Judaism*. New York: Doubleday, 2008.
Frei, Norbert. "Auschwitz und Holocaust. Begriff und Historiographie." In *Holocaust: Die Grenzen des Verstehens. Eine Debatte über die Besetzung der Geschichte*, ed. Hanno Loewy. Reinbek bei Hamburg: Rowohlt, 1992, 101–09.
Friedlander, Henry. *The Origins of Nazi Genocide: From Euthanasia to the Final Solution*. Chapel Hill: University of North Carolina Press, 1995.
Friedländer, Saul. *Kurt Gerstein: The Ambiguity of Good*. New York: Alfred A. Knopf, 1969.
———. "On the Possibility of the Holocaust: An Approach to a Historical Synthesis." In *The Holocaust as Historical Experience*, ed. Yehuda Bauer and Nathan Rotenstreich. New York: Holmes & Meier, 1981, 1–21.
———. *Reflections of Nazism: An Essay on Kitsch and Death*. New York: Harper and Row, 1984.

———. "Nazism: Fascism or Totalitarianism." In *The Rise of the Nazi Regime: Historical Reassessments,* ed. Charles S. Maier, Stanley Hoffmann, and Andrew Gould. Boulder: Westview Press, 1986, 25–34.

———. *Memory, History, and the Extermination of the Jews of Europe.* Bloomington: Indiana University Press, 1993.

———. *Nazi Germany and the Jews 1933–1939: The Years of Persecution.* London: Weidenfeld and Nicolson, 1997.

———. "Mosse's Influence on the Historiography of the Holocaust." In *What History Tells: George L. Mosse and the Culture of Modern Europe,* ed. Stanley G. Payne, David J. Sorkin, and John S. Tortorice. Madison: University of Wisconsin Press, 2004, 134–47.

———. *Den Holocaust beschreiben. Auf dem Weg zu einer integrierten Geschichte.* Göttingen: Wallstein, 2007.

———. *The Years of Extermination: Nazi Germany and the Jews 1939–1945.* London: HarperCollins, 2007.

Friedländer, Saul, ed. *Probing the Limits of Representation: Nazism and the "Final Solution."* Cambridge, MA: Harvard University Press, 1992.

Friedman, Henry. *I'm No Hero: Journeys of a Holocaust Survivor.* Seattle: University of Washington Press, 1999.

Friedman, Philip. "Problems of Research on the European Jewish Catastrophe." In *The Catastrophe of European Jewry,* ed. Yisrael Gutman and Livia Rothkirchen. Jerusalem: Yad Vashem, 1976, 554–67.

Fritzsche, Peter. *Life and Death in the Third Reich.* Cambridge, MA: The Belknap Press of Harvard University Press, 2008.

Funkenstein, Amos. *Perceptions of Jewish History.* Berkeley: University of California Press, 1993.

Furet, François. *Interpreting the French Revolution.* Cambridge, UK: Cambridge University Press, 1981.

Furet, François, and Ernst Nolte. *Fascism and Communism.* Lincoln: University of Nebraska Press, 2001.

Fussell, Paul. *The Great War and Modern Memory.* New York: Oxford University Press, 1975.

Ganzfried, Daniel. "Die Geliehene Holocaust-Biographie—The Purloined Holocaust Biography," *Die Weltwoche.* 27 August 1998.

Garbarini, Alexandra. *Numbered Days: Diaries and the Holocaust.* New Haven: Yale University Press, 2006.

Gaston, Katherine Healon. "The Genesis of America's Judeo-Christian Moment: Secularism, Totalitarianism, and the Redefinition of Democracy." PhD dissertation, University of California-Berkeley, 2008.

Geden, Oliver. *Rechte Ökologie: Umweltschutz zwischen Emanzipation und Faschismus.* Berlin: Espresso Verlag, 1996.

Geertz, Clifford. "Thick Description: Toward an Interpretive Theory of Culture." In *The Interpretation of Cultures: Selected Essays.* London: Fontana, 1993, 3–30.

Gentile, Emilio. *Il culto del littorio: la sacralizzazione della politica nell'Italia fascista.* Rome-Bari: Laterza, 1993.

———. *Le religioni della politica. Fra democrazie e totalitarismi.* Rome-Bari: Laterza, 2001.

———. *Fascismo. Storia e interpretazione.* Rome-Bari: Laterza, 2002.

———. "Fascism and the Italian Road to Totalitarianism." *Constellations: An International Journal of Critical and Democratic Theory* 15, no. 3 (2008): 291–302.

Gerlach, Christian. "Extremely Violent Societies: An Alternative to the Concept of Genocide." *Journal of Genocide Research* 8, no. 4 (2006): 455–71.

Gilbert, Martin. *The Holocaust: The Jewish Tragedy.* London: Fontana, 1987.

Gilbert, Shirli. *Music in the Holocaust: Confronting Life in the Nazi Ghettos and Camps.* Oxford: Oxford University Press, 2005.

Gildea, Robert, Olivier Wieviorka and Annette Waring, eds. *Surviving Hitler and Mussolini: Daily Life in Occupied Europe.* Oxford: Berg, 2006.

Gitelman, Zvi, ed. *Bitter Legacy: Confronting the Holocaust in the USSR.* Bloomington: Indiana University Press, 1997.

Givoni, Michal. "Witnessing in Action: Ethics and Politics in Humanitarians without Borders." PhD thesis, Tel Aviv University, 2008.

Gochman, Kalman. *Class Reunion.* n.p., 1989 (in Hebrew).

Goebbels, Joseph. *Goebbels Reden 1932–1939.* Munich: Heyne, 1971.

———. *Die Tagebücher von Joseph Goebbels,* ed. Elke Fröhlich. Munich: Piper, 1996.

Goeschel, Christian. *Suicide in Nazi Germany.* Oxford: Oxford University Press, 2009.

Goldberg, Amos. "If this is A Man: The Image of Man in Autobiographical and Historical Writing During and After the Holocaust." *Yad Vashem Studies* 33 (2005): 381–429.

———. "One from Four: On What Jaeckel, Hilberg, and Goldhagen Have in Common and What is Unique about Christopher Browning." *Yalkut Moreshet* 3 (2005): 55–86.

———. "Trauma, Narrative, and Two Forms of Death." *Literature and Medicine* 25, no. 1 (2006): 122–41.

———. "The Victim's Voice and Melodramatic Esthetics in History." *History and Theory* 48, no. 3 (2009): 220–37.

Goldhagen, Daniel Jonah. *Hitler's Willing Executioners: Ordinary Germans and the Holocaust.* New York: Alfred A. Knopf, 1996.

———. *Worse Than War: Genocide, Eliminations, and the Ongoing Assault on Humanity.* New York: Public Affairs, 2009.

Goldhagen, Erich. "Weltanschauung und Endlösung. Zum Antisemitismus der nationalsozialistischen Führungsschicht." *Vierteljahreshefte für Zeitgeschichte* 24 (1976): 379–405.

Goltermann, Svenja. *Die Gesellschaft der Überlebenden. Deutsche Kriegsheimkehrer und ihre Gewalterfahrungen im Zweiten Weltkrieg,* 2nd ed. Stuttgart: Deutsche Verlags-Anstalt, 2009.

Gourevitch, Philip. *We Wish to Inform You that Tomorrow We Will Be Killed with Our Families: Stories from Rwanda.* New York: Farrar, Straus & Giroux, 1998.

———. "The Memory Thief." *The New Yorker,* 14 June 1999.

Graetz, Heinrich. "The Diaspora: Suffering and Spirit." In *Modern Jewish Thought: A Source Reader,* ed. Nahum H. Glatzer. New York: Schocken, 1977.

Green, Linda. "Fear as a Way of Life." In *Genocide: An Anthropological Reader,* ed. Alexander Laban Hinton. Oxford: Blackwell, 2002, 307–33.

Greenspan, Henry. *On Listening to Holocaust Survivors: Recounting and Life History.* Westport, CT: Greenwood Press, 1998.

———. *The Awakening of Memory: Survivor Testimony in the First Years after the Holocaust, and Today.* Washington, DC: United States Holocaust Memorial Museum, 2004.

Greif, Gideon. *Wir weinten tränenlos … Augenzeugenberichte der jüdischen "Sonderkommandos" in Auschwitz.* Cologne: Böhlau, 1995.

Griffin, Roger. *The Nature of Fascism.* London: Routledge, 1991.

———. *Modernism and Fascism: The Sense of a Beginning under Mussolini and Hitler.* Basingstoke: Palgrave Macmillan, 2007.

———. *A Fascist Century: Essays by Roger Griffin,* ed. Matthew Feldman. Basingstoke: Palgrave Macmillan, 2008.

Griffin, Roger, Robert Mallett, and John Tortorice, eds. *The Sacred in Twentieth-Century Politics: Essays in Honour of Professor Stanley G. Payne.* New York: Palgrave Macmillan, 2008.

Gringauz, Samuel. "The Ghetto as an Experiment of Jewish Social Organization (Three Years of Kovno Ghetto)." *Jewish Social Studies* 11 (1949): 3–20.

———. "Some Methodological Problems in the Study of the Ghetto." *Jewish Social Studies* 12 (1950): 65–72.

Gross, Jan T. *Neighbors: The Destruction of the Jewish Community in Jedwabne, Poland.* Princeton: Princeton University Press, 2001.

———. *Fear: Antisemitism in Poland after Auschwitz.* New York: Random House, 2006.

Gross, Raphael. *Anständig geblieben: Nationalsozialistische Moral.* Frankfurt/M: S. Fischer, 2010.

Grossman, David. *See Under: Love.* London: Picador, 1989.

Grossmann, Wassili, and Ilja Ehrenburg. *Das Schwarzbuch. Der Genozid an den sowjetischen Juden.* Reinbek bei Hamburg: Rowohlt, 1994.
Guha, Ranajit. *Elementary Aspects of Peasant Insurgency in Colonial India.* Durham: Duke University Press, 1999.
Gurjewitsch, Aaron J. *Das Weltbild des mittelalterlichen Menschen.* Munich: C. H. Beck, 1996.
Gutman, Yisrael. *The Jews of Warsaw, 1939–1943: Ghetto, Underground, Revolt.* Bloomington: Indiana University Press, 1982.
Gutman, Israel, and Bella Gutterman, eds. *The Auschwitz Album. The Story of a Transport.* Jerusalem: Yad Vashem, 2002.
Habermas, Jürgen. *The Philosophical Discourse of Modernity.* Cambridge, MA: MIT Press, 1987.
Haffner, Sebastian. *Germany: Jekyll and Hyde.* London: Libris, 2005.
Hamann, Christoph. *Visual History und Geschichtsdidaktik. Bildkompetenz in der historisch-politischen Bildung.* Herbolzheim: Centaurus, 2007.
Hartman, Geoffrey H. *Scars of the Spirit: The Struggle against Inauthenticity.* New York: Palgrave Macmillan, 2002.
Hartog, François. "Le témoin et l'historien." In *Évidences de l'histoire: Ce que voient les historiens.* Paris: Gallimard, 2005.
Harvey, Elizabeth. *Women and the Nazi East: Agents and Witnesses of Germanization.* New Haven: Yale University Press, 2003.
Hatzfeld, Jean. *Machete Season: The Killers in Rwanda Speak.* New York: Farrar, Straus & Giroux, 2003.
Hayes, Peter. "Auschwitz, Capital of the Holocaust." *Holocaust and Genocide Studies* 17, no. 2 (2003): 330–50.
———. *From Cooperation to Complicity: Degussa in the Third Reich.* Cambridge, UK: Cambridge University Press, 2004.
Hayes, Peter, and John K. Roth, eds. *Oxford Handbook of Holocaust Studies.* Oxford: Oxford University Press, 2010.
Heer, Hannes, Walter Manoschek, Alexander Pollak, and Ruth Wodak, eds. *The Discursive Construction of History. Remembering the Wehrmacht's War of Annihilation.* Basingstoke: Palgrave Macmillan, 2008.
Helfand, Kenneth. *Defiant Gardens: Making Gardens in Wartime.* San Antonio: Trinity University Press, 2006.
Herbert, Ulrich, ed. *National Socialist Extermination Policies: Contemporary German Perspectives and Controversies.* New York: Berghahn Books, 2000.
Herrnstein Smith, Barbara. *Belief and Resistance: Dynamics of Contemporary Intellectual Controversy.* Cambridge, MA: Harvard University Press, 1997.
Herzberg, Abel J. *Between Two Streams: A Diary From Bergen-Belsen.* London: Tauris Parke, 1997.
Hilberg, Raul. *The Destruction of the European Jews,* 3 vols. Chicago: Octagon, 1961.
———. *Perpetrators, Victims, Bystanders.* London: Secker & Warburg, 1993.
———. *The Politics of Memory: The Journey of a Holocaust Historian.* Chicago: Ivan R. Dee, 1996.
———. *Sources of Holocaust Research: An Analysis.* Chicago: Ivan R. Dee, 2001.
Himmler, Heinrich. *Geheimreden 1933 bis 1945 und andere Ansprachen.* Frankfurt/M: Propyläen Verlag, 1974.
Hirsch, Marianne, and Leo Spitzer. "Gendered Translations: Claude Lanzmann's *Shoah.*" In *Claude Lanzmann's Shoah: Key Essays,* ed. Stuart Liebmann. New York: Oxford University Press, 2007, 175–90.
Hoffmann, Detlef. "Das Gedächtnis der Dinge." In *Das Gedächtnis der Dinge. KZ-Relikte und Denkmäler 1945–1995,* ed. Detlef Hoffmann. Frankfurt/M: Campus, 1998, 6–35.
Hoffmann, Jens. *„Das kann man nicht erzählen"—„Aktion 1005". Wie die Nazis die Spuren ihrer Massenmorde in Osteuropa beseitigten.* Hamburg: Konkret, 2008.
Holquist, Peter. "Violent Russia, Deadly Marxism? Russia in the Epoch of Violence, 1905–1921." *Kritika: Explorations in Russian and Eurasian History* 4, no. 3 (2003): 627–52.

Honneth, Axel. *Pathologies of Reason: On the Legacy of Critical Theory.* New York: Columbia University Press, 2009.
Horkheimer, Max, and Theodor Adorno. *Dialectic of Enlightenment.* Stanford: Stanford University Press, 2002.
Horowitz, Sara. *Voicing the Void: Muteness and Memory in Holocaust Fiction.* Albany: SUNY Press, 1997.
Höss, Rudolph. *Death Dealer: The Memoirs of the SS Kommandant at Auschwitz.* New York: Da Capo Press, 1996.
Howell, Martha, and Walter Prevenier. *From Reliable Sources: An Introduction to Historical Methods.* Ithaca: Cornell University Press, 2001.
Hunt, Lynn, ed. *The New Cultural History.* Berkeley: University of California Press, 1989.
Hutton, Christopher M. *Race and the Third Reich: Linguistics, Racial Anthropology and Genetics in the Dialectic of Volk.* Cambridge, UK: Polity Press, 2005.
Huyssen, Andreas. *Present Pasts: Urban Palimpsests and the Politics of Memory.* Stanford: Stanford University Press, 2003.
Ioanid, Radu. *The Holocaust in Romania: The Destruction of Jews and Gypsies Under the Antonescu Regime, 1940–1944.* Chicago: Ivan R. Dee, 2000.
Isaac, Benjamin. *The Invention of Racism in Classical Antiquity.* Princeton: Princeton University Press, 2004.
Jäckel, Eberhard. *Hitler's World View: A Blueprint for Power.* Cambridge, MA: Harvard University Press, 1981.
Jacoby, Karl. "'The Broad Platform of Extermination': Nature and Violence in the Nineteenth Century North American Borderlands." *Journal of Genocide Research* 10, no. 2 (2008): 249–67.
Jaffee, Martin S. "The Victim-Community in Myth and History: Holocaust Ritual, the Question of Palestine, and the Rhetoric of Christian Witness." *Journal of Ecumenical Studies* 28, no. 2 (1991): 223–38.
Jakobson, Roman. "Closing Statement: Linguistics and Poetics." In *Style in Language,* ed. Thomas Sebeok. New York: MIT Press, 1960, 353–57.
Jansen, Christian, and Arno Weckbecker. *Der "Volksdeutsche Selbstschutz" in Polen 1939/40.* Munich: R. Oldenbourg, 1992.
Joffroy, Pierre. *Der Spion Gottes. Kurt Gerstein: Ein SS-Offiziers im Widerstand?* Berlin: Aufbau Verlag, 2002.
Judt, Tony. *Postwar: A History of Europe since 1945.* London: William Heinemann, 2005.
Kallis, Aristotle. *Fascist Ideology: Territory and Expansion in Italy and Germany (1919–1945).* London: Routledge, 2000.
———. *Genocide and Fascism: The Eliminationist Drive in Fascist Europe.* London: Routledge, 2008.
Kalthoff, Jürgen, and Martin Werner. *Die Händler des Zyklon B: Tesch & Stabenow: Eine Firmengeschichte zwischen Hamburg und Auschwitz.* Hamburg: VSA, 1998.
Kane, Anne. "Reconstructing Culture in Historical Explanation: Narratives as Cultural Structure and Practice." *History and Theory* 39, no. 3 (2000): 311–30.
Kansteiner, Wulf. "Success, Truth, and Modernism in Holocaust Historiography: Reading Saul Friedländer Thirty-Five Years after the Publication of *Metahistory.*" *History and Theory,* Theme Issue 47 (2009): 29–53.
Kant, Immanuel. *Groundwork of the Metaphysics of Morals,* ed. Mary McGregor. Cambridge, UK: Cambridge University Press, 1997.
Kapferer, Jean Noël. *Rumors: Uses, Interpretations, and Images.* New Brunswick: Transaction, 1990.
Kaplan, Chaim A. *Scroll of Agony: The Warsaw Diary of Chaim A. Kaplan.* New York: Macmillan, 1965.
Kaplan, Marion A. *Between Dignity and Despair: Jewish Life in Nazi Germany.* New York: Oxford University Press, 1998.

Kassow, Samuel D. "Vilna and Warsaw, Two Ghetto Diaries: Herman Kruk and Emmanuel Ringelblum." In *Holocaust Chronicles: Individualizing the Holocaust through Diaries and Other Contemporaneous Personal Accounts,* ed. Moses Shapiro. Hoboken: Yeshiva University Press/ KTAV, 1999, 171–216.

———. *Who Will Write Our History? Emmanuel Ringelblum, the Warsaw Ghetto, and the Oyneg Shabes Archive.* Bloomington: Indiana University Press, 2007.

Katz, Steven T. *The Holocaust and Historical Context.* Oxford: Oxford University Press, 1994.

Kermish, Joseph, ed. *To Live with Honor and Die with Honor! Selected Documents from the Warsaw Ghetto Underground Archives "O.S." ("Oneg Shabbat").* Jerusalem: Yad Vashem, 1986.

Kershaw, Ian. *The Nazi Dictatorship: Problems and Perspectives of Interpretation.* 4th ed., London: Arnold, 2000.

Kévorkian, Raymond. *Le Génocide des Arméniens.* Paris: Odile Jacob, 2006.

Kielar, Wiesław. *Anus Mundi: 1,500 Days in Auschwitz Birkenau.* New York: Times Books, 1980.

Kiernan, Ben. *The Pol Pot Regime: Race, Power and Genocide in Cambodia under the Khmer Rouge, 1975–79.* New Haven: Yale University Press, 1996.

———. *Blood and Soil: A World History of Genocide and Extermination from Sparta to Darfur.* New Haven: Yale University Press, 2007.

King, Magda. *A Guide to Heidegger's Being and Time.* Albany: SUNY Press, 2001.

King, Richard H., and Dan Stone, eds. *Hannah Arendt and the Uses of History: Imperialism, Nation, Race and Genocide.* New York: Berghahn Books, 2007.

Kissi, Edward. "Genocide in Cambodia and Ethiopia." In *The Specter of Genocide: Mass Murder in Historical Perspective,* ed. Robert Gellately and Ben Kiernan. Cambridge, UK: Cambridge University Press, 2003, 307–23.

Klein, Peter, ed. *Die Einsatzgruppen in der besetzten Sowjetunion 1941/42.* Berlin: Edition Hentrich, 1997.

Klemperer, Victor. *LTI: Notizbuch eines Philologen.* Leipzig: Reclam, 1975 [1947].

———. *I Shall Bear Witness: A Diary of Victor Klemperer 1933–1941.* London: Weidenfeld and Nicolson, 1998.

Koch, Gertrud. "Der Engel des Vergessens und die Black Box der Faktizität. Zur Gedächtniskonstruktion in Claude Lanzmanns Film *Shoah.*" In *Die Einstellung ist die Einstellung. Visuelle Konstruktionen des Judentums,* ed. Gertrud Koch. Frankfurt/M: Suhrkamp, 1992, 155–69.

Konstan, David. "Anger, Hatred, and Genocide in Ancient Greece." *Common Knowledge* 13, no. 1 (2007): 170–87.

Koonz, Claudia. *The Nazi Conscience.* Cambridge, MA: Harvard University Press, 2003.

Korczak, Janusz. *The Warsaw Ghetto Memoirs of Janusz Korczak.* New Haven: Yale University Press, 1978.

Kott, Jan. Introduction to *This Way for the Gas, Ladies and Gentlemen,* by Tadeusz Borowski. New York: Penguin, 1976, 11–26.

Kruk, Herman. *The Last Days of the Jerusalem of Lithuania,* ed. Benjamin Harshav. New Haven: Yale University Press, 2002.

Kulka, Otto Dov. "The 'Reichsvereinigung' of the Jews in Germany 1938/9–1943." In *Patterns of Jewish Leadership in Nazi Europe 1933–1945,* ed. Yisrael Gutman and Cynthia J. Haft. Jerusalem: Yad Vashem, 1979, 45–58.

Kushner, Tony. "Holocaust Testimony, Ethics, and the Problem of Representation." *Poetics Today* 27, no. 2 (2006): 275–95.

LaCapra, Dominick. *Representing the Holocaust: History, Theory, Trauma.* Ithaca: Cornell University Press, 1994.

———. *History and Memory after Auschwitz.* Ithaca: Cornell University Press, 1998.

———. *Writing History, Writing Trauma.* Baltimore: Johns Hopkins University Press, 2001.

———. "Historical and Literary Approaches to the 'Final Solution': Saul Friedländer and Jonathan Littell." *History and Theory* 50 (2011): 71–97.

Lang, Berel. "Is It Possible to Misrepresent the Holocaust?" *History and Theory* 34, no. 1 (1995): 84–89.
———. *Heidegger's Silence*. Ithaca: Cornell University Press, 1996.
———. *Holocaust Representation*. Baltimore: Johns Hopkins University Press, 2000.
———. *Philosophical Witnessing: The Holocaust as Presence*. Waltham, MA: Brandeis University Press, 2009.
Langer, Lawrence L. *Holocaust Testimonies: The Ruins of Memory*. New Haven: Yale University Press, 1991.
———. *Admitting the Holocaust: Collected Essays*. New York: Oxford University Press, 1995.
Lanzmann, Claude. *Shoah: An Oral History of the Holocaust*. New York: Pantheon, 1985.
Lappin, Elena. "The Man with Two Heads." *Granta* 66 (1999): 7–65.
Laqueur, Thomas W. "We Are All Victims Now." *London Review of Books,* 8 July 2010.
Lara, María Pía. *Narrating Evil: A Postmetaphysical Theory of Reflective Judgment*. New York: Columbia University Press, 2007.
Leitner, Isabella. *Fragments of Isabella: A Memoir of Auschwitz*. New York: Thomas Y. Crowell Company, 1978.
Lekan, Thomas, and Thomas Zeller, eds. *Germany's Nature: Cultural Landscapes and Environmental History*. New Brunswick: Rutgers University Press, 2005.
Lemkin, Raphael. *Axis Rule in Occupied Europe: Laws of Occupation, Analysis of Government, Proposals for Redress*. Washington, DC: Carnegie Endowment for International Peace, 1944.
———. *Raphael Lemkin's Thoughts on Nazi Genocide: Not Guilty?,* ed. Steven L. Jacobs. Lewiston: Edwin Mellen Press, 1992.
———. "Totally Unofficial Man." In *Pioneers of Genocide Studies,* ed. Samuel Totten and Stephen L. Jacobs. New Brunswick: Transaction, 2002.
———. "Tasmania." *Patterns of Prejudice* 39, no. 2 *(2005):* 170–96.
Lengyel, Olga. *Five Chimneys: The Story of Auschwitz*. London: Granada, 1983.
Leociak, Jacek. *Text in Face of Destruction: Accounts from the Warsaw Ghetto Reconsidered*. Warsaw: Żydowski Instytut Historyczny, 2004.
Levene, Mark. "The Experience of Genocide: Armenia 1915–16 and Romania 1941–42." In *Der Völkermord an den Armeniern und die Shoah,* ed. Hans-Lukas Kieser and Dominik Schaller. Zurich: Chronos, 2002, 423–62.
———. *Genocide in the Age of the Nation-State*. Vol. 1, *The Meaning of Genocide*. London: I. B. Tauris, 2005.
Levi, Primo. *The Periodic Table*. London: Abacus, 1984.
———. *If This is a Man and The Truce*. London: Abacus, 1987.
———. *The Drowned and the Saved*. London: Abacus, 1988.
———. *The Black Hole of Auschwitz*. London: Polity Press, 2005.
Levin, Nora. *The Holocaust: The Destruction of European Jewry 1933–1945*. New York: Thomas Y. Crowell Company, 1968.
Levinas, Emmanuel. "To Love the Torah More than God." *Judaism: A Quarterly Journal of Jewish Life and Thought* 28, no. 2 (1979): 216–33.
Levine, Hillel. *In Search of Sugihara: The Elusive Japanese Diplomat Who Risked his Life to Rescue 10,000 Jews from the Holocaust*. New York: Free Press, 1996.
Levy, Daniel, and Natan Sznaider. *The Holocaust and Memory in the Global Age*. Philadelphia: Temple University Press, 2006.
Lewyn, Bert, and Bev Saltzman Lewyn. *Holocaust Memoirs: On the Run in Nazi Berlin*. Philadelphia: XLibris, 2001.
Leys, Ruth. *Trauma: A Genealogy*. Chicago: University of Chicago Press, 2000.
Lindeman, Yehudi, ed. *Shards of Memory: Narratives of Holocaust Survival*. Westport, CT: Praeger, 2007.
Longerich, Peter. *Politik der Vernichtung: Eine Gesamtdarstellung der nationalsozialistischen Judenverfolgung*. Munich: Piper, 1998.

———. *Holocaust: The Nazi Persecution and Murder of the Jews.* Oxford: Oxford University Press, 2010.
Lorenz, Chris. "Comparative Historiography: Problems and Perspectives." *History and Theory* 38, no. 1 (1999): 25–39.
———. "Model Murderers: Afterthoughts on the Goldhagen Method and History." *Rethinking History* 6, no. 2 (2002): 131–50.
Lower, Wendy. *Nazi Empire-Building and the Holocaust in Ukraine.* Chapel Hill: University of North Carolina Press, 2005.
Lozowick, Yaacov. *Hitler's Bureaucrats: The Nazi Security Police and the Banality of Evil.* London: Continuum, 2002.
Lyotard, Jean-François. *Heidegger and "the jews."* Minneapolis: University of Minnesota Press, 1990.
Maechler, Stefan. *The Wilkomirski Affair: A Study in Biographical Truth.* New York: Picador, 2001.
Maier, Charles S. *The Unmasterable Past: History, Holocaust, and German National Identity.* Cambridge, MA: Harvard University Press, 1988.
Mallman, Klaus-Michael. "Der qualitative Sprung im Vernichtungsprozeß. Das Massaker von Kamenez-Podolsk Ende August 1941." *Jahrbuch für Antisemitismusforschung* 10 (2001): 239–64.
Mamdani, Mahmood. *When Victims Become Killers: Colonialism, Nativism, and the Genocide in Rwanda.* Princeton: Princeton University Press, 2001.
Mankowitz, Zeev W. *Life Between Memory and Hope: The Survivors of the Holocaust in Occupied Germany.* New York: Cambridge University Press, 2002.
Margalit, Avishai. *The Ethics of Memory.* Cambridge, MA: Harvard University Press, 2002.
Maritain, Jacques. "La passion d'Israël" (1944), reprinted in *Le mystère d'Israël et autres essais.* Paris: Desclée de Brouwer, 1965, 203–04.
Mark, Ber. *The Scrolls of Auschwitz.* Tel Aviv: Am Oved, 1985.
Marrus, Michael R. *The Holocaust in History.* London: Penguin, 1989.
Mason, Tim. *Nazism, Fascism and the Working Class.* Cambridge, UK: Cambridge University Press, 1995.
Matlok, Siegfried, ed. *Dänemark in Hitlers Hand. Der Bericht des Reichsbevollmächtigten Werner Best über seine Besatzungspolitik in Dänemark.* Husum: Husum Verlag, 1988.
Matthäus, Jürgen. "Controlled Escalation: Himmler's Men in the Summer of 1941 and the Holocaust in the Occupied Soviet Territories." *Holocaust and Genocide Studies* 21, no. 2 (2007): 218–42.
Mazower, Mark. *Hitler's Empire: How the Nazis Ruled Europe.* London: Allen Lane, 2008.
McCarthy, Justin. *Death and Exile: The Ethnic Cleansing of Ottoman Muslims, 1821–1922.* Princeton, NJ: Princeton University Press, 1995.
McNeill, John Robert. *Something New Under the Sun: An Environmental History of the Twentieth-Century World.* New York: W. W. Norton, 2000.
Megill, Allan. *Historical Knowledge, Historical Error: A Contemporary Guide to Practice.* Chicago: University of Chicago Press, 2007.
Melson, Robert. "Choiceless Choices: Surviving on False Papers on the 'Aryan' Side." In *Gray Zones: Ambiguity and Compromise in the Holocaust and Its Aftermath*, ed. Jonathan Petropoulos and John K. Roth. New York: Berghahn Books, 2005, 91–100.
———. *False Papers: Deception and Survival in the Holocaust.* Urbana: University of Illinois Press, 2000.
Michman, Dan. "One Theme, Multiple Voices. The Role of Linguistic Cultures in Holocaust Research." In *The Holocaust: The Unique and the Universal: Essays Presented in Honor of Yehuda Bauer*, ed. Shmuel Almog et al. Jerusalem: Yad Vashem, 2001, 8–37 (in Hebrew).
———. *Holocaust Historiography: A Jewish Perspective.* London: Vallentine Mitchell, 2003.
———. "Introducing more 'Cultural History' into the Study of the Holocaust: A Response to Dan Stone." *Dapim* 23 (2009): 69–75.
———. *The Emergence of the Jewish Ghettos during the Holocaust.* New York: Cambridge University Press, 2010.

———. "Is There an Israeli School of Holocaust Research? The Holocaust and the study of Antisemitism in the State of Israel." *Zion* 74 (2010): 219–43 (in Hebrew).
Millu, Liana. *Smoke over Birkenau*. Evanston: Northwestern University Press, 1991.
Mintz, Alan. *Popular Culture and the Shaping of Holocaust Memory in America*. Seattle: University of Washington Press, 2001.
Miron, Guy. "Bridging the Divide: Holocaust Research vs. Jewish History Research—Problems and Challenges." *Yad Vashem Studies* 38, no. 2 (2010): 155–93.
Morsink, Johannes. *The Universal Declaration of Human Rights: Origins, Drafting, and Intent*. Philadelphia: University of Pennsylvania Press, 1999.
Moses, A. Dirk. *German Intellectuals and the Nazi Past*. Cambridge: Cambridge University Press, 2007.
———. "Raphael Lemkin, Culture, and the Concept of Genocide." In *The Oxford Handbook of Genocide Studies*, ed. Donald Bloxham and A. Dirk Moses. Oxford: Oxford University Press, 2010, 19–41.
———. "Redemptive Anti-Semitism and the Imperialist Imaginary." In *Years of Persecution, Years of Extermination: Saul Friedländer and the Future of Holocaust Studies*, ed. Christian Wiese and Paul Betts. London: Continuum, 2010, 233–54.
———. "Paranoia and Partisanship: Genocide Studies, Holocaust Historiography and the 'Apocalyptic Conjuncture.'" *The Historical Journal* 15, no. 2 (2011): 553–83.
Moses, A. Dirk, ed. *Genocide and Settler Society: Frontier Violence and Stolen Indigenous Children in Australian History*. New York: Berghahn Books, 2004.
———. *Empire, Colony, Genocide: Conquest, Occupation, and Subaltern Resistance in World History*. New York: Berghahn Books, 2008.
Moses, A. Dirk, and Dan Stone, eds. *Colonialism and Genocide*. London: Routledge, 2007.
Mosse, George L. *The Nationalization of the Masses. Political Symbolism and Mass Movements in Germany from the Napoleonic Wars through the Third Reich*. Ithaca: Cornell University Press, 1991.
———. *The Fascist Revolution: Toward a General Theory of Fascism*. New York: Howard Fertig, 1998.
Moyn, Samuel. *A Holocaust Controversy: The Treblinka Affair in Postwar France*. Waltham, MA: Brandeis University Press, 2005.
———. "Ordinary Memory." *Jewish Review of Books* 1 (2010).
Münz, Christoph. *Geschichtstheologie und jüdisches Gedächtnis nach Auschwitz: Über den Versuch, den Schrecken der Geschichte zu bannen*. Frankfurt/M: Stadt Frankfurt, 1994.
Musial, Bogdan. *Deutsche Zivilverwaltung und Judenverfolgung im Generalgouvernement: Eine Fallstudie zum Distrikt Lublin 1939–1944*. Wiesbaden: Harrasowitz, 1999.
Myers, David. *Re-Inventing the Jewish Past: European Jewish Intellectuals and the Zionist Return to History*. New York: Oxford University Press, 1995.
Netz, Reviel. *Barbed Wire: An Ecology of Modernity*. Middletown, CT: Wesleyan University Press, 2004.
Neumann, Boaz. "The Phenomenology of the German People's Body (*Volkskörper*) and the Extermination of the Jewish Body." *New German Critique* 106 (2009): 149–81.
———. *Die Weltanschauung des Nazismus: Raum, Körper, Sprache*. Göttingen: Wallstein, 2010.
Neumann, Franz. *Behemoth. Struktur und Praxis des Nationalsozialismus*. Frankfurt/M: Fischer, 1984.
Nichanian, Marc. *The Historiographic Perversion*. New York: Columbia University Press, 2009.
Noakes, Jeremy, and Geoffrey Pridham, eds. *Nazism: A Documentary Reader*. Vol. 3, *Foreign Policy, War and Racial Extermination*, rev. ed. Exeter: Exeter University Press, 1997.
Nolte, Ernst. *Three Faces of Fascism : Action Française, Italian fascism, National Socialism*. New York: Mentor, 1969.
———. *Der europäische Bürgerkrieg 1917–1945: Nationalsozialismus und Bolschewismus*. Berlin: Propyläen, 1987.
Nora, Pierre. "Mémoire et identité juives dans la France contemporaine." *Le Débat* 131 (September–October 2004): 24.

Novick, Peter. *The Holocaust in American Life.* New York: Houghton Mifflin, 1999.
Nunpa, Chris Mato. "Dakota Commemorative March: Thoughts and Reactions." *The American Indian Quarterly* 28, nos. 1–2 (2004): 216–37.
Ogorreck, Ralf. *Die Einsatzgruppen und die "Genesis der Endlösung."* Berlin: Metropol, 1996.
Oktem, Kerem. "Reconstructing Geographies of Nationalism: Nation, Space and Discourse in Twentieth Century Turkey." DPhil thesis, Oxford University, 2006.
Oliner, Samuel P., and Pearl M. Oliner. *The Altruistic Personality: Rescuers of Jews in Nazi Europe.* New York: Free Press, 1988.
Orth, Karin. *Das System der nationalsozialistischen Konzentrationslager: Eine politische Organisationsgeschichte.* Hamburg: Hamburger Edition, 1999.
Paldiel, Mordechai. *The Path of the Righteous: Gentile Rescuers of Jews during the Holocaust.* Hoboken: KTAV, 1993.
Palgi, Phyllis, and Henry Abramovitch. "Death: A Cross-Cultural Perspective." *Annual Reviews in Anthropology* 13 (1984): 385–417.
Passmore, Kevin. "Poststructuralism and History." In *Writing History: Theory and Practice,* ed. Stefan Berger, Heiko Feldner, and Kevin Passmore. London: Arnold, 2003, 118–40.
Patterson, David. *Sun Turned to Darkness: Memory and Recovery in the Holocaust Memoir.* New York: Syracuse University Press, 1998.
———. *Along the Edge of Annihilation: The Collapse and Recovery of Life in the Holocaust Diary.* Seattle: University of Washington Press, 1999.
Pätzold, Kurt, and Erika Schwarz, eds. *Tagesordnung Judenmord: Die Wannsee-Konferenz am 20. Januar 1942: Eine Dokumentation zur Organisation der "Endlosung."* Berlin: Metropol, 1992.
Paxton, Robert O. *The Anatomy of Fascism.* New York: Alfred A. Knopf, 2004.
Payne, Stanley G. *A History of Fascism 1914–45.* Madison: University of Wisconsin Press, 1995.
———. "Fascism—A 'Generic' Concept?" In *The Fascism Reader,* ed. Aristotle Kallis. London: Routledge, 2003, 82–88.
Pearce, Andy. "The Development of Holocaust Consciousness in Contemporary Britain, 1979–2001." *Holocaust Studies* 14, no. 2 (2008): 71–94
Perdue, Peter. "Erasing the Empire, Re-racing the Nation: Racialism and Culturalism in Imperial China." In *Imperial Formations,* ed. Ann Laura Stoler, Carole McGranaham and Peter Perdue. Santa Fe: School for Advanced Research Press, 2007, 141–72.
Perl, Gisella. *I Was a Doctor in Auschwitz.* New York: Ayer Company, 1948.
Petersen, Roger. *Understanding Ethnic Violence: Fear, Hatred, and Resentment in Twentieth Century Eastern Europe.* Cambridge, UK: Cambridge University Press, 2002.
Phayer, Michael. *The Catholic Church and the Holocaust, 1930–1965.* Bloomington: Indiana University Press, 2000.
Phayer, Michael, and Eva Fleischner. *Cries in the Night: Women Who Challenged the Holocaust.* Kansas City: Sheed & Ward, 1997.
Pohl, Dieter. *Nationalsozialistische Judenverfolgung in Ostgalizien: Organisation und Durchführung eines staatlichen Massenverbrechens.* Munich: R. Oldenbourg, 1997.
———. "Schauplatz Ukraine." In *Ausbeutung, Vernichtung, Öffentlichkeit,* ed. Norbert Frei, Sybille Steinbacher, and Bernd Wagner. Munich: Saur, 2000, 135–73.
Pois, Robert A. *National Socialism and the Religion of Nature.* London: Palgrave Macmillan, 1986.
Poliakov, Léon. *The History of Anti-Semitism.* Vol. IV, *Suicidal Europe, 1870–1933.* Philadelphia: University of Pennsylvania Press, 2003.
Poznanski, Renée. *Jews in France during World War II.* Hanover: University Press of New England, 2001.
Presner, Todd. "Subjunctive History: The Use of Counterfactuals in the Writing of the Disaster." *Storiografia: Rivista annuale di storia* 4 (2000): 23–38.
Ranciére, Jacques. "Are Some Things Unrepresentable?" In *The Future of the Image.* London: Verso, 2009, 109–38.
Reichel, Peter. *Vergangenheitsbewältigung in Deutschland. Die Auseinandersetzung mit der NS-Diktatur von 1945 bis heute.* Munich: Beck, 2001.

Reiter, Andrea. *Narrating the Holocaust*. London: Continuum, 2000.
Ricoeur, Paul. *Time and Narrative*, vol. 1. Chicago: University of Chicago Press, 1984.
Ringelblum, Emmanuel. *Notes from the Warsaw Ghetto: The Journal of Emmanuel Ringelblum*. Jerusalem: YadVashem, 1983.
Ringelheim, Joan. "Women and the Holocaust: A Reconsideration of Research." In *Different Voices: Women and the Holocaust*, ed. Carol Rittner and John K. Roth. St. Paul: Paragon House, 1993, 373–420.
Robins, Nicholas A., and Adam Jones, eds. *Genocides by the Oppressed: Subaltern Genocide in Theory and Practice*. Bloomington: Indiana University Press, 2009.
Roseman, Mark. "Surviving Memory: Truth and Inaccuracy in Holocaust Testimony." *Journal of Holocaust Education* 8, no. 1 (1999): 1–20.
———. *The Past in Hiding*. London: Penguin, 2000.
Rosenfeld, Oskar. *In the Beginning Was the Ghetto*. Evanston: Northwestern University Press, 2002.
Roskies, David G. *Against the Apocalypse: Responses to Catastrophe in Modern Jewish Culture*. Cambridge, MA: Harvard University Press, 1984.
———. *The Jewish Search for a Usable Past*. Bloomington: Indiana University Press, 1999.
Roskies, David G., ed. *The Literature of Destruction: Jewish Responses to Catastrophe*. Philadelphia: Jewish Publications Society, 1989.
Rosman, Moshe. *How Jewish Is Jewish History?* Oxford: Littman Library of Jewish Civilization, 2009.
Rössler, Mechtild, and Sabine Schleiermacher, eds. *Der "Generalplan Ost": Hauptlinien der nationalsozialistischen Planungs- und Vernichtungspolitik*. Berlin: Akademie, 1993.
Rothfels, Hans. "Augenzeugenbericht zu den Massenvergasungen. Dokumentation." *Vierteljahreshefte für Zeitgeschichte* 1 (1953): 177–94.
Rubenstein, Joshua, and Ilya Altman, eds. *The Unknown Black Book: The Holocaust in the German-Occupied Soviet Territories*. Bloomington: Indiana University Press, 2008.
Rubin, Miri. "What is Cultural History Now?" In *What is History Now?*, ed. David Cannadine. Basingstoke: Palgrave Macmillan, 2002, 80–94.
Runia, Eelco. "Burying the Dead, Creating the Past," *History and Theory* 46 (2007): 313–25.
Rupnow, Dirk. *Täter-Gedächtnis-Opfer. Das "Jüdische Zentralmuseum" in Prag 1942–1945*. Vienna: PicusVerlag, 2000.
———. "'Ihr müßt sein, auch wenn Ihr nicht mehr seid': The Jewish Central Museum in Prague and Historical Memory in the Third Reich." *Holocaust and Genocide Studies* 16, no. 1 (2002): 23–53.
———. *Vernichten und Erinnern. Spuren nationalsozialistischer Gedächtnispolitik*. Göttingen: Wallstein, 2005.
———. *Aporien des Gedenkens. Reflexionen über "Holocaust" und Erinnerung*. Freiburg i.Br: Rombach, 2006.
———. "Racializing Historiography: Anti-Jewish Scholarship in the Third Reich." *Patterns of Prejudice* 42, no. 1 (2008): 27–59.
Rüsen, Jörn. *History: Narration-Interpretation-Orientation*. NewYork: Berghahn Books, 2005.
———. "Humanism in Response to the Holocaust—Destruction or Innovation?" *Postcolonial Studies* 11, no. 2 (2008): 191–200.
Rüsen, Jörn, ed. *Meaning and Representation in History*. NewYork: Berghahn Books, 2006.
Sahlins, Marshall. *Islands of History*. Chicago: University of Chicago Press, 1985.
Sanders, Mark. *Ambiguities of Witnessing: Law and Literature in the Time of a Truth Commission*. Stanford: Stanford University Press, 2007.
Saunders, John Joseph. *The History of the Mongol Conquests*. Philadelphia: University of Pennsylvania Press, 2001.
Sax, Boria. *Animals in the Third Reich: Pets, Scapegoats, and the Holocaust*. NewYork: Continuum, 2000.
Scales, Len. "Bread, Cheese and Genocide: Imagining the Destruction of Peoples in Medieval Western Europe." *History* 92 (2007): 284–300.

Schaller, Dominik, and Jürgen Zimmerer, eds. *The Origins of Genocide: Raphael Lemkin as a Historian of Mass Violence*. London: Routledge, 2009.

Schmoll, Friedemann. "Die Verteidigung organischer Ordnungen: Naturschutz und Antisemitismus zwischen Kaiserreich und Nationalsozialismus." In *Naturschutz und Nationalsozialismus*, ed. Joachim Radkau and Franz Uekötter. Frankfurt/M: Campus, 2003, 169–82.

Seeber, Eva. "Der Anteil der Minderheitsorganisation 'Selbstschutz' an den faschistischen Vernichtungsaktionen im Herbst und Winter 1939 in Polen." *Jahrbuch für Geschichte der sozialistischen Länder Europas* 13, no. 2 (1969): 3–34.

Seidman, Naomi. "Elie Wiesel and the Scandal of Jewish Rage." *Jewish Social Studies*, n.s. 3, no. 1 (1996): 1–19.

Shenfield, Stephen D. "The Circassians: A Forgotten Genocide?" In *The Massacre in History*, ed. Mark Levene and Penny Roberts. Oxford: Berghahn Books, 1999, 149–62.

Sierakowiak, Dawid. *The Diary of Dawid Sierakowiak: Five Notebooks form the Łódź Ghetto*, ed. Alan Adelson. London: Bloomsbury, 1997.

Sloterdijk, Peter. *Sphären: Plurale Sphärologie*. Vol. 3, *Schäume*. Frankfurt/M: Suhrkamp, 2004.

Soyinka, Wole. *The Burden of Memory, the Muse of Forgiveness*. New York: Oxford University Press, 1999.

Specter, Matthew G. *Habermas: An Intellectual Biography*. Cambridge, UK: Cambridge University Press, 2010.

Spector, Shmuel. "Aktion 1005—Effacing the Murder of Millions." *Holocaust and Genocide Studies* 5, no. 2 (1990): 157–73.

Spencer, Jonathan. "Symbolic Anthropology." In *Encyclopedia of Social and Cultural Anthropology*, ed. Alan Barnard and Jonathan Spencer. London: Routledge, 2002, 535–39.

Spiegel, Gabrielle. "History and Post-Modernism." *Past and Present* 135 (1992): 194–208.

Spiegelman, Art. *Maus: A Survivor's Tale*, 2 vols. New York: Penguin, 1986, 1991.

Stauber, Roni. *The Holocaust in Israeli Public Debate in the 1950s: Ideology and Memory*. London: Vallentine Mitchell, 2007.

Steinbacher, Sybille. *"Musterstadt" Auschwitz: Germanisierungspolitik und Judenmord in Ostoberschlesien*. Munich: K. G. Saur, 2000.

———. *Auschwitz: A History*. London: Penguin, 2005.

Steiner, George. *Language and Silence: Essays 1958–1966*. London: Penguin, 1967.

Sternhell, Zeev. "How to think about Fascism and its Ideology." *Constellations: An International Journal of Critical and Democratic Theory* 15, no. 3 (2008): 280–90.

———. *The Anti-Enlightenment Tradition*. New Haven: Yale University Press, 2010.

Stiglmayr, Alexandra, ed. *Mass Rape: The War against Women in Bosnia-Herzegovina*. Lincoln: University of Nebraska Press, 2004.

Stone, Dan. "The Sonderkommando Photographs." *Jewish Social Studies* 7, no. 3 (2001): 131–48.

———. *Constructing the Holocaust: A Study in Historiography*. London: Vallentine Mitchell, 2003.

———. *Responses to Nazism in Britain 1933–1939: Before War and Holocaust*. Basingstoke: Palgrave Macmillan, 2003.

———. "The Historiography of Genocide: Beyond 'Uniqueness' and Ethnic Competition." *Rethinking History* 8, no. 1 (2004): 127–42.

———. "Raphael Lemkin on the Holocaust." *Journal of Genocide Research* 7, no. 4 (2005): 539–50.

———. *History, Memory and Mass Atrocity: Essays on the Holocaust and Genocide*. London: Vallentine Mitchell, 2006.

———. "Holocaust Historiography and Cultural History." *Dapim* 23 (2009): 52–68.

———. *Histories of the Holocaust*. Oxford: Oxford University Press, 2010.

———. "Beyond the Mnemosyne Institute: The Future of Memory after the Age of Commemoration." In *The Future of Memory*, ed. Rick Crownshaw, Jane Kilby, and Antony Rowland. New York: Berghahn Books, 2010, 17–36.

———. "Genocide and Memory." In *The Oxford Handbook of Genocide Studies*, ed. Donald Bloxham and A. Dirk Moses. Oxford: Oxford University Press, 2010, 102–19.

———. "*Nazi Germany and the Jews* and the Future of Holocaust Historiography." In *Years of Persecution, Years of Extermination: Saul Friedländer and the Future of Holocaust Studies,* ed. Christian Wiese and Paul Betts. London: Continuum, 2010, 343–57.
———. "Beyond the Auschwitz Syndrome: Holocaust Historiography after the Cold War." *Patterns of Prejudice* 44, no. 5 (2010): 454–68.
———. "Surviving in the Corridors of History or, History as Double or Nothing." In *Federman's Fictions: Innovation, Theory and the Holocaust,* ed. Jeffrey R. Di Leo. Albany: SUNY Press, 2011, 203–13.
———. "Defending the Plural: Hannah Arendt and Genocide Studies." *New Formations* 71 (2011): 46–57.
———. "Memory Wars in the 'New Europe.'" In *The Oxford Handbook of Postwar European History,* ed. Dan Stone. Oxford: Oxford University Press, 2012, 714–31.
Stone, Dan, ed. *The Historiography of the Holocaust.* Basingstoke: Palgrave Macmillan, 2004.
———. *The Historiography of Genocide.* Basingstoke: Palgrave Macmillan, 2008.
———. *Genocide and Philosophy,* special issue of the *Journal of Genocide Research* 13, nos. 1–2 (2011).
———. *The Oxford Handbook of Postwar European History.* Oxford: Oxford University Press, 2012.
Stout, Harry S. *Upon the Altar of the Nation: A Moral History of the Civil War.* New York: Penguin, 2006.
Stover, Eric. *The Witnesses: War Crimes and the Promise of Justice in the Hague.* Philadelphia: University of Pennsylvania Press, 2005.
Struve, Kai. "Ritual und Gewalt—Die Pogrome des Sommers 1941." In *Synchrone Welten. Zeiträume jüdischer Geschichte,* ed. Dan Diner. Göttingen: Vandenhoeck & Ruprecht, 2005, 225–50.
Sutton, Philip W. *Nature, Environment and Society.* Basingstoke: Palgrave Macmillan, 2004.
Szeintuch, Yechiel. *Isaiah Spiegel—Yiddish Narrative Prose from the Lodz Ghetto.* Jerusalem: Magnes Press, 1995, 7–92 (in Hebrew).
Szwajger, Adina Blady. *I Remember Nothing More: The Warsaw Children's Hospital and the Jewish Resistance.* New York: Pantheon Books, 1990.
Tal, Uriel. "Forms of Pseudo-Religion in the German *Kulturbereich* Prior to the Holocaust." *Immanuel* 3 (1973–74): 68–73.
———. *Religion, Politics and Ideology in the Third Reich: Selected Essays.* London: Routledge, 2004.
Tanay, Emanuel. "On Being a Survivor." In *Bearing Witness to the Holocaust, 1939–1989,* ed. Alan Berger. Lewiston: Edwin Mellen Press, 1991, 17–31.
Tewes, Ernst. "Seelsorger bei den Soldaten 1940-1956. Aufzeichnungen und Erinnerungen." In *Das Erzbistum München und Freising in der Zeit der nationalsozialistischen Herrschaft,* vol. 2, ed. Georg Schwaiger. Munich: Schnell und Steiner, 1984, 244–87.
Thomson, Ian. *Primo Levi.* London: Hutchinson, 2002.
Tobias, Jim G. „Ihr Gewissen war rein; sie haben es nie benutzt". *Die Verbrechen der Polizeikompanie Nürnberg.* Nuremberg: Antogo, 2005.
Tooze, Adam. *The Wages of Destruction: The Making and Breaking of the Nazi Economy.* New York: Allen Lane, 2006.
Traverso, Enzo. *Understanding the Nazi Genocide: Marxism after Auschwitz.* London: Pluto Press, 1999.
———. *The Origins of Nazi Violence.* New York: The New Press, 2003.
———. *Le Passé, modes d'emploi: Histoire, memoire, politique.* Paris: La Fabrique, 2005.
———. *À feu et à sang. De la guerre civile européenne (1914–1915).* Paris: Stock, 2007.
———. "Interpreting Fascism: Mosse, Sternhell and Gentile in Comparative Perspective." *Constellations: An International Journal of Critical and Democratic Theory* 15, no. 3 (2008): 303–19.
Traverso, Paola. "Victor Klemperers Deutschlandbild." *Tel Aviver Jahrbuch für deutsche Geschichte* 26 (1997): 307–44.
Trunk, Isaiah. *Judenrat: The Jewish Councils in Eastern Europe under German Occupation.* New York: Macmillan, 1972.

Tsahor, Ze'ev. "Ben-Gurion's Mythopoetics." *Israel Affairs* 1, no. 3 (1995): 61–84.
Tuck, Richard. *The Rights of War and Peace: Political Thought and the International Order from Grotius to Kant.* Oxford: Oxford University Press, 1999.
Unger, Michal. *Łódź: The Last Ghetto in Poland.* Jerusalem: Yad Vashem, 2005 (in Hebrew).
Utitz, Emil. *Psychologie des Lebens in Konzentrationslager Theresienstadt.* Vienna: Verlag A. Sexl, 1948.
van Alphen, Ernst. "Caught by Images: On the Role of the Visual Imprints in Holocaust Testimonies." *Journal of Visual Culture* 1 (2000): 205–22.
van Gennep, Arnold. "The Rites of Passage." In *Death, Mourning and Burial: A Cross-Cultural Reader*, ed. Antonius C. G. M. Robben. Malden, MA: Blackwell, 2004, 213–23.
Ventrone, Angelo. *Il Nemico Interno. Immagini, parole e simboli della lotta politica nell'Italia del Novecento.* Rome: Donzelli, 2005.
Veyne, Paul. *Writing History: Essay on Epistemology.* Manchester: Manchester University Press, 1984.
Visweswaran, Kamala. "The Interventions of Culture: Claude Lévi-Strauss, Race, and the Critique of Historical Time." In *Race and Racism in Continental Philosophy*, ed. Robert Bernasconi with Sybol Cook. Bloomington: Indiana University Press, 2003, 227–48.
Waller, James. *Becoming Evil: How Ordinary People Commit Genocide and Mass Killing.* Oxford: Oxford University Press, 2002.
Waxman, Zoë Vania. "Unheard Testimony, Untold Stories: The Representation of Women's Holocaust Experiences." *Women's History Review* 12, no. 4 (2003): 661–77.
———. *Writing the Holocaust: Identity, Testimony, Representation.* Oxford: Oxford University Press, 2006.
———. "Towards an Integrated History of the Holocaust: Masculinity, Femininity, and Genocide." In *Years of Persecution, Years of Extermination: Saul Friedländer and the Future of Holocaust Studies*, ed. Christian Wiese and Paul Betts. London: Continuum, 2010, 311–21.
———. "Testimony and Silence: Sexual Violence and the Holocaust." In *Feminism, Literature, and Rape Narratives: Violence and Violation*, ed. Zoe Brigley and Sorcha Gunne. London: Routledge, 2010, 117–29.
Weber, Eugen. *Varieties of Fascism: Doctrines of Revolution in the Twentieth Century.* New York: Van Nostrand, 1964.
Wegner, Bernd. "Erschriebene Siege. Franz Halder, die ‚Historical Division' und die Rekonstruktion des Zweiten Weltkrieges im Geiste des deutschen Generalstabes." In *Politischer Wandel, organisierte Gewalt und nationale Sicherheit. Beiträge zur neueren Geschichte Deutschlands und Frankreichs*, ed. Ernst Willi Hansen, Gerhard Schreiber, and Bernd Wegner. Munich: R. Oldenbourg, 1995, 287–302.
Weinrich, Harald. *Lethe. Kunst und Kritik des Vergessens*, 3rd ed. Munich: Beck, 2000.
Weissman, Gary. *Fantasies of Witnessing: Postwar Efforts to Experience the Holocaust.* Ithaca: Cornell University Press, 2004.
Wells, C. J. *German: A Linguistic History to 1945.* Oxford: Oxford University Press, 2003.
Welzer, Harald. *Verweilen beim Grauen. Essays zum wissenschaftlichen Umgang mit dem Holocaust.* Tübingen: Edition Diskord, 1997.
Weschler, Lawrence. *A Miracle, a Universe: Settling Accounts with Torturers.* New York: Pantheon, 1990.
Westermann, Edward. *Hitler's Police Battalions: Enforcing Racial War in the East.* Lawrence: University of Kansas Press, 2005.
White, Hayden. "Figural Realism in Witness Literature." *Parallax* 10, no. 1 (2004): 113–24.
———. "Introduction: Historical Fiction, Fictional History, and Historical Reality." *Rethinking History* 9, nos. 2–3 (2005): 147–57.
Wiener, Jon. "History as Obligation: An Interview with Friedlander." *Dissent* (web), 5 July 2007, http://dissentmagazine.org/online.php?id=29.
Wiese, Christian, and Paul Betts, eds. *Years of Persecution, Years of Extermination: Saul Friedländer and the Future of Holocaust Studies.* London: Continuum, 2010.

Wiesel, Elie. "Jewish Values in a Post-Holocaust Future: A Symposium." *Judaism* 16, no. 3 (1967).
———. *One Generation After.* New York: Random House, 1970.
———. *A Jew Today.* New York: Vintage, 1979.
———. *Evil and Exile.* Notre Dame: University of Notre Dame Press, 1990.
———. *All Rivers Run to the Sea:* Memoirs. New York: Knopf, 1995.
———. *Night.* New York: Hill and Wang, 2006.
Wieviorka, Annette. "On Testimony." In *Holocaust Remembrance: The Shapes of Memory,* ed. Geoffrey H. Hartman. Oxford: Blackwell, 1994, 23–32.
———. *The Era of the Witness.* Ithaca: Cornell University Press, 2006.
Wildt, Michael. *Generation des Unbedingten: Das Führungskorps des Reichssicherheitshauptamtes.* Hamburg: Hamburger Edition, 2002.
———. *Volksgemeinschaft als Selbstermächtigung: Gewalt gegen Juden in der deutschen Provinz 1919 bis 1939.* Hamburg: Hamburger Edition, 2007.
Wilhelm, Hans-Heinrich. "Antisemitismus im Baltikum." In *Die Normalität des Verbrechens: Bilanz und Perspektiven der Forschung zu den nationalsozialistischen Gewaltverbrechen,* ed. Helge Grabitz, Klaus Bästlein, and Johannes Tuchel. Berlin: Edition Hentrich, 1994, 85–102.
Wilkomirski, Binjamin. *Fragments: Memories of a Childhood, 1939–1948.* London: Picador, 1996.
Williams, John Alexander. *Turning to Nature in Germany: Hiking, Nudism, and Conservation, 1900–1940.* Stanford: Stanford University Press, 2007.
Winter, Jay. *Remembering War: The Great War Between Memory and History in the Twentieth Century.* New Haven: Yale University Press, 2006.
Wippermann, Wolfgang. *Faschismustheorien. Die Entwicklung der Diskussion von den Anfängen bis heute.* Darmstadt: Wissenschaftliche Buchgesellschaft, 1997.
Wollaston, Isabel. *A War Against Memory? The Future of Holocaust Remembrance.* London: SPCK, 1983.
———. "'What Can—and Cannot—Be Said': Religious Language after the Holocaust." *Journal of Literature and Theology* 6, no. 1 (1992): 47–57.
———. "'Memory and Monument': Holocaust Testimony as Sacred Text." In *The Sociology of Sacred Texts,* ed. Jon Davies and Isabel Wollaston. Sheffield: Continuum, 1993, 37–44.
Woodley, Daniel. *Fascism and Political Theory: Critical Perspectives on Fascist Ideology.* London: Routledge, 2010.
Wróbel, Piotr. "Hitler's Helpers? The *Judenräte* Controversy." In *Lessons and Legacies.* Vol. IV, *Reflections on Religion, Justice, Sexuality, and Genocide,* ed. Larry V. Thompson. Evanston: Northwestern University Press, 2003, 152–62.
Young, James E. *Writing and Rewriting the Holocaust: Narrative and the Consequences of Interpretation.* Bloomington: Indiana University Press, 1990.
———. "Between History and Memory: The Uncanny Voice of the Historian and the Survivor." *History and Memory* 9, nos. 1–2 (1997): 47–58.
Young, James E., ed. *The Art of Memory: Holocaust Memorials in History.* Munich: Prestel, 1994.
Zagorin, Perez. "History, the Referent, and Narrative: Reflections on Postmodernism Now." *History and Theory* 38, no. 1 (1999): 1–24.
Zeitlin, Froma I. "The Vicarious Witness: Belated Memory and Authorial Presence in Recent Holocaust Literature." *History & Memory* 10, no. 2 (1998): 5–42.
Zelkowicz, Yosef. *In Those Terrible Days: Notes from the Lodz Ghetto,* ed. Michal Unger. Jerusalem: Yad Vashem, 2002.
Ziesing, Hartmut. "A Flowery Paradise in Auschwitz: The Garden of the Kommandant of Auschwitz, Rudolf Höß." *Centropa* 4, no. 2 (2004): 142–46.
Zimmermann, Moshe, ed. *On Germans and Jews under the Nazi Regime: Essays by Three Generations of Historians.* Jerusalem: Magnes Press, 2006.
Žižek, Slavoj. *Did Somebody Say Totalitarianism? Five Interventions in the (Mis)use of a Notion.* London: Verso, 2001.

Contributors

Doris L. Bergen is the Chancellor Rose and Ray Wolfe Professor of Holocaust Studies at the University of Toronto. Her publications include *Twisted Cross: The German Christian Movement in the Third Reich* (1996); *War and Genocide: A Concise History of the Holocaust* (2003); *The Sword of the Lord: Military Chaplains from the First to the Twenty-First Centuries* (ed., 2004); and *Lessons and Legacies VIII: From Generation to Generation* (ed., 2008).

Donald Bloxham is Professor of Modern History at Edinburgh University. He is author of *Genocide on Trial* (2001); the Raphael Lemkin Award-winning *The Great Game of Genocide: Imperialism, Nationalism and the Destruction of the Ottoman Armenians* (2005); and *The Final Solution: A Genocide* (2009). He is also co-author with Tony Kushner of *The Holocaust: Critical Historical Approaches* (2005), and co-editor with A. Dirk Moses of the *Oxford Handbook of Genocide Studies* (2010).

Alon Confino is Professor of History at the University of Virginia. He has written substantially on nationhood, memory, and historical method and narrative in Germany and modern history. His article "Narrative Form and Historical Sensation: On Saul Friedländer's *The Years of Extermination*," was published in *History and Theory* (October 2009), and his book *Foundational Pasts: The Holocaust as Historical Understanding* was published by Cambridge University Press in 2012. He recently finished a book titled, *A World Without Jews: Germans' Memories of Jews in the Third Reich*.

Federico Finchelstein is Associate Professor of History at the New School for Social Research and Eugene Lang College of The New School in New York City. He is the director of the NSSR Janey Program in Latin American Studies. Professor Finchelstein is the author of four books on fascism, the Holocaust, and Jewish history in Latin America and Europe. His latest book is *Transatlantic Fascism: Ideology, Violence and the Sacred in Argentina and Italy, 1919–1945* (2010).

Saul Friedländer is Professor of History at UCLA and the incumbent of the 1939 Club Chair in Holocaust Studies. He has published widely on National Socialism and the Holocaust, most recently, *Nazi Germany and the Jews: The Years of Persecution, 1933–1939* (1997) and *The Years of Extermination: Nazi Germany and the Jews, 1939–1945* (2007). For the latter volume, Friedländer was awarded the German Book Trade Association Peace Prize (*Friedenspreis*) and the Pulitzer Prize.

Amos Goldberg is a senior lecturer in Holocaust Studies at the Hebrew University of Jerusalem and a co-editor of the bilingual (Hebrew and English) interdisciplinary journal *Dapim: Studies on the Holocaust*. He has published on various theoretical and historiographical issues in regard to the Holocaust. His forthcoming book (in Hebrew) deals with Jewish autobiographical writings during the Holocaust.

Wulf Kansteiner is Associate Professor of History and Judaic Studies at SUNY Binghamton. He has published articles on collective memory, trauma theory, and German intellectual and media history in *History and Theory, German Politics and Society, New German Critique, Rethinking History, History of the Human Sciences,* and the *Journal of Contemporary History*. He is the author of *In Pursuit of German Memory: History, Television, and Politics after Auschwitz* (2006).

A. Dirk Moses is Professor of Global and Colonial History at the European University Institute, Florence, and Associate Professor in the Department of History at the University of Sydney. His current interests are in world history, genocide, the United Nations, colonialism/imperialism, and terror. He is the author of *German Intellectuals and the Nazi Past* (2007). His anthologies include *Genocide and Settler Society: Frontier Violence and Stolen Indigenous Children in Australian History* (2004); *Empire, Colony, Genocide: Conquest, Occupation and Subaltern Resistance in World History* (2008); and *The Oxford Handbook of Genocide Studies* (co-edited with Donald Bloxham, 2010).

Samuel Moyn is Professor of History at Columbia University, where he has taught since 2001. He is the author of *Origins of the Other: Emmanuel Levinas Between Revelation and Ethics* (2005); *A Holocaust Controversy: The Treblinka Affair in Postwar France* (2005); and *The Last Utopia: Human Rights in History* (2010).

Boaz Neumann is Assistant Professor in the Department of History, Tel-Aviv University. He works on topics including modern Germany, especially Weimar and the Third Reich, early Zionism, and Heidegger as historian. Recent publications include *Nazi Weltanschauung: Space, Body, Language* (Hebrew, 2001; German, 2010); *Being-in-the-Weimar-Republic* (Hebrew, 2007); *Nazism: History, Historiography, Methodology* (Hebrew, 2007); and *Land and Desire in Early Zionism* (Hebrew, 2009; English, 2011).

Dirk Rupnow teaches at the *Institut für Zeitgeschichte* at the University of Innsbruck. He is the author of *Aporien des Gedenkens. Reflexionen über "Holocaust" und Erinnerung* (2006); *Vernichten und Erinnern. Spuren nationalsozialistischer Gedächtnispolitik* (2005); *Die "Zentralstelle für jüdische Auswanderung" als Beraubungsinstitution* (2004) (with Gabriele Anderl); *Täter – Gedächtnis – Opfer. Das "Jüdische Zentralmuseum" in Prag 1942–1945* (2000); and *Judenforschung im Dritten Reich. Wissenschaft zwischen Politik, Propaganda und Ideologie* (2011). He is the editor of *"Judenforschung": Zwischen Wissenschaft und Ideologie* (co-edited with Nicolas Berg and Dan Diner), in *Simon Dubnow Institute Yearbook* 5 (2006); *Pseudowissenschaft. Konzeptionen von Nichtwissenschaftlichkeit in der Wissenschaftsgeschichte* (co-edited with Veronika Lipphardt, Jens Thiel, and Christina Wessely, 2008); and *Zeitgeschichte ausstellen in Österreich. Museen – Gedenkstätten – Ausstellungen* (co-edited with Heidemarie Uhl, 2010).

Dan Stone is Professor of Modern History at Royal Holloway, University of London. His recent publications include *The Historiography of Genocide* (ed., 2008); *Histories of the Holocaust* (2010); and *The Oxford Handbook of Postwar European History* (ed., 2012).

Zoë Waxman is a Lecturer in History at Royal Holloway, University of London. Previously she taught at Oxford University. She is the author of *Writing the Holocaust: Identity, Testimony, Representation* (2006), and numerous articles relating to the Holocaust. Her research interests include Holocaust testimony and representation, memory, and gender. She is currently writing a book exploring women's experiences of the Holocaust, to be published by Oxford University Press.

Hayden White is University Professor of the History of Consciousness, Emeritus, in the University of California and former Professor of Comparative Literature at Stanford University.

Index

A
Acton, Lord, 4–5, 7, 8, 10, 11
Adam, Uwe, 239
Aegean Islands, 187
Africa, 164, 264
Agamben, Giorgio, 139
Aktion 1005, 63
Aktion Reinhard, 63
Albigenses, 278
Algeria, 283
Allardyce, Gilbert, 262
Aly, Götz, 38, 53, 82
Amalek, 282
American Civil War, 130
American Indians, 284
Améry, Jean, 259
amida, 84, 95
Amsterdam, 209
Anatolia, 235, 238, 239
Ankersmit, Frank, 7, 10, 12, 14
Annales, 6, 79
anti-fascism, 260
antisemitism, 34, 35, 37, 50, 53, 55, 65, 74, 83, 90, 134, 160, 164, 165, 184, 186, 210, 211, 212, 213, 215, 216, 217, 218, 222, 224, 234, 243, 244, 247, 251, 259, 261, 274, 286
Antonescu, Ion, 242, 243, 249
Apache Indians, 283
Arendt, Hannah, 1, 50, 72, 93, 95, 119, 120, 262, 265
Aristotle, 197
Armenian genocide, 171, 235, 238, 240–41, 244, 273, 276

Armenians, 171, 238, 239, 240
   massacres of (1894–96), 238
Arnold, Matthew, 12, 49
Aryanization, 67
Asch, Shaul, 93
Assyrians, genocide of, 235
Auerbach, Rachel, 90, 91, 92
Augustine, 132
Auschwitz, 15, 29, 37, 65, 67, 69, 72, 82, 106, 112, 113, 114, 115, 117, 120, 121, 146, 149, 153, 165, 166, 167, 172, 183, 187, 198–200, 207, 208, 217, 260
   as "*anus mundi*", 112
   as model German town, 117
   "capital of the Holocaust", 116
Auschwitz Album, 71
Austin, J. L., 196–97, 198
Austro-Hungarian Empire, 234, 246
Ayers, Edward, 33

B
Baden Baden, 36
Badiou, Alain, 265
Baeck, Leo, 87
Bajohr, Frank, 11, 13, 183
Balkans, 235, 236, 237, 246
Balkan Wars (1912–13), 235, 238
Ball, Karyn, 11–12, 14
Baltic States, 160, 248, 249
Ban Ki-moon, 168
barbed wire, 112–14
Bar Levav, Avriel, 92
Baron, Salo, 272
Bartov, Omer, 82, 160

Bataille, Georges, 51
Bauer, Yehuda, 83, 84, 262
Bauman, Zygmunt, 111
Bäumler, Alfred, 54
Będzin, 163
Belarus, 247
Belgium, 212, 215, 216, 218
Bełżec, 63, 249
Ben Gurion, David, 129, 273
Benigni, Roberto, 193
Bereza-Kartuska, 182
Bergen-Belsen, 114
Bergman, Hugo, 87
Beria, Lavrentii, 283
Berkhofer, Robert, 3, 55
Berlin-Baghdad Railway, 239
Berlin Treaty (1878), 238, 248
Berning, Bishop, 183
Bessarabia, 242, 248, 249
Bettelheim, Bruno, 114
Betts, Paul, 47, 56
Białystok, 276
Białystok Ghetto, 47
Bielski, Tuvia, 162
Bielski brothers, 168
bio-politics, 118
Blackbourn, David, 47, 106
Blanchot, Maurice, 52
Blobel, Paul, 63
Bloch, Marc, 79, 89
Bloxham, Donald, 10, 11, 150, 285–86
Blumenthal, Nahman, 90, 93–94
Bolshevik Revolution, 248
Borges, Jorge Luis, 144, 258–59, 265
Bosnia, 170, 236
Bourdieu, Pierre, 84, 95
Bramwell, Anna, 101
Breisach, Ernst, 50
Brieman, Yerahmiel, 94
Britain, 9, 102, 212, 235, 237, 238
Brod, Max, 87
Broszat, Martin, 181, 186, 223
Browning, Christopher, 8, 10, 11, 82, 83, 137, 150, 160, 195, 217
Brussels, 209
Buchenwald, 151, 170
Buczacz, 160–61
Bukovina, 242, 248, 249
Bulgaria, 216, 236, 238, 248, 252
Burke, Edmund, 159

Burke, Peter, 44–45, 47, 48, 49, 50, 80
Burkhardt, Jakob, 79
Burleigh, Michael, 263
Burrin, Philippe, 50
Bury, J. B., 5

C
Cambodia, 171
Canada, 169
Carthage, 277, 282
Cathars, 273
Catholic Church, 83, 188
Caucasus, 237, 238, 239, 240, 283
Certeau, Michel de, 181
Chalk, Frank, 273
Chamberlain, Houston Stewart, 54
Chartier, Roger, 5, 32, 48
Chechens, 283
Chełmno, 170, 185
China, 282
Christianity, 132–33, 134–35, 139–40, 216, 234, 273
Cicero, 284
Circassians, 237, 283
Clendinnen, Inga, 35, 144
Clinton, Bill, 171
Cohen, Boaz, 90
Cohen, Jeremy, 132
Cohn, Norman, 54
Cold War, 47, 69, 132, 135, 138, 236
  and Holocaust memory, 132–33, 135, 138
Collingwood, R. G., 51
Committee of Union and Progress, 238, 239, 240, 241
Communism, 169, 247
concentration camps, 67, 114, 143, 145, 148, 151, 153, 264, 274
  liberation of, 68
Confessing Church, 185, 188
Confino, Alon, 4, 8, 13, 47, 48, 52, 53, 54, 55, 56, 79, 137
Conrad, Joseph, 164
Conservation Associations (Germany), 111
Consistoire (France), 187
Crimea, 237
Crimean Tartars, 237
Croatia, 212, 216, 246, 247, 249, 250
Cru, Jean Norton, 128

Crusades, 278
Cuba, 163
cultural history, 11, 12, 13, 24, 34, 35, 39, 44–56, 79, 80, 86, 87, 95, 96
Czechoslovakia, 248
Czerniaków, Adam, 92, 163

D
Dachau, 151
Dante, 199, 207
Darfur, 170
Darnton, Robert, 80
Darré, Richard Walther, 101
Dawes, James, 130
Dawidowicz, Lucy, 50, 146, 149, 150
Dean, Carolyn, 46
De Felice, Renzo, 262
Defiance (Zwick), 168
Degesch, 115
Denmark, 216
Derrida, Jacques, 12
Des Pres, Terrence, 153
Deutscher Bund Heimatschutz, 104
Didi-Huberman, Georges, 62, 71, 72
Diner, Dan, 12, 186, 273
Dinur, Benzion, 90
Dissent, 130
Dobruja, 248
Doctorow, E. L., 219
Doerner, Bernward, 183
Douglas, Mary, 92
Dragon, Shlomo, 120
Dresden, 209
Du Bois, W. E. B., 274
Durkheim, Emile, 278

E
Eatwell, Roger, 263
Echternkamp, Jörg, 183
Eck, Nathan, 90
Eghigian, Greg, 47
Eichmann, Adolf, 65, 129
    trial of, 130
Einsatzgruppen, 116, 160, 216, 241, 248
Eley, Geoff, 29
Elias, Norbert, 285
Eliot, T. S., 220
Ellenbogen, Marianne, 150
Enlightenment, 37, 233, 235, 272, 274
environmental history, 47, 118

epistemology, 4, 12, 13, 74, 81, 129, 130, 136, 194, 203, 220, 222
Ernest, Stefan, 210
Estonia, 164
Euthanasia program, 63
Evans, Richard, 51

F
Facing History and Ourselves, 162
Fanon, Frantz, 274
Farbstein, Esther, 80
fascism, 1, 118, 234, 255–66 *See also* Italian Fascism
    Argentine, 260
    as reaction to Marxism, 257
    as tool of capitalism, 256
    Brazilian, 260
    centrality of antisemitism to, 259
    generic definition of, 256–58, 261, 265
    German, 256, 265
    historiography of, 255–56, 262, 263, 265
    Japanese, 256
    Latin American, 256
    Romanian, 260
    "sacred" aspects of, 263–64
Fasolt, Constantin, 6
Fassin, Didier, 139
Febvre, Lucien, 79
Fein, Helen, 165
Felman, Shoshana, 148
Ferderber-Salz, Bertha, 152
Finchelstein, Federico, 11
Finkelstein, Norman, 158
Finland, 187, 221
Fischer, Eugen, 54
Fischer, Max, 112
Foucault, Michel, 95, 113, 205
France, 102, 133–36, 165, 212, 215, 216, 247, 252
Frank, Anne, 148, 163
Frank, Hans, 243
Frankfurt Auschwitz Trials, 47
Frankfurt School, 137, 265
French Revolution, 24, 32, 33, 184, 235, 248
Freud, Sigmund, 259, 265
Friedlander, Henry, 172

Friedländer, Saul, 1, 4, 8, 9, 10, 13, 25–26, 27, 38, 40, 46, 48, 52, 53, 56, 73, 80–82, 83, 85, 96, 130, 136–38, 145, 153, 192, 203–24, 261, 262
Friedman, Henry, 168, 169–70, 171
Friedman, Philip, 83
Friends of the Earth, 103
Fritzsche, Peter, 13, 29, 47, 56
Frye, Northrop, 204
Funkenstein, Amos, 129
Furet, François, 24, 32, 33
Fürle, Günther, 184
Fussell, Paul, 89

G
Galicia, 248, 249
Gandhi, Indira, 171
Garbarini, Alexandra, 39, 89, 95, 164
Gary, Romain, 44
gas chambers, 61, 65, 67, 68, 69–70, 72, 116
Gazeta Żydowska, 92
Geertz, Clifford, 45, 49
gender, 13–14, 35
Generalgouvernement, 243, 249
Generalplan Ost, 108
Genghis Khan, 278
genocide, 6, 34, 62, 64, 106, 160, 165, 168, 171, 194, 211, 223, 236, 245, 246, 256, 273, 275–82
  and fascism, 255–56
  and memory, 62, 285
  as "security measure", 283, 284
  colonialism and, 37, 274
  rape in, 171
  "subaltern", 282
  types of, 236
genocide studies, 4, 37, 171, 236, 275, 285
Gentile, Emilio, 263, 264
Gerlach, Christian, 171
German Christians, 184
German Evangelical Church, 184–85, 188
German South–West Africa, 113
Gerstein, Kurt, 63, 64, 215
Ghetto Fighters' Museum, 90
ghettos, 11, 46, 61, 80, 85, 86, 89, 91, 92, 95, 108, 114, 143, 148, 153, 208, 242, 244
  as "*Judenreservat*", 110
  language in, 94
Giftpilz, Der (Hiemer), 110
Gilbert, Martin, 145
Gilbert, Shirli, 80, 95
Gildea, Robert, 47
Ginzburg, Carlo, 192
Globocnik, Odilo, 63, 64
Gochman, Kalman, 114
Goebbels, Joseph, 29, 101, 187, 211, 213, 249
Goldberg, Amos, 11, 13, 39, 55, 137–38, 261
Goldhagen, Daniel, 12, 29, 38, 52, 68, 130, 160, 195
Gospel of John, 131
Gradowski, Zalman, 146–47, 149, 154
Graetz, Heinrich, 272, 273, 274
Greco-Turkish War (1921–22), 235
Greece, 216, 244, 248
Green, Linda, 96
Greenpeace, 103
Griffin, Roger, 263
Gringauz, Samuel, 90
Gross, Jan T., 168
Grossman, David, 23
Grzywacz, Nachum, 148
Günther, Hans F. K., 54
Gurevich, Aron, 95
Gutman, Yisrael, 83, 84

H
Habermas, Jürgen, 265
Haeckel, Ernst, 107, 119
Haffner, Sebastian, 56
Hahn, Otto, 188
Halder, Franz, 71
Hartman, Geoffrey, 56, 152
Hausner, Gideon, 129
Hegel, G. W. F., 194, 257
Heidegger, Martin, 119–20, 257
Helphand, Kenneth, 80
Hempel, Carl, 5
Herbert, Ulrich, 26
Herder, Johann Gottfried, 93
Herero genocide, 38, 273
Herf, Jeffrey, 38, 50, 187
hermeneutics, 146
Herzberg, Abel, 114
heuristics, 5, 11, 130

Heydrich, Reinhard, 214, 250, 251
Hilberg, Raul, 81, 82, 143, 145, 149, 150, 158, 163, 170, 171, 172, 186
Hillesum, Etty, 163
Himmler, Heinrich, 63, 64, 65, 70, 71, 107, 108, 109, 112, 147, 164, 187, 222
    on *Lebensraum,* 109–10
Hippler, Fritz, 65
Hirsch, Marianne, 56
Hirt, August, 66
historical theory, 3, 4, 5, 6, 8, 9, 10, 11, 12, 13, 14–15, 23, 25, 28, 33–34, 39–40, 45, 46, 48, 81, 148, 152, 190–91, 193, 194, 197, 201, 203, 204–06, 218, 221, 222, 236, 257, 275
historische Sinnbildung, 10
History & Memory, 52
History and Theory, 49
Hitler, Adolf, 36, 50, 51, 55, 56, 63, 64, 66, 102, 111, 164, 185, 187, 210, 211, 213, 218, 244, 245, 249–50, 251, 259, 284
    "prophecy" of 30 January 1939, 249, 251
Hitler Youth, 52
Holocaust
    and European history, 233–52
    and fascism, 255, 258, 261–62, 265
    and genocide, 38, 170, 236, 245, 272, 281
    and world history, 262, 272–86
    archives of, 181
    art, 9, 191, 192
    as "decontamination", 115–16
    as ecological project, 102, 106–118
    as European event, 39, 182, 185, 208, 220
    as incomprehensible, 68, 73, 145
    as meaningless, 50, 52
    as "sacrifice", 259
    as "test case", 48, 49
    bystanders, 159–62, 215, 221
    children in, 93, 148, 160, 163, 165, 167
    Christian writings on, 133–36
    collaboration in, 216, 217, 220, 222, 247, 248, 265
    commemoration of, 9, 13, 63, 73, 74, 128, 158–72
    consciousness, 9, 23, 24, 25
    dehumanization in, 113
    denial of, 1, 48, 198, 206
    economics and, 53
    education, 158, 159, 162, 163
    fiction, 5, 9, 191, 192
    help during, 161
    hiding during, 148, 150, 153, 164, 166
    historiography of, 2, 3, 8, 10, 11, 12, 14, 23–24, 25, 26, 27, 28, 29–30, 32, 34, 35, 37, 38, 39, 47, 48, 49, 50, 52, 53, 55, 73, 82, 90, 96, 136, 138, 182, 186, 194, 201, 203–04, 209, 212, 220–21, 222, 255, 262, 263, 265, 286
    integrated history of, 181–89, 203, 209, 217, 221
    Jewish research during, 87, 183
    lessons of, 158, 159, 169, 170
    moral ambiguity in, 161–62, 169
    origins of, 26, 53–54, 56, 82, 182, 208, 209, 210, 224
    perpetrators, 5, 14, 28, 46, 54–55, 56, 61, 62, 64, 66, 67, 73, 74, 79, 80, 82, 159, 160, 162, 164, 165, 167, 215, 217, 220, 221, 222, 223, 265, 273
    photographs, 39, 65, 68, 69, 71–72
    problem of judgment, 1
    rescue during, 162, 165, 206, 218
    resistance to, 55, 84, 143, 183, 220. *See also* amida
    survival in, 83, 150–51, 209
    survivors, 14, 24, 73, 82, 143, 149, 151–52, 153, 167, 182, 206
    "territorial solution", 241
    uniqueness of, 24, 62, 170, 190, 201, 262, 272, 273, 274, 275, 278, 285
    victims, 12, 13, 39, 46, 51, 61, 62, 64, 66, 67, 72, 74, 80, 81, 82, 95–96, 120, 138, 145, 150, 159, 165, 167, 184, 191, 204, 208, 209, 212, 220, 221, 222, 261, 265
    women and, 14, 160
    Zionist understanding of, 206, 273
Holocaust (TV series), 68
Holocaust Commemoration Day (UN), 168, 273
Holocaust Studies, 11, 12, 25, 55, 191

Honneth, Axel, 265
Höss, Hedwig, 117
Höss, Rudolf, 116, 117–18
Huguenots, 276
Huizinga, Johann, 79
Hungary, 70, 212, 243, 247, 248, 249, 251, 252
Hunt, Lynn, 86, 92
hypothetic-deductive method, 7

I
Iaşi pogrom, 247
I. G. Farben, 116
industrial revolution, 235
Institute of Contemporary History (Munich), 181
intentionalism and functionalism, 27, 38, 39–40, 50, 51
Iraq, 170
Israel, 85, 152, 170, 273, 275
Israeli school of Holocaust history, 83, 84, 85, 90
Italian Fascism, 256, 260, 262
Italy, 216, 234, 256, 286

J
Jaffee, Martin S., 139
Japan, 286
Japanese Christians, 273, 276
Jay, Martin, 2
Jeckeln, Friedrich, 249
Jedwabne, 168–69
Jena, 87
Jenkins, Keith, 48
Jesus, 131–32, 134, 135
Jewish history, 55, 82, 83, 84, 85, 90, 95, 146, 182, 272–73, 274, 276
    institutional perspective on, 83, 85
Jews, 13, 24, 28, 34, 35, 51, 52, 66, 82, 84, 86, 183, 276
    and Nazi legislation, 40, 108, 163
    and Western civilization, 273
    as nation, 83
    as "racial undesirables", 108, 110, 111
    as witnesses in Christianity, 132–33, 134, 135–36, 139–40
    Dutch, 188
    funerary rites of, 92
    Hungarian, 71, 252
    in Austro-Hungarian Empire, 246–47
    lack of connection to land, 111
    Orthodox, 188
    Polish, 242
    responses to Holocaust, 51, 55, 87, 146, 147, 182
    Soviet, 241
    suicide in Nazi Germany, 163
    Volhynian, 246
Job, 131–32, 170
Jonassohn, Kurt, 236
Joyce, James, 219
Judenforschung (research on Jews), 65
Judenräte (Jewish Councils), 47, 163, 187
"Judeo-Bolshevism", 241, 246, 247

K
Kafka, Franz, 87
Kamenets-Podolsky, 249
Kane, Anne, 49, 51, 53
Kansteiner, Wulf, 13, 136–37, 138, 192
Kant, Immanuel, 167, 195
Kaplan, Chaim, 89, 93, 147, 150, 154, 260
Kaplan, Marion, 130
kapos, 164, 165, 172
Kassow, Samuel, 85, 91
Katzmann, Friedrich, 249
Kermish, Yosef, 90
Kershaw, Ian, 26
kiddush hashem, 55
Kiernan, Ben, 171
Kindertransport, 153
King, Magda, 120
King, Martin Luther, 127, 132
kitsch, 9, 75, 96, 191
Klemperer, Eva, 40
Klemperer, Victor, 33, 40, 93, 163, 218
Klüger, Ruth, 218
Kolnai, Aurel, 51
Königsberg, 164
Koonz, Claudia, 79
Korczak, Janusz, 93
Koshar, Rudy, 56
Krakow, 166
Krieck, Ernst, 54
Krüger, Friedrich, 71
Kruk, Herman, 164, 169
Kurds, 238

Kushner, Tony, 150
Kyrgyz, 237

L
LaCapra, Dominick, 6–7, 10, 12, 56, 79, 138, 263, 264
Lang, Berel, 12, 192
Langer, Lawrence, 12, 153
Lanzmann, Claude, 23, 72, 170
Laqueur, Walter, 223
Latin America, 129
Latvia, 247, 248
Laub, Dori, 148, 149, 150
law, 129–30
Lazarus, Moritz, 93
Le Chambon-sur-Lignon, 165
Leitner, Isabella, 120
Lekan, Thomas, 47
Lemkin, Raphael, 272, 275–86
Lengyel, Olga, 166, 167
Leociak, Jacek, 92, 95
Lessons and Legacies conference, 172
Levene, Mark, 286
Levi, Primo, 40, 113, 145, 146, 149, 151, 167, 184, 193, 198, 200, 207, 260, 265
Lévi-Strauss, Claude, 49
Lewyn, Bert, 149
Leys, Ruth, 139
liberalism, 186, 256
Life is Beautiful (Benigni), 168, 193
Lindbergh, Charles, 213
Linden, Herbert, 63, 64
linguistic turn, 7, 204
Lithuania, 146, 169, 212, 216, 247, 248
Littell, Jonathan, 5, 219
Łódź Ghetto, 91, 94, 95, 146, 172, 188, 208, 209
  disease in, 146
  Encyclopedia of the, 94
London, 209
Longerich, Peter, 10, 183
Lower, Wendy, 55
Lublin, 63, 241, 249
Luther, Martin, 132
Luther, Martin (German Foreign Office), 250
Lwów Ghetto, 208
Lyotard, Jean-François, 12, 50, 120

M
Macedonia, 248
Madagascar, 241
Maier, Charles, 51
Majdanek, 64, 115
Mallmann, Klaus-Michael, 249
Manchus, 282
Mann, Thomas, 54
Margalit, Avishai, 127, 131
Maritain, Jacques, 134, 136
Marx, Karl, 194, 204
Marxism, 24, 118, 186, 256, 257
Mauriac, François, 134, 135–36
Maus (Spiegelman), 23, 163, 193
Mazower, Mark, 27, 38
Megill, Allan, 2
Mein Kampf (Hitler), 36, 103
Meitner, Lise, 188
Melson, Robert, 166
Melville, Herman, 131, 196
memory, 11, 12, 13, 14, 24, 35–36, 39, 46, 55–56, 74–75, 127, 132–33, 135, 149, 151, 158, 285
Memory Studies, 36
Menecke, Friedrich, 164
Mengele, Josef, 164, 165
Merin, Moshe, 163
Michelet, Edmond, 136
Michelet, Jules, 204
Michman, Dan, 39, 83
military chaplains, 161–62
Millu, Liana, 165
minorities, 235, 248
Mintz, Alan, 85
Mokotow, 166
Mommsen, Theodor, 11
Monde, Le, 136
Mongols, 282, 284
Morrison, Toni, 196
Moscow, 185
Moses, Dirk, 37, 233
Mosse, George, 53, 54, 263, 264
Mucha, Stanisław, 70
Mufti of Jerusalem, 250
Murderers Are among Us, The (Staudte), 69
Mussolini, Benito, 260, 264

N
Naftalin, Henrik, 94
Nagel, Thomas, 129

Napoleonic Wars, 219
narrative, 2, 5, 6, 7, 11, 25, 28, 32, 37, 45, 50, 51, 55, 81, 151, 185, 192, 203–04, 205, 221
narratology, 204
Naturschutzparke, 111
Nazism, 9, 13, 24, 26, 27, 29, 30, 36, 51, 52, 53–55, 56, 79, 101–121, 186, 234, 258–59. *See also* Third Reich
    and Christianity, 29, 31, 211–12
    and environmentalism, 101–121
    and German culture, 29, 31, 34, 40, 51, 79, 245
    and German Romanticism, 108
    and language, 93
    and politics of memory, 61–75, 147–48
    and war, 252
    as form of fascism, 257, 259–60, 262
    concept of *Lebensraum,* 106, 108, 111, 112, 116, 118, 119
    unrelated to fascism, 261–62
Neff, Emery, 11
Netherlands, 215, 244
Netz, Reviel, 112–13
Neumann, Boaz, 11
New York Times, 94
New Zealand, 103
Nietzsche, Friedrich, 194
Night (Wiesel), 133–34, 144, 162
Night Porter, The (Cavani), 193
NKVD, 247
Nobel Peace Prize, 130, 143
Nolte, Ernst, 257
Nora, Pierre, 133
Normandy invasion, 197
Novick, Peter, 128, 170
Nuremberg rallies, 26
Nuremberg Trials, 47, 129

O
Obama, Barack, 127, 130
O'Hare McCormack, Anne, 94
Öktem, Kerem, 239
Oneg Shabbat, 72, 85, 91, 147, 148
Operation 14f13, 164
Organisation of Ukrainian Nationalists, 247

Ottoman Empire, 234, 235, 236, 237, 240, 246, 251. *See also* Anatolia, Armenians, Armenian genocide, Assyrians, Circassians
    Christians in, 238, 242, 246, 251
    Muslims in, 237, 238
    Orthodox Christians in, 235–36

P
Palestine, 85, 187, 215, 241
Palestinians, 274
Parallax, 199
Paris, 209
Passmore, Kevin, 7
Patterson, David, 143–44, 145
Payne, Stanley, 263
Pequots, 273
Peres, Shimon, 273, 274
Perl, Gisela, 152
phenomenology, 118
Pianist, The (Polanski), 168
Pinkiert, Motel, 92
Podchlebnik, Mordechai, 170
Pohl, Dieter, 183
Poland, 71, 85, 112, 146, 152, 160, 161, 164, 165, 187–88, 212, 216, 242, 243, 244, 247, 248, 249, 250, 277
Poliakov, Léon, 54
Polish Underground, 182
Pope Pius XII, 83
Portugal, 212
postmodernism, 4, 7, 10, 11, 48, 49, 218, 219
Postone, Moishe, 12
Prague, 65, 67, 87, 94, 147
Preysing, Bishop, 185, 188
Proust, Marcel, 219
psychoanalysis, 6, 81
Pynchon, Thomas, 196

R
realism, 2, 46, 74
Rechtman, Roland, 139
Red Army, 164, 283
Regensburg, 36
Reich Nature Protection Law, 102, 105
Reiter, Andrea, 152
relativism, 48, 192
representation, 4, 5, 7–8, 9, 23, 25, 35, 40, 49, 55, 56, 61, 64, 68, 73, 74, 75,

168, 184, 185, 190, 194, 195, 207, 219
Ricoeur, Paul, 5, 205
"Righteous among the Nations", 165
Ringelblum Emmanuel, 72, 85, 93, 147
  on Nazism, 93
Ringelheim, Joan, 168
Roma, 241, 242, 245
Roman Empire, 276, 282, 284
Romania, 169, 212, 242, 243, 245, 246, 247, 248, 249, 250, 251, 252
Romanov Empire, 234, 235, 236, 237, 283 See also Russia
Roseman, Mark, 150
Rosenberg, Alfred, 250
Rosenfeld, Gavriel, 56
Rosenfeld, Oskar, 94, 95
Rosenzweig, Franz, 132
Roskies, David, 80, 146, 147
Rosman, Moshe, 46, 55, 80
Rothberg, Michael, 46
RSHA, 10, 52, 65, 109, 250, 251
Rubin, Miri, 46
Rumkowski, Chaim, 163
rumors, 88–89
Rupnow, Dirk, 37
Rüsen, Jörn, 3, 4
RuSHA, 52
Russia, 216, 234, 236, 238, 239. See also Romanov Empire
Russian civil war, 236, 283
Rwandan genocide, 171, 251

S
SA, 114
Sahlins, Marshall, 49
Salonika, 216
Samuel, Marion, 82
Sapetowa, Karolcia, 168–69
Schindler, Oskar, 162, 165
Schindler's List (Spielberg), 68, 70, 153, 168, 193
Schmitt, Carl, 111, 275
Schneider, David, 45
Schulz, Bruno, 208
SD, 52, 65
Seidman, Naomi, 133–34
Seifert, Alwin, 112
Senesch, Hannah, 163
Serbia, 241, 244

sexuality, 6, 14, 53
Shanghai, 163
Shema (Levi), 198–99
Shoah (Lanzmann), 23, 72, 170
Sierakowiak, Dawid, 146, 147, 148, 149, 154
Sikhs, 171
Singer, Oskar, 94
slave labor, 106, 186
slave trade, 274
Slavs, 106, 108, 109
Slovakia, 164, 212, 247, 248, 249, 250
Social Darwinism, 108, 235
Sonderkommandos, 70, 71, 72, 118, 120, 135, 146, 148
  testimony of, 146–47, 148
source critique, 5, 6, 11, 184
South Africa, 113, 129, 162
  apartheid in, 162
Soviet Union, 26, 65, 113, 185, 234, 241, 242, 243, 244, 245, 246, 247, 248, 249, 250, 283, 286
  Volga Germans in, 246
Soyinka, Wole, 274
Spain, 9, 212, 264, 276
Speech Act theory, 196–97, 198
Spengler, Oswald, 194
Spiegelman, Art, 23, 163, 193
Spielberg, Steven, 68, 70, 153, 193
SS, 52, 63, 107, 112, 115, 147, 166, 243, 244, 249, 250, 251
  and racial policy, 107
  plans for *Ostwall,* 241
Stalingrad, 251
Stalinism, 234, 273
Stanislavow, 249
Starachowice, 8, 82, 150
Stauber, Roni, 90
Staudte, Wolfgang, 69
Steinbacher, Sybille, 116, 117
Steiner, George, 93, 144
Steiner, Jean-François, 135–36
Steinthal, Heimann, 93
Sternhell, Zeev, 262
Stone, Dan, 25, 37, 79
Stosberg, Hans, 117
Stout, Harry, 130
Stover, Eric, 129
Stroop Album, 71
Sugihara, Chiune, 162, 165

Suwałki, 146
Sweden, 188, 277
Switzerland, 182
Symchuck, Julia, 169
Szeintuch, Yechiel, 80
Szpilman, Władysław, 168
Szwajger, Adina Blady, 165–66, 167

T
Tacitus, 284
Tal, Uriel, 54
Tamerlane, 278
Tashkent, 163
testimony, 13, 73, 82, 93, 128, 137, 143–54, 184, 191, 192, 201, 208, 218, 223, 224
    as historical source, 137, 144, 150, 151, 152, 153, 184, 191
    as "sacred", 143, 144, 151, 154
    historians' attitudes to, 145, 149, 150
Tewes, Ernst, 162
The Hague, 209
Theresienstadt, 87, 88, 209
Third Reich, 13, 28, 29–30, 31, 34, 36, 37, 39, 50, 65, 182, 186, 207, 243–44, 286. *See also* Nazism
    Animal Protection Law, 102
    as concentration camp, 114
    as conservative, 105
    as totalitarian, 104
    bureaucracy of, 209, 211
    collective memory in, 35–36, 37, 39, 64, 66
    Foreign Office, 249, 250
    Four Year Plan, 105
    idea of *Heimat* in, 30
    institutions of, 52, 53, 66, 245
    "Jew-free", 243
    knowledge of Holocaust in, 183, 217
    memory of, 35
    propaganda in, 211, 217
    racial ideology in, 30, 31, 32, 34, 38, 54, 164, 187
    scorched earth policy of, 105
    Volksgemeinschaft, 51, 105, 117
    "voluntaristic turn" and, 51
Thirty Years War, 72, 278
Thrace, 239, 248
Tocqueville Alexis de, 33

Tolstoy, Leo, 219
Toynbee, Arnold, 194
Trachtenberg, Joshua, 54
transitional justice, 129
Transnistria, 169, 242
Transylvania, 166
trauma, 56, 64, 81, 128, 130, 138, 139, 167
Treblinka, 63, 135–36, 147, 163
"Treblinka Affair", 133, 135–36
Trocmé, André, 165
Trocmé, Magda, 165
Tuck, Richard, 284
Turin, 260
Turkey, 163
Turner, Victor, 45

U
UCLA, 192, 207
Uekoetter, Frank, 47
Ukraine, 160, 161, 169, 216, 246, 247, 248, 249
    famine in, 283
United Nations, 168, 273
United Nations Convention on the Prevention and Punishment of the Crime of Genocide (1948), 234, 278, 285
United Nations Declaration on Human Rights (1948), 285
United States, 13, 80, 85, 90, 113, 152, 212, 286
    entry into war, 210
    Holocaust memory in, 128
United States Holocaust Memorial Museum, 171
Upper Silesia, 106
Urals, 241, 250
US Army Historical Division, 71
USSR, *see* Soviet Union
Utitz, Emil, 87–88

V
Van Gennep, Arnold, 92
Versailles Treaty, 111
Veyne, Paul, 2, 6, 23
Vichy France, 187
Vidal-Naquet, Pierre, 136
Vienna, 94
Vilna Ghetto, 164, 208, 209

Volkov, Shulamit, 81
Volksdeutsche, 108, 109, 164
von Verschuer, Otmar, 54

W

Wadowice, 161
Waffen-SS, 250
Waldenses, 278
Wallenberg, Raoul, 162, 165
Wannsee Conference, 250
Warburg, Aby, 79
Warsaw Ghetto, 65, 71, 72, 85, 86, 91, 92, 93, 135, 147, 150, 163, 165, 167, 188, 209, 260
    Christians in, 188
Waxman, Zoë, 13
Wedding, 172
Wehrmacht, 28, 61, 71, 115, 186, 223
Wehrmacht Exhibition, 62, 68, 69, 71
Weimar Republic, 36, 51, 104
Welzer, Harald, 217
Westerbork, 188
White, Hayden, 1, 2, 3, 7, 8, 12, 13, 14, 48, 185, 204–07, 219, 220, 223, 224
Wiepking-Jürgensmann, Heinrich Friedrich, 112
Wiesel, Elie, 52, 133, 143, 144, 145, 152, 153, 162, 171
Wieviorka, Annette, 73, 128, 129, 131, 153
Wilckens, Heinrich, 111
Wildt, Michael, 36
Winter, Jay, 128, 131
witnessing, 127–40, 148, 191
    theological, 131–32
    "vicarious", 135
Wittgenstein, Ludwig, 236
Wollaston, Isabel, 148
Woolf, Virginia, 219
World War I, 32, 36, 72, 89, 113, 128, 216, 235, 237, 246
    Central Powers, 239
World War II, 14, 26, 27, 31–32, 47, 73, 94, 102, 103, 105, 115, 128, 133, 134, 193, 221, 234, 236, 238, 242, 246, 277, 285
    Axis Powers, 243, 246, 251, 252
    environmental catastrophe, 105
Wurm, Bishop Theophil, 188
Württemberg, 48

WVHA, 52

Y

Yad Vashem, 90, 163
Yahil, Leni, 220
Yiddish, 85, 93–94, 135, 152
YIVO, 91, 94
Young, James, 143–44, 150
Yugoslavia, 171, 236, 248

Z

Zagorin, Perez, 48
Zeit, Die, 81
Zeitlin, Froma, 135
Zelizer, Barbie, 56
Zelkowicz, Yosef, 91, 94
Zimmerer, Jürgen, 37
Zionism, 48, 275, 277
Žižek, Slavoj, 265
Zyklon B, 63, 112, 115–16

www.ingramcontent.com/pod-product-compliance
Lightning Source LLC
Chambersburg PA
CBHW072144100526
44589CB00015B/2077